I0592304

Albert Barnes

Lectures on the Evidences of Christianity in the nineteenth Century

Albert Barnes

Lectures on the Evidences of Christianity in the nineteenth Century

ISBN/EAN: 9783337176129

Printed in Europe, USA, Canada, Australia, Japan

Cover: Foto ©ninafisch / pixelio.de

More available books at **www.hansebooks.com**

LECTURES

ON THE

EVIDENCES of CHRISTIANITY

IN

THE NINETEENTH CENTURY.

DELIVERED IN THE MERCER STREET CHURCH, NEW YORK,
JANUARY 21 TO FEBRUARY 21, 1867.

ON THE

"ELY FOUNDATION" OF THE UNION THEOLOGICAL SEMINARY.

By ALBERT BARNES,

AUTHOR OF

"NOTES ON THE NEW TESTAMENT," "NOTES ON THE PSALMS,"
ETC., ETC.

NEW YORK:

HARPER & BROTHERS, PUBLISHERS.
FRANKLIN SQUARE.

UNION THEOLOGICAL SEMINARY,

NEW YORK.

THE ELY LECTURESHIP

ON

𝔗𝔥𝔢 𝔈𝔳𝔦𝔡𝔢𝔫𝔠𝔢𝔰 𝔬𝔣 𝔠𝔥𝔯𝔦𝔰𝔱𝔦𝔞𝔫𝔦𝔱𝔶.

FIRST SERIES.

BY THE REV. ALBERT BARNES,

OF PHILADELPHIA.

PREFACE.

THIS course of Lectures on the Evidences of Christianity in the Nineteenth Century was delivered, by appointment, as the first course on the foundation established in the Union Theological Seminary by Mr. Zebulon Stiles Ely, of New York, in the following terms:

"The undersigned gives the sum of ten thousand dollars to the Union Theological Seminary of the city of New York, to found a lectureship in the same, the title of which shall be 'The Elias P. Ely Lectures on the Evidences of Christianity.'

"The course of Lectures given on this foundation is to comprise any topics that serve to establish the proposition that Christianity is a religion from God, or that it is the perfect and final form of religion for man.

"Among the subjects discussed may be—

"The Nature and Need of a Revelation;

"The Character and Influence of Christ and his Apostles;

"The Authenticity and Credibility of the Scriptures: Miracles and Prophecy;

"The Diffusion and Benefits of Christianity; and

"The Philosophy of Religion in its Relation to the Christian System.

"Upon one or more of such subjects a course of ten public Lectures shall be given at least once in two or three years. The appointment of the Lecturer is to be by the concurrent action of the directors and faculty of said seminary and the undersigned; and it shall ordinarily be made two years in advance.

"The interest of the fund is to be devoted to the payment of the Lecturers and the publication of the Lectures within a year after the delivery of the same. The copyright of the volumes thus published is to be vested in the seminary.

"In case it should seem more advisable, the directors have it at their discretion at times to use the proceeds of this fund in providing special courses of lectures or instruction in place of the aforesaid public lectures for the students of the seminary on the above-named subjects.

"Should there at any time be a surplus of the fund, the directors are authorized to employ it in the way of prizes for dissertations by students of the seminary upon any of the above topics, or of prizes for essays thereon, open to public competition.

"ZEBULON STILES ELY.

"*New York, May 8th*, 1865."

CONTENTS.

EVIDENCES OF CHRISTIANITY.

LECTURE I.

I HAVE been requested to deliver a course of lectures
in this seminary on the "Ely Foundation," on the "Evidences of Christianity." By the terms of that "Foundation" the course is to "comprise any topics that serve
to establish the proposition that Christianity is a religion from God, or that it is the perfect and final form
of religion for man." Among the subjects discussed,
as specified, may be,

"The nature and need of a revelation;

"The character and influence of Christ and his apostles;

"The authenticity and credibility of the Scriptures:
miracles and prophecy;

"The diffusion and benefits of Christianity; and

"The philosophy of religion in its relation to the
Christian system."

The course, by the terms of the "Foundation," is to
be comprised in Ten Lectures, and the general subject
which I shall endeavor to illustrate in this course will be
THE EVIDENCES OF CHRISTIANITY IN THE NINETEENTH
CENTURY. I have selected this as being in accordance
with the subjects suggested for the general course; as

A 2

sufficiently comprehensive to embrace the points which can be considered in so limited a course; as suggesting important inquiries in regard to the present relation of Christianity to the world; and as leading to the discussion of topics originated or matured in our own age, and difficulties suggested in this age, which must be met by those who are, by their office and by the purposes of their lives, to be regarded as the public defenders of Christianity.

Christianity now exists as among the undisputed great moral powers or forces in the world. It has a place among other powerful systems of religion, and among philosophical systems, deeply affecting the destinies of mankind. It has a history of its own—a history extending now through more than eighteen centuries, and leaving unmistakable evidence of its existence and its power on the general course of events. It is a "power" on the earth undeniably exerting a vast influence on human affairs.

It is very closely connected with liberty, with domestic arrangements, with civilization, with literature, with the arts of life, with manners, customs, and laws, with the governments of the nations, with the administration of justice, with the doctrine of human rights, with prevailing views of morals, with the prospects of the world in regard to the future, and with the religious hopes of individual men. It was among the things, even in its feeble beginning, which Tacitus could not pass over wholly in silence; one of the things which demanded all the talent of Mr. Gibbon to explain, and which now, whatever may be men's individual faith in it, must enter into every philosophical view which is taken of the present condition and prospects of the world.

In regard to many or most of those things referred to — civilization, literature, arts, manners, customs, laws, governments, the administration of justice, the doctrine of human rights, the prevailing views of morals, and the hopes of men in regard to the future, it has either originated them, or it has shown a decided affinity for them, combining readily with them when suggested, enlarging their sphere of influence, and seizing upon them for its own promotion and perpetuity in the world. In this respect it is unlike all other forms of religion, and has now become so incorporated with those things, and so identified with them, that it could not be *detached* from them without disturbing, if not destroying, the whole frame-work of modern society. The Christian religion was fatal to many things that entered into the notions of civilization, the laws, and the governments of the ancient world, as it will be to many of those things as they exist in other lands if it is propagated among them ; nor could those ancient things be restored, or those modern things be perpetuated, without an entire destruction of the Christian system.

It is a perfectly fair question for any one to ask, What is the origin of this system of religion ? and the question is one which the friends of the system may be held to answer. Is it of man ? Is it a development or outgrowth of some former system of religion ? Is it a necessary result of the progress of the race in civilization—on the same level, in this respect, with the comforts of domestic life, the blessings of liberty, the useful arts, the sciences ? Is it a well-executed imposture ? for such it must be if it is an imposture at all. Is it the result of delusion and fanaticism ? Is it expressive of the conscious wants of man, founded on a myth, and

wrought by human wisdom into a system that commends itself to enlightened understandings, and to
hearts troubled by sin and sorrow, as being all that
man needs?   Or is it of divine origin, as it claims to be
—a true revelation from God?

The Westminster Review (January, 1866) therefore
is perfectly right in asking the question, "How did
Christianity *originate?* Did it originate as an out-
coming of a natural order, or by a supernatural interference?"

The question implies that it had an "origin," that is,
a beginning at some time since man began to exist on
the earth.   It is not, as is implied in the question, coe-
val with man.   There was a time when it did not exist;
when there was no trace of it on the earth.   History,
in each and every ancient nation, so far as those nations
have a history, goes back to a period when Christianity
did not exist.   It was not in Egypt, in Assyria, in Bab-
ylonia, among the Chaldees, in the Teutonic nations,
among the early inhabitants of the British Isles.   Have
the annals of any nation preserved the record of its
origin, so that now, after the lapse of ages, and after it
has been matured in its present form, we can understand how it made its beginning in our world?   Did
the wants of men suggest it?   Did the friend of men
devise it?   Did the wisdom of God, seeing that it was
needful for man, reveal it?

It is with a view to furnishing an answer to these
questions that the Course of Lectures on the "Ely
Foundation" in this seminary has been established, and
that the range of topics which I have indicated has
been suggested as limiting the subjects to be discussed
in the Lectures, and specifying the field to be occupied.
The range is a wide one, and it can not be supposed, as

it was not designed, that the subjects should be exhausted in a single course. It is wisely intended that the course shall be continued from year to year, not by the same lecturer, but by new lecturers, with fresh minds and hearts, with new powers, with views taken from different stand-points, with the results of varied experience and observation, with illustrations drawn fresh from the experience of pastors in the work of the ministry, and especially with a designed reference to the wants of the world, and the state of the public mind *outside the Church*, as demanded by the progress of science, by new difficulties that spring up, by questions that have not before occurred that may need solution, by new forms of objection that may be made to the Bible, by new aspects of philosophy, presenting to the minds of thinking men new difficulties in regard to the Christian system.

I have selected as the main topic on which I propose to address you, leaving ampler fields to those who shall follow me, The Evidences of the Truth of Christianity in the Nineteenth Century:—at a time when eighteen hundred years have passed away since the evidence of its divine origin was first submitted to the world; when it has been tried in its applications to the wants of men during those eighteen hundred eventful years; now, in an age remarkable for its advancement, and when evidence on all subjects is examined by rules unknown to the world at the time when the evidences of the divine origin of the Christian system was first submitted to mankind, and by an acuteness of investigation far in advance of that age. As Christianity convinced the men of that generation of its divine origin, it can not be improper to inquire whether the evidence that was deemed satisfactory then in regard to its origin should be

regarded as satisfactory now. The lapse of eighteen
hundred years may at least *suggest* the inquiry whether
it had at first any claims to the attention which it received from mankind.

Under the general topic which I have suggested, I
propose to embrace the following subordinate topics as
comprehended in it: The limitations of the human mind
on the subject of religion; Historical evidence as affected by time; Historical evidence as affected by science; the evidence of Christianity from its propagation, as that evidence exists at present; Miracles—the
evidence in the nineteenth century that they were performed in the first; Prophecy, as that evidence exists
now; the inspiration of the Scriptures with reference
to the objections made to it at present; the personal
character and the incarnation of Christ; the religion
itself as adapted to the wants of man, as illustrated
in these eighteen hundred years; and the relation of
Christianity to the present stage of the world's progress
in science, civilization, and the arts.

I may be allowed, before entering upon the particular
subject before us at this time, to refer to a difficulty
which I very sensibly feel in undertaking this course
at all. It is the supposition which seems to be implied
in such a course that I could do any thing supplement-
ary to the instructions which are, in the regular course,
delivered from the Chair of Theology in this seminary.
The proprieties of the place and the occasion would not
allow me to speak, as my feelings would prompt me to,
of him who occupies that chair, and whose time is devoted, yet in the full vigor of life, to this very inquiry,
among others in his course, and who enjoys advantages
for instructing others in studies of this nature which
can not be expected from one whose time is so much
occupied with the routine of pastoral duties.

There are a few things, however, which I may be allowed to say in reference to what seems to be presumption in undertaking such a task, and which may be applicable to the very purpose of endowing such a lectureship, as well as to my own undertaking. (*a*) It is known to all that different views of the same subject may be taken by different individuals from the points of observation which they respectively occupy, and that it may require a comparison of many such views to obtain a complete idea of any one object or subject. From how many different points may a landscape, a waterfall, a mountain, an ancient castle be viewed, each presenting some different aspect to the painter, each varied, yet each true, and all entering into the proper and full conception of the object. On moral and historical subjects this is not less true than it is in reference to mountains, to valleys, to waterfalls, to piles of architectural beauty or grandeur. He makes no assumption for himself who surveys from his own point of observation what has been painted by another from his. In the position which he occupies, and in the work of art which he attempts, there is no implied reflection on another. (*b*) On the great subjects of religion and morals, one man's reflection, experience, and observation may suggest something of value which may not have occurred to another. His own mental structure may be different, his own habits of thought may be different, his own experience in the world may be different, his own opportunities of observation may be different; and it is no reflection on another one, though engaged in the same general purpose, to submit his own reflections to his fellow-men. (*c*) It may be true that, while there are great advantages, on such subjects, from the fact of being devoted to one great line of

study, as in a chair of theology, and in the ample acquaintance which may be derived from such a position
with all that has been written by others, there may be
advantages in the labors of a pastoral life, in frequent
contact with men, in meeting the difficulties in the
minds of those who are inquiring on the subject of personal religion, which may be of not less value in the
cause of truth than the more deliberate and learned instructions of a theological chair, and which may assist
those who are preparing for the work of the ministry
in meeting the actual difficulties which they are to encounter in the living world. (*d*) I may observe farther
that these Lectures are designed and expected, if I understand the purpose of the founder and of the directors of the seminary in making the arrangements for
their delivery, to be less studied, elaborate, scientific,
and philosophical than those which are delivered in
the regular course of instruction in the seminary, and
which are especially prepared for students of theology
as such. It is the purpose in the "Foundation" to form
a new connecting link between the seminary and the
churches, to impart instruction here which will not
only benefit those who are hereafter to be the guides
of the public mind, but also, in union with them, to do
something to diffuse just views on these subjects in the
community, and to aid those who are at present acting their parts in the world, as well as those who shall
be the actors in the next generation. (*e*) And, once
more, I may observe that neither my friend who occupies that chair nor myself will so exhaust the subject as
to leave nothing for our successors. In our own place
and generation we shall each find enough to do; in
their generation, those who come after us will find that
there is an ample field for all their talents in the work

to be done in their time. The Christian "apologists" of the early centuries, the opposers of Celsus, Porphyry, and Julian, had enough to do in their day; Grotius, Leland, and Clarke had enough to do in theirs; Butler, Lardner, Paley, and Chalmers in theirs; in our day a new field, demanding new powers and new arguments in answering new objections, is opened to us, and in time to come, until the period when Christianity shall triumph over all the earth, the enemies of Christianity will be careful to give, each in their age, enough for the public defenders of Christianity to do. We, in our age, have a work to do; those who come after us will have a work to do in theirs.

As introductory to the course which I propose to deliver, and as an argument on the general subject, it seems proper to consider the capabilities of the human mind in reference to the general subject to be considered. If man is capable himself of originating a system of religion that will be all that is needed to guide him in the duties of life, to sustain him in its trials, and to prepare him for the future world, that fact would, of course, prove a revelation to be unnecessary, and would at the same time prove that all pretended revelations are false, since it can not be supposed that God would give by miracle a special revelation when he had already furnished, in another mode, all that is needful for man, or that there would be *two* methods of communicating the divine will on the same subject. On other subjects than religion this principle is every where observed. God does not give special revelations on those subjects which are quite within the range of the human powers, and where there may be a healthful exercise of those powers in ascertaining what is true and what is good. If, for the sake of example, it be admitted that God specially instructed Adam in regard to the appropriate names of the beasts of the field and the fowls of the air (Gen., ii., 19), or that he, with his own hands, made for Adam and Eve "coats of skins and clothed them" (Gen., iii., 21), or that he taught Noah how to construct the ark, or that he endowed Bezaleel and Aholiab with special wisdom in building the tabernacle, "to devise cunning works, to work in gold, and silver, and brass" (Ex., xxxi., 3–6), yet it is certain that this is not the ordinary method in which he endows men for the useful or the ornamental arts of life, nor is this the method on which this subject is referred to in the Bible. The principle every where assumed in the Bible, and a principle on which undeniably the whole Bible is formed, whether that book is a revelation or not, is that, where men have ample powers to accomplish what is needful for themselves, there is no special instruction given by revelation. No book is more destitute of information on the common arts of life, on agriculture, music, and the sciences, on political economy and the forms of government, on the arts of raising grain, of working metals, of mining, or of cooking food, on the structure of ships, wagons, roads, or canals, than the Bible. All these are left to the invention of men, to be wrought out in the proper employment of their own powers, with the presumption that man is competent to this; that he needs no special instruction, and that his own good will be best promoted by the exercise of his own powers on these subjects.

The principle is, that the Bible does not attempt to give knowledge on subjects which men may find out themselves. Agriculture, grafting, planting, architecture, fishing, ploughs, hammers, harrows, machinery, printing, railroads, steam, the telegraph—all these in due time; all by the skill of man. Man is competent to these things. There is no need of a revelation. The world, in its infancy, was not prepared for these things, and a revelation in regard to them would not have been understood. It was better to raise up men from time to time who would strike out great inventions when the world needed them than to communicate the knowledge by revelation; it was better that the human intellect should be sharpened and disciplined by these discoveries; it was better that men should be stimulated by the hope of useful inventions; and it was better that the knowledge of them should be brought on the stage when they would fit into human society, than to anticipate all, and render the human powers flaccid and useless by a revelation anticipating these things.

If religion is of the same nature as this; if man is equally competent to solve the great questions of religion that pertain to him, then it is plain that religion would have been left in this manner, and that a revelation being unnecessary, none would have been given, and consequently that all pretended revelations are false. The enemies of the Bible, therefore, are pursuing a legitimate line of thought in endeavoring to show that man has all the powers necessary to ascertain what is needful to be known of God, and consequently that the Bible and all other pretended revelations are false.

In considering now the particular subject before us —the limitations of the human mind on the subject of religion—it will be proper to direct your attention first to the limitations on the subject from the nature of the human mind itself, and then the illustrations which have been furnished by the results of the experiments which have been made.

The particular thoughts necessary to be presented under the first of these topics—the limitations on the subject from the nature of the mind itself—are the following: those limitations in the faculties of the mind in respect to the processes of reasoning; the limitations in the power of intuition; and the limitations in the instruments which man employs in his discoveries, or in enlarging the scope of his natural vision.

(1.) The powers of mind — created mind — mind as found in man—seem vast, are vast. It is not necessary for us, in exalting revelation, or in showing the necessity of revelation, to disparage or underrate those powers. The developments of mind in the ordinary processes of society, and in the discoveries which men have made in the sciences, lifting the whole race to a higher level, have been amazing. This is especially so when God, departing from the ordinary course of things, creates a great intellect as he originally created great mountains, or rocks, or oceans, or as he creates great worlds as illustrations of what he can do; as showing how he might have made the race; as showing, perhaps, how he does make other races; as furnishing a higher illustration than ordinary of what he himself is, lifting man, as by a sudden elevation, toward himself. Thus, in the upheavings of the lands in the old geological periods, in general the lands upheaved were low plains or elevated plateaus on a level, or gentle eminences diversifying the landscape, or here and there loftier mountains—the ranges of the Andes, the Alleghanies, the Apennines, the Alps, while at great intervals there stands the lofty Dhavalagiri, the Chimborazo, the Sorata of Nevada, and Mont Blanc, rising far into loftier atmospheres, as a few men, like Newton, stand far above the ordinary individuals of the race.

There are men—a few men—of such capacity that they seem to approach almost all subjects with equal ease; men who have by intuition, as Pascal had, what other men secure by slow processes and by long-continued trial; who begin where other men leave off; "many-sided" men, to whom all subjects appear equally easy, and with whom it seems to be a mere matter of will and choice what particular department they shall pursue to make themselves immortal.

But, while this *appears* to be so, the range of subjects on which any man, however richly endowed, may distinguish and immortalize himself, is very limited, and is confined within very narrow and very carefully-defined boundaries. There is, and there has been, no "universal genius." There is, and there has been, no man whose capacities are equally adapted to all the subjects of science and art, of poetry, rhetoric, and eloquence; of war, of statesmanship, of invention, and of practical life, in which they might equally acquire distinction. Society, indeed, required in its adjustments that within a limited range the powers of a man might be adapted —perhaps equally adapted—to any one of a number of pursuits; that in any one of them within that range he might be successful or might excel. This was necessary, in order that at any one time there might be talent enough on the earth for all the necessary objects of life, and that there might be, within a reasonable range, the liberty of a choice—a concession to human freedom and responsibility. But the range *is* a limited one, and within that a man must make his choice. He must be a farmer, *or* a seaman, *or* a mechanic, *or* a musician, *or* a poet, *or* a merchant, *or* a philosopher, *or* an artist; he

can not be all. Between perhaps four or five of these
he must make his choice, and within that range he
must determine how *his* life is to be spent. It is rare
that a man is distinguished in more than one of these
things. Michael Angelo was, indeed, distinguished,
perhaps equally, as a painter, sculptor, and architect;[*]
Shakspeare was equally distinguished in comedy, in
farce, and in tragedy; and there is now one living man
among us—a foreigner[†]—who, it is said, has already,
in four separate and distinct departments of science,
achieved in each a reputation, a like distinction in any
one of which would have placed him at the head of
that particular science. This "play" or this variety of
endowment is given to men not only that they may
have a choice, but that there may be at any one time
on the earth talent enough for all that talent is to do
in that one age.

Again, there is a necessary limitation in regard to
the *attainments* which men may make, as compared
with what remains that is as yet unknown. We all
remember the remark of Newton, "child-like sage;"[‡]

* This idea is expressed on his tomb in the church of Santa
Croce, in Florence. Beneath the monument there are three statues,
personifying *Painting, Sculpture,* and *Architecture,* and at the base of
the monument an inscription, of which the following is a part:

> "Michaeli Angelo Bonaratio
> E vetusta Simoniorum Familia.
> *Sculptori, Pictori et Architecto*
> Fama omnibus notissimo."

† Agassiz.

‡ "I do not know what I may appear to the world, but to myself
I seem to have been only like a boy playing on the sea-shore, and
diverting myself in now and then finding a smoother pebble or a
prettier shell than ordinary, while the great ocean of truth lay all
undiscovered before me."—*Brewster's* Life of Newton, pp. 300, 301,
Harper's ed., 1832.

and we remember, too, the sarcastic remarks of Pope on the discoveries of Newton himself, showing how little, after all the discoveries made by him, as compared with the knowledge of higher intelligences, may be, and what, in this respect, is the general condition of mankind on the subject of knowledge:

> "Superior beings, when of late they saw
> A mortal man unfold all nature's law,
> Admired such wisdom in an earthly shape,
> *And showed a Newton as we show an ape.*"

After all, how limited is the range of human thought and knowledge! We are to remember that ordinarily man is compelled to spend one third of the length of life in acquiring what has been known before, and putting himself in a position to *begin* his own investigations, as if one preparing to explore distant continents should be compelled to spend one third of his days in reaching it; we are to remember that any man is liable to be cut down at any moment, his career of brilliant discovery but just begun; we are to remember that the faculties of man begin soon to decay, and that the imbecility of age, if life is lengthened out, is almost like the imbecility of childhood—life ending as it began; we are to remember that the active average life of man, in which he must do all that he is to do, is but little over twenty years; and we are to remember, also, that the range of his inquiries is limited by the fact that they must be within the scope of his reason, where he may have instruments to aid him, and where he may have the light of other ages to guide him. But what if there are boundless fields wholly beyond that range; if there are worlds which he can not penetrate; if there is an infinity in God in reference to which he has no faculties or powers to investigate or understand it? The question has been well asked, "Why may there not be a whole sphere of existence, embracing the relations and the communion between God and man, with which natural science has no concern, and in which its dictation is as impertinent as the dictation of theology in physics? Why may not spiritual experience, and an approach to the divine in character, be a necessary means of insight into the things of the spiritual world, as scientific instruments and scientific skill are necessary means of insight into the things of the material world?"*

And, after all, what does man *know* of the universe? How little does he *know* of his own little world, its history, its origin, in component parts? What does he *know* of matter, of oxygen, of galvanism, of life? And what does he *know* of Jupiter, of Saturn, of Mars, of Sirius, of the moon, of the sun, of the inhabitants that dwell there, and of their history? How few are the words necessary to be employed in telling *all* that he knows of those worlds? And what does he know of the millions of worlds in that *nebula* to which our own solar system belongs, or of the countless millions that constitute the other "islands" that float in the immensity of space?

(2.) The next thought in relation to the point now before us pertains to the subject of *intuition*—to the question whether, though his range be limited in regard to subjects in which he is required to use *instruments* and *calculation*, man may not be endowed with a higher power, that shall bring directly within the sphere of his vision the great spiritual truths which it is necessary for him to understand.

* Lectures on the Study of History, by *Goldwin Smith*, Professor of Modern History in Oxford, p. 85.

This inquiry would open the whole subject of transcendentalism, and would embrace a range of thought which could not be entered on now. The only point material to the inquiries in this course of Lectures would be, whether there is such a power in man that the great truths of Christianity, as disclosed in the Bible, could have been the result of such an endowment, and could be traced to such a source.

It could hardly be necessary to argue this question here, since the mere *statement* of the matter may seem to be all that is necessary on the subject, and will, to most minds, settle the question. It is obvious that a claim of this kind *must* be a claim, in some sense, to an equality with God, since it implies a power that properly belongs to God, of looking into the whole nature of things, and since it implies a power also equal to that which must be supposed to pertain to God, if there be a God, of determining what is needful for man to know on the highest subjects, of determining what God *would* communicate if he made a revelation, and of declaring what God would be, and should be, and, therefore, of what he is. Obviously no one could do this who was not himself divine.

Still, as the claim is set up, and as men, on the ground of this, not only presume to judge of a revelation when one is proposed, and to determine whether it is worthy of credit alike in its general character and in the details, and as they claim the power, on the same grounds, to determine that a revelation is *not* necessary to man, and that, therefore, all pretensions to " book-revelation" are to be rejected at once, it may not be improper to make a few remarks on the subject.

(*a*) There can be no doubt that, to a certain extent, there *is* this power in man of looking directly at truth,

B

or, to make the assertion larger, that it is of the nature of mind, as such, to do this—the mind of God, and of all minds made in his image. We can not conceive of God without this power; we can not doubt that he could endow created mind with this power as well as with any other power, making it thus in his own image, or so that it would represent or express himself; and we can not limit him in regard to the extent to which he *could* endow mind in this as well as in any other respect, except that it can not equal his own infinity. There *must* be a limit, or all beings thus made would be *gods*, and instead of one God, the universe would be full of gods.

But that God has this power of looking at once into truth, of understanding its nature, of separating it from error, without the slow process of reasoning, there can be no doubt.

(*b*) That man has this power, to a certain extent, is apparent from our own consciousness. The belief in mathematical axioms or first principles is founded on this. We look at the truth at once without any medium or intermediate idea. We could not be assisted in this *by* any intermediate idea. We could not be made to doubt the truth by any objections that could be urged. That the whole is greater than a part, that the whole is equal to the sum of all the parts, that if equals are added to equals the sum will be equal, are points which do not and can not depend on reasoning, nor *could* we reason at all if there were not such points on which all men agree.

(*c*) But it is obvious that the *range* of this must be very different in different minds; nor, as has been already intimated, is it possible where, short of infinity, the limit *might* be made. To the mass of men the number of such truths is not large. To some minds truths, which to others could be learned only as the result of labored reasoning, are a mere matter of intuition. To most minds, for example, in studying Euclid, after a very few statements of that kind which are laid down as maxims or axioms which all men will assent to, every successive proposition is believed *only* as the result of clear demonstration in some labored process of reasoning; to Newton all these propositions were as axioms not demanding any proof, and read as axioms are; to Pascal they led on one another by a power of their own, which he represented, when a boy, on the floor by lines and bars of his own construction.

(*d*) As pertaining to religion, as in other matters, this subject presents itself in two forms: the one is that of *originating* truth, or declaring what truth *is;* the other is that, more common, of judging of truth when it is presented to the mind; of determining whether it *is* truth, and of rejecting it if it does not commend itself to the mind as true.* The latter is Rationalism, the former is the claim of Deism; both are comprised in the term Transcendentalism. Much of this is found in Plato, more of it in Kant; much in all Transcendentalists and Rationalists; more by most men in judging in regard to the evidences of a revealed religion than they are aware of; much is properly exercised in examining the claims of any religion, true or false. There are

---

* Thus Wegscheider represents the claims of Rationalists: "They claim for sound reason the power of deciding upon any religious doctrine whatsoever, derived from a supposed supernatural revelation, and of determining the argument for it, to be made out only according to the laws of thought and action implanted in reason."— Inst. Theol., § 10, quoted in *Mansel,* Limits of Religious Thought, p. 234, 235.

certain convictions engraven on the human mind in regard to truth to which I shall have occasion to advert
in another part of this course,* which *must* be met by
a pretended revelation, or it can not be received.
There is much in man that contributes to the reception
of a system of truth in a revelation when it is proposed,
and that gives it a power over the soul which nothing
can destroy.   It is in a large degree owing to this that
a true religion makes its way in the world, and in a
large degree also it is owing to this that the world is
kept from being imposed on by the pretensions of a
false religion.

(*e*) When we ask, however, whether this is sufficient
—whether this is all that man *needs*, we are met by
such answers as the following. (1.) There is no agreement among those who rely on this as to what *is* the
true system.   From Plato downward to Kant and
Comte, men have speculated on this point, and in regard to what is claimed under this system—the " true,"
the " absolute," the "infinite"—as to what God is, what
man is, or what is the moral system of the universe, it
is impossible to refer to *any* system on which men have
speculated at all, in respect to which there is a greater
variety of opinion, or in which more that is incompre-
hensible has been proposed to the faith of mankind.   It
would be very easy for any one to make extracts from
Hegel and from Kant so far above common apprehen-
hension, so mystical, so difficult of interpretation, so
destitute of apparent meaning, as to turn the whole
matter into ridicule if it should be held seriously that
this was to be the faith and the guide of mankind at
large.   Besides, who is to decide which is the true system ?   Or who, holding one system on this theory, has

* In the IXth Lecture.

a right to call in question the truth of the system preferred by another? (2.) But it is to be observed farther that there are—there must be, truths lying beyond the range of intuition—of man's powers. Only the infinite can look into and comprehend the infinite. There were profound depths in the minds of Newton and Bacon which a child of four years of age could not fathom—which no man could fathom who had not a mind like theirs. It is a matter of the plainest common sense likewise that there must be profound depths in the mind of God which none can fathom who is not the equal of God. Can the arms of a child wield and govern the world? Can a quart-measure take in that which would fill the great "tun" at Heidelberg? Could Loch Katrine contain all the waters of the ocean? There must be truths respecting God which man *can not* know unless God shall reveal them. There are things in the mind of the stranger that we casually meet, though on the same level with ourselves, which we can not know unless he shall choose to disclose them. He has the power of hiding them forever from our knowledge.

(3.) There is one other thought on this point of the subject. I have adverted to the limitations of the faculties of the mind in the ordinary processes of reasoning and in the power of intuition. I shall now advert to the defect in the limitation of the *instruments* which man employs in his discoveries, or in enlarging his scope of natural vision. The point now to be made is, that the means or instruments which man employs so successfully in enlarging the range of his natural powers do not disclose or reveal God. Those means or instruments are, in the first place, limited to their own particular range of discovery, and can be employed only in that direction, or can not be employed to aid man in more than one particular line. The telescope discloses wonders, but it can not be employed by the chemist, the metallurgist, the engineer. The tests of the chemist and his blow-pipe accomplish wonders, but they can not be employed in the purposes of astronomy. The electrical machine accomplishes wonders, but it can not be employed to determine the distance and magnitude of the planets, the height of the atmosphere, or the cause of the tides. Least of all can any of these be employed on moral subjects. They can not determine the great questions about God, and the nature of the human soul, and the destiny of man in distant worlds. The astronomer directs his glass to the blue fields of ether, and brings suns and systems to view before unknown to man, but he does not see God on his throne. The electrical machine may be turned forever, throwing out a continuous stream of light, but it does not reveal God, or cast a ray of light on the destinies of the human soul. All these are limited to their proper objects—all come short of revealing God.

Such, then, are some of the limitations of the human mind as suggested by the nature of the case.

We turn to the next general point proposed to be considered, to the illustrations which have been furnished on the subject by the experiment which the world has been making to answer the great questions which it must be the province of a revelation to answer, if a revelation is given to man.

This need not detain us long, though the subject is one that might be pursued to much greater length than the limits of these Lectures will allow.

The general remark to be illustrated is, that the trial

has been made, and so made that it is not necessary that it should be repeated.

If a revelation was to be given to man; if it be assumed for a moment that such was the divine purpose, it would seem to be not an unreasonable expectation that man himself should be allowed to make the experiment to see whether he could do without one; that is, whether such a revelation was *necessary* for man. This may be presumed to be reasonable, because (*a*) it would settle a great question forever, disposing man to receive and believe the revelation if he himself failed, and (*b*) it would be in accordance with the ordinary method of the divine arrangements in other things. Whatever man *can* do, it is, as before remarked, left for him to do; and whatever God may do for man, it is commonly preceded by the effort of man himself in that direction. Great discoveries in science and art are thus left for man to accomplish, if they are within his power; if the ordinary powers of man are insufficient for them, God creates and brings upon the stage some great mind, endowed in that direction beyond the ordinary powers of man, like Bacon or Newton, Watt or Fulton, Whitney or Morse, elevated above common men on these subjects as Isaiah or David were above ordinary men in the knowledge of spiritual things.

The trial on this subject, as it has actually occurred in the world, has related to two points: to the powers of man in relation to religion in general, and to those powers in relation to a "book-revelation."

In regard to the former of these, the powers of man in relation to religion in general, I remark, first, that the *time* allowed to man for the experiment was sufficiently long to permit the experiment to be fairly made. If we assume now that Christianity had its

origin at the time commonly ascribed to it, about
eighteen hundred years ago, then, according to the
common chronology, there were four thousand years
previous in which the experiment was to be made.
According to Chevalier Bunsen, Lepsius, and others
of that school, there were not far from twenty thousand years from the time when man appeared upon
the earth. It could not be denied that, taking either
position, the time was sufficiently long to admit of a
fair trial on this subject in regard to the capability of
the human powers to devise a system of religion; for,
if man could not devise a system that would meet his
wants in that time, it might be reasonably doubted
whether he could do it at all. It may be added also,
that, on the supposition that vast and eternal interests
were connected in any way with embracing a *true* system of religion, it might be difficult to reconcile it with
any just notions of benevolence in the Deity if the
time had been longer, and if those interests were exposed to farther peril. Indeed, one great difficulty now
to be explained, on the supposition that the revelation
of a plan of salvation was delayed so long, is to reconcile that fact with the benevolence of God, leaving,
during that long period, the eternal welfare of so many
millions of souls to be jeoparded by the delay in giving
a revelation to man: a difficulty which has its parallel,
however, in the fact that so many millions were suffered to die of pestilence, of the plague, and of fever, before the healing art was in any way perfected, and
while the substances constituting the *materia medica*
of the world were actually in existence, but were as
yet undiscovered by man.

  The next thing to be observed in regard to this trial
is, that the character of the mind mainly employed in

the experiment was all that could be demanded *in* such an experiment. If we were asked which of the *classes* of mind that have existed on the earth would be best adapted for original investigations of this nature, we should say that the qualifications would be most likely to be found in the Hindu mind, the Arabic, the Greek, and the Teutonic. These, indeed, in some respects run into each other, and may perhaps be regarded as of the same type or class; but of all the intellects that God has made in the world, a great question of this kind could be more *safely* intrusted to these classes of mind than to any other.

Now, laying out of view at present all reference to the others, it may be said that of these classes of mind the *Greek* was better adapted to this inquiry than either of those which have been referred to. That mind was, in some respects, the best that the world has seen—as if God had created it for the very purpose of settling forever this great inquiry. For acuteness, for depth, for accurate analysis, for subtle philosophical distinctions, for fervor, and for enthusiasm—being equally fitted for eloquence, for poetry, and for philosophy—that mind stands pre-eminent among all that God has made. The Greeks had a language, too, fitted, above all others spoken among men, for such inquiries—a language in which the highest conceptions of philosophy and religion could be better expressed than in any other, and in which the nicest shades of thought could be perpetuated—the language, in fact, adopted by the authors of the New Testament under, as we believe, the guidance of the Holy Ghost—*selected* from all the languages of the world as best adapted to express the great ideas of the Christian Revelation.

The Greeks, too, gave themselves to this inquiry,

fully impressed with its importance and its vastness, *as if* under the impression themselves that the great problem had been intrusted to their hands. They were not insensible to the magnitude of the questions at issue, and alike in their mental acuteness, in their language, and in their zeal, they have shown that the great problem was well intrusted to their hands. If the question were now asked, To what people of all lands and ages such a question could be best submitted? there would be but one answer—that the question whether man could originate or discover a religion that would be fitted for human wants in all ages could be most appropriately and safely lodged with the Greeks.

The *result* of the trial is now before the world. The trial is complete. It is not to be repeated. Whether Christianity is true or false, it may be assumed now that a more *hopeful* trial could not now be entered on; it may be assumed that if there is no *revelation* given to man, then man, on the subject of religion, must give himself up to despair.

There *is* no system of religion that man has devised that meets the wants of the race; there is none, unless it be Christianity, that the race in its progress will care to perpetuate. None of the religions which man originated before the Christian era, if we except Hinduism and Buddhism, have now an existence in the world, and it will not be pretended by those who reject the Christian revelation that these meet the wants of men, or that they can be perpetuated in the advancing periods of the world.

All the others have perished—perished with the empires where they were originated; perished with the priesthood to which they gave power; perished with the temples and altars which time has overthrown—

perished never to be revived.   The temples of Baalbec and Karnak will not be rebuilt; the altars of Mexico will not be reconstructed; the Parthenon will not be repaired; and the Pantheon will not again welcome the gods of all nations.   These ancient systems of religion were dying out when Christianity appeared, and would have died at any rate.   It is a fine remark of Augustine that "Christ appeared to the men of a decrepit, dying world, that while all around them was fading, they might receive through him a new, youthful life."*   It was not in the power of Julian, with all the influence and wealth of the world at his command, to quicken the old Roman Paganism into life again; it was the task of Mr. Gibbon to record the dying out of the *old* system, whatever might be his record in regard to the *new*.

In particular, it pertains to my argument to remark that the system of the *Greeks*, the result of the highest wisdom of man, has departed forever.   That religion has ceased altogether; the "elegant mythology" of the Greeks, as Mr. Gibbon calls it, has passed away. There is not a vestige of it remaining.   There is not now an altar, even in Athens, where Paul saw so many, where a heathen god is worshiped; there is no one there erected to an "unknown God."   Every altar that stood there in the time of Paul has long since been overthrown, not to be rebuilt; the splendid temples on which his eye rested when he stood on Mars' Hill have disappeared.   Even the Parthenon is in ruins, and there has not been vitality enough to perpetuate it in its beauty as a work of art; as a structure for the worship of Minerva it is to be entered no more forever.

There was nothing in the ancient religion of Greece,

* *Neander*, Church History, i., 77.

or in her philosophy as bearing on religion, that the world could lay hold of as worth perpetuating, and the religion of Greece, the highest result of human wisdom —of the speculation of the profoundest and acutest intellect of the world—has departed; the ruin of the ancient religion is universal. Not more entire is the ruin of kingdoms, dynasties, empires—of thrones and palaces—than is the ruin of temples and altars. All lie in promiscuous ruin: Karnak, Baalbec, Birs Nimroud in Babylon; the splendid temples in Athens and in Corinth; the temples of Jupiter, and Janus, and Apollo—all in Rome save the little temple of Ceres and the Pantheon—all are in ruin. No part of the world is now influenced in the slightest degree by the Egyptian, the Persian, the Assyrian, the Roman, the Greek religions, by the religion of the Druids, or of any of the old Teutonic or Scythian races.

It would be but carrying out this view to remark that the world, as left to itself, has made no advances since. Hinduism indeed survives, but it has made no progress, and it has not commended itself to man as the religion which he needs as civilization advances. Buddhism survives, but it also has made no progress in character, or in adapting itself to the wants of man, since it started from India and spread over China. Nor have men who have rejected Christianity, and renounced the ancient Paganism, although they have shown that they are abreast or ahead of the world in other things, devised a system of religion that would meet the wants of man, or that would commend itself to mankind as worthy to be perpetuated. Mr. Hume and Mr. Gibbon proposed no new system; Shaftesbury, Bolingbroke, Hobbes of Malmesbury, Morgan, proposed none; the system of Lord Herbert commended itself to but few minds in his own age, and now commends itself to none. The world has not shown that it is satisfied with the views of Hegel and Kant, of Strauss, of Renan, and of Comte. But my present purpose does not require me to pursue this argument.

It remains only to make a remark on the other thing suggested in regard to the limitations of the human mind—that limitation as illustrated in the attempt to give to man a "book-revelation"—to accomplish what the Bible claims to accomplish. The inquiry is, what, in the failure of *reasoning* on the subject, has man produced claiming to be a "book-revelation" from God, or to supply what reason has not shown itself able to supply.

It must be assumed here that those efforts *are* the result of the unaided human intellect, for a contrary supposition, or an admission that they are *inspired*, would not, of course, bear on my argument. For the sake of argument, at least, it may be admitted that they are the result of unaided human genius. The question is, whether they meet the wants of man ; whether they supply what Grecian wisdom could not supply ; whether men will be likely to attempt any thing more with any prospect of success.

The powers of the human mind have exhausted themselves in regard to a "book-revelation" in the Sibylline oracles, the Zendavesta, the Vedas and Shasters, the Koran, and the Book of Mormon—chiefly in the Koran.

It can not be denied that in some of these there is vast power ; it can not, with reason, be supposed that in respect to a pretended revelation these are to be surpassed, or that these pretended revelations are to be superseded by those of human origin that will better meet the wants, or that will have higher claims to the faith

of men. Including the Bible now in the number of
books that claim to be a revelation from God, it may be
assumed that, if *that* is on the same level with respect
to its origin, the human powers have exhausted themselves, and that the question whether man can devise
what shall be received as a revelation from God is
closed forever, and that the choice of that which shall
guide the race is limited to these. If the Bible is of
divine origin it determines the matter that there is to
be no other, for it claims to be final on the subject, and
man must, therefore, embrace the Sibylline oracles, *or*
the Zendavesta, *or* the Shasters, *or* the Bible, *or* the
Koran, *or* the Book of Mormon, *or* have no revelation.

In respect to the question now before us, however,
the Bible is to be put aside, for we are inquiring into
the capacities of the human mind on the subject *apart*
from the Bible—from Christianity.

The question for the infidel is whether he shall embrace one of the other books referred to, or whether he
shall attempt to originate one of a higher order that
will more perfectly meet the wants of men, or whether he shall reject all claims of pretended revelations
whatever.

The remark which I am now making is, that the powers of the human mind have *exhausted* themselves in
these efforts, and that it is hopeless now for an impostor to produce a " book-revelation," or such a pretended book, that shall be so far in advance of the rest of
the world as to meet the wants of mankind, or that
shall control as many millions of the human race as
these books do or have done, or that shall have the
prospect, as we believe the Bible has, of securing the
ultimate faith of all men.

Take, for example, the best of these books—the Koran. What prospect is there now—what possibility—that *man* shall originate a book claiming to have divine authority, that shall control as many millions of the human race as that book has done, and does now? For that book has formed the faith of nations. It has controlled armies, and directed wars, and made laws, and laid the foundations of empires. It has ruled for a thousand years some of the most acute, profound, energetic, active portions of mind that God has made. It controls now one hundred and sixty millions of minds. How many are controlled by Lord Herbert, by Bolingbroke, by Kant, by Hegel, by Comte? *We* may not be able, indeed, to read that book, either in the original language or in a translation, but we can not but respect it. The late Mr. Everett said that *he* had often attempted to read it, but had been unable to accomplish it; and all of us who attempt it, after a few pages or chapters, coincide with his remark, and lay down the book. But it *is* read, and read as the Bible is, by millions too, as giving them law, and forming their faith, and we can not but respect it. We can not but feel an interest in *any* book that has power to hold one hundred and sixty millions of the human race in subjection, and to mould the institutions and laws of so large a portion of mankind. There is more to interest us in that fact than there was in the power of Alexander, who subdued the world by arms; or in the power of the Autocrat of Russia, who rules by hereditary right; or in the power of Napoleon, who held nations in subjection by a most potent and active will. For, in such cases, there is living power, and there are vast armies, and there are frowning bulwarks, and there are the means of crushing and destroying men. But the dominion of the Koran is THE

DOMINION OF A BOOK—a silent, still, speechless thing that has no will, no armies, no living energies, no chainshot, no cannon, and yet it exerts a power which the monarch and the conqueror never wields. It lives, too, when monarchs and conquerors die. It rules advancing generations, and subdues their wills too. It moulds their opinions, leads them to temples of worship, and restrains their passions with a power which monarchs never wielded. It guides them in life, and is the last book which they consult, or call to remembrance, on the bed of death; and I think it will not be denied that I am justified in the conclusion that the powers of the human mind have exhausted themselves in that direction; that no man—not even Comte—can hope that it is within the range of his powers to originate a system that shall exert an influence on mankind as wide as the Koran, or that, displacing the Bible, and the Koran, and the Zendavesta, and the Shasters, shall disclose a system of religion that shall meet the wants of all mankind.

I infer from these remarks that the powers of man have exhausted themselves in this direction; that the human mind is limited on the subject of religion; that there are boundaries which it does not pass; that, if man is to have light to guide him to his Maker, it must be found, not in the recorded results of human thinking hitherto; not in any intuitions to which the human powers may rise; not in any books of human devising claiming to be a revelation, but in a "book-revelation" that comes direct from God—not in the Sibylline oracles, or in the Zendavesta, or in the Shasters, or in the Koran, but in the Bible.

LECTURE II.

HISTORICAL EVIDENCE AS AFFECTED BY TIME.

HISTORICAL criticism is comparatively a modern sci-ence. For the introduction and establishment of this science we are undoubtedly mainly indebted to the Germans, who, to whatever extent they may have car-ried it into Rationalism in theology, or skepticism in the classics, have unquestionably laid down, among much that is false, the true principles that are to be applied to the writings of the ancients.

Niebuhr, in the Preface to his History of Rome, says: "The History of Rome was treated, during the first two centuries after the revival of letters, with the same pros-tration of the understanding and judgment to the writ-ten letter that had been handed down, and the same fearfulness of going beyond it, which prevailed in all the other branches of knowledge. If any one had pre-tended to examine into the credibility of the ancient writers, and the value of their testimony, an outcry would have been raised against such atrocious presump-tion. The object aimed at was, in spite of every thing like internal evidence, to combine what they related. At the utmost, one authority was made to give way in some particular instance to another; and this was done as mildly as possible, and without leading to any far-ther results. Here and there, indeed, a man of an inde-pendent mind, like Glareanus, broke through this fence; but inevitably a sentence of condemnation was forth-with pronounced against him. Besides, the persons who did so were not the most learned; and these bold attempts were not carried with consistency throughout. In this department, as in others, men of splendid abilities and the most copious learning conformed to the narrow spirit of their age."

Wolff had, indeed, applied a spirit of unsparing criticism to the writings of Homer; Bentley had continued the application of these principles; Glanvil, who has been termed by a modern critic " the first English writer who had thrown skepticism into a definite form,"* had applied these principles to the prevailing belief in his time in sorcery and witchcraft; Bayle carried them to almost universal skepticism; Niebuhr applied them to the Roman History.

Glanvil, in order to test the historical evidence in regard to the miracles of the New Testament, proposed to make the trial on the belief in witchcraft in his time, as being contemporary, and as making it peculiarly easy to test the credibility of the supernatural; "for," said he, " things remote or long past are either not believed or forgotten; whereas, those being fresh and new, and attended with all the circumstances of credibility, it should be expected that they would have most success upon the obstinacy of unbelievers."†

The general grounds on which this criticism is founded are such as the following: That the witnesses for ancient facts lived in a remote and uncritical age; that they were not, when they lived, subjected to a cross-examination; that they have long since died and can not now be examined; that it was for the interest and attractiveness of their story to relate the marvelous, since most of their historic productions were recited in public, and none were allowed to contradict them; that

* Biographie Universelle.   † Lecky, Hist. of Rationalism, i., 133.

there were few contemporary historical documents with which they could be compared; that there was a love of the marvelous, and a prevailing belief in the supernatural, which was to be gratified; that time has effected changes in the public mind in most or all these respects; and that now, in a more critical age, and on the coolness of calm reflection, and with tests to separate the marvelous from the real, it is proper to apply to *all* ancient writings the principles of criticism suggested by the present advanced position of the world.

Time *has* made changes affecting historical testimony. All is not now believed that has been believed in former ages—nor should it be; all is not believed that is recorded—nor should it be. The world is less credulous than it once was; it is more disposed to examine what is proposed for belief; it has advantages which it once had not for this; it demands evidence which it did not once demand; it applies an unsparing criticism to what was once accredited as undoubted truth. It has learned that many false records have come down to us from the past; that there have been errors in transcribing ancient documents; that many of those documents have been corrupted by design, if an object was to be gained by it—if the glory of a nation or a hero was to be exalted, if the claims of a religion were to be established, if the interest of a party in the state, or in philosophy, was to be promoted; and it has learned that many of the documents which have come down to us from ancient times are forged documents; that there have been myths, legends, and fables wrought into history; that there have been fancied records of dynasties and heroes stretching back an almost illimitable number of years; that there have been details of unreal battles, of imaginary dynasties, and of fancied wonders;

that there have been apocryphal histories and apocryphal gospels.

Especially there has been a change on the whole subject of the supernatural.   In the early ages of the world
the relation of a supernatural event did nothing to im-
pair the general credit of the history, and the record of
such an event was received with as little skepticism as
a statement in regard to the ordinary events of the
world.   It does not appear that the statements of Livy
respecting the marvelous events attending the foundation of Rome and its early history impaired the general credit of his history, or lessened the public faith in
his statements in regard to things occurring under the
operation of natural causes.   It may be presumed, on
the contrary, that such statements of the marvelous
commended his history to a stronger credence, as being
in accordance with the common belief respecting the
foundation of empires, and as indicating the special favor of the gods toward the nation—a nation started on
a loftier career, and under better auspices, which could
refer to special divine interpositions in its behalf; which
could prove that even the gods were present when the
foundations of its walls and of its Capitol were laid.

All this has passed away.   An unsparing criticism
has swept all those marvels from the early history of
Rome, and in doing this, it demands that all the records
of marvels in the early history of nations should be regarded as fabulous.   To such an extent has the principle been carried, in fact, that the claim that "miracles"
or marvels have occurred in any period of the history
of the world is to be regarded as proof that the entire
history, and all that is dependent on it, is false.   Renan,
in his "Life of Jesus" (p. 17), says of the Gospels: "Let
the gospels be in part legendary: that is evident, since

they are full of *miracles* and the *supernatural ;*" that is, the fact that "miracles" and the "supernatural" are recounted there is to be regarded as undoubted proof that they are in a great degree "legendary"—on the same level with the first portion of the history of Livy, or with the early records of Egypt.

So, again, in a passage apparently approved by the Westminster Review* as a just principle, he says, "It is an absolute rule of criticism not to admit into history any narrative of miraculous incidents. This is not the result of any metaphysical system; it is simply a fact of observation. No such facts have ever been established, and all alleged miracles resolve themselves into illusion and imposture. All miracles that may be made the subject of examination vanish away."

The demand is now—a demand which this age is to consider, for it affects every question about a revelation, and is vital in its bearings on Christianity—that this shall be regarded as a universal rule in history; or, that the claim that a miracle has been wrought shall at once set aside all the evidences adduced in favor of the truth of any historic record.

To nothing have the principles of a stern historical criticism been more rigorously applied than to the books of the New Testament. All that has been said about legends, and marvels, and interpolated manuscripts, and forged documents, and unknown authorships, has been said about those books. All that has been said about statements being contradictory to each other, or to independent contemporaneous statements; about witnesses as incompetent to give testimony, or as not cross-examined, or as long since dead; about the ability of a more advanced age of the world to judge of a record

* Quoted in the Westminster Review, Oct., 1866.

that has come down from the mists, and through the
mists, of the past—all this has been said of what is affirmed as fact in the New Testament. A more unsparing criticism has been employed *because* the events
referred to are of a religious nature; and a portion of
the scientific and historic world—a portion not small—
is hastening to the conclusion, as a universal canon of
criticism, that the fact that any pretended history records a "miracle" is full demonstration that the history is false.

The question suggested by these criticisms is a *fair*
question; a question which men have a right to ask; a
question which the believer in miracles may be held to
answer. The value of evidence *is* affected by time.
One age may be much more competent to examine the
credibility of testimony than another. A subsequent
generation may be much better qualified to examine
such testimony than that in which the event was said
to have occurred. It may be easier to ascertain the
exact truth in regard to an event at a subsequent period
than when it occurred, as the movements and positions
of forces engaged in a battle can be best understood
and explained when the smoke of the battle has cleared
away. Statements apparently contradictory may be
explained and reconciled; different accounts may be
sifted and compared, and the result of all credible testimony may be combined in one. It is ever to be remembered that *the historic statement of an event is what
it is reported to be by all who witnessed it, and who have
made a record in regard to it ; not the statement of an
individual.* The historic statement in respect to the
decline and fall of the Roman Empire is what it is reported to have been by the great multitude of authors
and writers whom Mr. Gibbon had before him in com-

posing his history. His task was tó select, compare, reconcile, arrange, and combine into that *one* harmonious and magnificent history which he has given to mankind, all that was credible in that multitude of writers as bearing on the events of history, not to reproduce merely the statement of any *one* of those authors. The Scripture narrative of an event is what it is reported to have been by *all* the sacred writers, and the task of an expositor of the Bible is to compare, reconcile, arrange, and combine these also into one harmonious whole. The real narrative in regard to the life of the Redeemer is not what it is reported to be by Matthew, *or* Mark, *or* Luke, *or* John—it is the statement of all of them combined.

It is also a very pertinent question—a question which we may be held to answer—in what manner a religion, urging its claims now on the ground of the evidence on which Christianity advanced *its* claims, and on which it undoubtedly made its way in the world eighteen hundred years ago, would be met *in* this age—in this nineteenth century. Would it now; if the same evidences of its divine origin were urged, be received as a religion from God? Would it make its way in the world in this age as it did then? Would the evidences of its miracles be received in this scientific and critical age as they were in that comparatively uncritical, unscientific, and credulous age—an age when men were disposed to believe in the marvelous, and when the belief in the supernatural interposition of the gods in human affairs was the common belief of men? Was the evidence of the miracles ever thus subjected to such tests as they would be now, or as they ought to have been; would they convince men now as they did then? If it be admitted that the religion was propagated and embraced then on evidence that seemed to be satisfactory to mankind, would it be embraced, and could it be propagated now, on the same evidence? Would not that evidence be subjected to a more rigid and just scrutiny, and would it not, *therefore,* be rejected? If so, should it not be rejected now?

"Let a thaumaturgist," says Renan,[*] "present himself to-morrow with testimony sufficiently important to merit our attention; let him announce that he is able, I will suppose, to raise the dead; what would be done? A commission composed of physiologists, physicians, chemists, persons experienced in historical criticism, would be appointed. This commission would choose the corpse, make it certain that death was real, designate the hall in which the experiment should be made, and regulate the whole system of precautions necessary to leave no room for doubt. If, under such conditions, the resurrection should be performed, a probability almost equal to certainty would be attained. However, as an experiment ought always to be capable of being repeated, as one ought to be capable of doing again what one has done once, and as, in the matter of miracles, there can be no question of easy or difficult, the thaumaturgist would be invited to reproduce his marvelous acts under other circumstances, upon other bodies, in another medium. If the miracle succeeds each time, two things would be proven: first, that supernatural acts do come to pass in the world; second, that the power to perform them belongs or is delegated to certain persons. But who does not see that no miracle was ever performed under such conditions; that always hitherto the thaumaturgist has chosen the subject of the experiment, chosen the means, chosen the

* Life of Jesus, p. 44, 45.

public; that, moreover, it is, in most cases, the people themselves who, from the undeniable need which they feel of seeing in great events and great men something divine, create the marvelous legends afterward."

It may be added, as illustrating this feeling, that the world is beginning to demand an altogether different class of evidences of Christianity from that which satisfied the generations that preceded us, and although the authors, some of them at least, who satisfied those generations of the truth of the Bible, have scarcely passed away, yet that Grotius de Veritate, and Paley's Evidences, and Lardner's Credibility, and Chalmers's Evidences of Christianity, are beginning to be regarded as books pertaining to the past—books that performed their work well enough in their own time, but which are soon to be reckoned with the obsolete defenses of Christianity in the times of Porphyry, Celsus, and Julian, or in the times of the British deists of the seventeenth century. Whatever might have been the value of that evidence, and that mode of argumentation, in a former age, and however such arguments may have convinced the world in former times, it is now held that we are not at liberty to demand that the same credit shall be given to the arguments in this age. "Let the thaumaturgist," Renan would say, " work over the miracle in *our* times in such a manner as to satisfy an age far different from that when the miracles were pretended to have been wrought."

It becomes, therefore, very important to inquire whether, on the alleged facts on which Christianity was first propagated, and which were regarded eighteen hundred years ago as sufficient evidence to prove that the religion was from God, and under which the religion actually spread over the world, it may be commend-

C

ed to mankind now? Or has time so rectified the judgment of mankind on the subject of testimony as to show that the evidence was valueless then, and should be regarded as valueless now, and that the religion was in fact propagated under a delusion?

This is a fair question. This introduces the subject of this Lecture. It will be illustrated under two heads:

The general principles on the subject.

The application of those principles to the Christian testimony.

The general subject to be illustrated is, EVIDENCE AS AFFECTED BY TIME.

Evidence as bearing on things to be believed—which is its proper province—must pertain to subjects as mathematical, as legal, as scientific, as moral, as historical.

No one would pretend that on these subjects precisely the same kind of testimony would be demanded; no one would maintain that the evidence, to be satisfactory to the mind, must be precisely the same; no one would affirm that all would be equally affected by time, or that the same rules are to be applied in estimating their value.

In mathematics, time makes no change in the force and value of the evidence by which a proposition is established. If it be granted that shorter methods may be used, or that new methods of demonstration may be discovered, as the Algebraic process, or Logarithms, or Fluxions, or the Differential Calculus, yet these do not demonstrate that the former evidence was false, or unreliable as far as it went, or that that for which it was employed as a demonstration was false. It must be— it can not be otherwise—that Euclid believed that in a right angled triangle the square of the hypothenuse is equal to the sum of the squares on the two sides, on the same evidence on which we believe it, and the proof on which he relied, as far as it was proof, is as forcible now as it was then. Time does nothing to affect that evidence. It neither confirms nor impairs it. The evidence is to us precisely what it was to the human mind eighteen hundred years ago, and it will be the same to the end of the world. We believe it not because Euclid believed it, or because there is evidence that it *was* believed then, or because the truth of the proposition was propagated on the ground of the evidence then employed, but because the proof to our minds is precisely, neither more nor less, what it was to the first mind on which the truth of the "forty-seventh" proposition dawned. The proof can not be added to or diminished; and that proof will go down to the end of the world, whatever changes may occur in the laws of criticism, or in any advances which may be made in the capability of judging of evidence. Many new truths may be discovered and added to this, but time does not change the faith of mankind in this.

In legal matters, time does not necessarily or materially affect evidence. It affects the manner of arriving at it; the question as to what *is* legal testimony; the determination about the credibility of witnesses; the question how far interest in the case, or relationship to the parties, shall affect their credibility; the mode of examination, in open court or in secret; the credit due to the young, to those of feeble mind, or to those who may be partially insane; the competency of witnesses in general; but the evidence itself is not affected by time. The evidence that Titus killed Gaius in the time of Augustus, and that he was properly convicted and punished, is not modified by the lapse of eighteen hundred years, and by all the changes which have occurred

in the world in that time. If the evidence then relied
on established the fact so that, under the laws, Titus
was justly punished, it establishes it now, so that it
ought to go into history, and to be believed in all coming time; to become one of the cases of precedents establishing the principles on which justice is to be administered in every future age.

In scientific matters, the principles are the same. Testimony or evidence is not likely to be affected in any
way on these subjects; for, in general, we do not believe the facts of science on the evidence of testimony.
Although it is true that the mass of men credit the facts
of science—in Astronomy, Geology, Chemistry, and in
the kindred sciences—so far as they come before them
at all for belief, on the ground of testimony, yet it is
also true that these great truths and facts can be subjected to experiment and observation by any one that
chooses.   Galileo *testified* that there were moons apper-
taining to Jupiter.   That he did so testify can be easily
established by history; that there are moons revolving
around the planet is a matter, however, not depending
on the credibility of his testimony, or on the historical
records of that time, but can be verified by any one by
looking through a telescope.

Time sets aside, indeed, many things in science which
were once assuredly believed. But it is not done because the testimony is doubtful; it is because the observations were not accurately made, or because there
were false theories, or because better instruments, and
a more varied and prolonged observation, have shown
exactly what the facts were and are. But time, for
example, has not affected the evidence in regard to
the facts connected with the celebrated "Eclipse of
Thales," on which so much has been written, and which

has been the subject of so much discussion among astronomers — neither the fact in regard to the *effect* of that eclipse as stated by Herodotus, or the fact that Thales predicted it. Herodotus says (book i., ch. lxxiv.) that there was· a war between the Lydians and the Medes, and that, after various turns of fortune, " in the sixth year a conflict took place ; and on the battle being joined, it happened that the day suddenly became night. And this change," says he, " Thales of Miletus had predicted to them, definitely naming the year in which the event took place. The Lydians and the Medes, when they saw day turned into night, ceased from fighting, and both sides were desirous of peace."*

Time, in regard to this event, has undoubtedly shown that the *theory* which Thales held in regard to astronomy was a false theory; that the prediction implied no *very* accurate knowledge of the heavens; that probably *all* his knowledge on the subject was derived from the observation of the periodical times when eclipses occur; and that probably also *all* that he predicted was the *year* when this eclipse would take place, not the hour, the day, nor even the month; but time has not set aside the evidence in regard to the *fact.* Thus time may establish the truth of a scientific event, but not the cause of it; the fact may be demonstrated by testimony to the end of the world, but the testimony does nothing to establish the *causes* of it. On this point, however, time may do this: while the testimony as to the fact is unaffected, it *may* do much to show what was, or was not the cause of the event. Time may show that what was regarded as miraculous and supernatural when it happened, took place in the ordinary operations of nature, and the " dim eclipse" which, at the

* *Whewell's* History of the Inductive Sciences, vol. i., p. 509.

time of its occurrence, "with fear of change perplexed
monarchs," may take its place among ordinary events,
to be explained in accordance with ordinary and well-
understood laws. The fact existed as recorded; time
has changed the views of men in regard to the cause,
and reduced it from a marvelous to an ordinary operation of nature. What armies would now be stayed in
battle by an eclipse of the sun? Of ancient facts now
as reported to us in history, we give credit to the facts
as reported; we explain them as we choose. The facts
we admit. Here we pause. All in regard to the explanation is as much under our control as it was under
the control of those who have reported the facts to us.

In regard to moral subjects—to philosophy—the same
remark is to be made. We receive the statement that
certain opinions in morals, in philosophy, in religion
were held; we embrace those opinions or not, as we
choose; we explain and defend them in our own way.
It can not be denied, as a matter of historic verity, that
Plato, in the Gorgias, argues in favor of the immortality of the soul. The fact that he at times *seems* to hold
this is not to be set aside. But no one of us believes
the doctrine *because* he thus testified to it, and no one
believes it on the ground of the *proof* or *evidence* which
he adduces in favor of it. Time holds on to the fact
that such opinions were held; it sets aside, it may be,
all the arguments on which the opinion was held, or
reverses entirely the faith in the doctrine itself. That
the schoolmen held certain opinions we do not doubt;
that they were defended by great prolixity and by marvelous subtilty of argument, any one may have evidence
of who chooses to look into the ponderous tomes that
so calmly now repose in dust in the alcoves of our great
libraries, like ancient knights incased in armor in old

cathedrals; but who feels bound to believe their opinions; who feels bound to make himself acquainted even with the terms of their logic—the weapons with which they dealt their heavy blows?

There remains the question as to the bearing of these remarks on historic records—the records of *facts* pertaining to ancient times. This point will lead to a matter of much interest, and one which specially pertains to us, the question about the *facts* in regard to the miracles of the New Testament.

It is this kind of evidence which is mainly affected by time; this which leads into the whole region of historical criticism.

The manner in which this evidence is affected by time, and the reasons why there is occasion for the modern science of historical criticism, will be made plain by a few remarks.

The following things, then, are to be taken into the account in estimating the value of ancient historical testimony: (*a*) The imperfect observation in regard to the facts that are recorded. (*b*) The disposition for the marvelous in the early periods of history. (*c*) The character of the witnesses for competency, veracity, credibility, candor, honesty, freedom from selfish ends. (*d*) National vanity; not a few histories being in fact designed to exalt the glory of one nation over its rivals. (*e*) The nature of the subject; for on some subjects men are much more honest and credible than on others. Such are, or may be, for example, the views which men have on the subject of religion, that no reliance almost could be placed on their testimony in regard to the facts that pertain to it. The narrative would be certain to be colored by the views entertained on the subject, and the largest allowance would be necessary in estimating the value of the historical record. (*f*) The voluntary corruption of records for national, private, or party purposes. (*g*) The slow accumulation of errors in the process of transcription of records—small at first, and few in number, yet unavoidably perpetuated and multiplied by time. (*h*) The number of false or apocryphal histories that may be written for various purposes, as the long imaginary histories of the dynasties of Egypt and India, or the apocryphal Gospels.

Time affects all these things; and the work of historical criticism when the world becomes sensible that these have accumulated, and that the true should be separated from the false, becomes a work so vast as to be properly dignified with the name of *science*. Nothing demands more learning, patience, acuteness, sagacity, candor, and impartiality than such a work, and he who, in history, contributes any thing to separate the true from the false, and to give the world a correct record of the past, is to be classed among the benefactors of mankind.

In looking at these things, and contemplating the uncertainties and the corruptions of history, it becomes a question whether *any* facts pertaining to the past can be placed on the same level with those which are occurring in our own time, and which come under our own observation, or the observation of our contemporaries; or whether all the alleged facts of ancient history are to be classed among myths and legends; or where, *if* there is true history, the region of legend ends and that of history begins; and *if* legend, myth, and fable reign at all in the past, what is the *extent* of the dominion? Does it terminate with the legends of Livy? Does it cease with the stories of the interventions of the gods in battle, and in the foundation of cities and empires? Or does it embrace also the account of the Creation and Fall in Genesis; the record of the deluge; of the overthrow of Sodom; of the wonders of Egypt; of the wandering of the Hebrews in the desert; of the miracles of Gideon and Samson — the records of the Gospels, and of the acts of the apostles?

Is there *any thing* that can be *known* of the past?

There is a limit to skepticism in regard to the events of the past, as there is a limit to skepticism on all subjects. Valuable in its place, and valuable as an attribute of the human mind, yet there is a boundary which the Author of that mind has fixed, beyond which it is not allowed permanently to pass, and the world, sooner or later, works itself right on this subject, as it does on all others.

There are facts which historical criticism can not effect, and to which skepticism, even that of the most destructive nature, can not be applied. There are facts which Mr. Hume and Mr. Gibbon found in the past, and which Niebuhr found, and which are never henceforward to be called in question. The question in secular history is, what is their limit? The great question in religion, a question which Strauss, and Renan, and Lepsius, and Bishop Colenso, and the authors of the "Essays and Reviews," and the writers in the Westminster Review, are endeavoring to help us to solve, is whether the proper limit will exclude the facts in the Life of Jesus, and the miracles of the Old and New Testaments?

Let us now inquire for a moment what principles are to be applied to the solution of the historical question.

The world has settled down into a general view on the subject as to what is necessary to establish *faith* in an ancient fact, and when those things are found, the

C 2

faith of the world is, from the constitution of the human mind, as firm as it is in well-established contemporaneous events—it may be said as firm as when an event occurs under our own eyes; for we no more doubt that Cæsar fell by the hands of assassins in the senate-house, or that Xerxes crossed the Hellespont, or that the Persians were defeated at Marathon and Salamis, than that Washington fought at Trenton, or that Lord Cornwallis surrendered at Yorktown, or that the tide of rebel invasion was turned back at Gettysburg, or that the rebel General Lee surrendered to General Grant.

Such things occur as entering into history, in such cases, as the following:

(*a*) When the witnesses are competent, and have a proper opportunity of observing the facts; that is, where the facts are the proper subject of testimony *as facts*, or as actual occurrences, and not as matters of fancy and opinion.

(*b*) When the witnesses concur in the general statement of the fact, though they may vary in the circumstances or details.

(*c*) When there is no motive for deception or imposture. We do not see, for example, that Tacitus had any motive for either, and hence almost no part of his narrative has ever been called in question.

(*d*) When the facts recorded are strongly against the religious faith of the narrator, or when he would *wish* that the facts were otherwise. It is this which gives such value to the statement of Mr. Hume that "England owes whatever of civil liberty it enjoys to the influence of the Puritans"—a fact which we are morally certain he would have wished to be otherwise, and which he would have kept back if he could have done it as an honest historian; and this it is, with other things, which

gives so great value to the "History of the Decline and
Fall of the Roman Empire," for many of the facts recorded by Mr. Gibbon were undoubtedly such as a skeptic in religion would have wished to have been otherwise; in respect to many of those stated, Mr. Gibbon
could not but see that the world would regard them
as furnishing proof that the religion was of Divine origin; of many of those stated, therefore, it required all
his great talents to explain them on the supposition
that the religion was false. Yet he recorded them,
without suppressing what was true, or interpolating
what was false, or perverting what had occurred, leaving it to himself and to other skeptics to explain them
as they could.

(e) When the facts referred to, and which are said to
have occurred, furnish the most easy and natural explanation of the existing state of things, or go into existing events as the cause does into the effect, and are indispensable to the solution of what actually exists in
the world. There are, undoubtedly, numerous things
existing in the world—in the civilization, the arts, the
laws, the religion—for which the alleged facts in history
are the most natural explanation, and which are, in fact,
indispensable to the explanation. The main facts which
are said to have occurred in the life of Mohammed furnish the best explanation of the opinions, the laws, the
customs, the religious belief of a hundred and sixty millions of the human family; nor can those opinions, laws,
and customs be explained except on the supposition
that those facts actually occurred.

(f) When those facts are commemorated, and the
knowledge of them is perpetuated by monuments, coins,
medals, games, festivals, processions, and celebrations
from age to age; when, without the supposition of those

facts, all those things would be unmeaning, or would be wholly inexplicable. The annual observance of the fourth day of July in this country is founded on the Declaration of Independence, and can not be explained except on the belief of the facts as history states them. The division of the lands in England is founded on the fact that there was a "Doomsday Book," and that the lands were apportioned in accordance with that. The establishment of the Feudal System in England, the form of the government for ages, the tenure by which land is held, and the distinction of ranks, is founded on the fact that William the Norman was victorious at the battle of Hastings, and that the country was apportioned among his barons; nor can the laws in regard to real estate in England for eight hundred years be explained except on that supposition. The boundaries of the old thirteen states of the Union can be explained only on the supposition, which history states, that charters were granted to the colonies by the crown, fixing those boundaries—for there are no natural boundaries between Massachusetts and New Hampshire; between Connecticut and Massachusetts; between Pennsylvania and New York; between Virginia and North Carolina. The Tower of London can be explained only by a belief in the great facts of history as recorded in the books. What mean those standards taken in war, those old suits of armor, shields, and bows, and battle-axes, but that the nation once was as history represents it to have been? How came they there? Who invented them? Who had power to persuade the nation that all these had been used in wars and conquests? And what mean those blocks, made as if for beheading men, and those axes, unless it were true that Lord Russell, and Sir Walter Raleigh, and Algernon Sidney were actually beheaded? Who placed them there? Who has been able to persuade the nation that they represent bloody realities?

Thus facts come to us about which the world does not doubt; reports of ancient things which can not be explained except on the supposition that the main facts as alleged by history are true. So the fossil remains of the earth—the coal-beds—the extinct remains of races swept off in times far remote—preserved in enduring rocks, and laid far below the surface of the earth—are, like these old pieces of armor in the Tower of London, memorials of what the history of our world has been. The geologist, a laborious and most useful historian, is performing, by toil and sorrow, what the conductor through the Tower of London does in explaining the history of the past.

Things, therefore, may be, and are made true in regard to the past. No man has any more doubt that Cæsar was assassinated than he has that Mr. Lincoln was.

It remains to consider the application of these principles to the particular subject of Christianity—the question whether time has so affected the evidence in regard to the facts on which Christianity is based as to render those facts unworthy of belief.

I have already remarked that a more unsparing criticism has been applied to the historic records of Christianity than to any other records pertaining to the past. All that has been alleged against any other history has been urged against the books of the New Testament; all the charges which have been elsewhere alleged of incompetency on the part of witnesses; of defective observation; of personal interest; of corrupted manuscripts; of apocryphal writings; of inconsistencies and

contradictions; of uncertain authorship; of improbability in regard to the events; of mistakes and errors, have
been and are alleged in regard to the Evangelists.

To the ordinary difficulties in regard to ancient records, there is, in reference to the New Testament, this
additional difficulty, greatly augmented by the change
in the views of the world on the subject of the supernatural and the marvelous, that the narrative requires
us to believe in miracles—not merely that Jesus lived,
and taught, and was a good man, and founded Christianity, as Strauss and Renan admit, but that he cast
out devils; that he healed diseases by a word; that he
raised the dead; that he raised himself from the grave
and ascended to heaven—as the difficulty of believing
the record of Livy in regard to the foundation of Rome
would be greatly augmented if we were required to believe his legends about Romulus and Remus, or the miracle when a yawning chasm appeared in the city threatening its very existence, and the closing of the chasm
by the self-sacrifice of the gallant Curtius throwing himself into it clad in full armor.   No one can be required,
it would be said, in this sharp, keen, searching, scientific age, to believe what men readily believed in the fabulous periods of history, when the belief in the supernatural prevailed every where; when eclipses were
portents and prodigies; when, in ignorance of the laws
of nature, it was believed that the heavenly bodies were
moved by angels; that all atmospheric changes were
effected by angels; that a special angel was assigned
to every star and every element; when it was believed
that comets were precursors of calamity, and that a
special comet, ominous of evil, preceded the death of
such men as Cæsar or Constantine, or that such a comet
appeared before the invasion of Greece by Xerxes, be-

fore the Peloponnesian War, before the civil wars of
Cæsar and Pompey, before the fall of Jerusalem, before
the invasion of Attila, and before the coming of famine
and pestilence.* A more relentless criticism by far has
been applied to the New Testament than was applied
by Wolff to the Iliad, or by Niebuhr to the History of
Rome. And what strange, unhistorical theories are
held in regard to the four Evangelists! Those Evangelists contain indeed fragments of truth. There is
enough of truth in them to account for the origin of
Christianity. But they are without order or arrangement. They are of uncertain date or authorship. They
are to be rearranged and reconstructed. The portions
added are to be eliminated; the deficiencies are to be
made up by sagacity; the improbable parts are to be
discarded; all that is miraculous is to be regarded as
fabulous and legendary. The system of Christianity is
a "myth," having for its basis a very uncertain personage, of sufficient reality to suggest the mythical actions
ascribed to him, as in Strauss; or Jesus was a real personage, the real founder of Christianity, a young man
of vast originality, of wonderful genius, slowly made
conscious of his own powers, wrought up tò enthusiasm
unexpectedly to himself, to believe that he was to change
and reform the world, and acting on the borders of insanity, as in the romance of Renan.

What, then, is to be believed? What are the principles, as matters of history, which are to guide us?

Christianity, as we shall see in a subsequent Lecture,
has a history as marked and definite as any other; an
origin, a development, a progress, an array of facts that
belong to it alone. England has a history: its institutions; its judicial arrangements; its trial by jury; its

* *Lecky*, History of Rationalism, i., 289, 290.

writ of Habeas Corpus; its government by King, Lords, and Commons. Mohammedanism has a history. There is that which is *real* which has gone into the religion of Islam; which makes it what it is; that without the knowledge of which its facts can not be explained. So has Christianity.

The principles which are to be applied to this subject, as connected with the train of thought in this Lecture, must now be stated in few words.

(1.) The same principles of historical criticism must be applied to the books of the New Testament as to other books: no sharper, no more lax; no more severe, no more indulgent. No favor should be shown to them because they claim to be sacred books; nor should they be approached with any prejudice, or any suspicion, on that account. The question is not what the book *is about;* it is whether it *is true.* It is possible, in the nature of things, that a book *may* record correctly the account of the healing of a blind man, or the raising of a man from the dead; and, if such events have actually occurred, it is not to be *assumed* that a correct record can not be made of them, for such a record is as possible as the record of a battle or a record of travels. And, on the other hand, it should not be claimed that such a record, even when it describes the resurrection of the Redeemer from the grave, laying the foundation of the hope of immortal life for man, is to be exempt from the profane hands of criticism, or that a man is guilty of presumption, profaneness, or blasphemy who approaches such a record as he does the writings of Livy or Tacitus. Perhaps it should be said that the very importance of the subject, and the very sacredness of the subject, and the vastness of the interests at stake, should make the search into the genuineness and the accuracy of the narrative more keen and skeptical—as the claim of a title to a peerage or a vast estate would be examined more carefully than the title to the office of a justice of the peace or to a few acres of ground; or as one would examine more carefully the evidence that a ship was so constructed as to bear him safely across the ocean, than he would the capability of a skiff to sport with on a pond.

That there has been a delusion on this subject, on both sides, there can be no doubt. The facts that the books of the New Testament are regarded as sacred; that they pertain to religion; that faith in them has been for ages imbedded in the hearts of men; that the hopes of men are founded on them; that the consequences of finding that they are false would be terrible—leaving man without hope—darkening the world, dark enough at any rate, by the gloom of absolute despair—these facts, it can not be denied, have influenced many in regard to the manner in which they should approach those books. To them, too, it seems to be an act of profaneness—a crucifying again of the Lord of glory—to approach the account of the sufferings, the death, and the resurrection of the Redeemer with the same rules with which we approach the account of the plague in Athens by Thucydides, and to apply the same rules to the one which we apply to the others. Despite every effort to the contrary, we can not but have a different feeling, apart from any thing in the spirit and design of the men, toward Strauss and Renan, from what we have toward Wolff and Niebuhr; for we can hardly help feeling that *they* have profanely, like Uzzah, touched the ark of God. In the one case, we feel that no great interests are at stake, whether the narrative is true or false; in the other is involved all that is dear and sacred to the souls of men.

Yet the sacrifice must be made; the feeling that this is irreverence and profaneness must be overcome. Every man has a right to approach the most sacred records of the Bible with the same severe and stern rules of criticism with which the love of truth would impel him to approach any ancient records whatever. Nay, every man is bound to do it; for higher interests than any which are involved in an inquiry into the title to a peerage or an estate, or any involved in recorded facts in regard to the rise and fall of empires, are at stake. It is to be remarked, indeed, that it is not inconsistent with historical candor that a man should approach the records of the New Testament with the *hope* that they may be found to be true, just as a man may approach the examination of the evidence that the title to his farm is good, or of the news which he has received of the safety of a son that he had supposed was lost at sea, or as he may look on the evidence that his slandered wife is chaste, with the *hope* that the evidence will be found to be true. It is not, it can not be wrong in me to *desire* to find evidence that there is a God and a Savior; that I am to exist forever; that a way of redemption has been provided for sinners; and that there is a world of glory and purity beyond the grave. Nor is such a desire incompatible with candor in the examination of the evidence; for the very greatness of the hope, and of the interests at stake, should, and naturally will, make the mind calm and candid.

(2.) The great facts of Christianity *are* indisputably established, and this has been done by the ordinary methods of historic evidence. Those facts have gone into history as all other ancient facts have done, and the history of the world can not be explained or understood without admitting their reality. The condition of the world as it is now has grown out of those facts, and that condition can no more be explained without the admission of the truth of those facts than the Constitution and laws of England can be explained without admitting the truth that Alfred reigned, or that William the Norman conquered at Hastings and divided the kingdom among his followers, or that from John great concessions were obtained by his barons at Runnymede.

The facts to which I now advert in regard to Christianity as established by evidence are such as the following: (a) That it had an origin far within the limits of well-established history. It has not always been upon the earth. There have been centuries—many centuries—in the history of the world in which it had no existence, and when no germ existed from which it could have been developed. We can go back to the times of which Berosus, Thucydides, Livy make mention, and we can be certain that it did not then, either in germ or in development, exist upon the earth. (b) The time *when* it appeared, or when it was originated, is also a matter of history. The disputed passage in Josephus, if that is genuine, demonstrates it. The *undisputed* passage in Tacitus proves it beyond a question. The fact that the time of its origin is not made a question with Celsus, Porphyry, or Julian, confirms this. The record of Mr. Gibbon puts the matter beyond all doubt. It was a necessity in his historical purpose that he should trace the history of Christianity from its origin, and he has done it. (c) The main facts of the birth, the life, the character, and the death of the Founder of Christianity are matters of history. Strauss does not deny the reality of the existence of Jesus, though the things ascribed to him are "mythical;" Renan does not deny

his existence, or the main facts of his history, though
he has his own way of telling the story. The whole of
his romance is founded on the admission of the main
facts of his life. Jesus was an historical person. There
is the most marked distinction between him and Mars,
and Apollo, and Minerva; between him and King Ar-
thur, and Lear. The fact of his having lived is as clearly established as that of Alexander; the fact of his death,
and the manner of his death, as that of Cæsar. (d) The
fact that Christianity was *propagated*, or was spread
through the world from small beginnings, is established
by history. Its progress from land to land can be
traced; the steps of its movement can be marked on a
map from the time of its humble beginning till it mount-
ed the throne of the Cæsars. Nothing is more definite
and certain in history than the facts about its origin,
and its propagation in the world. Mr. Gibbon has
traced it as clearly and as honestly as he has the career
of his favorite Julian, and the facts have gone into the
undisputed history of nations. (e) History has established the fact that the religion was propagated on the
ground of the belief in the miracles which were alleged
to have been wrought in attestation of its truth, and
especially on the belief that its Author, having been put
to death on a cross, rose again from the dead. Whatever may be the truth in regard to those miracles, and
the fact of that resurrection, no one can doubt that these
things were put forward; that the belief of them was
made essential to the reception of the system; and that
its propagation is to be explained on the ground that
these things were believed to be true; and that it can
not be explained on any other ground. No one, not
Mr. Gibbon, or Renan, or Strauss, has attempted to explain the fact of the propagation of Christianity on the

ground that no claim was set up in regard to the resurrection of Jesus, or on the ground that the claim thus
set up was false. Assuredly the people of the Roman
empire, when they embraced Christianity, did it in the
belief that its Author had been raised from the dead,
and the belief of this was vital to the reception and ex-
tension of the system. The religion could not have
been propagated had it not been for this belief, and it
is equally clear that the account of this *could* not have
been inserted in the narrative respecting the founder
of the system afterward; that is, if it should be supposed that the religion had been propagated *without*
this belief, it would have been impossible to make this
an article of faith afterward. How could it be inserted
in the original records? How could men be made to
believe that a doctrine never adverted to in the propagation of a system had been, in fact, the main thing in
commending it to the world? (*f*) Once more: These
points are not affected materially by the questions
whether miracles were wrought, or whether Jesus was
actually raised from the dead. The point which I am
making is, that the religion was propagated on the *belief* of those things, not on the ground of their *truth.*
How far the fact that the world *believed* in the reality
of the miracles, and that great multitudes of all classes
abandoned their ancient systems of religion, and embraced Christianity as true, on that belief, *proves* that
the miracles were real, is another point which it is proper to argue with an infidel in its proper place. But
that is not the point now before us.

(3.) In looking at the question how far the evidence
of ancient facts is affected by time, I adverted, under
the general inquiry, to these circumstances—when the
, witnesses are competent, and have a proper opportuni-

ty of observing the facts; when there is no motive for deception or imposture; when the facts narrated are against the religious faith of the narrator; when the facts referred to furnish the most easy and natural explanation of existing things; and when these facts are commemorated and perpetuated by monuments, coins, medals, games, festivals, processions, and celebrations; that is, when they go into the very structure of society, and when it is no more easy to *detach* them from existing things than it was to *detach* the name of Phidias from the statue of Minerva without destroying the image. You can not explain the history of the world without the supposition that Cæsar was put to death by the hand of assassins.

It remains only to apply this principle, in few words, to Christianity.

Suppose, then, it were not true that Cæsar was put to death; suppose that the facts which I have adverted to in regard to Christianity, in its history, are false; what follows? What is to be done then? What is the proper work of the man who does not believe this?

On the principles now laid down, we have the same confirmation of the main facts of the history of Christianity which we have of the death of Cæsar, the life of Alfred, and the conquest of England by William the Norman, though on a wider scale, and affecting more deeply the course of history and the condition of the world; for, in the existing state of things on the earth, for one such thing that goes to establish those secular facts, and to make the supposition of their reality indispensable to the explanation of existing things, there are ten, at least, that go to confirm the truth of the main facts of the New Testament. Hard is the task of the skeptic who denies the reality of the death of Cæsar, in the senate-house, or of the existence of Alfred, or of the conquest of William the Norman; harder by far the task of the skeptic who denies the realities of the life and death of Jesus. For, in this case, he must suppose that all history, secular and sacred, has been corrupted and is unreliable; he must suppose that Christianity sprang up without any adequate cause, and at a time unknown; he must suppose that it made its way in the world on what was known to be false-hood; he must suppose that men every where embraced the system manifestly against their own interests, and with nothing to satisfy them of its truth; he must leave unexplained the conduct of thousands of martyrs, many of them of no mean name in philosophy and in social rank; he must explain how it was that acute and sub-tle enemies, like Celsus, Porphyry, and Julian, did not make short work of the argument by denying the truth of the main facts of the Christian history; he must ex-plain the origin of the numerous monuments in the world which have been reared on the supposition of the truth of the great facts of Christian history—the ancient temples whose ruins are scattered every where, the tombs and inscriptions in the Catacombs at Rome, the sculptures and paintings which have called forth the highest efforts of genius in the early and the mediæval ages, and the books that have been written on the sup-position that the religion had the origin ascribed to it in the New Testament; he must explain the observance of the first day of the week in so many lands, and for so many ages, in commemoration of the belief that Christ rose from the dead; he must explain the observance of the day which is supposed to commemorate the birth of the Redeemer, as one would have to explain the ob-servance of the birthday of Washington, on the suppo-

sition that Washington was a "myth," and the observance of the fourth day of July on the supposition that
what has been regarded as a history of the American
Revolution was a romance; he must explain the ordi-
nance kept up in memory of his death for nearly two
thousand years on the supposition that the death of
Christ never occurred on the cross at all; he must explain the honor and the homage done to the cross every
where—as a standard in war, as a symbol of faith, as
a charm or an amulet, as an ornament worn by beauty
and piety, as reared on high to mark the place where
God is worshiped, as an emblem of self-sacrifice, of love,
of unsullied purity—the cross in itself more ignominious than the guillotine or the gibbet—for why should
men do such things with a gibbet if all is imaginary?
—and he must explain all those coins, and medals,
and memorials which crowd palaces, and cabinets, and
churches, and private dwellings, and which are found
beneath decayed and ruined cities, on the supposition
that all these are based on falsehood, and that in all
history there has been nothing to correspond to them
or to suggest them. Can the fossil remains of the Old
World, the ferns in coal-beds, and the forms of fishes
imbedded in the rocks, and the bones of mammoths, and
the skeletons of the Ichthyosaurian and Plesiosaurian
races, be explained on the supposition that such vegetables, and such land and marine monsters never lived?
Will the geologist who happens to be an infidel in religion allow us to urge this in regard to those apparent
records of the former history of the world? Will he
then demand that all in history, in monuments, medals,
tombs, inscriptions, customs, laws, sacred festivals, religious rites, that *seem* to be founded on the truth of the
great facts of Christianity, shall be explained on the

supposition that no such facts ever occurred? that all this is myth, and fable, and delusion?

Hard would be the task of the infidel if he were to undertake this. It was too much for Mr. Gibbon, and he therefore set himself to the work of showing how, *on the admission of these main facts*, the propagation of the religion could be explained on the supposition that it had *not* a divine origin; it was too much for Strauss, and he therefore set himself to the task of showing how, on the supposition that Jesus lived, the system of Christianity could be made to grow around a few central truths, representing in imagined action the ideas of deceivers and impostors; it was too much for Renan, who, admitting the main facts in the New Testament, and attributing to the founder of the system unequaled genius, and a power of which he became slowly conscious, accompanied with much self-delusion, attempted to show how he originated a system designed to overturn all existing systems, and a system that did accomplish it. Each and all of these things go to confirm the position which I have endeavored to establish in this Lecture, that time does not materially affect the evidence of the great facts of history; that what was properly believed at the time when the events occurred may be properly believed now; that if the historic records were lost, we could reproduce many of the leading events of the history of the world. In particular, if the New Testament were destroyed, we could reproduce, from other sources, the main facts pertaining to the life and death of the Founder of Christianity, on which the religion was propagated and received, and the great features of the system as it was first propounded to the world.

How far the principles laid down in this Lecture bear

D

on the subject of miracles, and how far it is necessary
to assume the correctness of the records of miraculous
events in the New Testament, to explain the fact that
the religion was propagated in the world, and has been
continued to the nineteenth century, will be considered
in the application of these principles in the subsequent
Lectures.

LECTURE III.

HISTORICAL EVIDENCE AS AFFECTED BY SCIENCE.

THE subject of this lecture will be Historical Evidence as affected by Science, particularly the relation of Science to Christianity as affecting the evidence of its divine origin.

There is a wide-spread apprehension among many of the friends of Christianity that Science, in its progress, may set aside the evidence that the Bible is a system of revealed truth, and that, if the point is not already reached, it may soon be, when they will be found to be incompatible with each other, and when it will be impossible to reconcile them. There is probably more apprehension on this subject among the true friends of Christianity than they would like to avow to themselves or to others, and there is more dissatisfaction with the attempts which are made to remove the difficulties, and to reconcile the two, than they would think it prudent to admit. There is many a skeptical thought in a Christian's mind which he would be unwilling to utter, for he would not be desirous that his friends should know how much he is perplexed on the subject, and he would not think it right to expose the faith of others to the shock which would be felt if they knew what was passing through his mind. "Oh the temptations," said Dr. Payson, "which have harassed me for the last three months! I have met with nothing like them in books. I dare not mention them to any mortal, lest they should trouble him as they have troubled

me; but should I become an apostate, and write against
religion, it seems to me that I could bring forward objections which would shake the faith of all the Christians in the world. What I marvel at is that the Arch-
deceiver has never been permitted to suggest them to
some of his scribes, and have them published." "My
difficulties," said he in a letter to a friend, "increase
every year. There is one trial which you can not know
experimentally. It is that of being obliged to preach
to others when one doubts of every thing, and can
scarcely believe that there is a God. All the atheisti-
cal, deistical, and heretical objections which I meet
with in books, are childish babblings compared with
those which Satan suggests, and which he urges upon
the mind with a force which seems irresistible. Yet I
am often obliged to write sermons, and to preach, when
these objections beat upon me like a whirlwind, and almost distract me."* Cecil has made a similar remark:
"I have read," said he, "all the most acute and serious
infidel writers, and have been surprised at their poverty. The process of my mind has been such on the subject of revelation that I have often thought Satan has
done more for me than for the best of them; for I have
had, and would have produced, arguments that appeared to me far more weighty than any I ever found in
them against revelation."† In this respect, as in others,
a good man is often in the situation in which the Psalm-
ist was, when, in deep perplexity about the justice of
the divine dealings, he said, "If I say I will speak thus,
behold, I should offend against the generation of thy
children."—Psa. lxxiii., 15. He is therefore silent, hop-
ing almost against hope, that his apprehensions may not
be well founded, and yet not daring to push the inves-

* *Payson's* Works, vol. i., p. 379, 380, ed. Portland, 1846.
† Works of Rev. *Richard Cecil,* vol. iii., p. 110.

tigation farther himself. He is, in this respect, like the mariner who fears to examine his ship lest he should find the wood-work of the bottom eaten through, and nothing between him and the waters but the thin sheathing of copper; or the invalid who fears to have his lungs examined from the apprehension that the examiner may find there the unmistakable beginnings of a fatal disease; or the merchant who fears to examine his books from the apprehension that he will find himself to be a bankrupt. The ship, therefore, unexamined, moves on, the slight cough is borne as well as it can be, and the man of business tries to be calm under the apprehension that, if the truth were known, he would be found to be not worth a farthing.

There is a secret confident feeling on the part of not a few men devoted to scientific pursuits that all this is so, and that these fears in regard to Christianity are well founded. In not a few things, in his apprehension, the statements of the Bible and the disclosures of Science have been demonstrated to be irreconcilable, and he smiles complacently at the efforts made by the friends of religion, and especially by ministers of the Gospel, to harmonize them. He feels a confident assurance that one difficulty on the subject will succeed another, and that if a plausible solution of one discrepancy is suggested, Science will suggest a dozen where the points will be irreconcilable. He has that kind of carelessness, therefore, which a man has in playing a game of chess when he feels that, though his adversary may extricate himself out of some small difficulty in the move, yet the general course of the game is certain, and he can afford to be calm; or which the commander of the armies of the Union might have felt before Richmond, when, though there might have been a temporary reverse, yet the great plan of the campaign was de-

veloping itself, and the final overthrow of the enemy
was certain. So, it is to be feared, not a few men feel
about the final overthrow of Christianity by Science.
They do not exult. They do not care to use the language of triumph. They do not boast of victory : they
smile within, and calmly await the result.

Under these circumstances, it becomes a very important matter to inquire what tendency, if any, there is in
this direction, or what Science has done, or can do, to
render the statements in the Bible incredible. The exact point for consideration on the subject may be easily
understood. There are many things, it would be said,
which were not regarded as incredible at an early period of the world, or which men readily received as
real under the prevailing forms of belief, which Science
ultimately shows to be utterly incredible, and which it
removes from the faith of mankind. By the same process it may remove *all* that is marvelous or supernatural, and thus ultimately destroy every vestige of an argument for the divine origin of the religion.

An illustration will make this point plain. There was
nothing, it would be said, in the statements of Livy
about the prodigies which he records at the foundation
of Rome, or in the early periods of the Roman history,
which was contrary to the existing belief at that time,
which the prevailing views of the nature of evidence
rendered unworthy of belief, or which was a departure
from what was expected to be, and what was understood to be, the course of affairs on the earth. It was
an age of the supernatural and the marvelous. The
world was prepared to receive these accounts. There
was universal faith in superior beings; in the fact that
they often interposed directly in the affairs of men ; that
empires were founded, that battles were decided, and
that the world was controlled by these supernatural

agencies. There were no settled principles of Science contrary to the belief in prodigies, in sorcery, in divination, in necromancy, in demonology, in the reappearance of the dead.

Time has made important changes in regard to these alleged facts. It has reduced them to legends and myths, and the historical critic diminishes the number of things to be believed by mankind by the whole region of the supernatural. Science has taught what may be regarded as credible and what as incredible, and the reader of Roman history no longer feels himself bound to embrace these early marvels as a part of the true history of Rome.

The same thing, it is now alleged, has occurred in regard to the record of miracles and marvels in the Bible. In the early history of the world, and at the time, and in the countries where the books of the Bible were composed, there was nothing in those miracles and marvels which was inconsistent with the prevalent modes of belief, or with the knowledge of the universe as then understood. Faith in the miraculous and the marvelous was then the normal state of belief. All that could not be explained on natural principles—and there were as yet but few things that could be thus explained—was supposed to be the result of supernatural intervention. Eclipses, comets, meteors, earthquakes, the pestilence, the storm, and the tempest—all these and similar things were supposed to be the result of direct supernatural interposition. Demonology, sorcery, astrology, witchcraft, necromancy, furnished all the explanations which men had of events lying beyond the range of ordinary experience, and the groves, the waters, the hills, the valleys became filled with supernatural influences and beings. When the Bible was composed, it is said, there was nothing inconsistent with such belief, and nothing in its statements to shock the general faith of mankind, or to violate any of the known laws on which the world is governed. It was not then regarded as more wonderful than other things were supposed to be, and, therefore, not incredible, that God should make man from the dust of the earth; or that He should form a woman from the rib of a man; or that a serpent should speak in human language; or that an ass should use human speech; or that the sun and moon should be made to stand still in their course that a battle might be finished; or that the dead should appear; or that the earth should heave, and the sun be darkened, when the Savior died.

But Science now has gone far to establish the reign of universal law, to remove these marvels from the faith of men, to displace the belief in supernatural agencies, and to bring all things under the dominion of law; and the question occurs whether all those things which were once regarded as marvelous are not now to be reduced to the same rank as the marvels in Livy, or are not to take their place on the same level as the ancient belief in sorcery, astrology, necromancy, and witchcraft. So "Rationalism" demands, and so no inconsiderable part of the scientific world is disposed to assert.

It requires now some boldness in a man who wishes to stand well in the scientific world to avow his belief in the events of this kind recorded in the Bible. There are very many scientific associations before which such a man would hesitate in an attempt to explain and vindicate the first four chapters in Genesis, and in relation to which he would prefer silence to any distinct utterance of his own opinion; and a minister of the Gospel in this age encounters a difficulty which would not have been felt in a more credulous age—than he would have done at a time when such events pervaded all history, and when faith in such events entered into the creed of all men. Some, in this state of things, prefer to be silent on the whole subject; some wait for more full developments; some tremble at the announcement of a new discovery in Science as if another prop was to be taken from the faith; some are willing to hide the naked and offensive statements in the Bible under the garb of allegories and myths; some are willing to concede the fact that there *was* ignorance on the part of the sacred writers on those subjects, and they endeavor to calm down their own apprehensions by the supposition that the sacred writers were not inspired on those subjects, and were, therefore, as liable to be mistaken as other men.

The subject has become, therefore, a very important one to be examined in a consideration of the argument on the Evidences of Christianity, and any man would render a valuable service to the Christian world who could make suggestions that would calm down the anxieties of the minds of good men, and who could show that Science has not yet reached a point that need alarm the friends of the Bible.

The subject, in its highest bearings, is far beyond my ability, and were that not so, it could not be exhausted in a single Lecture. But it may be possible to suggest some thoughts on points on which the friends of Science and Revelation may have a common understanding, and which may do something to repress apprehension on the one hand, and exultation on the other. I approach this subject—as many of those whom I address will in their subsequent lives—under all the disadvantages produced by the common feeling that a minister of the Gospel is little qualified to grapple with these difficulties; that his studies lie apart from those which are

pursued in the schools of Science; that in no one of the
sciences can he be supposed to be as much at home as
he is in his own particular department, or as a scientific man is in his; and perhaps it would be urged with
special force—and I certainly feel and admit that consideration fully in my own case—that a man who received his education nearly half a century ago, and
then an imperfect one, can not be supposed, in the active pursuits of another profession, to have kept pace
with the advancements of Science in that remarkable
half century, or to be competent to speak to those who
have devoted their lives to those pursuits. All this I
feel and admit; and yet, on the other hand, it may be
that something has occurred to such a man in his own
reading and profession, as bearing on the subject, which
may not have occurred to one engrossed in another
profession as he has been in his.

I shall, therefore, submit some remarks to you designed to illustrate the relation of Science to Christianity as affecting, in the nineteenth century, the evidence of its truth.

L There must be entire harmony between the proper
deductions of Science and a revelation from God. On
most of the subjects of revelation, indeed, it is to be presumed that the communications made would be such as
not to admit of comparison with what Science teaches,
for it must be presumed that, if a revelation is given at
all, it will be, for the most part, on subjects which lie
beyond the range of man's natural powers, and the
points of actual contact on the high themes of theology
and the disclosures of Science must therefore be few.
In fact, in a revelation from God designed to guide man
in the duties of religion and in a preparation for another world—which must be the main design of a revelation—it is to be presumed that the points of contact

would be mostly incidental. Revelation is not given to teach geography, geology, anatomy, astronomy, chemistry, but religion.

Still, it is right to assume and to demand that, where there are any statements in a book that claims to be a revelation from God, on the subjects of Science, incidental or otherwise, they must and will be in accordance with what is disclosed by an accurate investigation of the works of God. The friends of revelation must admit this; the enemies of revelation may hold them to it.

This position is self-evident and indisputable except on a supposition which the friends of Science will not allow us to make, and which we have no right and no desire to make, that the Maker of the world, according to the doctrine of the Manichees, was a different Being from the Supreme God. In such a case, indeed, under the dualistic system of Zoroaster and the Manichees, it would be conceivable that a direct revelation from the Supreme Being might contain principles not reconcilable with the facts which Science would exhibit as derived from the actual creation. There is, indeed, another supposition which may be adverted to, where the same result would follow—that there is something in God which is not properly expressed in the works of creation, in the course of events, or in our moral nature, but that, when those higher things in God are understood, they will *reverse* many of our conceptions now of that which is right and that which is wrong; of that which is true and that which is false; of that which is to be loved and of that which is hated. Such an idea has been suggested by one of no less authority than Mansel.

But we can not be at liberty to avail ourselves of

this idea in extricating ourselves from any difficulty arising from the conflict of revealed religion and Science, for right is right, and wrong is wrong, every where, and we can not believe that the Great Creator has stamped upon the intellect and the conscience of men a universal lie, so creating them that they are under a necessity of believing that to be right which he knows to be wrong, and which he himself knows they will ultimately perceive to be wrong, and, therefore, we are shut up to the necessity of admitting and maintaining that between a true revelation and the fair deductions of Science there *must* be harmony. This idea, moreover, we urge in all our endeavors to overthrow the false religions of the heathen, and of this we purpose, in our missionary efforts, to make great use in showing that the books among them which claim to be a revelation can not be from the true God.

The enemies of the Christian religion may therefore hold us to this, and may insist on it, that if the statements in the Bible are contradictory to the disclosures of Science, and can not by fair means be shown to be in harmony with them, the Bible must be given up in its pretensions to being a revelation from God.

II. A second principle may be stated as indisputable, that the deductions of Science are to be admitted as true, wherever they may lead, or on whatever they may impinge.

This principle, also, is so clear that it is difficult to make it more plain by any illustration. We are so made that we *must* admit this; all our plans, and all our hopes, are based on this. All that, as friends of religion, we have a right to demand on the subject is, that the things which we are to believe, which may or may not affect religion, shall *be* true deductions of

Science. They must not be mere theories; they must not be conclusions based on a partial and imperfect observation of the facts in the case; they must not be views embraced manifestly with a purpose to destroy the credit of revelation; they must be points about which there can be no dispute, and in reference to which there will be no presumption that time and farther observation will set them aside. If the belief of the forty-seventh proposition of the first book of Euclid will destroy the faith of mankind in the Bible, be it so. We can not help it. But it is to be observed, on the other side, that there have been a thousand things assumed to be scientific truths, and which were in conflict with the statements of revelation, which time, better instruments, and farther investigation have shown to be false.

It is to be admitted and expected that Science, in its progress, will set aside many things existing in the world pertaining to common matters, and it is not less to be presumed that it will set aside many things that have been supposed to be connected with religion, and that this may at the time shock or shake the faith of many believers in the Bible, as if all were lost. Thus a good axe or hoe, made on scientific principles, sets aside those which may have been long in use; the printing-press set aside the apparatus for copying; the power-loom sets aside the hand-loom; the spinning-jenny sets aside the domestic wheel; the reaping machine sets aside the sickle and the scythe; the sewing machine sets aside, to a large extent, the common use of the needle.

In like manner, books are set aside as valueless except as records of history. Every new discovery renders the old book of less value, until it becomes worthless. Galen and Hippocrates cease to be of value in medicine; Mela and Strabo in geography; and Ptolemy in astronomy. Thus old machines, old books, Indian relics, and suits of ancient armor, become fit occupants of old libraries and of museums—the lumber, the *débris* of former times. The very fact that a book is "rare" is *prima facie* proof that it has been superseded by something better, and is worthless; and every writer on Science, and most of those on any subject in literature, must lay his account with the expectation that in that very department some man will make a brighter discovery, or write a better book, that will place what he has done among the things that the world will "willingly let die." Scientific men must accept this, and must toil on in their generation with the feeling that this is to be the end of their labors.

The same principle is applicable to religion. As in its own proper department Science makes its way regardless of opinions before held, and reputations won, and glory deemed to be immortal, and garlands that were supposed to be unfading, and patents secured, and money invested, and corporations strong and powerful, so Science will make its way on whatever it may impinge, however it may affect the faith of men, whatever it may do in disrobing priests and throwing down altars, and changing temples of worship to other purposes, and disturbing established investments, and whatever ruins it may strew in its path.

The religious part of the world must make up its mind to accept all the disclosures of true Science, however they may impinge on its articles of faith. If the facts of Science are hopelessly irreconcilable with the statements of the Bible, but one result can follow. The Bible will be abandoned. The truths of Science will stand. At first it will be abandoned by the scientific world, and then it will retain what hold it can be made to retain on the masses of men as the result of education, or tradition, or priestly power, or the conscious want of some religion; but, sooner or later, though slowly, it will lose its hold on mankind, as the belief in necromancy, demonology, sorcery, witchcraft, and magic, was at first embraced by all men, and then, as Science advanced, lost their hold on those who were capable of explaining the phenomena of the world on scientific principles, retaining still their hold on the masses, until Science, diffused every where, removes all faith in sorcery and magic from the world.

III. In forming a correct estimate on this subject, there are, however, certain things to be taken into the account, of which the friends of religion have a right to avail themselves, and to demand that they shall be regarded as important elements in determining the judgment of mankind.

(1.) One of those things is the *uncertainty* of Science, at least as bearing on the points at issue between science and revelation.

It may startle some to hear the expression, "the uncertainty of Science." It may demand some boldness, and may do not a little to peril a man's reputation, to use such an expression. We have been so much accustomed to the word "*exact*," as connected with the sciences, and have been so taught to believe that a mathematical demonstration must be absolutely certain, and have hence so hastily applied the same idea to all other demonstrations in Science, that we have learned to confine the words "*moral*" or "*probable*," as applied to evidence, to other subjects altogether, and hence it has come to be understood that an important distinction,

in this respect, is to be made between the evidence of
a scientific proposition and that for a revelation: the
words "exact" and "certain" to be applied exclusively
to the one; the words "moral" and "probable" only belonging to the other.

But, on this subject, it is important that such things
as the following should be borne in mind:

(a) When we look at the past in history, what is
more vague and uncertain than the "sciences" as they
have been held among men? What "science" now is
the same that it was two thousand years ago? What
has been more shifting, undefined, and unstable than the
"sciences" as they have been actually held? Let any
man read so common a book as Whewell's "History of
the Inductive Sciences," and instead of rising from the
perusal with the idea that Science is "exact," "certain," and "stable," he will be much more likely to institute a comparison between it and the ever-changing
sands on the shores of the ocean than with the fixed
and everlasting hills.

And again: On what points, outside of the small circle of the mathematical demonstrations, is Science "certain?" What is light? What is matter? What is galvanism? What is gravitation? What is attraction?
What is heat? What is life? How many are the original elements of matter? In what proportions do they
combine, and by what power are they held in combination? How many are the worlds that roll above us?
What is the duration of our own globe? When, and
how was it formed and moulded? And what "exact"
changes has it undergone? Is there any one of these
and numberless kindred points on which the views of
scientific men are settled and "certain?" Is there any
one on which there are not as many different and shad-

ówy opinions as there are on the doctrine of the Trinity or Incarnation? On the one subject of geology so early as the year 1806, the French Institute counted more than eighty theories hostile to Scripture history, not one of which has stood to the present day How many such theories have appeared and vanished since?

(b) And what is the *range* of scientific knowledge? How soon does man get to the extent of his faculties, and what vast oceans of knowledge lie now unexplored, as in the time of Newton? In one sense the knowledge of man is indeed vast, and all the epithets which we can use in describing it are deserved. But what does man *know?* He sees but a little way around him, and beyond all is dark. What does he know of the distant worlds? What does he know of the sun, or the moon, or the planets, or the fixed stars, or the comets? What is their history? What their compositions? What the character of their inhabitants, if they have any? What can he tell about the nearest fixed star? It is not a *knowledge* of that star to be able to determine its "parallax," or to be able to determine that the ray of light that comes to our eyes from that star, informing us of its existence, has been traveling twenty thousand years to give us the information, and that therefore the star itself may have ceased to exist twenty thousand years ago. And of the worlds beyond such a star what does man know? The truth is, that we have but just opened our eyes on a universe that in its creation demanded all the power and the wisdom of an Infinite God. Man— the wisest man—the man of farthest grasp—the man who has accumulated most, has but just left his cradle. But a few days ago he knew not any thing, not even the name of father or mother. He could neither speak nor stand. He knew not that a candle would burn his finger if he put it there. By slow degrees he learned to creep, and then to walk. He began to utter sounds which were kindly construed into language. He lisped, and hesitated, and then achieved a great victory by being able to utter a few simple monosyllables. And then how soon he thinks that he knows all about the universe so vast, and the God who made it. Thus a fine writer, speaking of the sum of Physical Science, says:

"Compared with the comprehensible universe and with conceivable time, not to speak of infinity and eternity, it is the observation of a mere point, the experience of an instant. Are we warranted in founding any thing upon such data, except that which we are obliged to found on them, the daily rules and processes necessary for the natural life of man? We call the discoveries of Science sublime; and truly. But the sublimity belongs not to that which they reveal, but to that which they suggest. And that which they suggest is, that through this material glory and beauty, of which we see a little and imagine more, there speaks to us a Being whose nature is akin to ours, and who has made our hearts capable of such converse. Astronomy has its practical uses, without which man's intellect would hardly rouse itself to those speculations; but its greatest result is a revelation of immensity pervaded by one informing mind, and this revelation is made by astronomy only in the same sense in which the telescope reveals the stars to the eye of the astronomer. Science finds no law for the thoughts which, with her aid, are ministered to man by the starry skies. Science can explain the hues of sunset, but she can not tell from what urns of pain and pleasure its pensiveness is poured. These things are felt by all men—felt the more in proportion as the mind is higher. They are a part of human nature; and why should they not be as sound a basis for philosophy as any other part? But if they are, the solid wall of material law melts away, and through the whole order of the material world pours the influence, the personal influence, of a spirit corresponding to our own.

"Again, is it true that the fixed or the unvarying is the last revelation of Science? These risings in the scale of created beings, this gradual evolution of planetary systems from their centre, do they bespeak mere creative force? Do they not rather bespeak something which, for want of an adequate word, we must call creative effort, corresponding to the effort by which man raises himself and his estate? And where effort can be discovered, does not spirit reign again?

"A creature whose sphere of vision is a speck, whose experience is a second, sees the pencil of Raphael moving over the canvas of the Transfiguration; it sees the pencil moving over its own speck, during its own second of existence, in one particular direction, and it concludes that the formula expressing that direction is the secret of the whole."*

(c) Again, it is to be borne in mind that there are subjects of knowledge, and they may be most momentous in their nature, that lie wholly beyond the range of Physical Science, and must ever lie there. Science has its sphere; beyond that sphere it has no instruments, no knowledge.

The great subjects of theology are of this character, and must ever be. The anatomist and the chemist do not profess to teach theology; nor do they teach it. Their investigations throw no light on the doctrine of the immortality of the soul; on the questions about a

* Lectures on the Study of History, by *Goldwin Smith*, pp. 86-88.

future state; on the inquiry how a sinner may be reconciled to God. The electrial machine throws out no light on those subjects; the scalpel of the anatomist does not even disclose the source of life; the glass of the astronomer does not penetrate far enough into the distant ether to reveal the throne of God. How far, then, Science should presume to speak of that which is wholly beyond its range, may be a fair question. How far it should sit in judgment on that which lies wholly without its sphere, is an equally fair question. Geology, chemistry, metallurgy, have their sphere—wide, noble, honorable; but the atonement, the incarnation, the Trinity, the fall of man, the work of redemption, pertain to another sphere, not less wide, noble, honorable. Each one in its place.* Each one to be honored. Each one to contribute any thing, every thing it can to the other, and to the whole; but each one to be confined to its proper sphere.

It may yet be seen that there is a "division of labor" in the departments of human action more wide than is commonly supposed to be implied in that modern discovery of wisdom. Each pin-maker labors in his own department, and the man who makes the head does not interfere with him who cuts the wire, or him who sharpens the point; each gun-maker labors in his own department, and he who makes the stock does not interfere with him who makes the barrel, or the rod, or the bayonet, or the hammer to the lock. All work in harmony; all contribute to the result, for the work of one fits into the work of another, as if all were the work of one man.

It is certain that in Science each department will communicate nothing but that which pertains to itself; that chemistry is not to be learned in the dissecting-

* No sutor supra crepidam.—*Plin.*

room of the anatomist, or music by the telescope, or
moral philosophy by the examination of fossils; and it
is equally certain that none of those sciences will communicate to man what he needs to know about the immortality of the soul; that the question about the resurrection of the dead is not to be decided by an examination of the rocks; that the blow-pipe of the chemist,
and the hammer of the geologist, do not reveal to a sinner the way of salvation.

(d) Again, the past experience of the world should be
allowed to teach men of science modesty and caution.
It should not be forgotten that there is no opinion so
extravagant and wild that it has not been at some time
embraced by philosophers, by men of science;* and it
should not be forgotten that a very large part of the
doctrines held in science in past times have been found
by more accurate observation to be absurd, and have
been dropped by the way, and are now numbered and
classified with the huge monsters—themselves not less
monstrous—the ichthyosaurians and the plethiosauri-
ans of the old geological periods of our world's history.
It is to be remembered, also, that the world has gone
through a long experience on the very subject now before us, the bearing of Science on revelation, and that
not one new discovery has been made in Science which
has not at the time been supposed to impinge on some
doctrine of revealed religion, and which has not caused
momentary alarm to the friends of religion, and momentary triumph to its foes.   Yet Christianity has survived them all.† So it *may be* in regard to the sciences

* Nihil tam absurde potest, quod non dicatur ab aliquo philosophorum.—*Cicero*, de Divinatione, ii., 58.

† See this admirably illustrated in *Wiseman's* Lectures on Science
and Revealed Religion, ed. Andover, 1837.

as understood now, and to those which remain to be disclosed in the advancing periods of the world.

(e) One other thing may be adverted to. It may be that the facts of Science are not as well established as they are claimed to be. Which of them is, in fact, settled? Which of them is complete and perfect? Is geology? It is, as yet, in the cradle. Is astronomy? How little of the universe is surveyed and known. Is chemistry? What chemist is there who stops where he is, and supposes that his work is perfect, and that nothing remains to be known? Is anatomy? What anatomist lays down his scalpel, and feels that all stimulus to future discovery has ended? What book is there on *any* of the subjects of Science which can be safely stereotyped? What man is there who can feel assured that his profoundest speculations of this year will not be classed next year with the almanac which has had its day? The young men of each generation are stimulated to make attainments in Science, because there are vast fields yet unexplored; the traveler in unknown lands is cheered because a vast and inviting field is before him which the foot of man has never trod, and as he passes on in his obstructed way through fields of flowers new to the eye of man, and ascends streams on which man has never glided, and climbs the mountain-top on which a human being has never before stood, and looks abroad on rich valleys that still invite him, he is animated and excited by the fact that all this is unknown, nor would he thank any one, not even his Maker, to disclose all this to his view, and to stifle the ardor derived from the hope of future discoveries. So many a patient student of the heavens each night, when most mortal eyes are locked in slumber, is looking out from the watch-tower—the "observatory"—surveying the heavens with the hope that some new star may be seen on which the eye of man has never rested, that shall solve some discrepancy of Science, or whose discovery may perchance place his name by the side of that of Le Verrier.

IV. A very material inquiry therefore meets us here. It is, What are we to *expect* on this subject? What have we a right to demand in a book submitting itself to us as a revelation from God? Suppose the scientific man entertains for a moment the idea that a "book-revelation" could be made, or that God would impart truths directly by inspiration beyond what man can discover by his unaided powers, what would he have a right to demand or expect? And how far would such a reasonable expectation correspond with what actually occurs in regard to the Bible?

It is not difficult to answer these questions.

(1.) We should *expect*—we should feel ourselves authorized to *demand*, in the sense that we could not receive it as a revelation otherwise—that the revelation should not contradict the disclosures of Science, as we expect that the disclosures made by the telescope will not contradict those made by the naked eye. The telescope, under the laws of vision, simply carries the vision farther, and extends it into regions beyond the natural range of the eye. But we anticipate this in regard to its disclosures, that while it reveals new worlds, it will reveal them as subject to the same laws which reign within the scope of our natural vision, and that we shall not, however vast may be the extent of our aided vision, or however deep we plunge into the distant ether, be conducted into the empire of another God. Such is the fact. The distant worlds, however far from us, and however vast, are subject to the same laws of light and motion which are observed on our own planet; nor even when we have passed our own solar system, and the nebula to which it belongs, and contemplate more vast and distant nebulæ, that seem to float as independent systems or *universes*, wholly separated from ours, do we come into the dominion of another Creator and another God.

So we expect of revelation. If God has given two books to men, the book of nature and the book of grace, a revelation through his works and an independent "book"-revelation by his word, we expect, we demand that they shall be reconcilable with each other. And, unless this is done, we are so made that we can not receive the latter.

(2.) We should expect that such a revelation would be confined *mainly* to the subject of religion. It is true that in such a revelation the truths of Science *might* have been disclosed as well as the truths of religion, for all this knowledge is in the mind of God, and he might have revealed a system of botany, or mineralogy, or anatomy, or chemistry, or astronomy that would have been perfect. But there were reasons which could easily be suggested why it was not desirable or wise that this should be; why the discoveries on these subjects should be left to the investigations of men themselves, and why they should be developed when the condition of the world would be such that society would be prepared for them, and when the world would appreciate them. There were reasons why the art of working metals should to some extent be known in the time of Tubal-Cain (Gen., iv., 22), but what would have been the value of a revelation of the use of the steam-engine, of the art of printing, or of the magnetic telegraph at that age of the world? It was wise and best that, when the world was prepared by its ordinary developments to be lifted to a higher level, men of extraordinary genius should be raised up to strike out the new inventions that would be demanded at that period of the world, for the real progress of the race would be better accomplished in this way than by a direct revelation from heaven. It was not for the good of the race, as I have endeavored to show in a former Lecture, that, on subjects which properly lie within the range of the human faculties, the knowledge which is needful for man should be communicated by a direct revelation from God, and hence what we should anticipate in such a revelation would be that it would be mainly confined to the subject of religion. In fact, it has never been made an objection to the Bible as a professed revelation that it does not deal with the subjects of Science, and does not claim to be an arbiter in its mooted questions.

(3.) We should expect and demand in a revelation that if there were incidental allusions or references to other subjects than the main subject of religion, they would be so made as to be in harmony with the information obtained on those subjects from other sources, or be susceptible of reconciliation with them. A skeptic would have a right to demand this; our own nature, as we are made, requires it. We act on this principle in the attempt to propagate our religion, and to set aside the revelations of other religions, and we regard it as a sufficient proof that they are false if we can show that they contradict the statenents of true Science.

(4.) Yet it could not be claimed that there should be no *apparent* conflict between the two. We do not go very far in the pursuit of knowledge on any scientific subject, on any question of history, on any matter of

F

philosophy, without finding that there is an *apparent* conflict between the disclosures made to us and the things already known or believed; and I need not say that a very material part of scientific study consists in the work of reconciling one thing with another, or in showing that there is real harmony where there is apparent discord. How slow and toilsome has been the process of reconciling the Copernican theory in regard to the movements of the heavenly bodies with admitted facts, or of reconciling the theory with apparent irregularities. And when has a new discovery been made that did not require a new adjustment? How long did astronomers wait, how deeply were they perplexed, in regard to certain irregularities in the planet Uranus, that was supposed to be the most remote in the system, until Le Verrier and Adams suggested that there was still another, sunk deeper in the depths of space, and as yet unknown, whose existence, size, and movements might reconcile and harmonize all?

(5.) Once more. On the subjects pertaining to Science in such a revelation, we should expect that the statements made would be in the common language used by men, and not in technical scientific terms. The reasons for this are obvious. Such truths could be made intelligible only by such language, and such language is used by scientific men themselves, even on subjects where they have the most accurate definitions. No greater jargon could be imagined—surpassing in apparent unintelligibleness and nonsense what occurred at Babel—than would be an attempt to hold conversation in the technical language of chemistry, of anatomy, or of medicine, and there is no surer proof of pedantry than such an attempt. "Language," said Talleyrand, " is for the purpose of concealing ideas;" and a revelation in scientific language would accomplish that beyond even the language of German transcendentalists. What would be the language of the world if reduced to scientific terms? By what cumbersome and unintelligible technicalities would men describe the rising or the setting of the sun, or the operations of walking, and seeing, and hearing, and eating, and cooking? Who could understand any thing of a rose if the technical language of botanists only were used, or of water, air, or earth, if only the technical language of chemistry were employed? In the words of Kepler: "Astronomy unfolds the causes of natural things; it professedly investigates optical illusions. Astronomers do not pursue this science with the design of uttering language. We say, with the common people, the planets stand still or go down; the sun rises and sets. How much less should we require that the Scriptures of divine inspiration, setting aside the common modes of speech, should shape their words according to the model of the natural sciences, and, by employing a dark and inappropriate phraseology about things which surpass the comprehension of those whom it designs to instruct, perplex the simple people of God, and thus obstruct its own way toward the attainment of the far more exalted object at which it aims."*

V. It is a very material question now, How far Science has affected the evidences of the truth of Christianity; how far it has rendered the proofs of its divine origin commonly relied on uncertain or doubtful; how far, if at all, it has rendered them valueless?

This is a very large subject—too large to be considered in the little time now remaining in this Lecture; and as, in some form, it will occur more than once

* Quoted in Lee on Inspiration, p. 370.

again in this course, a few suggestions only need now
be made.

The inquiry pertains to two points : What Science
has removed that was once *supposed* to be a part of
revelation; and Whether it has affected that which is
a real part of revelation, and which properly belongs
to it.

On the first of these points we now go hand in hand
with the skeptic and the doubter. Science *has* done
much, and perhaps the progress of civilization more,
in detaching from religion, and, if I may so say, from
the Bible—that is, from the Bible as it was formerly interpreted—much that would now, if it properly pertained to the Bible, be fatal to any claims to a divine origin. The Christian world has been indeed shocked and
alarmed as one after another of these things has been
assailed, for it was supposed that they were essential
to religion;—that they were incorporated in the Bible,
and that they were always to be regarded as essential
points of the Christian faith. The assault on these
things has been supposed to be an assault made by infidelity ; the skepticism produced in regard to them·
has been feared to be on the one hand, and claimed to
be on the other, the triumph of skepticism. But Science, in its progress, has disabused the minds of men on
these subjects, and has thus, in fact, been a helper, and
not a hinderer, in embracing the evidences of Christianity—an auxiliary, and not a foe—for it has shown
that in receiving the Bible men are not required to embrace what was once regarded as essential to the faith.
The question which remains for solution, and which is
agitated in this age, is, How far this is to go, and
whether all that is supernatural and miraculous in the
Scriptures is to be given up at the demand of Science,

in order that religion may commend itself to the faith of mankind.

The history on this subject is, in fact, the history of "Rationalism," in the broadest and best sense of that term. The subject has occupied and is occupying the attention of minds, partly among Christians and partly among skeptics, which must be admitted to be abundantly competent to grapple with it. Coleridge, among those that speak our language, perhaps began it; Sir David Brewster did much to disabuse the minds of men on the subject, and to relieve Christianity of a burden, in his "History of Magic;" Germany has made it prominent in its inquiries; Dr. Channing and Theodore Parker lent their aid to it in their way; and Buckle and Lecky, with different aims, have traced elaborately the course of thought in the history of the world on the subject.*

The sum is this: In the early periods of the world all things were full of marvels and wonders; all things not understood, and few things were supposed to be understood, were under the control of the supernatural. An eclipse was a prodigy, a miracle wrought for some special purpose; the plague and pestilence were prodigies brought upon men for special purposes; the gods constantly appeared acting in human affairs; the stars, by a potent influence, presided over the birth and death of individuals; the dead reappeared, and it was possible to make a compact with them for good or evil purposes; the groves, the hills, the streams, were full of dryads, and nymphs, and fauns; and the belief in charms

* Probably the best and most reliable history on the subject, as it is certainly the best written, is Lecky's "History of the Rise and Influence of the Spirit of Rationalism in Europe."

and incantations, in sorcery and witchcraft, was universal.

Time, science, and civilization have scattered most
of these delusions, and have reduced to regular laws
most of what was supposed to belong to the supernatural. The naiads, and fauns, and nymphs have disappeared; the groves have been unpeopled except in
poetry; the belief in sorcery and witchcraft has been
banished from the world; and the belief is cherished,
and the hope entertained by those who have been most
active in disenchanting the world, that *all* that has occurred, or that does now occur in our world, may be
traced to regular and fixed laws, excluding the supernatural altogether.

It is not difficult to understand what the *tendency* of
this process is, or what effect it is likely to have on
large classes of mind in regard to the miraculous and
the supernatural in the Bible. The real question is
whether this shall extend to all the events that have
occurred in our world; whether all the facts that have
taken place, including those which have occurred in
connection with events claimed to be miraculous, can
be reduced to regular laws; and whether all which can
not be so reduced shall not at once be regarded as delusion and imposture. Science and civilization having
done so much to drive sorcery, and magic, and witchcraft, and astrology, and necromancy, and superstition
from the world, and having gone so far to establish the
reign of regular law, the question is whether the triumph is not to be completed, and whether any thing is
to be left for direct divine intervention, and whether
we may not arrive at a point, or have not already
reached it, when it may be assumed as a maxim in
Science that any thing claiming to be miraculous is

at once to be rejected. Strauss reached that conclusion: "We may," says he, "summarily reject all miracles, prophecies, narratives of angels and demons, and
the like, as simply impossible and irreconcilable with
the known and universal laws which govern the course
of events."* The tendency on this subject no one can
doubt. That tendency has been described at length by
one who can not be supposed to have any wish in that
direction, but who has traced, with the hand of a master, the process by which the world has reached its present position in regard to the miraculous and the supernatural. Among other things he says: "Men are prepared to admit almost any conceivable concurrence of
natural improbabilities rather than resort to the hypothesis of supernatural interference; and this spirit is
exhibited not merely by open skeptics, but by men who
are sincere, though perhaps not very fervent believers
in their church. It is the prevailing characteristic of
that vast body of educated persons whose lives are
chiefly spent in secular pursuits, and who, while they
receive with uninquiring faith the great doctrines of
Catholicism, and duly perform its leading duties, derive
their mental tone and coloring from the general spirit
of their age. If you speak to them on the subject they
will reply with a shrug and a smile." "If we put aside
the clergy and those who are most immediately under
their influence, we find that this habit of mind [among
the Roman Catholics] is the invariable concomitant of
education, and is the especial characteristic of those
persons whose intellectual sympathies are most extended, and who therefore represent most faithfully
the various intellectual influences of their time." "All
history shows that in exact proportion as nations ad-

* Introduction to the Life of Jesus.

vance in civilization, the accounts of miracles taking
place among them become rarer and rarer, until at last
they entirely cease." These facts "show that the repugnance of men to believe miraculous narratives is in
direct proportion to the progress of civilization and the
diffusion of knowledge." "The plain fact is, that the
progress of civilization produces invariably a certain
tone and habit of thought which makes men recoil from
miraculous narratives with an instinctive and immediate repugnance, as though they were essentially incredible, independently of any definite arguments, and
in spite of dogmatic teaching." "Generation after
generation, the province of the miraculous has contracted, and the circle of skepticism has expanded. Of
the two great divisions of these events, one has completely perished. Witchcraft, and diabolical possession,
and diabolical disease have long since passed into the
region of fables. To disbelieve them was at first the
eccentricity of a few isolated thinkers; it was then the
distinction of the educated classes in the most advanced
nations; it is now the common sentiment of all classes
in all countries of Europe. The countless miracles that
were once associated with every relic and with every
village shrine have rapidly and silently disappeared.
Year by year the incredulity became more manifest,
even where the theological profession was unchanged.
Their numbers continually lessened until they at last
almost ceased, and any attempt to revive them has
been treated with a general and undisguised contempt.
The miracles of the fathers are passed over with an incredulous scorn or with a significant silence. The rationalistic spirit has even attempted to explain away
those which are recorded in Scripture, and it has materially altered their position in the systems of theology.

In all countries, in all churches, in all parties, among men
of every variety of character and opinion, we have found
the tendency existing. In each nation its development
has been a measure of intellectual activity, and has
passed in regular course through the different strata of
society. During the last century it has advanced with
a vastly accelerated rapidity; the old lines of demarca-
tion have been every where obscured, and the spirit of
Rationalism has become the great centre to which the
intellect of Europe is manifestly tending. If we trace
the progress of the movement from its origin to the
present day, we find that it has completely altered the
whole aspect and complexion of religion. When it began, Christianity was regarded as a system entirely beyond the range and scope of human reason; it was impious to question; it was impious to examine; it was
impious to discriminate. On the other hand, it was visibly instinct with the supernatural. Miracles of every
order and degree of magnitude were flashing forth incessantly from all its parts. They excited no skepticism and no surprise. The miraculous element pervaded
all literature, explained all difficulties, consecrated all
doctrines. Every unusual phenomenon was immediately referred to a supernatural agency, not because
there was a passion for the improbable, but because
such an explanation seemed far more simple and easy
of belief than the obscure theories of Science. In the
present day Christianity is regarded as a system which
courts the strictest investigation, and which, among
many other functions, was designed to vivify and stimulate all the energies of man. The idea of the miraculous, which a superficial observer might have once
deemed its most prominent characteristic, has been
driven from almost all its intrenchments, and now quiv-

E 2

ers faintly and feebly through the mists of eighteen hundred years."*

The friends of Christianity who still retain their faith in the miraculous do not deny that Science and civilization have done much to change the views of the world in regard to the marvelous, and that they have done much to disprove what was once held to be taught in the Bible. At the same time, however, the progress of a more correct exegesis has shown that many of these things are *not* taught in the Bible, and thus religion has been delivered from a burden which in the present state of the world it would not have been able to bear; for we could not now go before the world with the defense of witchcraft or sorcery as once held; or with the views of Turretin in regard to the creation, as, in his apprehension, taught in the Scriptures;† or with the views of Cosmas, of the sixth century, in regard to the structure of the universe.‡

* *Lecky*, History of Rationalism, vol. i., p. 160, 161, 162, 194, 195.

† " First," he remarks, " the sun is said in Scripture to move in the heavens, and to rise and set. 'The sun is as a bridegroom coming out of his chambers, and rejoiceth as a strong man to run a race.' 'The sun knoweth his going down.' 'The sun ariseth, and the sun goeth down.' Secondly, The sun, by a miracle, stood still in the time of Joshua, and by a miracle it went back in the time of Hezekiah. Thirdly, The earth is said to be fixed immovably. 'The earth also is established, that it can not be moved.' 'Thou hast established the earth, and it abideth.' ' They continue this day according to thine ordinances.' Fourthly, Neither could birds, which often fly off through an hour's circuit, be able to return to their nests. Fifthly, Whatever flies or is suspended in the air ought by this theory to move from west to east; but this is proved not to be true, from birds, arrows shot forth, atoms made manifest in the sun, and down floating in the atmosphere."

‡ "According to Cosmas, the world is a flat parallelogram. Its length, which should be measured from east to west, is the double

How far this is to proceed is now the great question between the friends and the enemies of the Bible—the one claiming that the miraculous and the supernatural are not to be abandoned; the other that nothing shall be received and believed by men which can not be explained by established and unvarying law. Here is to be the battle-ground of this generation, and perhaps of the next; for this warfare men are girding on their armor; for this conflict, as much as for any other, the young men who are preparing for the ministry must be prepared.

The great questions which now lie open, and which are, in their relations to Christianity and Science, to be examined and determined, are substantially these: The creation of the world—whether it was, in fact, created at all, as stated in the Bible, and in the order affirmed in the first chapter of Genesis; the antiquity of the human race — whether man existed upon the earth at

of its breadth, which should be measured from north to south. In the centre is the earth we inhabit, which is surrounded by the ocean; and this again is encircled by another earth, in which men lived before the deluge, and from which Noah was transported in the ark. To the north of the world is a high conical mountain, around which the sun and moon continually revolve. When the sun is hid behind the mountain, it is night; when it is on one side of the mountain, it is day. To the edges of the outer earth the sky is glued. It consists of four high walls rising to a great height, and then meeting in a vast concave roof, thus forming an immense edifice, of which our world is the floor. This edifice is divided into two stories by the firmament, which is placed between the earth and the roof of the sky. A great ocean is inserted in the side of the firmament remote from the earth. This is what is signified by the waters that are above the firmament. The space from these waters to the roof of the sky is allotted to the blest; that from the firmament to our earth to the angels, in their character of ministering spirits."—*Lecky,* History of Rationalism, vol. i., p. 277.

a period anterior to that which is fairly implied in the Bible; the origin of the race — whether the different types of men upon the earth have a common origin, and have been derived from a single pair, as is affirmed in the Bible, or whether men have sprung up in different centres, either as developed from inferior orders of creatures, or from independent created "heads" of the different races, the Caucasian, the Mongolian, the Ethiopian, the American; and the whole question of miracles—whether they are possible; whether a miracle can be believed, or whether the laws of nature are so fixed and unchanging that there never has been, and never can be, sufficient evidence of the direct interposition of the divine power to justify the belief that those laws have ever been set aside.

It remains now to be said that, whatever may be hereafter, Science has furnished no *demonstrations* on these points which should give the friends of religion real cause of alarm. It has *not* yet been demonstrated that the universe was not created, and in the order described by Moses; it has *not* yet been proved that man has been upon the earth for a period longer than that assigned by a fair interpretation of the Scripture record; it has *not* been shown that the races of men did not descend from a single pair; and the point has *not* yet been established that God has never interposed, since the creation, by his own direct power in controlling the condition of the world; that the sun and moon did *not* stand still at the command of Joshua; that Christ did *not* still the tempest by a word; that he did *not* recall Lazarus to life; that he did *not* himself rise from the dead and ascend to heaven. Science has not *yet* brought these alleged facts within its range, nor has it demonstrated that these facts could not be proved by proper historical testimony. These are *not* settled points in Science, as Kepler's great laws of motion are, or Newton's law of gravitation is. When they become such, and not till then, will there be a real conflict between Science and the teachings of the Bible. So matters stand on this subject in this nineteenth century.

The course of events thus far, while it has removed many *imaginary* things from the Bible, and relieved us from much that encumbered and embarrassed the argument for the truth of revelation—as it has removed many imaginary things from the secular history of the past, and has relieved us from many things that perplexed and embarrassed us in regard to past events— has, as yet, removed none of the *real* things affirmed in the Bible, and which, by just laws of exegesis, we are bound to maintain, as, on the parallel subject of secular history, it has not affected, and can not affect, the *real* events which belong to history. The future we can not anticipate. The past, at least, is secure. What Science is yet to do it is not ours to foresee. How this matter is to stand in the centuries to come, is, of course, beyond our positive knowledge. Whether Science can eliminate miracles as it has done sorcery, and magic, and necromancy, and astrology from the world, is to be the inquiry of future ages; a field of fair conflict between the friends and the enemies of revelation. History in its great facts is safe thus far; religion in its great facts is safe also—each with equal confidence may be safely intrusted to that Great Presiding Spirit that has preserved both up to the present time. It will remain, in a subsequent part of this course of Lectures—it may be demanded of us—it can not be evaded —to inquire whether the principles of Science which

have swept away so much once deemed marvelous and
supernatural, will sweep away the claim of all that is
miraculous; whether, in view of all that it has done, a
miracle can be properly regarded as a historical subject
of belief. That point will be reserved for a special subsequent Lecture.

LECTURE IV.

THE EVIDENCE OF CHRISTIANITY FROM ITS PROPAGATION.

THERE are two forms of religion in the world which owe their present existence and influence to the fact that they were at first *propagated* by direct effort. They are Christianity and Mohammedism. ⸍ In this respect they stand by themselves. The religion of the Jews had its origin with their own nation, and grew up with themselves, and identified itself with all their legislative, municipal, and military regulations—a growth among themselves, and not an accretion from surrounding nations. They indeed sought to make proselytes, but they never sought or expected to make their religion a universal religion. Moses labored to make the Jewish people a *religious people*, not to convert the surrounding nations, and at no period of their history did the Hebrews ever conceive the idea of converting the whole world to their faith. It was the religion of the Jewish nation, not the religion of the world.

The Egyptian religion was limited to the Egyptians, the Chaldean to the Chaldeans, the Assyrian to the Assyrians. It was a fundamental idea in the ancient Pagan religions that every nation had its own gods, and that those gods were to be respected by other nations. The Greeks did not go forth to convert the world to *their* Jupiter, Juno, or Mars, but were content that all others should do honor as they chose to their own national gods. In the Pantheon at Rome the idea was embodied in the very name and conception of the temple, that all the gods of the nations were to be recognized, and that all might have a place there provided they did not disturb or displace those who were recognized as the Roman divinities.

Christianity and Mohammedism, however, each alike started out on a different idea. They were to be propagated. They were to overstep the narrow limits of the people among whom they had their origin. They were, wherever they went, to displace other religions. They were to convert heathen temples to churches or mosques, or, if this could not be done, they were to disrobe their priests, and to empty them of worshipers, and to leave them tenantless. They were to throw down all altars; stop the effusion of blood in sacrifice every where; change all laws that recognized the existence of more gods than one; set up the worship of one God, and bring the nations of the earth under the influence of a " book-revelation"—the Bible or the Koran. They were both to be diffused by direct effort; and the idea of *propagation* was a fundamental idea in both—the one by the sword, the other by the influence of truth and love.

They began much alike. Both had their origin in an individual in whom alone was the germ of the religion—was *all* the religion; and both those founders of the respective systems were obscure—both poor, both uneducated, both without powerful alliances or armies. Neither of the religions was a development from any previous form of religion, or an outgrowth of existing views among men, or of any prevailing form of civilization, and neither of them would have started up as such an outgrowth or development in Persia in the time of Cyrus, or in Greece in the age of Pericles, or in

EVIDENCES OF CHRISTIANITY. 113

Rome in the time of the Antonines, or of any nation
now, if we can suppose that the existing nations had
their present forms of civilization or art without any
religion. Both had very small beginnings, and weari-
some weeks and months, and even years, passed away
before they became so rooted or accumulated such force
as to affect the established institutions, or to excite apprehension among the friends of existing systems of religion. The founders of both experienced similar opposition from their own families and friends, and made their
first converts among strangers; and both were greatly
persecuted. The one, to save his life in infancy, was
borne to a distant land, and was often obliged to resort
to measures derived from his higher nature to save his
life, and at last was put to death on a cross; the other
was compelled to flee from the place of his birth and
from his home, and to make a distant city the seat and
centre of his efforts to spread his religion. Neither
lived to see much more than the beginning of the diffusion of their religion, and the religion of both was
spread with rapidity over extended regions only when
they were no longer upon the earth to direct its diffusion in person. Millions of human beings have been
brought under the power of each; each has lived, since
its origin, through the revolutions of many centuries,
and amid all the advances which the world has made in
science and in art; each has given laws to nations; has
founded governments; has changed long-existing dynasties; has controlled kings on their thrones; has organ-
ized vast armies; has changed, if not made permanent,
the customs of the world. The banners of each in war
have waved over numberless battle-fields, often when
contending alone with other nations; often when ar-
rayed against each other; seldom in union against a

common foe. Both, though often attacked with the utmost violence, yet survive, and now together more deeply influence the destiny of the world than all other forms of religion combined.

Both these religions can not be true; both can not have been propagated because they were true. An argument for the divine origin of either from the fact of its propagation that would be equally applicable to both would prove nothing, and a very material question occurs whether there *is* any such peculiarity in the manner and fact of the propagation of the one as would demonstrate its divine origin, which would not be applicable to the other; or whether the mere propagation of a system of philosophy or religion, under any circumstances, proves that it is from God.

Without comparing the evidence in regard to the two, and reserving the remarks which distinguish and separate the two, so far as the argument is concerned, to the closing part of the Lecture, I shall endeavor, as its main purpose, to set before you the argument for the divine origin of Christianity as derived from its propagation.

This I shall do by illustrating the following points:

I. That the religion was propagated;

II. That the evidence or facts on which this was done was sufficient to account for its propagation, or to secure its propagation if such evidence existed; and,

III. That the fact of the propagation of Christianity, in the manner in which it occurred, can be explained only on the supposition that there was such evidence, and that the religion is from God.

I. The first point, as I have announced it—That the religion was *propagated*—has so far the appearance of being a truism that you may be surprised, perhaps, that

I have so far reflected on your understandings as to submit it as a proposition to be proved or even illustrated.
I mean by it, however, more than may strike you on its
mere announcement.

What I mean by it, and what is to be illustrated in
this argument is, (1.) That it was not a development
from any previous system of religion or from the state
of the world; and (2.) That it was propagated in the
manner and on the grounds which are stated in the
New Testament.

(1.) It was not a development from any previous system of religion or from the state of the world.

That there *are* things existing in society which are
of the proper nature of development from something
previously existing, or which have sprung into being
because the state of the world demanded them, can not
be called in question; and it can not be denied that
progressive civilization seems to follow, in some respects, the laws of development in the vegetable kingdom. It would be a curious and not unprofitable inquiry to ascertain what were the germs of the present
civilizations of the world, and by what laws they have
been unfolded. Society is thus *a growth*, formed of ac-
cretions from without, as plants are, in which the principle of life in the germ attracts to itself, and moulds
into the appropriate shape, under its own laws of life,
whatever is necessary to its full and perfect form. The
race thus, like the plant, is one, and the progress is stead-
ily and indefinitely onward.* It is, in itself, a fair question whether all existing things in society can be traced

---

* " Social advancement is as completely under the control of natural law as is bodily growth. The life of an individual is a miniature
of the life of a nation."—*Dr. Draper*, History of the Intellectual Development of Europe. *Preface.*

to this law of development or progress; and it is perfectly fair for any advocate of that theory to endeavor
to show that Christianity, so far as it indicates progress,
comes under that law. So far, in fact, has the principle
now adverted to been carried, that it has been held that
the great minds which have been thrown up from time
to time to meet great emergencies in the world, and to
lift the race to a higher level, have, in fact, been created
by circumstances, and are simply a development of
what may be in the germ of humanity; as the richest
fruit, under the highest cultivation, is but a *fair* development of what is in the germ from which it sprang.
In like manner it has been held, and it is quite material
for infidelity to hold it, that Christianity is but a simple development of a state of things to which the world
in its progress was coming; itself, in due time, to give
way to some higher development that shall spring out
of an advanced state of society, and that will better
than Christianity then represent the real progress of the
world—"Positivism," or some such form of religion.
According to such a theory, in the words of another,
"Christianity arose from a happy confluence of the
Greek and Roman with the Hebrew civilization." The
state of the world demanded a change in religion. The
old religions were dying or dead. The civilization of
the world was in advance of those religions, and *they*
must die, at any rate. But there were in them elements of religion representing the progress which the
world had made at that time, which might be mingled with the advanced principles in civilization, and
out of which a new system might spring that would
accompany the world in its progress for many generations, until, it also becoming decayed and effete, and
falling behind some distant age, some higher form of

religion would arise which would better represent an advanced period of the world.

Whether this is so is a fair question, and yet it would appear not to be of difficult solution.

It may be remarked in the outset that Christianity has not the *appearance* of being a development. It had no *growth*. It was perfect at the commencement as it came from its Founder, and as it was explained in the New Testament. It became fixed at once, and it has not changed. It has no doctrines now which it had not eighteen hundred years ago; and it had none then which it has not now, for it has lost none by the way. One of our main embarrassments in regard to it, as compared with the progress of the world, as we shall see in a subsequent Lecture, is that it is a *fixed* religion, not susceptible of change or modification. To that our adversaries hold us; from that we can not retreat. The form of Minerva was not more complete at her birth than Christianity was, and its form was no more susceptible of growing beauty than was hers. In proof that these things were so, I submit the following remarks:

(*a*) Christianity was not a development of the Pagan religions. It sprang up in a land remote from those religions; it has no features in common with them; it came, so far as they had life, into immediate and deadly collision with them. The Egyptian, the Babylonian, the Persian, the Greek, the Roman mythologies—which of them or what part of them is represented by Christianity? The temples, the priesthood, the sacrifices, the *morals*—which of them is represented by Christianity? Which of them welcomed its coming—which of them sprang forward to embrace it—which of them opened its temples for it?

(*b*) Christianity was not developed from Judaism,

unless it be in the sense, if the comparison be not too low, in which the chrysalis is "developed" into the butterfly, and the new insect emerges into a new form of being, the former life—the groveling caterpillar— dying altogether. Judaism died when Christianity appeared. Unlike the expiring worm, indeed, with the little life it had, it evinced a deadly antagonism to the new form—the new religion—and then it, like that worm, expired. Its altars were overthrown; its priests were disrobed; its temple was razed to the foundations; its sacrifices were rendered unmeaning, and ceased forever; its political economy was ended; its people were scattered to the ends of the earth, to be gathered as a nation no more. We as Christians, indeed, admit, in *our* sense of the term, that Christianity was "developed" in a certain sense from the Jewish religion; that the one had the same origin as the other; that the same life-blood flowed through both; that the Messiah of the one was adumbrated by the rites of the other; and that the one was, in the purpose of God, preparatory and introductory to the other. But this is not the sense in which the enemies of Christianity would say that Christianity was developed from Judaism; and in the sense in which *they* use the term it is in no manner true.

(c) It was not a development from the Greek philosophy, or from the Roman philosophy, the echo of the Greek. That philosophy, in common with other forms of philosophy, has, indeed, at times greatly influenced and modified Christianity as it has been held in the world; but the *systems* have been kept distinct, and have never been confounded. With both these before us now—for the records of the Greek and Roman philosophy have been, from some cause, almost as carefully preserved as the records of Christianity—we are enabled to make a comparison between what Socrates, Pythagoras, Zeno, and Plato taught, and what Jesus taught; and no germ of the latter is to be found in the former. It is impossible to take the teachings of the Greeks, and to show how the peculiarities of the Christian system could have grown out of them; and it·is morally certain that if Christ had not appeared in person, and if the world had retained its possession of the Greek philosophy, such a system as that of Christianity would have been forever unknown to men. From some cause, the Greek philosophy has quite as much affinity with the religion of the Koran as it has with the religion of the New Testament; for it was at Bagdad, in the time of the Caliphs, that it was preserved, when a dark night had settled down on Christian Europe; it was at Bagdad, in the palmy days of the religion of Mohammed, that it was most carefully studied; it was from Bagdad, as, in part, the result of the Crusades, that it was given again to Europe.

(*d*) Nor was it a development of the civilization which the world had attained at the time when it appeared. Christianity is not Greek civilization; it is not Roman; it is not Egyptian; it is not Persian; it is not Babylonian. In fact, the enemies of Christianity tell us that it set itself much *against* the civilization of the world when it appeared. It enjoined peculiar manners, and was austere, cold, dissocial, severe; it had no fine arts of its own, and it looked with disdain on the arts of polished life in Greece and Rome; it evinced no affinity for poetry, painting, or statuary, but looked with distrust on them all; it attempted no rivalship of the works of the great Greek masters, but aroused their hostility by eschewing and avoiding them; its own

works of art of that early age—needful for their public
assemblies, and needful to mark the places where martyrs slept— as in the catacombs of Rome, are of the rud-
est structure; and its connection with the arts—poetry,
painting, sculpture, architecture — was of the slowest
growth, and was the work of late, and not of early
years.   Moreover, there has been a deep conviction in
the minds of many of its best friends that the extensive
cultivation of the fine arts is not conducive to the
growth of a pure Christianity, but that such a cultivation is, from some cause, closely connected, in fact, with
a deterioration in doctrine, and with corruption in practical life.   Christianity at its beginning was what it
has ever been since.   Less by far than any other system that has influenced mankind has it been the result
of development and growth.

(e) Nor is it true that it is a development of civilization as the world has advanced since its Founder lived, and that it owes its present form to the
progress of the race.   In one breath we are told by
Comte and his followers that it falls behind the age;
that it is effete and obsolete; that the world now, in
its state of civilization, needs a better system, and
that it is the business of philosophy to reveal such a
system; in the next breath, by Buckle and his friends,
that it is the result of the progressive civilization
of the world, and has grown naturally out of the un-
foldings of the germs of civilized life.   " Can a fountain send forth at the same place sweet water and bitter?   Can the fig-tree bear olive-berries? either a vine
figs?   So can no fountain both yield salt water and
fresh."

Neither of these suppositions is true.   Christianity
has not outlived its influence on the civilization of the

world, nor has it obtained its influence because it is a development of the germs of civilization which the world in its progress is unfolding.

In one word, Christianity is not a "development" at all. It was mature and perfect at the beginning. Few of the great things which influence our world morally or physically are the result of "development." In the old geological periods, as we are now instructed, one was in no sense a "development" from the former; nor did the old in any form travel over into the new in an improved and more perfect growth. The old races were swept off absolutely, and new successive creations of plants and animals were brought upon the changed earth. Man at last appeared, not as a development, but as a new creation. So geology now teaches us. In the progress of society, of what is the printing-press a development? the railroad—the magnetic telegraph? Of what was the mind of Shakspeare, of Bacon, of Newton a development? What was there in the intellect of John Shakspeare, originally a glover, and then a skinner and wool-stapler* in Henly Street, in Stratford-on-Avon, that *developed* itself into Hamlet, and Lear, and Macbeth—that, in the language of Hugh Miller, "set such great thoughts bounding through the world?" What was there in the obscure and humble parson, the father of Newton, that "developed" itself into the science of fluxions, and the discovery of the great law of gravitation?

(2.) The facts in regard to the propagation of Christianity are well settled in history.

(a) It had its origin with Jesus of Nazareth. That fact is as clear as any fact in history; it is so clear that no one can doubt it; it is so clear that it has never been

---

* *Ulrici*, Dramatic Art of Shakspeare, p. 70.

F

denied.   Jesus of Nazareth was a real historical personage.   What he was, who he was, whence he came, what was the object of his coming, are other questions; but that he lived, that he taught, that he died—that he was born in the time of Augustus Cæsar, and died in the time of Tiberius—are points settled by all history.   Infidelity has not ventured to call these things in question.   And the most learned and able forms of skepticism have been employed in showing how, these facts being assumed, the growth and spread of Christianity can be explained.   The Jesus of Strauss is a real historical personage, around whom his disciples and followers have drawn the myths that have grown up into Christianity as it is; the Jesus of Renan is a real personage —an uneducated peasant, ignorant of history, of geography, of literature—unacquainted even with the history of the Herods of his own country, and a stranger to the history of Rome, yet a young man of remarkable and unparalleled genius, far beyond his own age, or any age—ultimately, as springing from the exertion of his own unconscious powers, conceiving the idea that he was the Messiah, and was, in a form before unknown, to set up the worship of the true God, and to change the religion of the world; the Jesus of Gibbon is a real personage, the influence of whose life and opinions on the world is to be explained in the best way in which it can be.

(b) This religion was propagated mainly by very humble men; by men who were uneducated; by men for the most part fishermen—having no original superiority above other fishermen on the shores of the Lake of Galilee, a rude and uncultivated region, or above fishermen as they are found now around Cape Cod or on the Banks of Newfoundland—among the last of men that would be selected for the work of religious missions, or for founding a religion, or for measuring strength with the philosophy of the world: men without rank, or position, or influence, except as they *created* it in the effort to spread the new religion; men belonging to a despised race—a race known indeed beyond the boundaries of their own narrow country, but mostly as slaves, and characterized by Tacitus as " the enemies of the human race;" men belonging to a nation that had produced nothing in sculpture, in painting, in philosophy, in arts, or in arms, to make them known abroad; men belonging to a race which heathen poets condescended to notice only with contempt.*

(c) The facts in the history of its propagation are as well settled as any other facts in history—so well settled as to admit of no skepticism in regard to them. There were no armies; there were no military leaders. The conquests of Christianity were not, certainly until it ascended the throne of the Cæsars, the result of bloody victories. The facts in regard to its propagation have been traced with great learning, impartiality, and fidelity by Mr. Gibbon, and accord, as stated by him, with all the other records that have been handed down to us. They have not been called in question by Strauss or Renan, and infidelity has not ventured, if it had any desire to do it, to found its attacks on Christianity on a denial of those facts. It was in Mr. Gibbon's path to state those facts, and he has done it without hesitation, and without an attempt to pervert them. In fact, he has traced that history in regard to the propagation of Christianity as the result of the labors of humble and unknown men, without influence or arms, *as* faithfully and impartially as he has described the

* Credat Judæus Apella.—*Horace.*

character of the Antonines or Julian, or as he has traced the history of the spread of the religion of Mohammed.

(d) The religion was propagated on the ground of miracles; on the affirmation that Christ rose from the dead; on the belief of the facts as they are stated in the New Testament. Whatever may be said about the truth on any of these points—whether, for example, Christ actually rose from the dead, or whether the hallucination of a woman has taught mankind to believe this, as Renan alleges: "The strong imagination of Mary Magdalene," says he, "has enacted a principal part. Divine power of love! sacred moments in which the passion of a hallucinated woman gives to the world a resurrected God"*—yet there can be no doubt that the religion was, in fact, propagated on the ground of the *belief* of the facts stated in the New Testament, and that if these had *not* been believed, the religion could not, and would not have been spread over the world. The New Testament is full of this, and history is full of it. Mr. Gibbon did not venture to call this fact in question, though he has stated it, as it became him to do with his views of religion, in connection with the fact, *as* undoubtedly true also, that for ages the belief prevailed in the Church that miracles continued to be wrought, and that "that belief must have conduced very frequently to the conversion of infidels."† The only point which I am now making is, that the religion was propagated and received in the world on the ground of the belief that the miracles of the New Testament were true, and especially on the belief that Christ rose from the dead.

* Life of Jesus, p. 357.
† See his statement in full in vol. i., p. 264–267, of his History, Harper's ed., 1829.

II. The second inquiry is, Whether the supposed evidence of the divine origin of Christianity, on which it was propagated, was of such a nature as to account for the facts in regard to its spread in the world ; to *justify* men in embracing it ; and to explain the causes of the great changes which it made. If those evidences were real, would they *explain* the facts which followed ; would they be such as to show that the action of the world in the case was right and wise ; would it be true that in subsequent times the race could look upon this part of its history with complacency and approbation ? for there is much, very much, in the past history of man on which we *can not* thus look, and which, for the honor of our nature, the historian of human affairs would be glad to forget.

It will not be practicable or necessary to dwell long on this part of the subject. It is, perhaps, the part of the argument which I am submitting to you which would be most readily yielded by those who deny the truth of the Christian religion.

What is to be supposed in the case is this, that the things which are revealed in the New Testament actually occurred as they are stated there, and that credible proof that they did actually occur was furnished to mankind—so furnished that the world actually received it *as* credible proof. Let it be supposed, therefore, that the things narrated in the New Testament actually took place, and that the world believed this—that Jesus lived ; that he was born and reared in the manner related ; that he taught ; that he proclaimed the doctrines which are attributed to him ; that he was pure and holy in his character ; that he answered the description of a long series of ancient predictions in regard to the Messiah ; that he healed the sick by mira-

cle; that he opened the eyes of the blind, and caused
the lame man to leap as an hart; that he cast out devils; that he raised the dead; that he was put to death
on a cross; that the earth trembled, and that the sun
withdrew his beams when he died; that he himself rose
from the dead and ascended to heaven—let these things
be supposed, and let them be credited by mankind.
The question then is, whether there was any thing in
the actual reception of the system which can not be
explained on this supposition; any thing that can not
be vindicated and justified as honorable to human nature? Is there any thing in it which the world ought
to desire to forget? Is there any thing in reference to
the actual changes which Christianity has made in the
affairs of nations which the historian of human affairs
would be at a loss in accounting for? Is there any
thing in the reception of Christianity which would
place the race on the same humiliating ground on which
the past history of the world in regard to sorcery, and
witchcraft, and necromancy, and imposture in general,
has placed it?

Nowhere would the explanation of things be so easy;
nowhere would the historian have more occasion to
congratulate himself than in assuming these as facts in
the explanation of the history of the world. How easy
would have been the task of Mr. Gibbon, how much
hard labor would it have saved him, if he had "seen
his way clear" to admit these things to be true!

I may be able, in the proper place, to show, that if the
things attributed to Mohammed in history actually occurred, or were real historical events, the changes which
were consequent on the introduction of his religion into
the world are susceptible of easy explanation. I attempt no more than this in the remarks now made in
regard to the establishment of Christianity.

(1.) These things *were* relied on: that Jesus lived; that he uttered great truths about God; that he taught the doctrine of the immortality of the soul, the resurrection of the dead, and the final judgment; that he wrought miracles in amazing numbers; that he raised the dead; that he himself rose from the dead; that he ascended to heaven; that he made an atonement for the sins of the world. The system never would have been preached at all if these things had not been believed to have occurred; it never would have been embraced if it had not been believed that they were true. The world *did* believe them; the world acted on the belief. Mr. Gibbon could not deny this; no man can now deny it. The reliance in spreading the Gospel was not on military power; on philosophy; on superior claims in science; on a higher civilization; on appeals to the passions of men; on the promise of temporal advantages; on necromancy, juggling, fortune-telling, or sorcery; on new theories about government and law. All the accounts agree in this, that it was not on these things, but on the belief of the truth of the facts of Christianity as we have them in the records of the New Testament now.

(2.) The old systems of religion sat loosely on the world, and the world was, in a certain sense, waiting for a new religion. This was undoubtedly the case in Judea, for the power of the Jewish religion was waning, and the nation was, on principle and in accordance with their prophecies, waiting for an important change in religion when their Messiah should appear. The same thing was substantially true elsewhere. There is undoubted truth in a remark which Mr. Gibbon makes, that the systems of religion prevailing in the Roman empire were all " regarded by philosophers as equally false, by statesmen as equally necessary, and by the mass of the people as equally true." It is also an undoubted fact, established on the well-known testimony of the writers of that age, that there was a general expectation prevailing that some remarkable person would soon appear whose coming would materially change the condition of the world. Thus Suetonius (ch. iv.) says: "An ancient and settled persuasion prevailed throughout the East that the fates had decreed some one to proceed out of Judea who should attain universal empire." Thus Tacitus (Annals, 5, 13), says: "Many were persuaded that it was contained in the books of their priests that at that very time the East should prevail, and that some one should proceed from Judea, and should possess the dominion." It is not, indeed, to be maintained that this expectation was universal, nor is it to be affirmed that Paganism or Judaism had lost their power altogether, for there was still vitality enough in both to arouse themselves to desperate efforts to destroy the new religion when it appeared, in furious storms of persecution.

Yet, that the power of the religions of the world as controlling mankind was waning, if not almost extinct, is the undoubted testimony of history. Mr. Gibbon, speaking of the influence of the prevailing religions on the public mind, makes the following, among other remarks: "We are sufficiently acquainted with the eminent persons who flourished in the age of Cicero, and the first Cæsars, with their actions, their characters, and their motives, to be assured that their conduct in this life was never regulated by any serious conviction of the rewards and punishments of a future state" (vol. i., p. 260). "The general system of their mythology," says he, "was unsupported by any solid proofs; and the wisest among the Pagans had already disclaimed its

usurped authority."—*Ibid.* "The doctrine of a future
state," he adds, "was scarcely considered among the
devout polytheists of Greece and Rome as a fundamental article of faith."—*Ibid.* In connection with these
remarks, and as illustrating the religious state of the
world when Christianity appeared, and as accounting,
in some measure, for its reception by mankind, he makes,
also, the following important observations:

"When Christianity appeared in the world, even
these faint and imperfect impressions" [respecting religion in the prevailing form] "had lost much of their
original power. Human reason, which by its unassisted
strength is incapable of perceiving the mysteries of
faith, had already obtained an easy triumph over the
folly of Paganism; and when Tertullian or Lactantius
employ their labors in exposing its falsehood and extravagance, they are obliged to transcribe the eloquence
of Cicero or the wit of Lucian. The contagion of these
skeptical writings had been diffused far beyond the
number of their readers. The fashion of incredulity
was communicated from the philosopher to the man of
pleasure or business, from the noble to the plebeian, and
from the master to the menial slave who waited at his
table, and who eagerly listened to the freedom of his
conversation. On public occasions the philosophic part
of mankind affected to treat with respect and decency
the religious institutions of their country; but their secret contempt penetrated through the thin and awk-
ward disguise; and even the people, when they discovered that their deities were rejected and derided by
those whose rank or understanding they were accustomed to reverence, were filled with doubts and apprehensions concerning the truth of those doctrines, to
which they had yielded the most implicit belief. The

F 2

decline of ancient prejudice exposed a very numerous
portion of human kind to the danger of a painful and
comfortless situation. A state of skepticism and sus-
pense may amuse a few inquisitive minds. But the
practice of superstition is so congenial to the multitude,
that if they are forcibly awakened, they still regret the
loss of their pleasing vision. Their love of the marvelous and supernatural, their curiosity with regard to future events, and their strong propensity to extend their
hopes and fears beyond the limits of the visible world,
were the principal causes which favored the establishment of polytheism. So urgent on the vulgar is the
necessity of believing, that the fall of any system of
mythology will most probably be succeeded by the introduction of some other mode of superstition. Some
deities of a more recent and fashionable cast might
soon have occupied the deserted temples of Jupiter and
Apollo, if, in the decisive moment, the wisdom of Providence [*sic*] had not interposed a genuine revelation,
fitted to inspire the most rational esteem and conviction, while, at the same time, it was adorned with all
that could attract the curiosity, the wonder, and the
veneration of the people. In their actual disposition,
as many were almost disengaged from their artificial
prejudices, but equally susceptible and desirous of a devout attachment, an object much less deserving would
have been sufficient to fill the vacant place in their
hearts, and to gratify the uncertain eagerness of their
passions. Those who are inclined to pursue this reflection, instead of viewing with astonishment the rapid
progress of Christianity, will perhaps be surprised that
its success was not still more rapid and still more universal."*

* Decline and Fall, vol. i., p. 280, 281.

(3.) The new system contained statements on points which men had desired to know, and on which they despaired of obtaining information from any other source. We shall see in a subsequent Lecture (Lecture IX.) that Christianity meets and satisfies original wants in man—wants in his very nature as a religious being, and wants as a fallen being—and that it supplies, in the great sacrifice which it reveals as made for sin, what men had been elsewhere seeking in vain. The remark which I am now making is, that the fact that those doctrines were *promulgated* and *believed* in the early propagation of Christianity, will go far to explain the fact that the religion was embraced, or to account for the success attending the efforts for its dissemination. Mr. Gibbon has himself shown this with great skill in reference to the doctrines of the immortality of the soul and of a future state, for he has made this one of the five causes which will explain the fact of the propagation of the Christian religion.* The point which I am now making is, that what was true of *those* doctrines is true of other doctrines of Christianity also. It is no less a fact that they met the wants and aspirations of men. And as we know that the religion *was* propagated and embraced on the belief of these truths, it follows that if it is assumed that they *were* true, the fact would go far to explain the reception of the religion in the world. The new religion met a conscious *want* of men in the failure of polytheism, and was embraced in part *because* it met such a want. That there is a God, one God ; that there is a Savior ; that the soul is immortal ; that there is a future state ; that the pardon of sin may be obtained, are truths which men had panted to know, but which had been found in no other

* Decline and Fall, vol. i., p. 259–264.

system, and which they had ceased to hope could be obtained in connection with philosophy or polytheism.

(4.) Men will sooner or later yield to that which seems to them to have the force of truth, or which they believe to be true. The foundation of this remark is, that there is that in the human mind, as we shall see in another part of this course (Lecture IX.), which corresponds with truth, or which is designed to secure the reception and influence of truth in the world, and this principle or law of our nature will explain the progress which truth on any subject has made. It is, moreover, the most cheering thing in regard to the future, for it makes it certain that truth on all subjects, religion as well as others, will ultimately be triumphant. It is to be admitted that there may be that in the mind itself which will temporarily resist this. There may be the prejudices of education, of bigotry, of country, of custom, of party, and of religion — the "idols" of the "tribe," of the "cave," of the "forum," and of the "theatre," as Lord Bacon calls them*— but those prejudices truth will overcome. There may be laws, customs, and vested interests; there may be the influence of a priesthood; there may be the resistance of a false philosophy; there may be all the power derived from hereditary rank; there may be all that there is in the passions of men, and the love of ease and indulgence; there may be all the power of a gross immorality, sanctioned by religion, by custom, and by law; and there may be all the power of a state or empire. All this Christianity encountered; most of this any new form of religion, or any new opinion in philosophy, will be likely to encounter in the world. Truth may seem to begin

* Idola tribus, idola specus, idola fori, idola theatri.—Novum Organum, lib. i., aphor. xxxix.

its way as by beating against adamantine walls. It may appear to accomplish no more than the ocean does with its raging billows against rock-bound coasts, or along the pebbly shore. It makes the attack, and then retires. If the pebble is removed a little inward, it will come back again; if the sand is washed a little, it at once fills up; if the solid rocks tremble, they still stand firm. Truth may seem to be stayed, and to die out; but it will not.

> "Truth, crushed to earth, will rise again;
> The eternal years of God are hers."

Time only is needed for its triumph. In due time it will be in the ascendant; and, great as was the opposition which Christianity met when first announced to the world, yet it did triumph, and the principle now laid down will account for the fact that it triumphed. The same principle, also, will account for the fact that it is kept up in the world; and the same principle makes it absolutely certain that it will ultimately prevail all over the earth.

(5.) A belief in miracles will convince men of the truth of a religion which they are wrought to establish, and faith in the miracles of the New Testament was one of the main grounds on which the system was embraced. The process of argument by which this is proved is a very brief one. It is simply that the human mind is so made that it *can not* believe that the laws of nature would be set aside to confirm a falsehood or to commend an impostor. Whatever may be true in regard to the converse of this proposition, whether the human mind is so made that it can believe that the laws of nature will be set aside to confirm a true system of religion, or to commend a true embassador from heaven to the world—which is now the great question in our conflict with scientific infidelity, yet there is a universal opinion—men *can not* believe otherwise—that God would not, and could not, interpose in this manner in behalf of an impostor and a false system of religion.   If the dead are raised, and if men believe that they are raised, then they will believe also that he who does this is invested with special power by God, and has a special commission from him, for created power does not raise the dead.

Mr. Gibbon has been at considerable pains (vol. i., p. 264–267) to illustrate the fact that "supernatural gifts, even in this life, were ascribed to the Christians above the rest of mankind," and "must have conduced to their own comfort, and very frequently to the conviction of infidels;" and he has made it a point to consider *when* these marvelous powers ceased in the Church. Mr. Lecky, with a different purpose, and with great ability, has engaged in the inquiry when miracles really ceased in the Church, and has described the prevailing state of mind on the subject at the present time (History of Rationalism in Europe, vol. i., p. 155–202); but, whenever it ceased, no one can doubt, not even Mr. Gibbon, that the *belief* that such miracles were wrought would account for the spread of the Gospel.   Indeed, that, as has been remarked, is one of the main points by which he accounts for its diffusion in the Roman empire.

I can not but be justified, therefore, in the conclusion which I draw from these things, that if the miracles ascribed to the Savior were wrought, this fact will account for the spread of Christianity in the world, and will justify its reception.   Somehow the mind of man is so made that such a result *must* follow.

(6.) The belief of the things on which Christianity was propagated would account for all the facts which occurred in the conversion of men; in their forsaking sin; in their yielding to the claims of virtue; in the reformations of morals and of life which followed in the path of the apostles. That men *did* forsake their sins, and that they *did* lead upright and pure lives under the influence of this system, is a simple matter of historic truth which no one would call in question. It is apparent on the face of the New Testament; it has come down to us in sacred history; it is confirmed by what occurs now; and it is established by what, with some, would be a more decisive authority than all the rest, that of Mr. Gibbon; for he would have given a different representation of the influence of Christianity on morals if God, while he allowed him to be an *infidel* in religion, had not made him *faithful* as an historian.

Of the five causes on which, according to him, the reception of Christianity in the world can be explained without the necessity of admitting its divine origin, the purity of its morals is one. It became necessary, therefore, in such an argument, to show that the early Christians were distinguished for their pure moral character, and that Christianity, in fact, promoted the reformation of mankind. This point has been elaborated by him with consummate skill (vol. i.; p. 267–271). If there is a sneer on his face while he writes, and an underlying sarcasm as his pen moves so smoothly, it is no more than we were to expect; but the *fact* is one which could not but be stated in an honest account of the Decline and Fall of the Roman Empire. The use to be made of it was another question for him, as it is for us; but historic verity *demanded* of Mr. Gibbon that the statement should be made, as it is made, that "the primitive Christian demonstrated his faith by his virtues" (vol. i., p. 267), and that full credit should be given

to the statement that " when the Christians of Bithynia
were brought before the tribunal of the younger Pliny,
they assured the proconsul that, far from being engaged
in any unlawful conspiracy, they were bound by a solemn obligation to abstain from the commission of those
crimes which disturb the private or public peace of society—from theft, robbery, adultery, perjury, and fraud"
(vol. i., p. 267, 268), and that " the friends of Christianity may acknowledge," says he, " without a blush, that
many of the most eminent saints had been before their
baptism the most abandoned sinners" (vol. i., p. 267).

Now, if the system of Christianity is true, such facts
would occur just as it is stated that they did occur;
that is, it would produce precisely such effects as these,
for its doctrines are designed to produce such effects.
It needs no argument to show that these effects must
follow from such a system of doctrines, and the causes
and effects in such a case would be commensurate with
each other; in other words, the supposition of the truth
of Christianity would account for the facts in its propagation.

(7.) In like manner, the supposition of the truth of
the facts in Christianity would, if they were believed,
shake the faith of men in the old systems of religion; for,
if Christianity was true, these systems were of course
false, and men would perceive it and abandon them:
an event which actually occurred, and which can thus
be satisfactorily explained.

(8.) On the same supposition, also, all the arrangements for a priesthood, and for the offering of sacrifices,
alike among the Jews and the heathen, would be seen
to be useless and unnecessary, and would soon lose their
hold on men—as was the fact.   The Jewish priesthood,
as a priesthood, ceased almost immediately on the in-

troduction of Christianity; the altar was overthrown, the temple was demolished, and Judaism expired. The same effect followed among the heathen. The fires ceased to burn on the altars; the priests were disrobed; the temples were closed; the vast fabric of superstition melted away. This effect undoubtedly followed on the preaching of Christianity, for it is attested by all history, and it was an effect which *must* follow if Christianity was true. The supposition that it was true, or was believed to be true, will account for the effects which actually followed.

(9.) On the same principle, also, it would follow that all the laws made for the support of Paganism would soon become obsolete, and would lose their power, so that they could not be revived, and so that it would become necessary to adjust the laws to the new order of things. If the religion should lose its hold on the people; if the temples and the altars should be forsaken; if the priesthood should become powerless; if the Lares and the Penates should be treated as useless lumber; if the Dies Fasti should cease to attract the people; if faith in the gods should cease, then all the laws which upheld those things would be unmeaning and powerless, and the legislation of the state would be adjusted to the new religion: an event which actually occurred, and which is susceptible thus of an easy explanation.

(10.) It would also follow, however, that there would probably be a *conflict* between the two systems, and that, while there was power on the one side and feebleness on the other, there would be an attempt to sustain the one and to destroy the other by power—the power of the state; for, if Christianity was true, there was that in it which would not yield to the dictation of civil power; and if Paganism was expiring, it would

rouse its remaining strength to put down the new system. This actually occurred, as might have been anticipated, and the supposition of the truth of Christianity will account for all the persecutions which attended its early propagation.

(11.) And once more: The new religion, if it was
from God, or if it was believed to be from God, would
make martyrs, and the supposition of its truth will
account for all that occurred in the history of martyrdom. All that is recorded of their patience, calmness,
firmness, tenacity, *obduracy*, OBSTINACY, if men please,
can be accounted for if it be supposed that the religion
was from God. When Pliny wrote to the Emperor Trajan that, having failed in the attempt to secure a recantation from the accused Christians, he ordered them to
death, because, whatever might be their general conduct, he thought that such " *inflexible obstinacy*" ought
to be punished, he was but recording a fact that *must*
have occurred on the supposition that Christianity is
true.* The religion required just such sacrifices, and
just such firmness as Pliny described. It would produce just such calmness, firmness, obduracy, obstinacy,
among its true friends. It would *make* confessors and
martyrs. It would produce just such effects as were
actually produced in tens of thousands of instances in
the attempt to propagate it, and, therefore, the cause is
commensurate with the effect.

* " I have taken," says Pliny to Trajan, "this course with all who
have been brought before me and have been accused as Christians.
Upon their confessing to me that they were, I repeated the question
a second and third time, threatening also to punish them with death.
Such as still persisted I ordered away to be punished; for it was no
doubt with me, whatever might be the nature of their opinion, that
contumacy and inflexible obstinacy ought to be punished."—*Lardner's
Works*, vii., p. 23, ed. London, 1829.

The supposition of the divine origin of Christianity, therefore, would furnish an easy and natural solution of all the recorded facts which occurred in its propagation, alike in regard to the great numbers that embraced it, the spirit with which it endowed them, and the changes which it made in the world.

III. The remaining inquiry is, Whether the propagation of Christianity can be explained on any other supposition than that it is from God.

This inquiry, to make the argument complete, would properly resolve itself into two parts: the question whether the propagation of Christianity could be explained on the supposition that it is *not* from God; and the question whether the other system referred to in the beginning of this Lecture—the only one that in this respect can come in competition with it — would not furnish the same argument as to a divine origin.

Can the propagation of Christianity be explained on the supposition that it is an imposture?

The only labored attempt to show this has been by Mr. Gibbon, and he has exhausted the subject. Nothing has been left to be added by succeeding skeptics. The explanation of the remarkable facts connected with the subject of Christianity was in Mr. Gibbon's path in describing the Decline and Fall of the Roman Empire. He could not avoid it; and we have no reason to suppose that he wished to avoid it; for when, in the solitude of night, in the summer-house of his garden at Lausanne, he had finished his work, and laid down his pen, and took several turns in a covered walk of acacias, meditating on what he had done, there was, perhaps, no part of the work on which *he* would look with more satisfaction than on the chapters (xv., xvi.) in which he describes "the progress of the Christian religion, and the sentiments, manners, numbers, and conditions of the primitive Christians," and "the conduct of the Roman government toward the Christians."—Vol. i., p. 249–329.*

He could not avoid this inquiry. The spread of Christianity was too important a fact in the history of the world, and was too closely connected with the downfall of the empire to permit him to pass it by; and though the same facts might have been recorded

---

* "It was on the day, or rather night of the 27th of June, 1787, between the hours of eleven and twelve, that I wrote the last lines of the last page, in a summer-house in my garden. After laying down my pen, I took several turns in a *berceau*, or covered walk of acacias, which commands a prospect of the country, the lake, and the mountains. The air was temperate, the sky was serene, the silver orb of the moon was reflected from the waters, and all nature was silent. I will not describe the first emotions of joy on the recovery of my freedom, and perhaps the establishment of my fame," etc.—Miscellaneous Works of *Edward Gibbon, Esq.*, vol. i., p. 170, ed. Dublin, 1796. In illustration of the feelings of satisfaction with which Mr. Gibbon regarded these two chapters of his History, I may refer to his remarks in his "Life and Writings" *after* those chapters had been attacked by Mr. Davies, of Oxford, by Bishop Watson, by Dr. Priestley, Sir David Dalrymple, and Dr. White, of Oxford. As the result of the whole, he says, "Had I believed that the majority of English readers were so fondly attached to the name and shadow of Christianity; had I foreseen that the pious, the timid, and the prudent would feel, or affect to feel, with such exquisite sensibility, I might perhaps have softened those invidious chapters, which would create many enemies, and conciliate few friends. But the shaft was shot, the alarm was sounded, and I could only rejoice that, if the voice of our priests was clamorous and bitter, their hands were disarmed from the powers of persecution." "Let me frankly own that I was startled at the first discharge of ecclesiastical ordnance; but, as soon as I found that this empty noise was mischievous only in the intention, my fear was converted into indignation; and every feeling of indignation or curiosity has long since subsided in pure and placid indifference."—Mis. Works, vol. i., p. 153, 156.

with another mode of explaining them, or with no attempt to explain them, yet the principles of Mr. Gibbon would not permit him to suggest the explanation that it came from God, and a bare statement of the facts as they occurred, with no explanation, would have made an impression on mankind which those principles would lead him to counteract if he could. The diffusion of Christianity *seemed* to attest its divine origin. It was an argument much relied on by Christians. On the mass of men the manner of its propagation has always made a deep impression in favor of its divine origin. That the religion is from God *seems* to be the most natural, philosophical, and obvious explanation of the facts in the case. If, therefore, it could be shown that the propagation of that religion could be accounted for on the supposition that it is not of God, or by mere natural causes constantly in operation among men, much might be done to loosen its hold on the world.

Mr. Gibbon has done his work well. No man could bring to the task greater learning, more patient industry, more impartial historical honesty, or more attractive eloquence in thought or in style. No man surpassed him in the knowledge of the vast lore treasured in ancient libraries, sacred and secular, that could be made to bear on the subject; no man has ever equaled him in understanding the power of a sneer. The argument, as he pursued it, is complete. No one will add to it; no one will improve it.

The points on which Mr. Gibbon relies in the explanation of the "Progress of the Christian Religion" are five in number: "The inflexible, and, if we may use the expression, the intolerant zeal of the Christians, derived, it is true, from the Jewish religion, but purified from the narrow and unsocial spirit which, instead of inviting, had deterred the Gentiles from embracing the law of Moses." "The doctrine of a future life, improved by every additional circumstance which could give weight and efficacy to that important truth." "The miraculous powers ascribed to the primitive Church." "The pure and austere morals of Christians." "The union and discipline of the Christian republic, which gradually formed an independent and increasing state in the heart of the Roman empire."

This is all. But I need not say that the force of these considerations is not seen by the mere announcement of their *titles.* It could only be seen in view of the very elaborate and ingenious argument with which these principles are illustrated.

Of course I could not, in the task assigned me, go into an examination of this argument, and you would not thank me for undertaking it. The world understands it, as the world understands the argument of Mr. Hume against miracles, that, however it is to be met or explained, it is not an argument to be greatly relied on by infidelity. The progress of Christianity in the world has not been perceptibly impeded by either; and the number of those influenced by either argument is small, mostly among those in early life, and to a great extent, if not entirely, those who were skeptics before. If a personal allusion may be allowed, I may be permitted to say that this was precisely the effect nearly fifty years ago on my own mind.

Some very general remarks on the reasons thus assigned for the propagation of Christianity may, however, not be unprofitable or improper.

(*a*) It is now to be admitted—it would be conceded universally—that these are *all* the causes that can be assigned for the propagation of Christianity on the supposition that the religion is on the same level with Mohammedism, or is false. No one has attempted to add to this argument; no one would be likely to attempt it. Mr. Gibbon exhausted the subject. It was to be presumed that he would state all the arguments which would occur to him, and it is certain that no arguments likely to bear on the subject would escape him. Infidelity can do no more in *this* argument, and the argument is complete.

> "Si Pergama dextrâ
> Defendi possent, etiam hâc defensa fuissent."
>
> Æn. ii., 291, 292.

There are no more arguments to be added to these. Historical research will add no more. German rationalism will add no more, and the warfare is transferred to other fields.

(*b*) It can not be denied that Mr. Gibbon has, in these statements, rendered an involuntary tribute of great value to Christianity, and has conceded much that may be referred to as an actual, though an indirect proof of its divine origin. It was much that the necessities of the case, and the claims of honest and impartial history, should extort from such a man, and in such connections, the concessions made in regard to the system; it is much that Christianity had laid the foundation *for* such an argument — an argument which Mr. Gibbon *could* not have urged in explanation of the continued prevalence of the Greek and Roman mythology in the world, or in explanation of the propagation of the Mohammedan system. It was much that he could refer, and was constrained to refer, to "the zeal of the early Christians;" to "the doctrine of a future life, improved by every additional circumstance which could give weight and efficacy to that important truth;" to "the

pure and austere morals of Christians;" and this, with
what was implied in the very nature of the argument,
and what is, in fact, conceded, that these things were
not found in the ancient systems of religion ; that paganism — human wisdom and philosophy — had never
originated these things so as to give permanency to
the ancient systems of religion, or to secure their propagation in the world.   " The general system of their
mythology," says he (vol. i., p. 260), " was unsupported
by any solid proofs, and the wisest among the Pagans
had already disclaimed its usurped authority.   The doctrine of a future state was scarcely considered, among
the devout polytheists of Greece and Rome, as a fundamental article of faith."   " The first book of the Tusculan
Questions," says he, " and the Treatise De Senectute, and
the Somnium Scipionis, contain, in the most beautiful
language, every thing that Grecian philosophy or Roman
good sense could possibly suggest on this dark subject ;"
and, as the result, he adds, " The writings of Cicero represent in the most lively colors the ignorance, the errors, and the uncertainty of the ancient philosophers
with regard to the immortality of the soul" (vol. i., p.
259).

The impression, in fact, made on the mind of Cicero
himself by the ablest argument that philosophy has
ever furnished for the immortality of the soul—that in
the Gorgias—is thus expressed in his own language, in
a passage which I shall have occasion to quote again:
" I know not how it is that when I read I assent ; but
when I lay down the book, and begin, by myself, to
think of the immortality of souls, all my assent glides
away."*

* *Marcus.* Num eloquentiâ Platonem superare possumus?   Evolve
diligenter ejus cum librum, qui est de animo: amplius quod desideres,

It is natural and proper now to ask whence had the Author of Christianity these views which commended his religion to the world, securing its propagation, and displacing all the results of human wisdom? Whence sprang these "pure and austere morals," so unlike what prevailed under the best forms of the Pagan religion, so superior to any of the systems of philosophers? Let it be supposed that Christianity is from God, and all this is plain. What will make it plain on any other supposition?

(c) It is to be admitted by us that Mr. Gibbon is right in the statement of the historical fact that these things *did* contribute materially to the spread of Christianity, for in embracing it men gave their assent to the fact that these things were so; they embraced it, among other reasons, *because* they believed that these things were so. They saw in these truths and results such a religion as man needs; they saw what was not to be found in any other system; they saw, or thought they saw *in* these things proof that a religion so pure, a religion that prompted to such zeal for the good of man, a religion which revealed the doctrine of immortality, must be from God. Were they far from truth and nature in such a supposition?

(d) In considering the question whether these causes alone would explain the facts of the propagation of Christianity, let it now be supposed that the system was false; that it was based on imposture and delusion; that Jesus never existed, or that he was an enthusiast, or that he was an impostor, or that his apos-

nihil erit. *Auditor.* Feci, mehercule, et quidem sæpius: sed nescio quo modo, dum lego, assentior; cum posui librum, et mecum ipse de immortalite animorum cœpi cogitare, assentio omnis illa elabitur. —Tusc. Quæst., lib. i., c. ii.

G

tles contrived the system with an intention to impose
on the world; that no miracles were wrought; that
Christ was *not* raised from the dead; that all this occurred in the most intellectual age of past time, when
the light of philosophy had just culminated in Greece
and in Rome, and before the long night settled down
on Europe in the Dark Ages; when of all ages it would
have been most easy to detect an imposture—and the
problem then would be, how could *such* a religion, under *such* apostles, and in *such* an age, accomplish these
things ? How *could* it overthrow the ancient systems
of mythology; set aside the ancient laws; change long-
established customs; render meaningless and void the
ancient sacrifices; disrobe an established priesthood;
throw down ancient altars; overcome the corrupt and
evil passions of men ; go into the scenes of domestic
life, and transform all around the fireside : how could
it remove Penates and Lares, and set up a Christian
altar in their place; lead men to abandon sins long in-
dulged, and to call things sinful which before were regarded as innocent; transform pollution to godly living, and lift up the degraded to a life of pure devotion
and self-sacrifice, and of such men *make martyrs ?* Yes,
make martyrs, for this it did by tens of thousands—the
young, the aged; the rich, the poor; the refined, the
uncultivated; the master, the slave; the man who had
been a philosopher, and the tender and delicate female
reared in luxury, and accustomed to the gayety and
the splendors of the court.

This is the problem; and the reasons assigned will
not, do not explain this. The mind is conscious of a
sad vacancy when these facts are before it, and these
reasons are assigned for those facts. It wants more ; it
must have more.

But add now the idea that all this was true—that things were as they are stated in the New Testament—and we have a cause that is commensurate with the effect, that settles all doubts, that makes all things plain.

And shall we now compare this system and these facts with that other system which infidelity would make parallel with this, and whose propagation the unbelievers would explain on the same principles—the system of Mohammed?

Well was it, though perhaps he was unconscious of the reason why it was so, that Mr. Gibbon did not attempt elaborately, as in the case of Christianity, to explain the causes of the rapid diffusion of that system. Those causes are patent on the face of the system and on the face of history. Yet Mr. Gibbon has, as in the case of Christianity, narrated with great exactness and fidelity the origin, the slow growth at first, the subsequent triumphs, and the influence of that system, as no other man has done or could do. But he has not ventured to suggest that its propagation might demonstrate that it was of divine origin, for that might have suggested a stronger argument for the propagation of the other system; he has not thought it necessary, as in the case of Christianity, to attempt an explanation of the causes of its diffusion, for that explanation, easy, natural, and satisfactory as it must have been, *might* have appeared too much in contrast with the explanation of the causes of the spread of Christianity, and, in thus accounting for the one, *might* have suggested to men that there was some sophistry in the explanation of the other.

But can the spread of Mohammedism be explained except on the supposition that it is from God? Has any historian ever found any difficulty on that subject;

or even felt himself embarrassed in regard to such an explanation? Is it more difficult than the explanation of the conquests of Cæsar or Alexander? If you add to the idea of conquest—of the triumphs of arms which you have in the conquests of Cæsar and Alexander—the idea that Mohammedism is a *religion*, and, therefore, meets one of the wants of mankind; that it affirms the doctrine that there is one God, and, therefore, in this respect, meets the highest wants of men; that it makes provision for the indulgence of some of the most powerful passions that rule in the human soul; that it makes prominent as an attraction the promise of sensual delights alike in this world and the world to come; that it imposes few restraints on the passions, and those only that are most easily evaded; that it falls in, in the main, with the whole course and tendency of human nature, and blends these indulgences with religion, and makes them part of the religion itself—if these things are before the mind, is it difficult to explain the spread and the permanency of the system? How different from a system of poverty, and humility, and self-denial; a system with nothing of military glory; a system originated not by one who was a splendid conqueror, but by one who was poor and despised, and was crucified between malefactors; a system going forth not under the blazonry of banners of conquest, but *as* if one should make the image of the *gallows* an emblem of his religion — for the *cross* was then more ignominious than the *gallows* is now; a system which required a renovated heart, and the renunciation of the passions, and a pure life! How different these two as making an appeal to mankind! In the language of another, "The enthusiasm by which Mohammedism conquered the world was mainly a military enthusiasm. Men were drawn to it at once, and without conditions, by the splendor of the achievements of its disciples, and it declared an absolute war against all the religions it encountered. Its history, therefore, exhibits nothing of the process of gradual absorption, persuasion, compromise, and assimilation that was exhibited in the dealings of Christianity with barbarians." And again: "One of the great characteristics of the Koran is the extreme care and skill with which it labors to assist men in realizing the unseen. Descriptions the most minutely detailed, and, at the same time, the most vivid, are mingled with powerful appeals to those sensual passions by which the imagination in all countries, but especially those in which Mohammedism has taken root, is most forcibly influenced."[*]

When we remember these things, and when we remember, "as modern criticism has shown from the state of the Arab mind and character in the period antecedent to the coming of Mohammed, that the race was fully prepared for its mission as soon as some principle should unite in one nationality the struggling and divided tribes of the Peninsula," it is not difficult to explain "the rapid expansion of the power of that religion, the brilliant and fugitive bloom of civilization which embellished the dominion of the Arabs," *without* the supposition that it was from God.[†]

* *Lecky*, Hist. of Rationalism, i., 235.

† Edinburg Review, vol. cxxiv., 1. The literature on this subject, in order to a full understanding of the causes of the rise and decline of this extraordinary power, may be found in the following works: *Gibbon*, Decline and Fall of the Roman Empire, chs. l., li., vol. iii., p. 360–460. Mohammed der Prophet, sein Leben und seine Lehre, von *Gustav Weil*, Stuttgardt, 1844. Life of Mahomet, and History of Islam to the Era of the Hegira, by *William Muir*, 4 vols., London, 1861.

The Mohammedan religion was in the line of human
nature; was in accordance with a previous state of the
public mind; was under the guidance of an eminent
military chieftain and his not less illustrious successor;
was connected with the founding of a mighty empire
—it appealed to the most powerful passions of men, and
yet, at the same time, gave to men what they pant for—
a god, a religion, a hope of immortality—and immortality, in its case, which was of all things most gratifying,
a prolongation forever of the pleasures of sense.   How
different from the Christian scheme!

Mohammedism rose, and spread, and flourished as
a religion constructed with eminent ability, and sustained by military power, and the love of national
glory; it is decaying and falling as a false religion
must do, not keeping up with the progress and wants
of the world; Christianity, as we shall see hereafter,
becomes more extended and wide-spread in its power
and influences as the world advances in civilization,
science, and the arts, and is the only system of religion
that has any promise, in itself, of spreading over the
nations, and of enduring to the end of human affairs.

Das Leben und die Lehre des Mohammed's, von *Adolf Sprenger*, 3
vols., Berlin, 1855–1865.

LECTURE V.

MIRACLES: THE EVIDENCE IN THE NINETEENTH CEN-
TURY THAT THEY WERE PERFORMED IN THE FIRST.

I PROPOSE, in this Lecture, to consider the evidence
in favor of the divine origin of Christianity as derived
from miracles. The particular point which I shall have
in view is the evidence as it exists in the nineteenth
century that miracles were performed in the first, or as
the evidence appeals to the men of this generation.
The remarks will have reference to the argument in the
present age of the world, and in view of the objections
which may be urged by those who deny the divine
origin of Christianity as derived from the present state
of science, and from the great changes which have occurred in the minds of men on the stability of the laws
of nature now after the lapse of eighteen hundred years
since Christianity was introduced, and on the whole
subject of supernatural interferences and agencies. It
is evident that the state of the argument must be somewhat different from what it was when Christianity was
first proclaimed, and that it would have been comparatively easy to convince men of the reality of such supernatural interferences as those on which Christianity
is based at a time when the belief in such interferences
was almost universal. There has been a growing confidence, as science has advanced, in the fixedness of the
laws of nature, and it is conceivable that the confidence
in the fixedness and stability of those laws *might* become so strong as to lead men to adopt it as a maxim

that all testimony in favor of miracles is to be at once
rejected. With many persons that point is already
reached. "We summarily," says Strauss (Intr. to the
Life of Jesus), "reject all miracles, prophecies, narratives
of angels and demons, and the like, as simply impossible
and irreconcilable with the known and universal laws
which govern the course of events." So Renan, and so
the Westminster Review, in passages which I have had,
or shall have occasion to refer to, adopt this as a maxim.
The question whether this is so is, perhaps, *the* great
question which is before mankind in this age; it is certainly a question which the friends of religion in this
age are to meet, and in reference to which the enemies of
religion are pressing very hard on the faith of the Church.

The essential idea of a miracle is that of an event
where the only antecedent is the divine *will* and the
divine *power*. Theologically considered, it is where
such an event occurs as performed in attestation of the
divine mission of him who performs it, and as showing
that he is authorized to proclaim the law, or to disclose
the will of God, as the credentials of an embassador
accredit him to a foreign court, and authorize him to
declare the will of the government which has sent him.

It is not difficult, therefore, to distinguish the idea
of a miracle from that of an ordinary event, and it is
not necessary, in order to obtain that idea, to inquire
whether it is a suspension of the laws of nature, as
theologians have commonly affirmed it to be, or a violation of the laws of nature, as Mr. Hume was pleased
to regard it, or as the introduction of a higher law of
nature adjusted to the occasion, as Dr. Thomas Brown
seems to have regarded it. If there are laws of nature
already in operation in relation to that on which the
miracle is performed, of course those laws would be

"suspended" for the time; whether in any case there would be a "violation" of those laws, or whether all that there is in the case is the introduction of higher laws, are points which, perhaps, are above us, and which would not, at any rate, help us in understanding the real nature of a miracle.

The idea is, that the only antecedent in the case is the divine *will*—the divine *power*. That is all that enters into the result. That covers and explains all. In the creation of the world, the only antecedent was the divine will—the divine power. It was not by any established laws; it was not by the use of subordinate agencies; it was not a development from things already existing. In the formation of new races upon the earth in the old geological periods preparatory to the introduction of man, and in the creation of man himself, the only antecedent in each case was the divine will—the divine power. One race was not developed from another, nor were the elements of the one taken as materials from which to form the other. One race was entirely swept away from the earth, to be succeeded by another, brought into existence in a similar manner, and by the same power. In raising the dead, the only antecedent in the case is the divine will—the divine power. There is nothing in the condition of the dead tending to that; there are no laws of nature operating in the grave in that line or direction; there is nothing in the condition of the dead—no germ—no hidden life —that can be developed into the new form of being. All the laws of "nature" in the case tend to a different result—to decomposition and permanent death; and if those laws continued to operate with no counteracting will or power, the dead would remain in their graves forever.

G 2

This is the essential idea in a miracle. The particular idea, as connected with the evidences of revealed religion, is that this power is put forth in attestation of one who claims to be a messenger from heaven, or in the establishment of some doctrine or truth to be believed by men. Whatever may be the difference of opinion as to the *fact* of such a divine interposition, there can be none on the question whether such a power, if exerted, would be a sufficient confirmation of a claim to a divine mission, or of the truth of a doctrine proposed to the faith of mankind. Men are so made that they could not believe otherwise, nor can they reason themselves into a contrary belief. Here, at least, the limits of skepticism are fixed and settled. God would not give this power to an impostor, nor would he put forth this power in defense of a falsehood. Men may believe that there is no God, but they can not believe that, if there is a God, he would raise the dead to confirm a lie or to deceive mankind. Whatever may be their views of God—Fetish, Polytheistic, Monotheistic, Deistic, Christian, Mohammedan, Buddhist, Trinitarian, Unitarian, they will agree in this. They are so made, and they can not think otherwise. Whoever made man, or however, or whenever he was formed, this idea was incorporated into his very nature. His Maker—known or unknown to us—*meant* that man should believe that if he interposed by his direct will and power, it would be in favor of truth, not of falsehood ; in favor of one sent from heaven, and not in favor of an impostor. So men have believed, and so they will believe to the end of time.

As to the *evidence* of the truth of miracles, the next question is not so much whether those in reference to which the claim would be made are established *by* suf-

FICIENT *testimony*, as whether they can be established *by* ANY TESTIMONY WHATEVER. In the language of Mr. Mansel (Aids to Faith, p. 16), "If it once be granted that testimony is admissible in the case, it is scarcely possible to conceive a stronger testimony than that which the Christian miracles can claim." Accordingly, Strauss and Renan *assume* that a miracle is simply impossible, and that *all* reference to miracles is to be entirely laid out of the question. Mr Hume also places the matter expressly on that ground. He says: "A miracle is a violation of the laws of nature; and as a firm and unalterable experience has established these laws, the proof against a miracle, from the very nature of the fact, is as entire as any argument from experience can possibly be imagined."—Essays, vol. ii., p. 108, ed. Phila., 1817. This, too, is the tendency of science, so far as science bears on the subject at all; for just in proportion as men approximate the position that the laws of nature are universal, fixed, and unchangeable, they approximate the position that no human testimony whatever could establish the truth of a miracle. "No testimony," we are told, on high scientific authority, "can reach to the supernatural; testimony can apply only to apparent, sensible facts; testimony can only prove an extraordinary and perhaps inexplicable phenomenon; that it is due to supernatural causes is entirely dependent on the previous belief and assumption of the parties."* And this *is* the question. In the language of Mr. Mansel, "The question is not the rarity of miracles—no one asserts them to be common; it is not their general improbability—no one asserts them to be generally probable; it is not that they need an extraordinary testimony as compared with other events

* Essays and Reviews, p. 107.

—such a testimony we assert they have. It is neither more nor less than their *impossibility ;* an impossibility to be established on scientific grounds, such as no reasonable man would reject in any other case — grounds such as those on which we believe that the earth goes round the sun, or that chemical elements combine in definite proportions. In this point of view the argument is altogether of a general character, and is unaffected by any peculiarities of probability or testimony which may distinguish one miraculous narrative from another. If the progress of physical or metaphysical science has shown beyond the possibility of reasonable doubt that miracles are *impossible ;* if, as seems to be the tendency of a recent argument, the assertion of a miracle is now known to be as absurd as the assertion that two and two make five,[*] it is idle to attempt a comparison between greater or less degrees of probability or testimony."[†]

In this connection, as showing what is the state of one class of minds on this subject, and perhaps as representing in fact more than would be willing to avow it, I may copy a remark and an illustration of Renan which I have before quoted (Life of Jesus, p. 43, 44, 45) : "None of the miracles," says he, "with which ancient histories are filled, occurred under scientific conditions. Observation, never once contradicted, teaches us that miracles occur only in periods and countries in which they are believed in, and before persons disposed to believe them. No miracle was ever performed before an assembly of men capable of establishing the miraculous character of an act. Neither men of the people nor men of the world are competent for that. Great precautions and a long habit of scientific research are requisite.

[*] Essays and Reviews, p. 141.   [†] Aids to Faith, p. 19.

"We do not say," he adds, in a passage which I have quoted before, "miracle is impossible; we say hitherto there has been none proved. Let a thaumaturgist present himself to-morrow with testimony sufficiently important to merit our attention; let him announce that he is able, I will suppose, to raise the dead, what would be done? A commission composed of physiologists, physicians, chemists, persons experienced in historical criticism, would be appointed. This commission would choose the corpse, make certain that death was real, designate the hall in which the experiment should be made, and regulate the whole system of precautions necessary to leave no room for doubt. If, under such conditions, the resurrection should be performed, a probability almost equal to certainty would be attained. However, as an experiment ought always to be capable of being repeated, as one ought to be capable of doing again what one has done once, and as in the matter of miracles there can be no question of easy or difficult, the thaumaturgist would be invited to reproduce his marvelous act under other circumstances, upon other bodies, in another medium. If the miracle succeeds each time, two things would be proven: first, that supernatural acts do come to pass in the world; second, the power to perform them belongs or is delegated to certain persons. But who does not see that no miracle was ever performed under such conditions; that always hitherto the thaumaturgist has chosen the subject of the experiment, chosen the means, chosen the public; that, moreover, it is, in most cases, the people themselves who, from the undeniable need which they feel of seeing in great events and in great men something divine, create the marvelous legends afterward."

Such are some of the feelings and views which the

defenders of miracles are to meet in the nineteenth century.

It is important, then, to remark here that Christianity is founded on a belief of the possibility and the reality of miracles, and on the belief that it is possible to establish the fact that they have occurred by testimony, as firmly as testimony can establish any other fact—that is, so as to make this the basis of faith and of action in our highest interests. No one who receives any thing on the ground of testimony can doubt that Christ claimed the power of working true miracles, as a proof that he came from God. "That ye may know that the Son of Man hath power upon earth to forgive sins, I say unto thee, Arise, and take up thy couch, and go into thine house."—Luke, v., 24. "If I with the finger of God cast out devils, no doubt the kingdom of God is come upon you."—Luke, xi., 20.

No one can doubt, also, that as Jesus claimed the power of working miracles, and appealed to them as proof of his divine mission, so his disciples believed that he actually did work miracles, and went forth to propagate his religion on that ground.

Still farther, no one can doubt, as I showed in the last Lecture, that Christianity *was* propagated on that ground, and that the belief that it was sustained by miraculous or supernatural agency was one of the main reasons why it was embraced at all, and why it made so rapid progress in the world.

In like manner, no one can doubt that the apostles claimed the same power, and that it was, also, on the belief that they had the power miraculously of speaking foreign languages, of healing the sick, and of raising the dead, that they spread the religion abroad among the nations.

No man can explain the things referred to in the New Testament, and claimed to be miracles, on any principles of optical illusion, of jugglery, of deception, of sleight of hand, of superior knowledge of physical laws, of an acquaintance with the secret powers of nature. Many things that were once regarded as miracles may be thus explained; many things once reckoned among the works of "magic," or that were regarded as supernatural, have been explained on principles of science, by Sir David Brewster, in his work on "Magic;" many of the tricks of jugglers, that may be above our power to explain them, are yet of easy explanation; many things may be produced in the laboratory of the chemist which may seem to be miraculous to the unlearned, but which are plain to the chemist himself; and many of the things relied on by impostors as proofs that they were from God, can be now easily explained. But the miracles of the New Testament *can not* thus be explained. Renan has indeed attempted to explain the healing of Peter's wife's mother, and the resurrection of Lazarus, and the alleged resurrection of Jesus, but the world will not accept such explanations. If the facts occurred, they are above the operations of any laws of nature. If the lame were made to walk; if the lepers were cleansed; if the eyes of the blind were opened; if diseases departed by a word; if the dead were restored to life, these things are above any natural laws, and the world will hold the whole to be deceit and imposture, or will believe that they were real miracles, that is, events where the only antecedent was the will and the power of God.

Whether Christianity could or could not have been originally propagated, as it is now to be kept up in the world, without miraculous agency, might be a fair question ; but it is certain that the experiment was *not* thus made, and that it was *not* thus propagated. The infidel *must* concede, at least, that it was, in fact, propagated on the belief that Christ really performed miracles, and that he himself was actually raised from the dead.

At this stage of the argument, therefore, the following points of statement and inquiry occur :

(1.) Is a miracle possible, that is, in the form in which the question must come before us, not, whether, supposing that there is a God—a being of almighty power who has framed and established the laws of nature—*he* could set aside his laws, and himself work without them, for no rational man could doubt that ; but whether there is by fate, or physical necessity, or otherwise, any such *ascertained* fixedness and stability of the laws of nature that it can not be believed that they *would* ever be set aside by the introduction of a higher power working without reference to them ?

(2.) Is it possible to establish the fact *if* a miracle has been wrought ? Can there be evidence which will properly set aside the presumption of the absolute uniformity of the laws of nature, as derived from experience, or the study of those laws, or from any other cause, that this has actually been done ? Is it not much more probable that men have been deceived, or have been imposed upon, than that those laws have been set aside for any purpose ? Has not the world been full of instances where testimony was false; have there been any corresponding instances or facts in the way in which the affairs of the world are actually managed, that might be considered as *parallel* to this, or that might be equally regarded as a departure from fixed and regular laws ?

(3.) Is the evidence adduced, even if a miracle has

been wrought, such as the case would require; such as the world might demand; such as would properly satisfy a man accustomed to reason on scientific principles; such as a geologist or astronomer would admit in regard to the condition of the earth in former ages, or the recorded phenomena of the heavenly bodies? Is the evidence such that it *ought* to convince us? Does the strength of the testimony at all correspond with the unusual and the improbable nature of the fact? May it not be demanded that the testimony shall be such as *would* correspond with the unusual and improbable nature of the fact; that, as there is the strongest presumption *against* the miracle, so the testimony ought to be not merely that which would establish an ordinary event, but such as would *overcome* this presumption against it?

(4.) A more material and important question still is, Whether there is any stronger evidence in favor of miracles than there is in favor of witchcraft, of sorcery, of the reappearance of the dead, of ghosts, of apparitions? Is not the evidence in favor of these as strong as any that can be adduced in favor of miracles? Have not these things been matters of universal belief? In what respects is the evidence in favor of the miracles of the Bible stronger than that which can be adduced in favor of witchcraft and sorcery? Does it differ in nature and in degree; and if it differs, is it not in favor of witchcraft and sorcery? Has not the evidence in favor of the latter been derived from as competent and credible witnesses? Has it not been brought to us from those who saw the facts alleged? Has it not been subjected to a close scrutiny in courts of justice—to cross-examinations—to tortures? Has it not convinced those of highest legal attainments; those accustomed to sift testimony; those who understood the true principles of evidence? Has not the evidence in favor of witchcraft and sorcery had, what the evidence in favor of miracles has *not* had, the advantage of strict judicial investigation, and been subjected to trial, where evidence should be, before courts of law? Have not the most eminent judges in the most civilized and enlightened courts of Europe and America admitted the force of such evidence, and on the ground of it committed great numbers of innocent persons to the gallows or to the stake?

I confess that of all the questions ever asked on the subject of miracles, this is the most perplexing and the most difficult to answer. It is rather to be wondered at that it has not been pressed with more zeal by those who deny the reality of miracles, and that they have placed their objections so extensively on other grounds. From the fact that it is so seldom referred to by skeptics, it is manifest that it does not strike them as it strikes me, and that they, from some cause, are not disposed to use it as I would, if I had no faith in miracles; and perhaps it may savor more of apparent candor than of wise prudence for a believer in the reality of miracles even to make the suggestion.

The argument might be made very strong, and if there were time to present it here, it might be done in such a manner that it might *seem*, at least, to be impossible to meet and refute it.

An extract or two from Lecky, in his History of Rationalism in Europe, will show the nature of the difficulty and the force of the objection, though the remarks made by him are in no way designed to support the cause of infidelity: "For more than fifteen hundred years it was universally believed that the Bible established, in the clearest manner, the reality of the crime [of witchcraft], and that an amount of evidence, so varied and so ample as to preclude the very possibility of doubt, attested its continuance and its prevalence. The clergy denounced it with all the emphasis of authority. The legislators of almost every land enacted laws for its punishment. Acute judges, whose lives were spent in sifting evidence, investigated the question on countless occasions, and condemned the accused. Tens of thousands of victims perished by the most agonizing and protracted torments without exciting the faintest compassion. Nations that were completely separated by position, by interests, and by character, on this one question were united. In almost every province of Germany, but especially in those where clerical influence predominated, the persecution raged with fearful intensity. Seven thousand victims are said to have been burned at Treves, six hundred by the single bishop of Bamberg, and eight hundred in a single year in the bishopric of Wurtzburg. In France, decrees were passed on the subject by the Parliaments of Paris, Toulouse, Bordeaux, Rheims, Rouen, Dijon, and Rennes, and they were all followed by a harvest of blood. At Toulouse, the seat of the Inquisition, four hundred persons perished for sorcery at a single execution, and fifty at Douay in a single year. Remy, a judge of Nancy, boasted that he had put to death eight hundred witches in sixteen years. The executions that took place at Paris in a few months were, in the emphatic words of an old writer, 'almost infinite.' The fugitives who escaped to Spain were there seized and burned by the Inquisition. In Italy a thousand persons were executed in a single year in the province of Como; in the other parts of the country the severity of the inquisitors at last created an absolute rebellion. In Geneva five hundred alleged witches were executed in three months; forty-eight were burned at Constance or Ravensburg, and eighty in the little town of Valery, in Savoy. The Church of Rome proclaimed in every way that was in her power the reality and the continued existence of the crime."

The writer from whom I have made this extract adds: "It is, I think, difficult to examine the subject with impartiality, without coming to the conclusion that the historical evidence establishing the reality of witchcraft is so vast and so varied that it is impossible to disbelieve it without what on other subjects we should deem the most extraordinary rashness. The defenders of the belief, who were often men of great and distinguished talent, maintained that there was no fact in all history more fully attested, and that to reject it would be to strike at the root of all historical evidence of the miraculous. The subject was examined in tens of thousands of cases, in almost every country of Europe, by tribunals which included the acutest lawyers and ecclesiastics of the age, on the scene at the time when the alleged facts had taken place, and with the assistance of innumerable sworn witnesses. The judges had no motive whatever to desire the condemnation of the accused; and as conviction would be followed by a fearful death, they had the strongest motives to exercise their power with caution and deliberation. In our day it may be said with confidence that it would be altogether impossible for such an amount of evidence to accumulate round a conception which had no basis in fact. If we considered witchcraft probable, a hundredth part of the evidence we possess would have placed it beyond the region of doubt. If it were a natural, but a very improbable fact, our reluctance to believe it would have been completely stifled by the multiplicity of the proofs."*

As materially bearing on the point before us, it would be important to inquire into the changes which have occurred in the world in regard to faith in the miraculous and the supernatural, and to ask to what this change *tends*, or how it bears on the subject of miracles. But I have not time or ability to do it, and it has been done in a manner which leaves nothing to be desired by Lecky.

Successively, by the slow progress of civilization; by the advances of science; by being able by natural laws to explain what were once regarded as portents and wonders; by a gradual cessation of faith in things that seemed to be established by incontrovertible evidence, eclipses, and meteors, and famines, and earthquakes, and comets, have been removed from the regions of the marvelous, and, in like manner, the faith of mankind in sorcery, and witchcraft, and magic has, to a great extent, passed away. If there are remains of this still lingering in the minds of men, and if new and strange things have been added to these in our age not less absurd and irrational than the faith in witchcraft and sorcery, these are not so general as materially to affect the question before us. It has not yet occurred, as far as I know, to infidelity to place the subject of "table-moving" and "spirit-rapping" on a level with the miracles of the New Testament.

It is a great question now—*the* great question of our age in regard to religion, and not less important in regard to science—*How far is this skepticism to extend?* What is its proper limit? Is the principle to become

* See *Lecky*, History of Rationalism in Europe, vol. i., pp. 28, 34, 36, 37, 38, 39.

so universal as to include *all* the facts claiming to be
of a supernatural nature which have actually occurred,
or which will occur in our world? Is it to embrace
the whole region of the miraculous and the supernatural, so as to exclude the idea of any direct agency on the
part of God, any phenomena—any changes—the antecedents in which are only the divine will and the divine
power? So it is maintained by Rationalists; such, too,
is the practical belief of many men whose lives are devoted to science.

The progress of things, the influences of civilization,
the discoveries of science in regard to physical laws,
have "*exorcised*" the world, if the expression may be
allowed, in regard to sorcery, witchcraft, magic, necromancy, portents and wonders in eclipses, storms, and
earthquakes; are these to "exorcise" the world in regard to mesmerism, spiritualism, spirit-rapping, and
table-moving; and are they also to "exorcise" it
in regard to the belief that Joshua caused the sun to
"stand still upon Gibeon," and the moon "in the valley
of Ajalon;" in regard to the stilling of the tempest on
the Sea of Tiberias; in regard to the healing of the lame
man at the pool of Bethesda; in regard to the opening
of the eyes of Bartimeus; in regard to the raising of
Lazarus from the grave; in regard to the resurrection
of the Redeemer himself?

So say the Rationalist and the skeptic, and here issue
is joined.

We approach, then, this great question in this form;
and my wish is to show you exactly how this matter
lies; what progress is made toward this result; what
there is to show that this result can never be reached,
and that, notwithstanding all this, the believer in the
miracles of the Bible has no cause of alarm as to any
such result.

I shall, in the remainder of this Lecture, first make some preliminary, or, rather, if you will allow the word, *eliminary** remarks, and then show you that this conclusion has not been reached, and that it is impossible for men to reach it, leaving in fact in the nineteenth century the evidence for miracles the same as that of ordinary well-authenticated facts in history on other subjects.

(*a*) The first remark is, that the universal belief in miracles and the marvelous; the ease with which such things are credited by men, the most enlightened as well as the unenlightened, statesmen, jurists, ecclesiastics, law-givers, sages—Socrates, Coke, Bacon, Hale, among numberless others—shows that a belief in the supernatural and the marvelous does not shock mankind; is not contrary to the laws of the human mind; is rather in accordance with some law of our nature that *looks* for such interventions, and seeks and expects to be gratified. It may be added, also, that this proves that men would naturally *expect* such an intervention if a revelation were made to mankind.—It is not safe to argue against a universal law of human nature; against deep convictions which have been implanted in the soul of man, and which seek expression in all ages and among all people. Such a method of reasoning will be found, sooner or later, to be fundamentally wrong. We may assume that our Maker did not constitute our being on a universal lie, or incorporate into our nature faith in a universal falsehood. This may be called credulity; superstition; the fruit of ignorance; prejudice. The material fact, however, is that the mind of man is so *made ;* and that this proves that He who made it designed so to endow it that it would not be shocked by the

* *Eliminating,* expelling; discharging; throwing off.—*Webster.*

marvelous and the supernatural, and that men should
be prepared to welcome the evidence of the truly miraculous when it is presented to them. It is to be
presumed, also, that if this is the original and normal
state of the human mind, there would be events under
the divine government which would properly correspond with this. The fact that men are made with eyes
adapted to vision is presumptive evidence that there
would be light corresponding with their structure, and
that there would be things to be seen; the original capacity of mankind for knowledge supposes that there
would be things to be known; that law of our nature
which demands society presupposes that there would
be other beings with whom friendships could be formed;
the natural desire of men to know God supposes that
there is a God to be known; the universal expectation
of miracles supposes that there would be miracles in
which man could believe.

(b) The second remark is, that the question so much
agitated, and so difficult of solution, at what time miracles ceased in the Church, and whether they were or
were not continued after the time of the apostles, does
not affect the question whether the miracles of the New
Testament were really performed; whether, for example, Jesus turned water into wine, or raised Lazarus
from the grave. If those miracles which were claimed
to be performed in the early Church were false; if those
claimed to be wrought by the Holy Coat at Treves
were true; if those wrought by the Emperor Vespasian,
and at the tomb of St. Francis Xavier, on which Mr.
Hume dwells so complacently, were true or were false,
it does not prove that God did not interpose by direct
power in giving a new religion to the world, and in furnishing attestations that the great messenger came from

him. If the Christian fathers worked miracles, it does not prove that Paul did not; if those claimed to have been wrought by the fathers were false, that does not prove that those which Christ claimed to have wrought were false also. If there have been false claimants to the crown of England, that does not prove that the claim of the present sovereign is unfounded.

(c) A third remark is, that it is assuming more than can be proved that direct divine interventions in the affairs of the universe have ceased now altogether, or that there are no events occurring in which the divine will and the divine power are the only antecedents. Proof on that point is obviously beyond the capacity of man. In the argument of Dr. Clarke on the Being of a God, it was remarked that, unless man was omnipresent, he could not possibly demonstrate that there was no God; for in that part of space beyond him, and which he could not penetrate, it was *possible* that there might be a God. In like manner we may say that, unless man now is omnipresent, and unless he can bring all the events which occur, seen and unseen, under the explanation of natural laws, it is *possible* that some of those events may be performed by the direct agency of God. Moreover, it is impossible to prove that God has in any way so pledged or committed himself to abide always by established and regular laws, and never to put forth his direct power in creation, in the government of worlds, or in their destruction, that man can assume this as an axiom or established truth, in relation to the present races of animals now on the earth, or in relation to any new races that he may bring upon the stage. At no one of the old geological periods of our world could it have been shown that God had "committed" or "pledged" himself that he would not sweep off the existing races,

II

and that he would create no more; nor does the fact of the uniformity of laws, so far as established yet, constitute any such " committal" on the part of God that he will not again interpose by his direct power in the affairs of the universe.   It is certain that there are many things occurring which science has not as yet been able to reduce to natural and regular laws, great as is the progress which has been made in that direction; it is equally certain that but a small part of our own world—land, water, air—has been explored; it is certain that man knows almost nothing of the manner in which things are done in distant worlds; and it is *possible* that in that vast region of the unknown there *may be* things occurring which are the direct and immediate result of the will and the power of God.   At all events, man is not in a condition to pronounce an opinion on that subject, and he violates one of the rules of sound philosophy when, from so narrow a basis of observed facts, he draws a sweeping and universal conclusion.

(*d*) A fourth remark is, that it is difficult to see why the facts in a miracle, if a miracle occurs, are not as susceptible of proof as any other facts.   If the sun stood still at the command of Joshua, the fact was in itself as susceptible of proof as that the sun seemed to move; if a lame man " leaped as an hart," there would be no more difficulty, one would suppose, in proving that *he* leaped than that any other man leaped; if one who was sick rose up and carried his couch, there would be no more difficulty in establishing such a fact in regard to him than in regard to another man; and if one who was dead was alive again, that fact, it would seem, would be susceptible of easy proof.   The testimony of credible witnesses that they had seen such a man as Lazarus in ordinary life would not be called in question; how would the testimony that they saw him after it was known or affirmed that he was dead vary the nature of the evidence? In what respects does the testimony differ? What *is* the testimony when one affirms that he has *seen* a certain person? How does that differ when the testimony pertains to the same person at another time, even after it was known that he was dead? If in the one case the fact can be established, why may it not in the other?

The *illusion* here, to use no harsher term, is in the supposition as to what is *seen* in the case. The objector to miracles supposes that it is necessary to *see the miracle itself*, and that, unless this is *seen*, there can be no proper testimony in the case. But no witness could possibly *see* two and two make four, *in the abstract*. No man pretends that he *sees* the changes which occur in the growth of a plant, or in the formation of the animal from the embryo, or the fowl from the egg. No man pretends to *see* the processes in the changes which occur in the laboratory of the chemist. In the last case, as substantially in all these cases, what is *seen* is the appearance of certain combinations of the elements of matter in one form, and then the appearance of the same elements of matter as they exist in new formations. The testimony of the chemist as to the existence of the *latter* would be as credible as his testimony in regard to the *former*, and would require no additional confirmation. No one would call the testimony in question because he had not *seen* the process of the transformation, or because there was a *power* there, lying back of the new form assumed, which he could not explain or understand. The facts in the case would in no manner be affected by this consideration, nor, in examining such a witness, would that consideration be allowed to affect the credibility of the testimony. *Suppose* that that power were the direct power and will of God—as for aught he knows it may be—would that affect the nature of the testimony of the chemist as to the reality of the visible change? And then suppose that he were called to give testimony as to the fact that a man was blind, and that a man saw, how does the fact that there may lie *between* the two things the power and the will of God affect the one case more than the other? There are difficulties *in* such a transformation which no one has been able to explain, but those difficulties in ordinary cases would not be allowed to be a bar to the reception of the testimony as to the preceding and the subsequent facts. Lazarus before his death and Lazarus after his death was precisely the same man; and it is difficult to see how the testimony in regard to him, if exactly the same, should be admitted in the one case and rejected in the other.

(*e*) One other remark. It is, that science, so far as it has gone, has demonstrated that the alleged miracles of the New Testament, if the facts occurred, can not be explained by the laws of nature, or that they could not have been wrought by any physical *laws*. Very many things, as we have seen, once deemed supernatural and miraculous, have been shown to be the production of the ordinary laws of nature, and have thus been removed from the region of the marvelous, and have taken their places among things well understood as being in accordance with regular laws. Eclipses, meteors, comets, earthquakes, the lightning, the *ignus fatuus* —things that once alarmed mankind, have thus, to a great extent, taken their places in the ordinary course of events. Æsculapius is no longer worshiped as the god of medicine, for it is no longer supposed that there is any direct and supernatural divine agency in the healing art; nor are Ceres or Neptune worshiped as if supernatural divine power were manifested in the rearing of fruits, or in regulating the storm, or in the ebbing and the flowing of the waters of the sea. The magician has given way to the chemist working by established laws. Marvels and wonders, therefore, have been greatly limited and diminished by placing these events under the operation of the regular rules of nature.

Science has *not* advanced so far, however, as to explain the miracles of the New Testament on any known principles, as it has in these matters, nor has it made any approximation to it. Nay, just so far as it has gone it has demonstrated that those miracles can not be explained on any principles known, or likely to be known, to science—gravitation, attraction, repulsion, electricity, galvanism, or the healing properties of vegetables or minerals. The chemist does not open the eyes of the blind by a touch; he does not heal the sick by a word; he does not raise the dead by the blow-pipe or by galvanism. In the language of Mr. Mansel, " The advance of physical science tends to strengthen rather than to weaken our conviction of the supernatural character of the Christian miracles. In whatever proportion our knowledge of physical causation is limited, and the number of unknown natural agents comparatively large, in the same proportion is the probability that some of these unknown causes, acting in some unknown manner, may have given rise to the alleged marvels. But this probability diminishes when each newly-discovered agent, as its properties become known, is shown to be inadequate to the production of the supposed effects, and as the residue of unknown causes,

which might produce them, becomes smaller and smaller.   We are told, indeed, that the 'inevitable progress
of research must, within a longer or shorter period, unravel all that seems most marvelous;'* but we may be
permitted to doubt the relevancy of the remark to the
present case, until it has been shown that the advance
of science has in some degree enabled men to perform
the miracles performed by Christ.   When the inevitable
progress of research shall have enabled men of modern
times to give sight to the blind with a touch, to still
tempests with a word, to raise the dead to life, to die
themselves, and to rise again, we may allow that the
same causes might possibly have been called into operation ten thousand years earlier, by some great man in
advance of his age.   But, until this is done, the unraveling of the marvelous in other phenomena only serves
to leave these works in their solitary grandeur, as
wrought by the finger of God, unapproached and unapproachable by all the knowledge and all the power of
man.   The appearance of a comet or the fall of an acro-
lite may be reduced by the advance of science from a
supposed supernatural to a natural occurrence; and this
reduction furnishes a reasonable presumption that other
phenomena *of a like character* will in time meet with a
like explanation.   But the reverse is the case with respect to those phenomena which are narrated as produced by *personal agency*.   In proportion as the science
of to-day surpasses that of former generations, so is the
improbability that any man could have done in past
times, by natural means, works which no skill of the
present age is able to imitate."†

With these general remarks on the subject of miracles, I proceed to state what is the form which the ar-

* Essays and Reviews, p. 109.   † Aids to Faith, p. 21, 22.

gument assumes in the nineteenth century, or, in the present age of the world, with all the advances which have been made in science; or what points have been established as bearing on the possibility and the credibility of the miracles of the New Testament.

I. The first remark is, that no such universality of the certain and fixed laws of nature as is claimed by those who deny the reality of miracles, has been ascertained and demonstrated; nor can it be. In other words, amidst the infinite number and variety of phenomena which have occurred in our world, and in other worlds, and which are now constantly occurring, it has not been demonstrated, and can not be, that there are none in respect to which the only antecedent is the direct will and power of God. To show that miracles are not possible, and not credible, it is necessary to do this. But this can not be done; for, if there is any thing made clear by science, it is that the human powers of observation and comprehension are not *vast* enough to establish so universal a proposition. The argument of Newton in regard to "gravitation" *could not* reach the point that there is, and has been nowhere, any matter that is not moved by another force. The laws of Kepler in regard to planetary motions are not so established in regard to their universality that there may not be, somewhere in the boundlessness of space, worlds held in being, and moved by other forces than these.

The remark now made, so obvious, demonstrates that no one can *prove* that the uniformity and fixedness of the laws of nature is so " universal" as to exclude the possibility of miracles ; for such a demonstration must take in all events, all worlds, all systems, all beings— angels and God as well as men. Our " experience," of which so much is made by Mr. Hume, pertains only to our own world and to men; it takes in nothing beyond. But, to be complete, the demonstration must take in all worlds, creatures, systems, ages, and cycles of ages, and must establish the fact that in all these things God never does perform, and never has performed, any act by his own immediate power or will, or that no world has been called into being, that no creature has been made, that no event has occurred, where the only antecedent in the case was the divine power and will. Obviously this is wholly beyond the power of man to demonstrate. There have been times in the history of the universe of which no records have come to us. How can man demonstrate what has or what has not been done, then? There are worlds which man has never seen by the naked eye or by the glass. How can he demonstrate what has been or has not been done in those worlds? There may be beings of whose "experience" man has no knowledge. How can he determine how they came into existence, or prove that among them there are not events produced by the direct power of God? There may be worlds and systems —"*nebulæ*"—that are so detached from our system that we can not demonstrate that the same laws which govern our system control them, or that, in the infinity of the divine resources, there may *not* be methods of controlling those worlds which are unknown here. How is man to determine that point? And, moreover, there may be a spiritual world—a world so detached from all matter, and so wholly independent of matter, that nothing can be inferred in regard to the laws which govern it from the laws of Kepler or Newton. Who can tell how God may act in that spiritual world? Who can demonstrate that in that world no event ever occurs where the sole antecedent is the divine power and the divine will?

As, therefore, no one can prove that there is no God unless he himself is infinite, and can be present in all the immensity of space at the same time, since where he is not there God may be, so it is true that no one can prove that the laws of nature are so fixed and universal that a miracle is impossible, unless he himself can take in the whole of the universe, since it may be true that beyond the sphere of his knowledge there are events the only antecedent of which are the will and the power of God.

The observation now made, if well founded, must meet all that has been said by Mr. Hume in regard to "experience," so far as that bears on the subject. When it is said by him that "as a firm and unalterable experience has established these laws, the proof against a miracle, from the very nature of the fact, is as entire as any argument from experience can possibly be imagined," the word "experience," if it has any meaning, must refer to experience that *embraces the whole subject;* that is, in relation to *all* the events to which the question of such uniformity would be applicable. But it is clear that among *men* there has been no such "experience." There have been, and there are, many events which lie quite beyond any such range of observation hitherto made; there are undoubtedly many things which have not as yet been reduced to any known laws, and it is yet an open question whether they can be; that is, whether the powers of men are adequate to the inquiry, and whether, if they are thus adequate, the events are of such a nature that they can be reduced to regular and fixed laws. In the earlier periods of the world, as already remarked, there were many things that passed under the name of "miracles" and wonders—phenomena which there was no way thus of

H 2

accounting for—whose causes are now familiar to us,
for in the ruder ages of the world they seemed to lie
wholly in the regions of the marvelous. As science advances, the circle of those marvelous works is contracted, and a large part of those wonders is reduced to the
dominion of fixed laws. The laboratory of the chemist
now exhibits many a phenomena which in the Middle
Ages would have been classed among the marvelous,
now reduced to the regular operation of law; and it
can not be doubted that there may be yet in nature
many a secret power that has not yet been made the
subject of scientific observation, or been brought under
the general word "*experience*." It can not be regarded
as improbable that many of those things *will* thus be
carefully observed, arranged, and classified, and that
they will be found to be under the control of fixed and
unchanging *laws;* but the world is not *yet* far enough
advanced to justify the assertion that the "experience"
of mankind extends to *all* these things. Not until this
is done, and not until that "experience" shall take in
the whole of the distant material worlds and systems,
and not until that "experience" shall take in also the
whole of the spiritual world, could it be affirmed that
it has been demonstrated by "experience" that there
may not be events the sole antecedent of which is the
will and the power of God. Man can not, therefore, as
yet, *prove* that miracles are impossible.

II. The second remark in regard to miracles, as a se-
quence of what has already been said, is, that the effect
of the progress of true science is to demonstrate that
the hypothesis which refers miracles to *unknown* natural causes is baseless; and that if the events occurred,
they were *real* miracles. The only possible opinions in
regard to the miracles of the New Testament are, that

they were not performed at all; or that they were performed, as those who wrought them declared, in virtue
of a supernatural power, and in attestation of their own
divine mission; or that they "are distorted statements
of events reducible to known natural causes." This
last was the solution suggested by Paulus, who proposed to explain them on "naturalistic" principles; it is
adopted substantially by Prof. Baden Powell;* and it is
the explanation of the causes of many of the events referred to as miracles in the New Testament offered by
Renan. But, as has been already remarked, and the remark deserves to be repeated, for it is vital to the whole
question, science makes no approximation to this solution, but its tendency has all been in the opposite direction—to *separate* these events more and more from the
common operations of nature. The "experience" of the
world, in the observation of events, has never gone toward the point that there is a secret power in nature to
raise the dead, and if the dead have been raised it has
been where the only antecedent in the case has been
the power and the will of God. "There remains," therefore, "only the choice between a deeper faith and a
bolder unbelief; between accepting the sacred narrative
as a true account of miracles actually performed, and
rejecting it as wholly fictitious and incredible."†

The case where it is alleged that one has been raised
from the dead may be referred to as an illustration of
this point. The case supposed is this: *First.* There
was actual—real death. It was not a swoon; not a disease that for a time produced the appearance of death;
not suspended animation — it was actual death. Such
is supposed in the case of Lazarus, and in the case of

* "On the Study of the Evidences of Christianity."
† Prof. *Mansel*, Aids to Faith, p. 23.

Jesus himself. *Second.* There was a restoration to
real life; the restoration of the same person; the
preservation of personal identity. It was not a phantasm; not an appearance; not a spirit; not an imma-
terial substance that deceived the senses. In the case
of both Lazarus and Jesus, it was a restoration to real
life of the same person. Both are represented as they
were before they died; both are recognized by their
friends; both eat, walk, talk, have the same sympathies,
friendships, affections as before; both are cognizable
in all these respects as they were before they died.
Third. Science does not do this; does not approach it.
There has never been an instance in the "experience"
of the world in which it has been done by natural laws;
there has never been an instance in which it has been
claimed that it has been thus done; there has never
been an instance in which there has ever been an approach to it. There have been instances of restoration
from suspended animation; there has been spasmodic
muscular action produced by galvanism; there may
have been a momentary inflation of the lungs; there
may have been even a smile produced on the countenance of the dead—the horrible appearance of laughter
in the sardonic grin, but there has been no real life, no
regular heaving of the lungs, no living real smile produced in one who has been actually dead. Thus far the
"experience" of the world on this subject has been as
"uniform" as any experience can be, that science lays
no claim to the power of raising the dead.

   III. My third remark in regard to miracles in their
relation to the laws of nature is, that there is a sense
in which those "laws of nature," so fixed and determined, are constantly set aside, or are "violated" by
the action of other "laws of nature," that is, they are

held absolutely in check so long as those other laws prevail. When the lightning strikes a tree, "it puts ₊an end to all the ordinary development of vegetation," and seems to be a bare conflict of "force with law." Yet it is also true that the lightning follows a law of its own, and that law seems to conflict with law, or that one law sets another aside, and that there are meteorologic laws to which both the lightning and the vegetation are subject.* The same thing is true when the wind raises up the waters of the ocean and piles them in mountains, or when the vapor is upborne and carried by the clouds over valleys and hills, or when the dust of the earth is raised up by the whirlwind—in each case suspending, or "violating," for the time, the law of gravitation, the most "universal" law in nature. This result is perhaps still more manifest in the principle of *life*, that mysterious and unknown principle which seems to have the power, during its continuance, of "violating" *all* the laws of nature. By that principle the chemical elements which enter into the composition of the oak are detached from their natural connections as they are found in the air, the earth, and the waters; the chemical laws which held them in those connections are suspended; they enter, under the principle of *life*, into new combinations, constituting now the component parts of a tree—the organic structure, the fibre, the bark, the branch, the leaf, the fruit—and they are held together *by* that principle of life by all the power needful to lift up the enormous mass from the earth, despite the law of gravitation, and to keep it steadfast against the influence of storms and tempests, century after century, until that principle of life shall loose its grasp and become extinct, and then, not before, the chemical laws re-

* Tracts for Priests and People, p. 342.

sume their power, and the old oak returns to gases and
to earths under the resumed operation of those laws.
The same thing is still more strikingly manifest in the
animal structure, under the principle of *life*. The elements that make up the human body—carbon, hydro-
gen, nitrogen, oxygen, phosphorus, lime, iron, sulphur,
sodium, potassium, magnesium — are all *detached* from
their natural connections in the air, the earth, and the
waters—in the animal, the vegetable, and the mineral
world—and are formed into an entirely *new* combination of bone, sinew, nerves, muscle, with a definite size
and shape, moulded and rounded, not by the physical
laws of nature, but *in spite* of those laws, by a principle
which "violates" them for the time, and holds them as
long as it pleases; and it is not until *life* decays, and
this new power *ceases*, that the natural chemical laws
resume their functions, not now in the form of the living man, but in the grave, where the human frame is
resolved into its natural elements. The chemical laws
resume their action as soon as life departs, and those
laws continue to act again until every particle that
composed the human frame enters, under those laws,
into new inorganic combinations, or until, under some
new principle of life, vegetable or animal, the process is
arrested midway, and new forms of life appear. All
over the earth, therefore, on the land, in the waters, in
the air, nothing is more common than that what are
called the "fixed and uniform laws of nature," those
laws which Mr. Hume informs us "a firm and unalterable experience has established," are, in fact, suspended
—"violated"—held in check and abeyance—by this
principle of *life*, where life is the *only* antecedent in
the result. That a higher power than life—*the* Life
itself, God — may not suspend them; that that higher

power may not suspend the laws which regulate *life* itself, or restore it, has *not* as yet been established by a "firm and unalterable experience."

IV. In order to a proper understanding of the subject, it is necessary also to take into consideration the element of the *will*, and the power consequent on that, in reference to the "laws of nature." However fixed and settled those laws may be, the power of the will in man is constantly operating to suspend or interrupt them, that is, constantly producing effects which are not to be traced to regular and fixed laws, and which would never be produced *by* those laws. In other words, the effects are not produced by the laws of matter, but the laws of matter are, for a time, as really *disturbed* as in the case of a miracle, and fail of striking us as being as remarkable and perplexing only because they are of constant occurrence. It might be said, indeed, that the *will* itself is subject to fixed laws, and that, after all, the effects are produced by regular and fixed laws; but it is not easy to demonstrate that point, and it is not to be *assumed* that this is so, or that in the operations of the will there is nothing which can not be reduced to fixed and unvarying laws. At any rate, whatever may be true on that point, it is not to be assumed that it is any more true in reference to the human will than it is in reference to the divine will, and the difficulty in the one case is, as to the point, the same as in the other. In either case it is the introduction of a new *power*, apart from all force in the mere physical laws of nature, which are regarded as so settled and fixed—"the work of an agent wholly independent of those laws, and who, therefore, neither obeys nor disobeys them." For the time being, so far as the result is concerned, the new agent, or the new power, sets aside or suspends the operation of those laws, and the result in the case is to be traced to the new and independent power. Whether God has reserved to himself the right to *interfere* with the regular laws of matter, as he has actually conferred it on man, is simply a question as to a *fact*, and not at all as to the *possibility* of the thing.

When a man, by the exertion of his will, raises his arm, or walks, or lifts a weight from the ground, he, in each case, *suspends* or *overcomes*, for the time, the law of gravitation, so far as he produces an effect which is not to be, and which can not be traced to that law—an effect which that law of gravitation could never in any circumstances produce, and which all the principles involved in the law of gravitation combine to *prevent*, and the effect produced is to be accounted for *wholly* by a power above and regardless of it — the power of the *will;* and in estimating the "experience" of the world in reference to Mr. Hume's argument, we are to take that part into the account as an important and a very common part of the "experience" of mankind — a matter of "experience" quite as common as that pertaining to the "firm and unalterable experience which has established those laws." When a man of his own will throws a stone into the air, "the motion of the stone, as soon as it has left his hand, is determined by a combination of purely natural laws, partly by the attraction of the earth, partly by the resistance of the air, partly by the magnitude and direction of the force by which it was thrown." But by what *law* came it to be thrown at all? By what law of *nature*—a law "fixed by an unalterable experience"—did it happen that it left its quiet bed on the ground; that the principle of *inertia* was overcome; that the law of gravita-

tion which held it there, and would have held it there
forever, was interrupted, and that it *commenced* its
course through the air? Neither the law of gravitation by itself, nor all the laws of nature put together,
would ever have caused it to leave the ground and com-
mence that flight through the air; but all the laws of
" *nature*," in fact, combined to resist this, as really as
the laws of " nature" combined to resist the raising up
of Lazarus to life, or as the laws of " nature" on the Sea
of Tiberias combined to keep up the storm, and to resist the power of Jesus, who commanded the winds and
the waves to be still. It remains yet to be *proved*, not
asserted, that when God's free will interposes to produce effects which are to be traced to that will alone,
there is a more *real* violation of the laws of nature than
there is when the human will interposes and produces
changes which are to be traced to that will alone. It
may be further added, that if the will of men *does* produce such disturbances and interruptions of the laws of
nature, then, so far from its being true, as Mr. Hume says,
that " a firm and unalterable experience has established
those laws," it is true that there is almost nothing that
is more *liable* to be disturbed, or that nothing is more
common than that there are effects produced which are
not to be traced to those laws, but where the only
known antecedent is *will*, and the *power* consequent on
will.

V. A fifth and final remark on the subject is, that the
progress of our world, and, as far as we know, the progress of the universe, has *not* been under the operation
of regular and fixed " laws." I mean that there are evidences of divine interposition apart from the operation
of such laws, and that the results are such as can not
be traced to those laws, but are to be traced to a direct

divine interposition, and that, *therefore*, miracles are not in themselves absurd or impossible.

There are two methods in which, subsequent to the act of creation, the existing state of things on the earth, and in the universe at large, as far as we know, has been produced: the one is by development, or the growth of things under natural laws; the other is by the introduction of a new order of things, into which no former state naturally runs, or which, in no proper sense, can be the result of any antecedents in nature, but which must be traced to a mere interposition of power.

That the former—that of *development*—exists, no one can doubt; and it can not be denied that this is the regular and ordinary course of things; that is, that there is something which, in the order of nature, *precedes* the effect; which is the *cause* of it; which *measures* it; which contains in embryo all that is produced. Thus the germ of the acorn is developed into the oak, and the ovum is developed into the crocodile, the ostrich, and the barn-yard fowl; thus the slumbering powers of the infant are developed into the physical strength, the poetic genius, or the eloquence of the man. In all such cases there is nothing *produced* which is not a fair *unfolding* of what existed in the germ; nothing which is the result of mere power *ab extra*. The precise limit of this class of operations in nature has not yet been fixed. It is well known that attempts have been made to explain all the phenomena of the universe on this principle. The author of the "Vestiges of Creation" regards this as a sufficient explanation of the origin of the worlds and systems which compose the universe; Dr. Darwin supposes that all the varieties of species on the earth can be explained on this principle; and in this manner it is supposed, as may be true, that new worlds are constantly forming, and that the nebulous masses are now resolving themselves into suns and stars. Perhaps it is not within the range of the human powers to determine the exact limits of this process, and to do it is not material for any purpose connected with revealed religion.

But, while we would concede all that true science can ask on this point, it is still a fact that this has not been the sole or the main agency by which our world exists as it is now. In very many respects it has made advances—has reached higher elevations from age to age—by some new *power*, the result of creative and supernatural agency, that has come in, over and beyond any thing that can be regarded as the result of development. That power lifts the world to a higher level, and can be best explained on the supposition that it is by direct divine interposition; that is, that the antecedent in the case is the will and the power of God, whether that be called *miracle* or not.

(a) The ordinary law is, as is claimed by the Atheist for the whole, by a gradual accumulation and development. Men record and preserve the results of past experience. The world gathers up the lessons of the experiments that are made; the history of failures and successes; the inventions in the arts and the discoveries in science; the issues of the experiments to abridge labor, to facilitate travel, to promote domestic comfort, to till the soil, to improve the wild fruits, trees, and grasses; in building houses, in machinery, in navigation. In like manner the world treasures up the wisdom of sages; the results of the battles for freedom; the experiments made in government; the methods of education; the rules of prudence that regulate domestic life. All these enter into civilization, and we now, in this age

and land, are enjoying the avails of all the past wisdom,
all the sacrifices, all the toils and perils, and all the discoveries of past ages.   Every philosopher has thought
for us; every legislator has legislated for us; every
traveler has traveled for us; every explorer of unknown
lands and seas has done it for us; every patriot has
fought and bled for us; every martyr has died for us.
Every one who has stricken out an invention in the arts
has done it for us, and every one who has made a discovery in science has done it for us.   Faust in the art of
printing; Gioia, of Amalfi, in discovering the properties
of the magnet; Galileo in constructing the telescope;
Watt and Fulton in applying steam to the purposes of
manufactures, or to travel by sea and by land; Franklin, who " wrested the lightning from heaven and the
sceptre from tyrants,"* and Morse, who applied the
laws of electro - magnetism to the communication of
thought, did it for us.   We recline on beds of down,
and sit down at tables loaded with luxuries, and dwell
in houses of comfort or magnificence, and travel rapidly
and safely over lands and seas, and breathe the pure air
of freedom as the result of the wisdom and toil of all
past ages.   The world gathers up the results of the
past, and rises gradually to a higher elevation; from
that point it does not go backward, for nothing thus
accumulated that is valuable is suffered to be lost.

Society and the world in this respect move slowly;
for often dark and dreary centuries elapse when the
world *seems* to make no progress—like those slow revolving ages, and cycles of ages, when the deposits
were made in the waters which now constitute the
rocks, or which, upheaved by some sudden convul-
sion, constitute the mountains, and bring the beds of

* Eripuit cœlis fulmen sceptrumque tyrannis.

ancient coal, deposited for man, to the surface of the earth.

(*b*) There is another method in which the world advances. It is not gradual, but sudden—*per saltum*—by impulse, not by development. It occurs when the affairs of the world are to be put on a higher level; when the slow process of accumulation, experience, and development would not meet the wants of the world; when the race is to be *lifted up* suddenly, as the mountains were lifted up, or as the bed of the ocean was suddenly raised to become the abode of races of living beings. Then God creates some great genius and brings it upon the earth. Then some great invention occurs which at once puts the race on a higher level. Then some discovery in science is made that affects at once all the interests of society; that opens new avenues of trade; that facilitates commerce; that diffuses intelligence; that levels mountains; that exalts valleys; that bridges streams or even oceans; that binds the nations into one. Then a new level is reached at once, which in the ordinary course of things would not have been reached for centuries, if it could have been reached at all. The world rises at once to a higher *plateau*, and moves forward *on* that, under the slow law of accumulation, till the time arrives when, by some new discovery or new invention, it rises still higher, never again to go backward.

The immediate and efficient antecedent in this is the will and the power of God. It is not by the development of a germ; it is not by the cultivation and expansion of that which before existed in embryo. Genius and talent are the creation of God—created when he pleases; lodged where he pleases; developed under such circumstances as he chooses. Be it poetry, eloquence, inventive power, skill in the fine or the useful arts, it is alike the creation of God.

It is *creation*—beginning anew, not development—*created*, not called into existence by circumstances. So God made the mind of Plato, of Socrates, of Newton, of Bacon, of Pascal, of Edwards, of Alfred, Charlemagne, Fulton, Cuvier, Columbus, Washington. The bringing of such minds upon the earth can be regarded as in no proper sense the result of such a "firm and un-alterable *experience* in establishing the laws of nature" as Mr. Hume speaks of; they are as much the result of a divine agency as the creation of the world, or as the healing of the blind man at the Pool of Bethesda.

So, too, the world advanced, as geologists now tell us, before it was fitted for the abode of man, by a series of successive *creations*. One race of beings was *swept away* —not developed into another. Each order of monsters had its day, and then passed off the stage to give place to a higher order. The essential *fact* on the subject, which no man who is properly informed will deny, and which is now stated by geologists as a part of the teaching of their science, is, that entire races were swept away, and were succeeded by others which were in no sense whatever *developments* of the former—new creations; new forms of being on the earth—crea-tures, or forms of being so distinct that the one could not have lived at all in the condition in which the earth then was, and the other was swept away because the earth had become fitted for a higher order of beings. The old monsters—the Plesiosaurian and Ichthyosau-rian races—have no *successors* on earth. The races were swept entirely away, and all that remains of them is found in the rocks. The fossils of the old geological periods reveal successive *creations*, not successive *devel-*

opments. So man appeared at last, not as a development of the ourang-outang or monkey, but as a new
creation—brought upon the stage by creative power
when the earth had been fitted up for his abode. In
all science there is probably no fact better established
than the one now adverted to, that the races were entirely swept off, not developed into new forms or races,
and that a new creation appeared, in no sense a resurrection from the old, and that, perhaps, in each case,
after an interval of millions of years.

Thus the world advances, also, by some new invention in the arts that can in no proper sense be regarded
as a "development" of a previous order of things, or as
the result of "fixed and certain laws." Such inventions
are often the result, perhaps always, of a *suggestion*
that comes into the mind, having nothing to do with
any thing that went before, that can be traced by no
law of association to any previous thought in the mind,
and whose origin no system of mental philosophy will
explain. The suggestion which gives birth to the invention is retained in the mind while a thousand others
are dismissed; it is reflected on; it is conned, matured,
experimented on, until the invention appears before the
world, modifying human affairs, raising the race to a
higher level, lifting it up on a new *steppe* or *plateau*,
along which it travels, or by the help of which it rises
higher, until some newer invention, still more brilliant
and important than any which preceded, shall lift the
race to a higher level still, and be the cause of a still
higher advancement. Thus the discoveries of the art
of writing, of printing, of gunpowder; of the properties
of the magnet, of the telescope, of the microscope, of the
application of steam, of the telegraph, have successively
modified human affairs, and put the condition of the

world on an elevation from which it can never descend
—not by "fixed laws;" not by "development;" not by
a "firm and unalterable experience," but by a new
power.

In like manner, some new disease sent direct from
God may materially modify human affairs.   The "*black
death*" that reigned in Europe, cutting off, as has been
estimated, during the six years of its continuance, twen-
ty-five millions, or a fourth part of the inhabitants of
Europe,* depopulating entire districts of country, and
spreading consternation every where — in what sense
was that a *development*, "under the laws of a firm and
unalterable experience," as Mr. Hume would say?   The
small-pox, the cholera—to what "laws," thus fixed and
settled by "experience," are they to be traced? Of what
previous disease were they the *development?*   Nothing
is more certain than that, up to the period of their appearing, the "experience" of the world — of the whole
world — was *against* the small-pox and the cholera,
much more than it had been against miraculous and supernatural agencies, and, according to the argument
which I am examining, all belief in those diseases is impossible or absurd.

The cases to which I have thus referred show that
God has not bound or pledged himself to govern the
world always, and in all circumstances, by the fixed
laws of nature; that he has not withdrawn from the
world and left it to do its work, as a vast machine, by
wheels, and springs, and cogs, and pulleys; that he has
reserved to himself the right to interfere when he has
important ends to accomplish, by his own free will, in
some manner corresponding to the fact, though far
above it, that *we* thus, by *our* will, interfere with those

* *Hecker's* Epidemics of the Middle Ages, p. 29.

laws; that, as there were occasions on which it was proper that he should interfere by new acts of *creative* power in the old geological periods of the world, and when the present order of things was to be inaugurated, so he may now interpose by acts of creation in the distant parts of the universe by bringing new worlds into being, and new orders of creatures upon them; and that, as there *have been* occasions when the affairs of the world were to be raised to a higher elevation by the creation and endowment of some mind by extraordinary powers, or by some brilliant discovery in science or invention in the arts, so there *may have been* occasions on which it was proper to interfere by the introduction of a new religion upon the earth, and by attesting its origin as from himself—by so far putting forth his own *will* and *power*, independeut of natural laws, and suspending those laws for the time, as to open the eyes of the blind, to unstop the ears of the deaf, to cause the lame man to leap as an hart, and to raise the dead from their graves.

Such are the facts in regard to miracles, as I understand them, and such is the state of the evidence on the subject in the nineteenth century.

I

LECTURE VL

THE ARGUMENT FOR THE TRUTH OF CHRISTIANITY, IN THE NINETEENTH CENTURY, FROM PROPHECY.

THE argument for the truth of Christianity or revealed religion, as derived from prophecy, is different,
in some very important respects, from the argument as
derived from miracles.

(1.) First. The miracles on which reliance is placed
occurred in past ages—in periods now far remote. It
is not claimed by the friends of the Bible that miracles
are now performed to establish its truth. Even in those
portions of the "visible Church" where it is claimed that
miracles are still performed, it is not maintained that
they are performed to confirm the general truths of revelation; to demonstrate that the prophets and apostles
were sent from God; or to prove that the Christian religion, as distinguished from other religions, is true, but
that they are wrought in favor of some dogma of the
Church; or in honor of the memory of some particular
saint; or to show that the church in which such miracles occur is the true Church, in contradistinction from
other associations which claim to be parts of the true
Church; in honor of the faith, or of the priesthood, of
some one branch of the Church of God.

The miracles, however, on which reliance is placed
for the proof of Christianity as such, occurred in a period now far in the past; they were witnessed by comparatively few persons; and the evidence that they
were performed at all comes to us under all the disad-

vantages of testimony transmitted through successive generations. We ourselves have not been permitted to witness the performance of a miracle in attestation to the truth of our religion, nor, when urging the claims to the divine origin of that religion from miracles, and seeking to convince our fellow-men of its truth on that ground, can we appeal to one actually wrought in their presence or in our own, as furnishing such a demonstration. It was, therefore, not difficult to construct the plausible argument of Mr. Hume against miracles—an argument so plausible that to this day it has not been found easy to detect its sophistry. But, whether that argument was well founded or was a sophism, no such sophism, and, at any rate, no such argument, can be suggested in regard to prophecy. It is a subject which we can investigate as eye-witnesses ourselves. We have the prophecy before us in fixed and permanent language, to be interpreted on principles universally recognized in the interpretation of language, and where the friends and the foes of the religion in defense of which they are adduced are supposed to be equally qualified to understand the use of language and the rules of exegesis, and to have an equal right to apply those rules. The very words of the prophecy may be carefully studied, and may be calmly compared with the facts to which it is claimed they are applicable. It is not like a miracle, to be seen at the exact moment of the occurrence or not at all; it is not like the word, the look, or the touch, that restores sight to the blind, or that heals diseases; it is not like the voice that stills the tempest, or that raises the dead, and then is silent forever. The witnesses of such scenes, and the actors in such scenes, pass from the world in a single generation, nor can we call them on the "stand" again to subject them to a rigorous "cross-examination." In prophecy, however, every thing can be examined with all the calmness required by the principles of the inductive philosophy. All is before us that there *is* in the case, and will remain there as long as we please. The words of the prophecy and the facts are neither of them evanescent, and are as fixed as the substances which the chemist coolly examines in his laboratory, or as the stars on which the astronomer gazes, night after night, at his leisure.

(2.) Second. In the argument from prophecy there can be no doubt about the *facts* in the case. In the argument from miracles, the main point of the inquiry relates to the *facts* themselves. If the alleged facts are admitted to have occurred—if Lazarus was actually raised from the dead—there would be no difference of opinion that would embarrass us in regard to the *argument;* that is, that it was an event produced by the immediate power and will of God, irrespective of natural laws. The whole effort of infidelity, therefore, in regard to a miracle, is to set aside the evidence that the fact occurred, not to deny the force of the argument derived from it if the fact is established. In prophecy, the argument assumes a different form. Respecting the main *facts* in the case there can be no question, and if there were a question, it could be readily examined and determined. If any man doubts whether Jerusalem and the Temple were destroyed, he has only to look into Josephus or Gibbon to satisfy his mind of the fact. If he doubts whether Babylon, Tyre, Petra, or Nineveh are in ruins, he has only to look into Volney, or Burckhardt, or Maundrell, or Layard, or to go to the places of their former magnificence, and seat himself amidst the ruins of their grandeur, and, "book in hand," compare, at his leisure, their present state with the predictions in the prophets. He may take his own time for the examination; he may look at the ruins fragment by fragment, and compare, with the minutest and most patient detail, the facts before him with the statements in the prophets. He may sit down to the argument with as much coolness as he would to a mathematical demonstration, and survey the evidence as calmly as he does that which enters into the inductive philosophy. In a miracle, a voice spake loud, solemn, and clear, as when the tempest was hushed on the Sea of Tiberias, or when Lazarus was raised from the grave, and then the voice died away. In prophecy, a voice speaks still from solitary Petra, from ruined Tyre, from the site of the Temple in Jerusalem, from the exhumed palaces of Nineveh, from the midst of the "wild beasts of the desert," and the "doleful creatures," and the "owls that dwell" in Babylon, and the "satyrs that dance there," and the "wild beasts that cry" in its "desolate houses," and the "dragons in its pleasant palaces,"* to all generations. From their deep silence; from the palaces where once was the sound of the viol and the harp; from the forsaken temples, an utterance is heard still responding to the ancient prophetic warning. We hear the cry of the "bittern" and the "owl" proclaiming the fulfillment of the prophecies of Isaiah; and the "dance of the satyr" and the "cry of the wild beasts" invite the world to contemplate the truth of the ancient predictions.

(3.) Third. There is another point of difference between miracles and prophecy. The proof from the former was complete in the time of the apostles; the proof from the latter is increased and strengthened

* Isaiah, xiii., 21, 22.

from age to age, and will be augmenting to the end of
the world. It is accumulating with every new fact in
history, and will go forward to meet the incredulity of
all coming times. In this respect these two sources of
evidence bear some resemblance to the demonstration
of God's wisdom and power in the creation of the world,
and in its providential government. The act of creation, grand and awful, when the "morning stars sang
together, and all the sons of God shouted for joy," was
an impressive demonstration of his power, a stupendous
miracle that put the question of his omnipotence forever to rest, as the stilling of the tempest and the
resurrection of Lazarus did that of the Savior. But
the wisdom of God, and the goodness of God, and the
mercy of God, shine forth from age to age, and the argument is presented fresh and new to each generation.
The evidence is repeated with each revolving year;
with each returning season; with each opening flower;
with the running stream; with the dews of the morning and the zephyrs of the evening; and with the conversion and salvation of each penitent sinner, as the
evidence of the truth of religion from prophecy meets
each coming generation, and will attend the race until
the proclamation "the kingdoms of this world are become the kingdoms of our Lord, and of his Christ; and
he shall reign forever and ever," shall be heard throughout the universe.*

God *might* have made the human mind—might have
made *all* created minds—so as to foresee the future as
well as to remember the past. In the nature of things
there is no more difficulty in the one case than in the
other; and, at all events, no one can prove that this is
impossible. God's own mind is thus constituted, if it

* Rev., xi., 15.

be proper to apply the words *future* and *past* to him; and, in creating other minds in the "image" of his own, it was, and must have been, a matter dependent on his will and wisdom whether they should be endowed in the same manner.

Man was made in the "image" of God. In the knowledge of the past, or in retaining the memory of the past, we see clearly that he *was*, in this respect, made in the "image" of his Creator. If he had been endowed with the power of looking into the future, the fact that he bore the "image" of his Creator would have been still more apparent and striking. In the purpose to create him in his "image," it was for God himself to judge *how far* that "image," in respect to power, and knowledge, and wisdom, in treasuring up the memory of the past, and in anticipating the future, was to be extended. Obviously there must be a limit in all these things immeasurably this side of his own infinity, whatever might be the *capacity* of man for extending this in an indefinite approximation in the future *toward* the infinity of God. There are lines which approach each other forever, but which never meet.

In regard to events lying in the past and in the future, God chose, in making man, that he should be endowed with the power of retaining the one, but with no power of looking directly into the other; as he chose, in regard to power, that that power on the part of man should extend only to those things which pertain to natural or physical laws, retaining the power above those laws of creating or destroying — the power of miracles — to himself. This arrangement, among other results, lays the foundation for furnishing a proof of a divine revelation, on the one hand by miracles, and on the other by prophecy—the power of setting aside the ordinary laws of nature at his pleasure in the one·case, and the power, in the other case, of foretelling what man otherwise could never know.

There were reasons, quite obvious in the main, why this should be so in respect to past and future events.

On the one hand, in reference to the past, it was of the highest importance to the well-being of man, if not to his very existence, to the progress of society, to all just views of responsibility, to the formation of his own character, that he should be so endowed as to gather up and retain the past—the past in his own individual experience; the past in the progress of society. Character is formed in this way by availing ourselves of our past attainments and past experience. Responsibility rests on this, for there could be no just and adequate views of retribution if all our thoughts, and plans, and words, and deeds were at once effaced forever, as the figures and letters that we trace in the sand on the seashore are by the next wave. To all just notions of responsibility, our thoughts, and words, and deeds must be as if " they were graven with an iron pen and lead in the rock forever" (Job,xix., 24). Society makes progress in this way by treasuring up the accumulated wisdom of the past—the results of all happy inventions, of all struggles for freedom, of all improvements in the arts, and of all the profound sayings of sages and philosophers. The present state of the world in civilization, in science, in the arts, in domestic comforts, in the enjoyment of liberty, in religion, is the result of the fact that man is endowed with the faculty of *memory*.

On the other hand, there would have been equal *disadvantages* in thus endowing man in regard to the future, enabling him to see the future as he can retain the past. Such an arrangement would have done much to stifle effort and to weaken the stimulus to enterprise and exertion, for much of that effort and that stimulus depends on the fact that a thing is unknown but may be known; that a discovery may be made that will contribute to wealth or fame; and that the human powers may find employment and pleasure *in* the discovery. Thus the young are stimulated to make attainments in literature and science, because there are vast fields yet unexplored, and to·a noble-minded youth it is all the better if not a ray of light has been shed upon them; nor would such a youth thank any one to stop the career of noble thought and the path of discovery by pouring down a flood of light on all those regions, so that no more should be left for the efforts of honorable ambition. It was this which animated Columbus when the prow of his vessel first crossed the line beyond which a ship had ever sailed, and plunged into unknown seas. Every wave that was thrown up had a new interest and beauty from the fact that its repose had never been disturbed before by the keel of a vessel; and when his eye first saw the land, and he prostrated himself and kissed the earth, his glory was at the highest, for he saw what in all ages was unknown before. So we are every where stimulated and animated by the unknown, by what is before us that may be gained, by the fields of new thought which man has never explored.* Farther, what a world of sorrow might this be if we saw the future as we remember the past! Who would desire it? Who would be willing that all that is to occur to him or to his family during a single year should be spread out before him on the first day of the

---

* Avia Pieridum peragro loca, nullius ante
  Trita solo; juvat integros accedere fonteis;
  Atque haurire.—*Lucretius.*

year? How many dwellings would such a knowledge fill with grief! If, at the beginning of a year, we knew that a beloved child was to sicken and die ; if the scene was all spread out before us ; if we saw the exact progress of the disease, and knew the exact hour when it would terminate fatally, how sad would be our feelings as we looked on that child ; how sad to us the weeks, and days, and hours, as the fatal hour drew on! How many dwellings in the land would be filled with grief, and how many would be the sorrows which would be added to a now wretched world!

God, therefore, while he has so far made us after his own "image" that we can retain the memory of the past, has mercifully limited our endowments in the other direction, and hidden the future, in a great measure, from our view.

Yet, while this is true as a great law, it is to be remarked, and the purpose of this argument requires especially that it should be before our minds in order that we may understand exactly what prophecy is, that there *are* certain endowments of the human mind which have reference to the future, and it is material so to distinguish them as to show that they do not amount to the idea, or invade the province of *prophecy*, or to show how prophecy is distinguished *from* those endowments.

The powers of the human mind, inspired or uninspired, as they are exercised in this world in relation to the future, must be arranged under the following heads : Hope, mathematical calculation, sagacity, prophecy.

Hope.—This has relation, indeed, to the future, but not to the *knowledge* of the future. It predicts nothing; it makes nothing certain. Hope, founded on a probability or possibility in regard to the future, on the common course of human events, or on special prom-

ises, does much indeed to stimulate men to effort, and
to cheer a dark and suffering world, but it does nothing
to determine the future, except as that future itself is
determined by efforts inspired by hope. It in itself
makes nothing certain. It gilds the future, indeed, with
much that is bright, but with that which is imaginary,
and which is, therefore, much of it a mere illusion. It
makes the world appear brighter than the reality, and
is a benevolent arrangement — one of those numerous
things which occur in the world, often *underlying* other
things, which show that the Creator of the world is a
benevolent Being, and intends, at the same time, to
stimulate human effort, to cheer man in his sad and
dark path, and to keep before him the prospect of a
brighter world than this. It is not, however, a deception. Though it does not always correspond with the
reality, though the anticipation is often brighter than
the result, though youth is cheered and stimulated
more than age is, or than youth would be if it had a
clear view of the reality of things, it is not a designed
illusion, for man is not kept ignorant of the fact that
there may be disappointment, and no promise which
God has made in the arrangements by which hope is
inspired is violated, for all those promises are made
with this condition well understood, and none which he
has *absolutely* made ever fail. The labor of the hus-
bandman *may* fail; the ship richly freighted *may* encounter a storm and sink in the ocean; health *may*
fail; life *may* be cut off before its plans are developed
and its hopes matured; the fig-tree may not blossom,
and there may be no fruit in the vines; the labor of the
olive may fail, and the fields may yield no meat; the
flock may be cut off from the fold, and there may be
no hind in the stalls (Habakkuk, iii., 17); yet still, on

the average, the promises of hope are sufficiently real
to stimulate effort, and to cheer and encourage man;
but it does not enable him to penetrate the dark future, and to tell what that *will be*.

Mathematical calculation.—Here, such is the stability of the laws of nature, that the knowledge of the future, within the sphere of such calculations, is minute
and absolute, provided the present system shall remain,
and provided God shall not interfere by his own direct
will and power to change it. To neither of these points
does it extend. But within its own sphere it is certain,
and is, except prophecy, the most absolute knowledge
which we have of the future.

In this we can not go beyond what the case will justify in our admiration of the endowments of man. The
knowledge thus within the grasp of the human mind
shows perhaps more than any thing else his wonderful
greatness and power. The position of the heavenly
bodies at any time, however remote in the future; an
eclipse of the sun or moon; the transit of a star; the return of a comet after, in a wild, eccentric course, it has
buried itself in the depths of ether, and traversed for
years or centuries those unfathomed regions—all these
show the greatness of man; show the greatness of the
God who made him, and who has made a system so accurate in its movements, and so vast and enduring.

Yet all this has a limit, and a limit far—far inside of
what prophecy undertakes to do. It is confined to
physical laws. It leaves out the whole element of *will*
—that on which so many of the events of prophecy actually turn—the will of princes, of statesmen, of warriors, of the numberless hosts of human beings engaged
in civil affairs or in battle, whose separate purposes may
enter into the result. It proceeds on the supposition

that the order of events will not be disturbed by the
divine will—a thing of which no astronomer can be
sure. It has little—nothing to do with the common affairs of life; with the things which enter into commerce,
arts, discoveries, inventions, improvements, poetry, eloquence, and song; with the duration of cities and empires; with the great men that may come and play
their part, and then disappear. Who among the gifted
men of our race can foretell these things?

Sagacity.—This is a power of penetrating the future
to a certain extent, given to man for important purposes; a power on which much of the success of the
life of an individual, and much of the prosperity of nations may depend. It has every evidence of being a
divine arrangement, for it lies in the direction of exalted genius, and can not be the result of mere education, training, or experience. In a humble form it exists in most minds; it is quite indispensable to the successful prosecution of business; it serves much to distinguish one man from another in the same calling in
life. The success of one merchant above another; the
success of one banker above another—nay, the success
of one farmer above another, may as often be traced to
that sagacity which looks into the future, and anticipates the changes in the commercial world which will
be likely to occur, as to any other endowment. In its
higher forms, as in cases like those of Burke and Canning, it seems almost to approach the region of inspiration and prophecy. In its humbler forms, and perhaps
in its higher forms, it is capable of cultivation by experience; by reading; by an increased knowledge of the
ordinary course of events; by a calculation of probabilities; by an acquaintance with the past. The states-
man combines his knowledge of the experience of the
world with his own power of penetrating the future;

the sagacity of the merchant is often almost the mere result of large and long observation and experience.

In either case, however, it never rises to certainty; it is never prophecy. It makes mention of no names; it specifies no dates; it enters into no particulars—no details. It draws out the plans of no battles or sieges on land, and no naval conflicts; it brings no actors by name on the stage; it describes no burning towns, no wasted fields, no permanent desolations, no future condition of cities, states, or empires. Burke's celebrated prediction of the consequences of a "Regicide Peace" is of the most general character; enters into no details; anticipates no history in dates and names, and leaves no impression on the mind of what the details would be. In one of the most splendid passages in the English language, Macaulay ventures a suggestion in regard to the time when London may be a scene of wide desolation, and imagines an inhabitant of New Zealand, on the ruins of London Bridge, sketching the ruins of St. Paul's. Speaking of the Roman Catholic Church, he says, in that passage: "She saw the commencement of all the governments and of all the ecclesiastical establishments that now exist in the world, and we feel no assurance that she is not destined to see the end of them all. She was great and respected before the Saxon had set foot on Britain—before the Frank had passed the Rhine—when Grecian eloquence still flourished at Antioch—when idols were still worshiped in the Temple of Mecca; and she may still exist in undiminished vigor when some traveler from New Zealand shall, in the midst of a vast solitude, take his stand on a broken arch of London Bridge to sketch the ruins of St. Paul's."*

* Review of *Ranke's* History of the Popes. Miscellanies, vol. iii., p. 320, 321.

This is splendid writing; this is eloquence of language; this is sublime in the description of what might —of what may occur. But it is not prophecy. If he had said that this *will be*, it would be prophecy; and if he had gone into detail, as Isaiah has done in regard to a city larger in its area than even modern London, and concerning which, at the time, there was as little probability that it would be a "vast solitude" as there is that London will be; if he had said, as Isaiah does, "It shall never be inhabited, neither shall it be dwelt in from generation to generation; but wild beasts of the desert shall lie there; and their houses shall be full of doleful creatures; and owls shall dwell there, and satyrs shall dance there; and the wild beasts of the islands shall cry in their desolate houses, and dragons in their pleasant palaces; I will make it a possession for the bittern, and pools of water; and I will sweep it with the besom of destruction, saith the Lord of hosts" (Isaiah, xiii., 20–22; xiv., 23), *this* would have been *prophecy*.

Except by prophecy—by direct inspiration of God—the power of man in regard to the future is limited by those things which have now been adverted to. His desires, indeed, his efforts have not been bounded by these things, nor has he been satisfied by this arrangement; for there is no one thing that he has more longed for, or for which he has struggled more, than to penetrate the dark veil which shuts out the future, and to make his own power in regard to the future correspond with his power over the past. By the interpretation of dreams; by consultation of the stars; by attempting to make compacts with the dead to induce them to disclose the secret which is supposed to be in their possession; by mysterious combinations of numbers; by oracles; by torturing nature to make it disclose the secret; by somnambulism; by spiritualism; by the flight of birds; by inspecting the entrails of animals; by the supposed visitations of the gods, and the return of the departed to the earth, men have sought to set aside the great law which God has ordained on this subject, but in vain. Man reaches distant worlds by the telescope; he whispers so as to be heard across continents, sending his thoughts beneath the waves of the ocean, and over deserts and mountains; he chronicles the centuries lying back of all recorded history, by which the earth was slowly moulded to be the residence of living beings; he marks with unerring precision the movements of far distant worlds, but not one thing in the future, even that which is nearest to him, can he learn; not one response can he get to all the modes in which he asks the question, *What is to be to-morrow?*

Prophecy is the only thing which discloses that, and to that we now turn with the inquiry whether, to any extent and for any purpose, God has lifted the veil and disclosed the future to man? If he has, it is a miracle, like any other miracle. The power to disclose the future, like the power to create a world or to raise the dead, is *beyond* the power of man. The limitation in the one case is in regard to *time;* in the other in regard to *power*. In either case, all beyond is of God. The one is miracle, the other is prophecy.

The following things are essential to prophecy:

First. That the prediction be *beyond* the power of man in penetrating the future; that it be not a vision of hope; that it be not the result of a mathematical calculation; that it be not within the limits of mere political sagacity. The inspiration of hope is not prophecy, for it makes nothing certain. The calculation of an eclipse is not prophecy, for it depends on fixed laws. The suggestions of sagacity are not prophecy, for they are not fixed and certain; they give no dates, no names, no details.

Second. It must be demonstrated that the prediction was before the event. Every man has a right to require that this shall be put beyond suspicion.

Third. The prediction must be *fairly* applicable to the event. It should not refer to one of many things to which it might be adjusted with equal ease, but to one thing, and *so* definite that it can not be adjusted to another, except as that other may be an unfolding of it. The prediction of the destruction of Babylon must be *of* Babylon, and so expressed that it shall describe that city in its future ruin, and not Tyre, Nineveh, Petra, Jerusalem, Rome.

Fourth. The language should be such that it will be unmistakable. Whether words or symbols are used, they must be such that by *fair*, not by *forced* interpretation, the prediction is applicable to the event. The enemies of revelation have a right to demand this; its friends are bound to show that it is so.

But there are some things of equal clearness which are *not* to be demanded, and which are essential to a just view of the subject, but which are not as likely to be conceded as these would be. It is important that we have a clear understanding with the enemies of revelation in regard to them also.

First. In order to prophecy it is not necessary that there should be an exact and minute specification of names, dates, and circumstances. The reasons of this are obvious: (*a*) If there were such an exact specification it would be possible to defeat the prophecy. (*b*) An event can be designated with sufficient certainty with-

out such an exact specification of names, dates, and circumstances.   (c) A predicted event, that seems obscure
before the event occurs, may become clear when the
event is accomplished.   Such may be the clearness of
the event, so entirely may it tally with the prediction,
so plain may become the statements in the prophecy
that seemed to be obscure, and so perfectly may the
facts in the event harmonize apparently contradictory
statements in the prophecy, that, while it would not
have been easy or possible, perhaps, to have made a
statement in detail beforehand of what would be, there
can be no doubt of what was intended in the prophecy.
Thus, for illustration, in the prophecies respecting the
Messiah, there *seemed* to be two classes of predictions
that were wholly irreconcilable, and that led to wholly
different expectations of what he would be.   One class
described him as a man in humble life ; a man of sorrows ; a man rejected, despised, put to death, buried.
The other class described him as the descendant of
David ; as one who would occupy his throne; as a
prince and a conqueror ; as triumphant; as reigning ;
as setting up a perpetual kingdom ; as going forth to
the conquest of the world ; as triumphing over all his
foes ; as successful and glorious in his work.   One class
of the prophecies described him as one who had all the
susceptibilities of a man, and who was subject to all the
infirmities of a man ; the other class described him as
the " mighty God," and the " Father of the everlasting
age" (Isa., ix., 6).   The Jews naturally, in carrying out
their ideas of national pride and glory, selected the latter view, and anticipated in their Messiah an illustrious
prince and conqueror — one who in his reign would
surpass even the magnificent reigns of David and Solomon.   They were never able when he appeared, nor

are they to this day, to blend the two descriptions in one person. The Christian sees no difficulty in the subject, for he finds, he thinks, all these things united in him who, "being in the form of God, thought it not robbery to be equal with God, but made himself of no reputation, and was made in the likeness of men; and being found in fashion as a man, he humbled himself, and became obedient unto death, even the death of the cross" (Phil., ii., 6–8).

What is here stated may exist to some extent under any circumstances, and in the plainest descriptions, from the nature of the human mind, and from the necessity of the case. A description of a person that we have not seen, or an event that we have not witnessed, may be very obscure before the person is seen or the event occurs, but plain enough, and so plain that the correspondence can not be mistaken, when the person is seen or the event occurs. Who ever obtained any correct idea of Niagara Falls by a description? Who, say to the most polished Greek and Roman mind, could have conveyed by mere description any idea of a printing-press, of a locomotive engine, of the magnetic telegraph? Who could convey to one born blind an idea of the prismatic colors, or to the deaf an idea of the sounds of the great organ at Harlaem?

As I suppose all students do, I had formed an idea of Rome from the descriptions which I had read in my early years. I had grown up with the idea until it became as definite in my own mind as the lanes, and roads, and fields, and streams of the quiet country-place where I was born. I could have drawn out a map of it, and could have located the Tiber, and the Vatican, and the Forum, and the Coliseum. When, some years ago, I was actually there, I had *two* Romes in my eye

—the Rome of my youth and of all my life, and the Rome of the reality, and nothing scarcely could have been more unlike than the two. Yet the Rome of the reality, in fact, corresponded with all the descriptions that I had read; all those accounts were blended and combined in it; and the Rome of my youthful imagination gradually gave way to the reality, so that I can recall it no more. So the anticipations of the Messiah grew up among the Hebrews. A distinct conception of him, apparently as drawn by the prophets, was formed in the national mind. When the reality appeared, he was, therefore, not recognized as the Messiah, and was rejected. To the present day that Messiah of the youth of the Hebrew people—the Messiah of the imagination—is before the unconverted Hebrew mind. To the converted Jew—to Saul of Tarsus—that imaginary Messiah passed away, and the Messiah of the reality became fixed in the mind, blending all the ancient descriptions in harmony. Paul, I think, refers to this illusion and this reality when he says of himself, " Though we have known Christ after the flesh, yet now henceforth know we him no more" (2 Cor., v., 16).

Second. In presenting the argument from prophecy, we may lay out of view the fact that many of the prophecies are yet difficult and obscure. Undoubtedly that may be so, and it is to be admitted that it is so. To a certain extent, for the reason already stated, *all* prophecies must be in a measure obscure until they are fulfilled, and, as there may be many which are not yet fulfilled, it is not to be denied that they may be obscure. But this fact does not affect those that are clear—clear either in the terms in which they are expressed, or made clear by the fact that they are fulfilled. They stand on their own basis, and are to be interpreted as if there were no other prophecies, whether real or obscure, true or false. Moreover, the fact that they are now obscure does not make it certain that they will always be so, or that even *they* may not, at some future time, have a place among those predictions so clearly fulfilled as to show that they had their origin in God.

It may be remarked, also, that what is now affirmed respecting prophecy is also true of the facts respecting science, or of knowledge of any kind. Many of the real truths of science are to us, as yet, *very* obscure, *very* dim and shadowy. They seem to be enveloped in a mist which we can not penetrate. They are not defined, even in their outlines, fully and clearly. There are many doubts, even in the best cultivated minds, in regard to them. The age of the world, for instance, is one such point. No one has been able to determine it by measuring the duration of the various periods which geology reveals as having succeeded each other, in the formation of rocks, and soils, and seas, since the creation, or since the *matter* of the earth was brought into being. Indeed, no approximation has been made to this, nor has any one ventured even to *conjecture* how long this has been.* But the obscurity on this point in no wise affects the clearness and the certainty of the facts which geology has disclosed in regard to the changes of the earth. The evidence of each one of these rests entirely on its own basis, quite independent of the inquiry about the times which have elapsed since those great changes commenced. Time, too, and farther inquiry *may* throw light on the questions which are still obscure, and they

* "The *actual* lengths of these ages it is not possible to determine even approximately. All that geology can claim to do is to prove the general proposition that *Time is long*." —*Dana's* Text-book of Geology, p. 244.

may, at some far-distant period in the future, take their
place among the clear and acknowledged truths of science, as the now obscure prophecies may among those
that are plain.

Third. For a similar reason, we may lay out of view
the question about the *interpretation* of many of the
prophecies as *forced* and *fanciful.* Undoubtedly they
are so, and it is a great abridgment of our task in interpreting prophecy that we are not required, in defending the divine origin of the predictions of the Bible,
to undertake the defense of those interpretations. For
the vagaries of the human mind; for the weaknesses of
religionists, however amiable; for idiosyncracies among
good men; for fanciful theories in regard to interpretation; for the failure of expectations founded on such
interpretations, prophecy itself is in no wise responsible, any more than science is for the failure of the experiments to secure perpetual motion or to construct a
flying machine. The world is quite full of Second Advent literature, much of it already occupying the same
place in our libraries which the ingenious plans for securing perpetual motion or constructing flying machines do in the Patent Office, but these no more affect
the reality of prophecy than those abandoned speci-
mens of visionary ingenuity and skill do the steam-boat
or the telegraph.

Fourth. For the purpose of the present argument,
also, we may lay out of view the manner in which the
sacred writers themselves quote the prophecies and apply the language of the Old Testament to the events recorded in the New, under the general form of quotation, ἵνα πληρωϑῇ (Matt., i., 22; ii., 15; iv., 14; xxi., 4;
xxvi., 56; xxvii., 35; Mark, xiv., 29; John, xii., 38, *et
sæpe*). In saying that these quotations may be laid out

of view, it is not admitted that they are on a false principle, or that they can not be vindicated, but that they do not affect the real question about prophecy. If it should be conceded that their manner of making these quotations could not be vindicated, still the admission would only affect the question of their own *inspiration*, not the main question whether there are prophecies of whose application there could be no doubt. The sole inquiry in regard to the passages that come under the form of quotation included in the words ἵνα πληρωϑῇ— "that it might be fulfilled"—would be whether this manner of quotation would be consistent with just views of inspiration. A solution of the difficulties on that point, or a failure to solve the difficulties, would in no way affect the more general inquiry whether there may not be prophecies which are encumbered with no difficulties of this nature. They must stand or fall on their own merit. The question of *inspiration* may be affected by this inquiry, but not the question of *prophecy*.

Laying these things, therefore, out of view, as in no way affecting the inquiry before us, I shall now proceed to make a few remarks on the evidence from prophecy of the truth of revelation as it appears in the nineteenth century. Of course the remarks must be few. I can not go in detail into an examination of the numerous predictions in the Bible in regard to the future.

The Bible, more than any other book, deals with the future.

(*a*) Philosophers and historians rarely venture into the region of the future, for it is not in their province. Their field is mainly the past; their range in regard to the future is limited to reflections and inferences from the past as to what the future, supposing that the world is governed by uniform laws, and that the

same causes will produce the same results, may be.
That luxury will corrupt and destroy a nation is one
of those general maxims derived from the experience
of the past, and it may therefore be predicted that
where luxury abounds it will produce the same effect
hereafter which it has done before.   But beyond such
general maxims philosophers and historians do not venture to go.   Mr. Gibbon deals with the past; Tacitus
dealt with the past; Mr. Hume and Lord Macaulay deal
with the past; and, profound as are the reflections of
these men, especially those of Tacitus, on human affairs,
on human nature as exhibited by the course of events,
and on what may be the destiny of nations or the advances of society hereafter, yet they never venture to
suggest what may be the boundaries of empires in times
to come; what new forms of dominion may arise; what
remarkable personages may appear and act their part
on the great theatre of human affairs; what cities may
be besieged or lands laid waste by war; what new
towns may be built, or at what periods of time great
and important events may be expected to occur.   Men
can calculate eclipses, but they do not venture to foretell how events will occur that are dependent on the
human will, or consequent on new discoveries and inventions in the sciences and the arts.   The Bible, however, deals as much and as freely with the future as
with the past, and the sacred writers do not hesitate any
more to describe what *will occur* than to record what
has happened.   The nearest approach to such predictions as occur in the Scriptures, in the ancient classic
writings, is probably found in the "Pollio" of Virgil
(Ecl. iv.), bearing, in some respects, a strong resemblance to some passages in Isaiah; but it would be
easy to show how far short this comes of *prophecy.*

(*b*) False religions do not deal much with the future. As Mohammed in his public life expressly disclaimed reliance on miracles as not necessary to the establishment of his religion, so, in the Koran, he has practically disclaimed reliance on prophecy as equally unnecessary. There are no predictions in the Koran corresponding with those of the Messiah in the Scriptures, or with those pertaining to Babylon, to Petra, to Tyre, to Edom, or to Jerusalem. Mohammed, perhaps, had sagacity enough to see that the truth of any such predictions would soon come to a practical test, for there is nothing on which men who wish to establish a permanent religion, or a permanent fame, will be so slow to venture as on predictions in regard to the future. The Bible, therefore, has laid itself open to detection as no other book has, if it is false, by its pretended disclosures of the future. Lord Bacon, in his will, said, "For my name and memory, I leave them to men's charitable speeches, and to foreign nations, and *to the next ages.*" The Bible, in all the reproaches cast upon it, has thus left its vindication to the "next ages"—to remotest periods and generations.

The nature of the argument I shall state now in few words. There is not time to go into detail, nor is it necessary for my purpose.

First. The sacred books describe things as they *now exist*—now, in this nineteenth century. The range of subjects to which this remark is applicable is very large, but the nature of the argument would be the same whether we take the whole range of subjects into the account, or confine our illustrations to a few of them. As the facts are not such that they could or would be called in question, it can not be alleged that any advantage would be taken, or any unfairness evinced, if we

K

confine onr attention to a very few of these things.
We may take, then, as a specimen—as a sufficient illustration—the condition of two celebrated cities in the
past, Babylon and Tyre. The remark which I am now
making is, that now, in the nineteenth century, the condition of those cities is what the prophets said *it would
be* more than two thousand years ago.

Babylon.—The prophets said that the following would
be its condition: "And Babylon, the glory of kingdoms,
the beauty of the Chaldees' excellency, shall be as when
God overthrew Sodom and Gomorrah. It shall never
be inhabited, neither shall it be dwelt in from generation to generation; neither shall the Arabian pitch his
tent there; neither shall the shepherds make their fold
there; but wild beasts of the desert shall lie there, and
their houses shall be full of doleful creatures, and owls
shall dwell there, and satyrs shall dance there. And
wild beasts of the islands shall cry in their desolate
houses, and dragons in their pleasant palaces; and her
time is near to come, and her days shall not be prolonged" (Isa., xiii., 19–22). "I will also make it a possession for the bittern, and pools of water; and I will
sweep it with the besom of destruction, saith the Lord
of hosts" (Isa., xiv., 23).

This *is* the condition of Babylon now, and *has been*
for centuries. Every part of this statement can be confirmed, and has been confirmed by travelers in the East,
and in regard to the *facts* there are no varying statements. My time will not allow me to go into detail in
showing the accuracy of this description; and it is unnecessary, for there are no differences of statements in
regard to what Babylon is, and has been for centuries.*

· * For details on this subject, if any are disposed to pursue it farther,
I may be permitted to refer to my Notes on Isaiah on these passages,
and to *Keith* on the Prophecies, p. 185–190, 218–235.

Tyre.—Of Tyre, the prophets said that the following would be its condition: "Thus saith the Lord God, Behold, I am against thee, O Tyrus, and will cause many nations to come against thee, as the sea causeth his waves to come up; and they shall destroy the walls of Tyrus, and break down her towers; and I will scrape her dust from her, and make her like the top of a rock: it shall be a place for the spreading of nets in the midst of the sea; for I have spoken it, saith the Lord God" (Ezek., xxvi., 3–5). "I will make thee like the top of a rock; thou shalt be a place to spread nets upon; thou shalt be built no more, for I the Lord have spoken it, saith the Lord God" (Ezek., xxvi., 14). "I will make thee a terror, and thou shalt be no more: though thou be sought for, yet thou shalt never be found again, saith the Lord God" (Ezek., xxvi., 21). This *is*, and *has been* the condition of Tyre for many centuries now, as might be shown by any number of witnesses. "The vicissitudes of time, or rather the barbarism of the Greeks of the lower empire," says Volney, "have accomplished their prediction. Instead of that ancient commerce," says he, "so active and so extensive, Tyre, reduced to a miserable village, has no other trade than the exportation of a few sacks of corn and raw cotton; nor any merchant but a single Greek factor, who scarcely makes sufficient profit to maintain his family." "The whole village of Tyre," he adds, "contains only fifty or sixty poor families, who live obscurely on the produce of their little grounds and a small fishery."—Travels, p. 212. Bruce describes Tyre as a "rock whereon fishers dry their nets." Of Tyre in its present condition, there is no more difference in the description of travelers than there is in the description of Babylon. The accordance of the facts with the prophetic statements could be easily established in the most minute details.

The remarks now made might be extended, with like accuracy of description, to Nineveh, Edom, Petra, Jerusalem, to the condition of the Hebrew people, I believe also to the fall of the Roman empire, the establishment of the kingdom of the Messiah, and the rise and character of the Papal power. But the discussion would be too extended, and would not add essential strength to the argument. Let us, therefore, in the consideration of the argument, confine ourselves to the two great cities now mentioned, and to the cities with which they were connected, and which rose from the same causes, and which by the same causes were made permanently desolate, as the prophets said they would be.

Second. What was predicted, and what has occurred, in regard to the cities to which I have referred as an illustration of the argument, was, in itself, in a high degree improbable. There was no reason why Babylon should become a scene of utter and permanent desolation; there was none why Tyre should cease to be an important sea-port, and should become a place on which the poor fisherman should spread his nets; and there was no probability that either would occur. A similar prophecy now, in regard to London or New York, would have as much probability as the prophecies respecting Babylon and Tyre had when they were uttered; and strange and improbable as Macaulay's description of the inhabitant of New Zealand standing on a broken arch of London Bridge, amid a scene of wide desolation, and making a sketch of the ruins of St. Paul's, seems to us, yet it is no more strange than the predictions of Isaiah and Ezekiel would have appeared to the men of their times in regard to Babylon and Tyre. Babylon, in its position, its strength, its resources, its trade, its wealth, its relation to the vast empire of which it was the capital, and the other empires of the East with which it was connected, had all the requisites of a great and permanent city; Tyre, in its harbor, its relation to the commerce of Asia, its situation on the Mediterranean, with no rival harbor on the whole of the eastern shores of that great sea, and its position between Asia and Europe, through which the commerce of the East must pass, had all the requisites of a permanent and rich sea-port; nor could it be shown that Liverpool or New York, in relation to the commerce of the world now, are more favorably situated than Tyre was then. The great traffic of the East—of the world —passed through it, and it must have seemed then that that traffic would continue to pass through it forever.

Third. The causes of the permanent ruin of these cities, and of the other cities in the same group—Petra, Tadmor, Baalbec—were such as could not then be foreseen. The foretelling of those causes was wholly beyond the existing state of knowledge at that age of the world—wholly beyond the range of human sagacity.*

The main cause of these great changes, and perhaps the sole cause of these permanent desolations, was the discovery of the Cape of Good Hope, and the consequent change which that event made in the commerce of the world. Babylon, and Tyre, and Petra, and Pal-

---

* In relation to these causes, which there was not time fully to state in the Lecture, I may be permitted to refer to an article on the "Ancient Commerce of Western Asia," in the Biblical Repository for 1840, and reprinted in the volumes entitled "Miscellaneous Essays and Reviews," published by Ivison and Phinney, 1855, vol. ii., p. 5–60.

myra were indeed in ruins before that event occurred,
but there was nothing in the nature of the case that
prevented their being *rebuilt again*, until the causes
which had made them great had ceased forever.   The
great and rich commerce of the East had been the prize
sought for by all ancient nations, and that commerce
had laid the foundation, or had given importance to the
cities and sea-ports which were in the line of its direction, as that commerce subsequently made Alexandria
and Venice, in a great measure, what they were.   The
discovery of the Cape of Good Hope—a new passage to
India — gave that commerce a new direction forever,
and sealed the truth of the prophecies—forever turned
it *from* Petra, and Palmyra, and Tyre, and Babylon, and
Alexandria, and Venice, as the ocean ships from Asia
to California, and the Pacific Railroad, *may* yet turn it
away from London and Liverpool.   There were no
causes when the prophets spoke that tended to make
Babylon, and Petra, and Tyre what they are, any more
than there were causes which could be foreseen to produce the malaria in the Pontine Marshes, desolating
Rome, or than there will be causes in the future which
could now be foreseen which will make Philadelphia or
London pools of water and the habitation of owls.
Mere political sagacity could never, in Palestine or any
where else, have foreseen the discovery of the Cape of
Good Hope, or the effects of the use of the magnetic
needle, or the changes produced by the railroad and
the steam vessel; nor could political sagacity have predicted the flowing in of the sand that permanently
blocked up the harbor of Tyre.

   Fourth. The prophetic statements to which I have
referred were written *before* the events occurred.   In
respect to some prophecies, as, for example, the predic-

tion of the beginning and the close of the Babylonish captivity, in which *both* the prophecy and the event are now far distant in the past, it may require no small amount of learning and argument to demonstrate that the prophecy was written *before* the event; in respect to the events now under consideration, no such study can be necessary, for it can not be made a matter of doubt. I believe, indeed, that it can be fully shown by the sternest literary criticism that the prophecies respecting Babylon and Tyre were written *before* the decline and fall of those great cities, and when they were, in fact, in the meridian height of their splendor; but, however that may be, there can be no doubt that they were written before the *present time*, and, therefore, anterior to their fulfillment as the fulfillment is now—*the fulfillment of absolute and perpetual desolation.* If it *could* have been foretold by natural sagacity, or by reasoning on the ordinary course of events, as probable or even certain, that they would be overthrown by war, or by time, or by changes in human affairs, yet how, by such sagacity, could it have been predicted that they would *be perpetually and permanently desolate?* How could the prominent *cause* of that perpetual desolation —the changing of the commerce of the world by a new route to the Indies, of which they at that time never dreamed—have been foreseen? And how, in any circumstances, could their *perpetual* desolation have been predicted? Do cities never rise again after they have been destroyed? Are they never rebuilt after they have been razed to their foundations by war? Jerusalem— how often was it rebuilt after it had been laid in ruins! Rome—how often has that been laid waste by fire; by invading armies; by the Goths and Vandals; by malaria; and yet how often it has been rebuilt again! Lon-

don—how often has the fire passed over it, and yet it
has risen to augmented wealth and grandeur! Lisbon,
destroyed by an earthquake—how soon did it rise
again! Why, then, are Babylon, and Tyre, and Petra,
and Tadmor, doomed to perpetual desolation? And
how could it be known that they would be? But there
they are, now, in this nineteenth century, precisely as
the prophets said they would be—piles of ruins; utter
desolations; the habitation of dragons, and satyrs, and
owls.

Fifth. It remains, then, in summing up what I have
said, to observe that these things are beyond the range
of the unaided powers of man. They are not a mere
guess, or a vague conjecture of what *might be*, like Macaulay's remark about the New Zealander; they are
positive affirmations of what *would be.* They can not
come under the province of *hope*, for their enemies could
have seen no ground of hope that they would be thus
permanently desolate. They are not the result of mathematical calculation, as the movements of the heavenly
bodies are, for ruined cities come under no such laws.
The predictions are not the result of political sagacity.
In particularity; in definiteness; in minuteness; in detail, they are wholly unlike the predictions of Burke
and Canning, for even Burke, wonderful as his sagacity
was, never ventured on any predictions that would correspond in detail with the events following the French
Revolution and the Regicide Peace. They are, therefore, the result of PROPHECY—the effect of a supernatu·
ral endowment of man, on a line similar to miracles; and
a confirmation now, like miracles, of the divine origin
of the book in which they are found.

The following, then, is the argument in this nineteenth century:

(a) There are the books containing these prophecies. They have come down to us from the far-distant past — the most venerable books in the possession of mankind. Those books do not pass away as their authors did. They live. They have lived for more than two thousand years. They will live on to all coming time. They do not change. Not a word is altered; not a letter is lost. They may be examined with the utmost patience and leisure of criticism, and the world is invited to the examination.

(b) There are the facts. The East is full of them. *They*, too, do not now change. Babylon and Tyre are what they have been for more than a thousand years, and they will remain what they are for more than a thousand years to come, except that the corroding tooth of time will slowly remove the proofs, as now found in their remains, that they once existed at all. They, too, may be examined as leisurely as the books. Travelers tell us what they are, and they do not vary in their statements. Any man, if he has any doubt on the subject, may go and examine those ruins. " I would," said a countryman of our own, when speaking of the ruins of a city in the East, " I would that the skeptic could stand, as I did, among the ruins of this city, and there open the sacred book, and read the words of the inspired penman, written when this desolate place was one of the greatest cities in the world. I see the scoff arrested, his cheek pale, his lip quivering, and his heart quaking with fear, as the ancient city cries out to him, in a voice loud and powerful as one risen from the dead; though he would not believe Moses and the prophets, he believes the handwriting of God himself in the desolation and eternal ruin around him."*

* *Stephens*, Incidents of Travel, etc., vol. ii., p. 76.

K 2

LECTURE VII.

INSPIRATION OF THE SCRIPTURES WITH REFERENCE TO THE OBJECTIONS MADE IN THE NINETEENTH CENTURY.

THE subject of this Lecture will be the inspiration of the Bible as an argument for the divine origin of Christianity, keeping before us, in the discussion, the main thought which lies at the foundation of these Lectures —the argument as it exists in the nineteenth century. The point of the inquiry is not what the argument for the inspiration of the Bible, and the consequent proofs of the divine origin of the system, would have been when the canon of the Bible was complete, and it was first submitted to the world, but what it is now, after the volume has been before the world for eighteen hundred years. It has been fairly tried. It may be presumed that all the objections that are ever to be made to its inspiration have been already made. It may be assumed that its teachings are understood, and that we now understand what its influence will be at any time, in any land, or in relation to any class of men, barbarous or civilized, or in its bearing on the morals, the manners, and the laws of men. It may be assumed, perhaps, that science will have nothing more formidable to oppose to its claims to inspiration than it has already alleged, and that no discoveries will be made in the ruins of ancient cities and towns, or in the structure of the earth itself, that will add any new facts to strengthen the argument against its divine origin.

What, then, is the evidence, in the age in which we live, that this book was inspired?

It would not be practicable in a single Lecture, on such a subject, to enter into details, and it is not my purpose to attempt it. This one subject itself might extend beyond the entire limit of this course of Lectures, and still be unexhausted; for the field is ample; the difficulties are great; there are important questions which are not yet settled; and perhaps, as compared with other subjects pertaining to the Bible, there is no more inviting field on which a student of the sacred Scriptures, who would wish to prepare something that might be the great work of his life, could more properly employ his talents than in endeavoring to determine the yet unsettled questions about the inspiration of the Bible. Into the questions, therefore, about the modes of inspiration; whether it extends to the words as well as to the matter; how far the sacred writers availed themselves of their own knowledge and observation, and the knowledge and historical records in existence when they wrote; how far, as inspired men, they are responsible for statements on other subjects than those pertaining to the immediate purpose of inspiration — the ordinary facts of history, or the statements of science; how far they were permitted to employ their own powers, and how this is consistent wth their being inspired; how the apparent discrepancies and contradictions in the book can be reconciled with the idea of inspiration — into these and kindred questions I do not propose largely to enter. I may be permitted, also, to say, that on some of these points there are difficulties which have not yet been met, and which perhaps none of us are prepared to meet.

I shall, therefore, limit my remarks to considerations of a very general nature, designed to show that the Bible can not have been the work of the unaided human powers, but that there are things pertaining to it which show that it must have come from God, or that it was inspired. In a parallel case, we might show that the worlds bear marks of having been made by God, and that any other theory would be incapable of defense, though there may be a thousand difficulties in our minds in respect to that creation, and a thousand things which we are not competent to reconcile and explain.

There are certain characteristics of mind which, however unnatural it may seem at first sight to place them together, appear to lie in the same *line*, or to have a relation to each other which has not yet been explained; where one closely borders on another; where one may be mistaken for another; and where, in describing the operations of the mind, there may be danger of ascribing that to one which properly belongs to another. I mention them in the following order: Genius; Inspiration; Insanity.

I mention them in this connection and this order, not because this order is always found, or because the one naturally develops itself into the other, or because the one is to be explained on the same principles as the other, but because there is a certain *resemblance* in them which would not be likely to be found in other characteristics of the human mind as bearing on the production of a work of art, or in relation to the developments of the highest forms of thought. The Bible is the creation of one of these. The word *inspiration* is often applied to the works of *genius;* among the Greeks, and the ancients generally, the idea of *inspira-*

tion, as at the oracle at Delphi, was closely connected with the ravings of *insanity*.

(1.) *Genius.*—This means "the peculiar structure of mind which is given by nature to an individual, or that disposition or bent of mind which is peculiar to every man, and which qualifies him for a particular employment; a particular natural talent or aptitude for a particular study or course of life—as a *genius* for history, poetry, or painting."—*Webster.* Hence it comes to be applied to superiority of mind, or to uncommon powers of intellect, particularly the power of invention.

This often seems to rise into inspiration, and, at any rate, lies along on the borders of inspiration, using that word now in the largest sense. Our life, if we would mark it in any case, is made up much of suggestions *ab extra*—from without. Those suggestions are numberless, and as varied as they are numberless; they are flitting and transitory; they come from some unseen quarter, and are apparently connected with each other by no laws of association, and by no laws that we can trace with what we have done or thought before. A few of them we retain at our pleasure; the mass we dismiss at once, as we do dreams. Genius consists, perhaps, not so much in the numbers or the nature of those suggestions as in the power or the disposition to retain them and to make a selection from them; to keep and combine those that may be the origin of great inventions, or that may be developed into some new discovery in science—that may lay the foundation of a great tragedy or a great epic. A thousand persons might have seen the spasmodic action produced in the muscles of the leg of a frog when in contact with a composition of zinc and acid, and never have thought of it again; but to Galvani it suggested an idea worth

pursuing.   Thousands of persons had seen an apple fall
from a tree, and had thought no more of it; to Newton,
according to the current tradition, it suggested an inquiry into the cause of its falling, and led to the discovery of the great laws by which the planets are held in
their places and by which the worlds revolve.   Thousands of persons had seen the operation of steam on a
small scale—in lifting the lid of a tea-kettle—and had
dismissed it without thought; to such a mind as that
of Watt it suggested the idea of power, of motion, and
is now changing the industry, the commerce, the civilization, and the religion of the world.

Yet who can tell whence these suggestions come into
our minds?   Who is their author?   By what laws do
they come, and by what laws do they go?   And by
what principles did Homer, and Shakspeare, and Newton retain them, and mould them till their development
had given undying lustre to their memory?

There are those who suppose that the inspiration of
the Bible is no more than this, and that it is to be explained on the same principle; not as derived from suggestions by the Spirit of God, but as suggestions of the
mind itself, the suggestions of genius.   Such persons—
and they are many now—like Theodore Parker, and
like Renan, do not deny the "*inspiration*" of the Bible,
but it is inspiration such as there was in Burns or in
Bacon; in Homer or in Milton; in Dante or in Michael
Angelo.   Shakspeare and Isaiah, Kant and Paul, differ
only in degree.

How closely the idea of genius and inspiration lie on
the same line may be seen from the meaning which the
word *genius* has acquired.   The ancients, in their use
of the word, did not attribute genius to a man's own
mind.   It was the good or evil spirit, or demon, which

was supposed to preside over his destiny in life; to direct his birth and actions; to be his guard and guide; to suggest thoughts to him; to impart to him wisdom. Socrates always referred what he had of wisdom that might be superior to that of other men, not to himself, but to his "*genius*"—the demon that pertained to him, that attended on him, that *inspired* him. The *genius loci* of the ancients was the presiding spirit of a place, the tutelary divinity, hence denoting the pervading spirit of an institution, a city, a society of men. The question before us is whether this will explain all that there was in Isaiah and John.

(2.) Inspiration in the proper sense of the term. Admitting now that there is such a thing, the present object is to distinguish it from genius—how it resembles it, and how it differs from it.   ·

(*a*) As we have seen, it resembles it. It is suggestive. It is *ab extra*. It is from some unseen quarter. It comes into the mind by no laws of association with the past, often apparently by no laws of association with the different *parts* of the suggestion, any more than the suggestions of genius have, or than dreams have. It contains great thoughts—what Lord Bacon calls "the seeds of things"—to be developed either by the study of the prophet himself, who is inspired, studying his own predictions as if they were those of another man, or, in after times, by events that shall occur, by higher revelations, or by the studies of uninspired men. Thus, of the prophets, one himself inspired has said, "Of which salvation the prophets have inquired and searched diligently, searching *what*, or *what manner of time* the spirit of Christ which was in them did signify, when it testified beforehand the sufferings of Christ, and the glory that should follow" (1 Peter, i., 11, 12). They gave themselves to the careful and profound study of their own prophecies, of the *meaning* of the words which had been suggested to them by the Spirit of God.

(*b*) Yet inspiration differs from genius. It is in *advance* of genius; it is *beyond* what lies in the range of genius. We suppose that no development of genius, no mere enlargement of any man's natural powers, however richly endowed, nothing which comes under the name of genius, would come up to what is implied in inspiration. However we may account for the "suggestions" which come into our minds, as I have said, *ab extra*, and especially the "suggestions" which come into the minds of men of genius, and which constitute the distinction between them and other men—suggestions on which the progress of the world in science and in art so much depends—or whether they can be accounted for or not, yet we suppose that the matter of *inspiration*—the "suggestions" to the mind of the prophet—*can be* definitely explained. They are not the suggestions of *genius*, but of the *Spirit of God*, breathing truths into the soul which would never occur to a human mind, however exalted, and securing, by a direct and special agency on the soul, the perfect accuracy of such suggestions. They are *as if* the Spirit of God spoke to men. There is a limit to genius. There is a point beyond which it does not go. It never comes up to inspiration, as mere human *power*, however great and wonderful, never comes up to a miracle. There is a point where that power stops short of a miracle, and that is *within* the power necessary to raise the dead; there is a point where genius stops short, and that is *within* the limit of inspiration. And yet it is a fair question, Why may not the genius which accomplished what Shakspeare accomplished embrace what Isaiah did as well as what Shakspeare did?

(3.) It may have seemed strange, perhaps, that I have suggested the word *insanity* as in any way connected with inspiration; as having any resemblance to that or to genius, or as lying in any respect in the same line; as if genius and insanity were in any way connected; as if men of genius were likely to be insane, as if all the insane were remarkable for genius; or as if the prophets uttered their predictions under the ravings of insanity.

It would take longer than the time will now admit of, without exhausting the whole time allotted to this Lecture, fully to explain and justify even the *introduction* of such a thought to your minds, or to show how they have been in any way connected or associated in the minds of men.

Perhaps even now the highest and best delineations of insanity have been drawn, not by Pritchard and others who have particularly studied and observed it, but by one who may almost never have seen an insane person, and who had not himself studied the subject, but by a man endowed, undoubtedly, with the highest genius that the world has known—as drawn in the character of Lear, Hamlet, Jaques, and in the tender sympathy, the knowledge of the disease, and of the proper mode of treatment of the disease expressed in the characters of Ophelia and Cordelia.[*]

The Savior himself was regarded by his kindred as insane: "And when his friends heard of it, they went out to lay hold on him, for they said, *He is beside himself*"—ἐξέστη (Mark, iii., 21). "Many of them said, He hath a devil, and is *mad*"—μαίνεται (John, x., 20).

---

[*] See "Shakspeare's Delineations of Insanity, Imbecility, and Suicide," by *A. O. Kellogg*, M.D., p. 1-114.

Paul was regarded as insane. "Festus said, with a
loud voice, Paul, thou art beside thyself—μαίνῃ—much
learning doth make thee mad;" more literally, "much
learning has *turned thee to insanity*"—εἰς μανίαν περι-
τρέπει (Acts, xxvi., 24). "Whether," says Paul, "we be
beside ourselves"—ἐξέστημεν—as we may seem to many
to be, *to be insane*—"it is to God"—in the cause of
God; that is, what we say as inspired men may seem
to men to be the mere ravings of insanity (2 Cor.,
v., 13).

It is well known to all that among the heathen the
ideas of inspiration and insanity were closely connected.
The opinion which was held by them on the subject is
beautifully stated by Plato: "While the mind sheds its
light around us, pouring into our souls a meridian splendor, we, being in possession of ourselves, are not under
a supernatural influence; but after the sun goes down,
as might be expected, an *ecstasy*, a divine influence, and
a *frenzy* falls upon us; for when the divine light shines,
the human goes down; but when the former goes down,
the latter rises and comes forth. This," says he, "is
what ordinarily happens in prophecy. Our own mind
retires on the advent of the divine spirit, but after the
latter has departed the former again returns" (quoted
in Bib. Repos., vol. ii., p. 163). Here Plato calls it "*an
ecstasy*," "*a frenzy*," bordering close, at least, on insanity.

In the common ideas respecting the Pythian oracle,
the conception of insanity, or raving madness, becomes
more distinct. Thus Lucan says: "She madly raves
through the cavern, impelled by another's mind, with
the fillets of the god and the garland of Phœbus shaken
from her erected hair; she whirls around the void
space of the temple, turning her face in every direc-

tion; she scatters the tripods which come in her way, and is agitated with violent commotion, because she is under thy angry influence, O Apollo."*

Virgil has given a similar description of a demoniacal possession of this kind :

"I feel the god, the rushing god! she cries—
While thus she spoke enlarged her features grew ;
Her color changed, her locks disheveled flew.
The heavenly tumult reigns in every part,
Pants in her breast, and swells her rising heart.
Still spreading to the sight the priestess glowed,
And heaved impatient of the incumbent god ;
Then to her inmost soul by Phœbus fired,
In more than human sounds she spoke inspired."†

It has been supposed by some that the true prophets were under an influence of this kind; that they were divested of intelligent consciousness, so that they were ignorant of what they uttered, and that the Spirit of Inspiration made use of them only as *organs*, or as unconscious agents to utter his truth. It is not my purpose to go into this inquiry; but I suppose, in common with the great mass of those who believe in the Bible, that, though they did not comprehend the *full* meaning of what they uttered (1 Peter, i., 10–12), yet that they

*   Bacchatur demens aliena per antrum
       Colla ferens, vittasque Dei, Phœbeaque serta
       Ercatis discussa comis, per inania templi
       Ancipiti cervice rotat, Spargitque vaganti
       Obstantes tripodes, magnoque exæstuat igne
       Iratum te, Phœbe, ferens.—Pharsalia, v.

†   Ait: Deus, ecce, Deus! cui talia fanti—
       Ante fores, subitò non vultus, non color unus,
       Nec comptæ mansere comæ ; sed pectus anhelum,
       Et rabie fera corda tument ; majorque videri
       Nec mortale sonans ; afflata est numine quando
       Jam propriore Dei.—Æn., vi., 46 seq.

had an intelligent understanding of what they saw or
spoke; that the prophet had *control* over his own mind
(1 Cor., xiv., 32); that he could speak or not, as he
pleased; and that in his inspired utterances he acted, as
at other times, as a conscious, voluntary, and intelligent
agent.   The true idea, probably, has been expressed by
Lowth: " Inspiration may be regarded, not as suppressing or extinguishing for a time the faculties of the human mind, but of purifying, and strengthening, and elevating them above what they would otherwise reach."
The reference which I have made to *insanity* is not at
all because it is believed that that was the condition of
the minds of the prophets, but as illustrating the fact
that it has been supposed that these states of mind lie
much in the same direction, or have points of resemblance not unworthy to be noticed.   The bearing of the
remarks on the subject before us is that the Bible, as
a composition, is to be traced as a whole, and in all its
parts, to *one* of these three things.   The question between the friends of the Bible and other men is to
which of these it is to be attributed.

It will be admitted by all that the Bible is not a
work of *ordinary* talent—of *mediocre* human powers.
If it is a production of mere genius, it is genius of the
highest order.   Every thing about it shows this: its
hold on mankind; its power to survive attacks; its perpetuated existence; its undiminished influence in the advances of civilization and the arts, and in the changes
of human opinion; its poetry; its eloquence; its unity
of purpose; its power of creating interest in the minds
of all classes of men—the most humble as well as the
most exalted, *and* the most exalted as well as the most
humble; the poor man, the rich man; the slave and
slave's master; the man of science, the man of refined

taste, and the newly-converted savage; the delicate female and the hardy warrior. It is a book that can not be destroyed; a book that does not become old, and that is not hidden away in the lumber of old libraries. It keeps its place among living men in ages when new books abound; it has its place, in regard to a living power, not with Strabo, and Galen, and Mela, and Abelard, and Duns Scotus, but with Milton, and Shakspeare, and Macaulay, and Burke—books that are "thumbed" and read; it is a book of influence, and has more influence on mankind now than Homer, and Plato, and the Koran, and Shakspeare—than Kant, and Locke, and Bacon altogether. *Is* it a work of mere genius?

I said that there are great questions about inspiration which are yet unsettled. I repeat, on account of its importance, and with the hope of stirring up some young man of this Seminary to the task, the remark that I have already made, that, in my judgment, there is no one department of Christian literature to which a young man could better devote himself, with the hope of producing something which the "world would not willingly let die," than the solution of those questions. They are beyond my range now—beyond my learning, my ability, and I shall not attempt to enter on them. What is inspiration at all? What is plenary inspiration? Is it suggestion, or superintendence, or control, or all combined? In inspiration, how far were the faculties of the men themselves employed? Were they kept from error on all subjects? In what sense was what they wrote on common matters inspired? To what extent in the Book is the Spirit of God "responsible" for the statements made? And how can the dates, and the genealogies, and the apparent inconsistencies and contradictions be reconciled with the proper idea of inspiration? These are questions in many of their bearings yet to be solved, and happy will be the man who shall be raised up to solve them.

Perhaps, at this stage of the argument, it might be said that the question whether the Bible *is* an inspired book can not be settled till these questions are determined, for they enter into the very essence of the question. It may seem to be so, and it might be difficult to show that it is *not* so. And yet it is not necessarily so. A thousand questions may be asked on any subject without affecting the main question. There may be questions asked about the Principia of Newton, and the correctness of his theories about light and colors, and "fits of easy transmission," and radiations of heat, which do not affect the question about the work as the work of a man in intellect at the very head of the race; there are many questions about the Iliad, yet unsettled, which do not affect the question whether the whole work is the production of one man; whether such a man as Homer ever lived; and whether the poem is made up of independent "rhapsodies" by different authors. The work is a whole by itself, and is a work of transcendent genius, however these questions may be settled.

May we not take some such view of the Bible, and find in that the evidence that it is *inspired* without being able as yet to solve all difficulties, as we find in other books, in a similar manner, the evidences of genius?

In regard to the argument now to be submitted to you, I would be willing to concede that no single one of the points which I shall suggest would of itself constitute a proof of such inspiration. The impression which I would hope to make would be derived from all of them combined. The point which I would desire

to leave for solution when I am through with the argument would be, *Whether these things could exist if the
Bible were not an inspired book?* I shall ask you to
remember that that which may not seem to be strong
in itself may be strong in its position. The braces
which help to sustain a lofty pile of architecture in a
cathedral, or the arch of a bridge, may be feeble in
themselves, yet these, combined and interlaced among
each other, may give strength that shall hold the lofty
structure or the massive bridge against the winds and
the currents forever.

I. The first remark which I make is, that this claim,
whatever it is, relates to a *class* of men, extending
through a long series of years, constituting a *unity* in
their productions, and making their productions properly *one book.* Whatever may be said of the productions of *uninspired genius, this* can not be said of them,
and this claim could not be set up for them. There is
no sense in which the Iliad, and the Paradise Lost, and
the histories of Herodotus and Gibbon, and the orations
of Demosthenes and Burke, constitute *one book.*

The Bible is *one book ;* not accidentally, or by being
bound together like a pile of old pamphlets which the
lover of pamphlets accumulates and binds up in one
volume, but by an *organic* unity ; a unity of spirit, design, harmony, purpose ; a unity in the sense of being
separate from all other books; a unity as distinct as if
it were the production of one man; a unity as complete
as the Iliad or the Paradise Lost—having a plan; having a beginning, a middle, and an end—a beginning, a
middle, and an end more complete, extending through
more years, and embracing a greater variety of characters and events than any other volume in the world—
its beginning the beginning of creation; its middle the

Incarnation and the Atonement; its end the consumma-
tion of the world's affairs.

The volume is made up, indeed, of a large number of
pamphlets, written by different men, in different languages, and at different periods. The writers were of
very different rank and character, from the magnificent
Oriental prince to the shepherd-boy and the fisherman
—from the man trained in the best schools of the age,
like Paul, to the man who could say of himself, "I was
no prophet, neither was I a prophet's son; but I was
an herdman, and a gatherer of sycamore fruit; and the
Lord took me as I followed the flock, and the Lord said
unto me, Go, prophesy unto my people Israel" (Amos,
vii., 14, 15). Some of them, indeed, had all the learning
of their own country, and not a little of that in foreign
lands, and some had none; some had traveled, but most
of them had not; some had conversed with sages of
other countries, but most of them had never seen a
philosopher or a sage.

What they wrote constituted substantially all the literature of the nation—its poetry; its learning; its history; its eloquence; its laws. At the time of the completion of the volume it was all that they had. If there
had been other books in existence, as the books of " Nathan the Prophet," and the "Prophecy of Ahijah the
Shilonite," and "the Visions of Iddo the Seer" (2 Chron.,
ix., 29), and "Shemaiah the Prophet" (2 Chron., xii., 15),
they had been absorbed into the volume, or had been
allowed to "drop out," as not pertaining to the design
of the one book that was to constitute the literature of
the nation. If, simultaneously with this, or in the interval when one part of the volume—the Old Testament—was completed, and the other part—the New—
was commenced, there was any thing that was, from

any cause, deemed worthy of preservation, it was carefully separated from the sacred books in the "Apocry-
pha;" if contemporaneously with the New Testament,
or subsequently, any other literature existed, as the
writings of Philo and Josephus, or the Talmud, this also
was carefully separated from, and never confounded
with, the one volume that constituted the peculiar literature of the nation.

There is, there has been no other nation where such
an organic literature has sprung up, the work of many
authors, extending through many years, and yet constituting one volume. The religion of China is in a
book written by one man—Confucius; the Koran is
the production of one man; for any thing that appears,
the Zendavesta had a similar origin. The books of India, indeed—the Vedas and the Shasters—have, in this
respect, some resemblance to the Bible, but, so far as
appears, they were the productions of a few authors,
and were composed in a brief period.

You can not *bind up* the literature of any other people, making one organic volume, as the Bible is bound
up. You can not thus bind up Grecian literature in
one volume. You have Homer, *and* Hesiod, *and* Herodotus, *and* Thucydides, *and* Aristotle, *and* Plato, *and*
Sophocles, *and* Æschylus, but they would not, and could
not make one volume, having a beginning, a middle,
and an end. There is no reason why it should *begin*
thus; why it should *advance* thus; and there is no
catastrophe at its close. It is not *one* book. They are
many books. There *is* no unity. They are not the
production of one *class* of men, except as the Greeks
in general were distinguished from the rest of mankind.

. In this view, too, the length of *time* is to be noticed
during which the composition was going on. The Bi-

L

ble is not the production of one age, so that it could be considered, as certain groups of writings may be, as the development of that age; it is the production of many ages, and the composition was quietly going on at the same time in which the most important changes and revolutions were occurring in the earth. During the time of its composition kingdoms rose and fell; great conquerors founded empires, acquired immortality, and they and their kingdoms passed away; new discoveries were made in science and in art; vast revolutions occurred in human affairs. Unaffected by these changes, the composition of the Bible was quietly going on, and the men engaged in the work calmly performed their task, as a man would in a cave, sheltered by rocks, while storms and tempests howled around him. For a period of sixteen hundred years from the composition of the first book—the book of Job—to the book of Revelation, that work was calmly advancing—the writers now appearing in groups, and the work now interrupted by intervals of hundreds of years, till the last declaration was uttered, "Surely I come quickly; amen. Even so, come, Lord Jesus;" winding up the volume and the work. The idea of unity is one that runs through all that period. The plan is slowly developed. The plan is finally consummated by one—John in Patmos— as unlike as can well be conceived in language, in attainments, in style, and manner, the man who at least sixteen hundred years before put pen to the whole work in the language, "There was a man in the land of Uz whose name was Job;" or, if Genesis was the first book written, as it is the first in the Bible now, in the language, "In the beginning God created the heaven and the earth." Meantime they never copied from one another. They never seem to have been conscious that there was a *plan* slowly developing itself. They never mutilated or shaped facts so as to fit in to such a plan; they never modified the statement of events so that they would *seem* to be a fulfillment of that plan. Moses, and David, and Isaiah, and Paul, and John are as independent of each other as Hesiod, and Homer, and Plato. The sacred writers were not a corporation, a company, a society, to *write up* a certain system, nor were there revisers of their writings so to shape and alter them as to secure unanimity and unity. The "Dunciad" was written by concert; the "Spectator" was written by concert; Pope's Homer was translated by different authors under his direction, and united by him in one; the German critics sometimes tell us that the Iliad itself was not written by *one* Homer, but by many; the dramas of Beaumont and Fletcher are always in one volume—"Beaumont *and* Fletcher"—apparently joint productions; but in the composition of the Bible each man pursued his own plan, for Moses, and Isaiah, and Paul were perfectly independent authors.

This is the more remarkable, because a great change occurred in passing from the Old Testament to the New. The old system, with all the peculiar laws and institutions pertaining to it, was to give way, and a new system to be introduced—Christianity *living* to be superinduced upon Judaism *dying*. The difficulty was how, in a system so unlike, and where one was to expire and the other to rise into life, the one could be made to appear to run into the other. Is Christianity a development of Judaism? Would men under their own guidance, and without some higher influence, have *developed* the old system—the Jewish system—the system of the prophets—into Christianity? Not at all. It would have been, under such a guidance, Judaism still; Judaism

refined and expanded, Judaism adapted to the whole
world, but Judaism still. And yet the New Testament
is a development—a filling up—a *completion* of the system of the Old, and the entire Book—the Bible—is *one*.
It is susceptible of easy proof that one part is the completion or complement of the other, as the two parts of
a tally, or as "complementary" colors; not as the Jews
would have done it, but as it was intended it should be.
There is a scheme commenced. There is an anticipation. There is a progress. There is a completion in
the Messiah. There is the unfolding of a plan running
in its statements through many centuries; one writer
in one age stating one thing, and another in another,
as if in one age one artist should have fashioned an arm,
and another a leg; one a hand, and another a foot; one
the nose, another the lips, another the chin; one the
form and size of the head, and another the body; and
all at last should have been put together in the form of
Minerva or Apollo.

The completion of the plan in the New Testament is
different from what a Jew would have made, but it *is*
a completion. He would have made the Messiah of the
New Testament a prince, a conqueror, a king; he would
not have made him a poor man, a despised man, a sufferer; the true completion was that he was indeed a
prince, a king, a conqueror, but that he was at the same
time, and eminently, poor, despised, and a sufferer. But
this accords, in fact, after all, with the Old Testament,
for he was to spring from the decayed family of Jesse and
David; he was to be despised and rejected of men; he
was to be a man of sorrows and acquainted with grief;
his grave was to be appointed with the wicked, but with
the rich man was he to be in his death, and yet he was
to be a conqueror and a king, with a dominion wider

than Cæsar ever won, and an empire more enduring than any of the dynasties of kings.

And if this is true, then there is this presumption in the case, that it was under the guidance of One Mind, that it is the product of one plan, that it is not the work of many minds acting independently or in concert, but that there was one presiding Intellect that guided all these writers, and adjusted all these parts one to another, as much as there must have been if there had been separate laborers working independently of each other, and through many centuries, in forming the different parts of the Venus de Medici or the Apollo Belvidere.

II. The second point will relate to a peculiarity in *books* as such, and in respect to which what has occurred to the Bible considered *as* a book can be best explained on the supposition that it is an inspired volume.

Books fall away in the progress of society; they drop out of notice; they accomplish their purpose; they are not missed. The peculiarity of the Bible on which I wish to remark, and from which I shall draw this part of my argument, is, that the Bible is *not* a book of this class. It does not drop out of notice; it has not accomplished its purpose; it does not fall away in the progress of events, it would be missed; it will not and could not be spared.

There are three classes of books of the kind that I now refer to.

There are, first, those which, though they are founded on truth, yet have no such merit as to make the world anxious to retain them. They have a local bearing and a local reputation, but have no claim on the general attention of mankind, and no merit that will convey them down from age to age. The old paths are strewed with these remains of literature, and advancing generations have no interest in gathering them up and preserving them; and any man that *makes* a book must lay to his soul—no very "flattering unction"—the idea that *probably* this will be the fate of the book that *he* makes. Commonplace books, poetry, novels, travels, biographies, histories, works of science, works on art, are thus dropped out of view and perish, or are preserved in the alcoves of a great library, or are among the rarities which antiquarians gather. The *prima facie* evidence in regard to an old book is that it is worthless, *because* it is rare; for if it had been valuable it would have been reprinted, and would *not* have been rare.

There are, secondly, those which have been *superseded* by better books on the same subject. Of these the number is already vastly large, and is constantly accumulating. Multitudes of books once useful have dropped away from the memory of mankind to be recovered no more—books that are gone with the volumes of Nathan the Prophet and Iddo the Seer (2 Chron., ix., 29)—books that have absolutely perished, while those that remain of that class go largely to swell the number of volumes on the shelves of our great libraries—books useful as illustrating the history of science and art, and the development of human affairs—books useful to the antiquarian, but books no longer useful as representing the real state of human knowledge. Science is enlarged. What was formerly regarded as science is no longer such; and the books of Galen, Hippocrates, Mela, Roger Bacon, occupy substantially the same place in science which the works of Abelard and Duns Scotus —may I not add Turretin—do in theology. The chemistry of the Middle Ages, the chemistry of Bagdad, was a different thing from the chemistry of Lavoisier, of

Priestley, of Black, and of Sir Humphry Davy; and the books even of *these* men are also vanishing fast, and are taking their places with those that are mainly interesting to the antiquarian alone.

There are, thirdly, books that are false in science, in philosophy, in the facts affirmed, that pass away, of course, when the truth is discovered. All the works of Ptolemy, and all the books founded on the Ptolemaic system of the heavens, ingenious, labored, and profound as they were, passed away, of course, when the Copernican theory was established; and those books now, like thousands of others, are of use only as marking the history of science, or as illustrating the powers of the human mind, or as showing, by contrast, the wonderful wisdom of the Creator in the actual structure of the universe and the beauty of the Copernican system.

The question now is, Whether the Bible is a book that belongs to either of these classes; a book to pass away with advancing knowledge, and in the progress of ages; a book to be dropped; a book that is to lie hidden in the alcoves of great libraries; a book that is to be of interest and value only to the antiquarian. If it is not so, then *why* is not so?

The Bible is *not* a book to be dropped and forgotten. Whatever may be said of it, it is *not* to occupy the same place as those books which, from any cause, the world is "willing to let die." It has held its place in the world longer than any other book or books, unless it be true that the writings of Confucius go back to as remote a period as the composition of the book of Job. It has passed through innumerable revolutions in governments, in opinions, in philosophy, in manners, customs, and laws. It has made its way in the world under all forms of government—monarchical, aristocratic, republican, democratic. It has held on its steady course when Aristotle was in the ascendant and controlled the mind of Europe, and when he was dethroned, and Plato rose in the ascendant. It has held its way in the great change from the Ptolemaic to the Copernican systems of astronomy, and in all the revolutions which have been made in science and the arts. Many of those arts and much of that science it has modified; many of the laws which rule among the nations, and no small part of the customs of social life among the most refined people, it has originated or shaped; it has seen systems of government and systems of religion pass away, and it still lives. The Bible, in the parts then composed, was among the books that influenced human affairs when Nineveh stood where its buried ruins now are; when Babylon was great and magnificent, where now the wild beasts of the desert lie down, and satyrs dance, and owls dwell, and dragons cry (Isa., xiii., 22); when Tyre was the mistress of the seas, now a place where the fisherman dries his nets; long before Hesiod and Homer sang; when uncivilized and savage men wandered over the Seven Hills on the Tiber, and when not a hut stood on the banks of the Thames.

·   The Bible has survived all attacks, and they have not been few or unskillful; *and it has now a hold on the world which it never had before,* and the world would now more unwillingly than ever before "let it die." It is translated into more languages than any other book; it has been transcribed more frequently, and with more care, than any other book; it is more frequently printed than any other book; it is more embellished with the highest ornaments of art than any other book; it lies on more tables in the dwellings of the intelligent and the refined than any other book. More cultivated minds have been employed in defending and illustrating it than any other book; more learning has been expended on it than on any other book; more keen and sagacious criticism has been employed on it than perhaps on all other books put together. More such minds are engaged in defending it now than ever were before. More men are employed in translating it, and more presses are at work in printing it than ever before. It is doing more to influence the world than it has done in any former age. It is working its way among the nations of the earth; changing customs and laws; originating institutions of learning and benevolence; modifying punishments; influencing the treatment of prisoners; breaking off the shackles of slavery; and elevating the character and position of woman, as it has never done before. It is recognized as authority in more colleges and schools than it has ever been before; and if there are more attacks made on it from scientific sources, it is also true that more defenders from the same source arise to show that it is not inconsistent with the best deductions of science. The simplest and most philosophical way of explaining all this is, that the book had a higher origin than man.

III. My third remark will relate to the place which the Bible has in history, and the point of the remark will be, that the Bible contains records and statements on historical subjects which can be best explained also on the supposition that it is an inspired book.

(1.) The first observation here is, that it is the only history of the world that traces human affairs up to their origin. Following back any other history, and endeavoring to ascertain the origin of things in the early transactions in our world, we soon come to the region of fable, of legend, of myth, of night; we reach a point where all anterior in the history is manifestly the work of the imagination or the invention of national pride. In Egypt, in India, in China, in the African tribes, in Mexico and Peru, and to a great extent in Greece, we soon come into the region of night; and even of Rome, who, since the work of Niebuhr, will affirm, notwithstanding the records of Livy, that we have any exact knowledge of what occurred in its early history? Begin, in your investigation of past events, where profane history begins, and you are plunged into the midst of a state of affairs of whose origin you know nothing, and where the mind wanders in perfect night and can find no rest. Kingdoms are seen, but no one can tell when or how they were founded; cities appear whose origin no one knows; heroes are playing their part in the great and mysterious drama, but no one knows whence they came or what are their designs; races of beings are seen whose origin is unknown, and the past periods of whose existence upon the earth no one can determine—races formed no one can tell for what purpose or by what hand. Vast multitudes of beings are suffering and dying for causes which no one can explain; one generation in its own journey to the grave treads over the monuments of extinct generations, and with the memorials of fearful changes and convulsions in the past all around it of which no one can give an account. Begin your knowledge of the past at the remotest period to which profane history would conduct you, and you are in the midst of chaos, and you can not advance a single step without plunging into deeper night—a night strikingly resembling that described in the oldest book in the Bible itself, and the oldest book in the world, as the abode of the dead: "The land of darkness and the shadow of death; a land of darkness as darkness itself;

and of the shadow of death without any order, and where the light is as darkness" (Job, x., 21, 22).

(2.) The Bible is the only book that explains the origin of things—the creation of the earth and the heavens—the creation of man, and the creation of the vegetables and animals that people the globe. True science does not pretend to explain those things; for, whatever false science may attempt, true science *pauses* before it reaches the point of the creation of *matter* or the origin of *life*. It *finds* matter, and it *finds* life, at the beginning of all its own investigations; nor do the labors of the chemist and of the physiologist go *behind* those facts as already existing to tell *how* they came into being. The Bible *does*.

(3.) The Bible, so far as secular *history* becomes intelligible, and at the point where it becomes intelligible, accords with and explains the existing state of things. The tenth chapter of Genesis, almost entirely a dry list of names—apparently as dry and unmeaning as the muster-roll of an army, or as Homer's list of heroes and ships in the first book of the Iliad—contains, in fact, the only clear and intelligible account of the peopling of our globe, and the origin of the nations that now dwell upon the earth. It is a document which could not have been fabricated any more than one beforehand could fabricate the names of the soldiers in an army, and yet it is the only document which we possess that tells how the world was divided and settled. The nations that dwell in Europe, in Asia, and in Africa can, for the most part, be distinctly traced up in their origin to the men whose names occur there; and without this dry document, all accounts of the peopling of the globe would be darkness and chaos.

(4.) The Bible explains facts that exist which would be otherwise inexplicable.

In a state of feeling now extensively prevalent among scientific men, there are many who would shrink from avowing their belief in the first four chapters of Genesis, and there are many who would desire to turn those chapters into myth and fable, as containing statements which no scientific man would literally receive. In a course of lectures, or even in preaching, it might seem to the view of many such men to argue more of recklessness than of prudence to select those chapters as the subject of illustration, and there are not a few having high claims to eminence in science who would turn away from the statements in those chapters as belonging wholly to myths and legends.

Yet *in* those chapters are contained all that we *know*, if we know any thing in regard to the origin of the real facts that exist in our world. We, who hold to the inspiration of the Bible, believe that the record in those chapters will explain the origin of all that now exists on earth; we are certain that if that explanation fails, we shall look in vain elsewhere for any explanation—to history; to the reasonings of philosophers; to the geologist; to the antiquarian; to the poets.

(*a*) Those chapters explain the origin of things—the creation of the heavens and the earth. Science does not explain the *creation* of the world—the origin of the universe. It has no facts on that subject with which to deal; its work commences when the work of creation is done; when matter already has a being, and when the laws of matter are already established. It explains the laws by which the elements of matter combine or are moved, not how they were made; it explains the proportion of the sixty or more substances of which our world is composed; the laws of the chemical elements; the laws of galvanism, of light, of heat, of electricity, of *life*—not how they were *made*.

(*b*) The Bible explains the *order* in which things were made on the earth. Till the discoveries in the recent science of geology, the world has been in the dark in regard to that order, and the naked statement in the first chapter of Genesis, appealing, up to that period—that is, for nearly six thousand years—to the mere *faith* of mankind, has been all that the world has had to rely on. Two things are remarkable in regard to that statement in the first chapter of Genesis, with all that there is *in* the chapter still unexplained and mysterious: one is, that the *order* of the creation as there stated corresponds with singular accuracy with the order as disclosed by geology; the other is, that geology now affirms, from the testimony of the earth itself, that there were successive *creations*, as is affirmed in Genesis; in other words, that one class of animals has not been *developed* from a previous order of beings. The Bible affirms thus; and if there is any one thing now clear in the developments of geology, it is, that one race was *swept off* to make way for another; and that one succeeded another in a certain order, and that *order* is the one found in the Bible; that man was the last in the series of the creations; and that there has been, in fact, no work of *creation*—no new matter formed—no new races of animals or vegetables brought upon the earth since man appeared. "Thus," says Moses, "the heavens and the earth were *finished*, and all the host of them" (Gen., ii., 1). How did Moses, or whoever was the author of the statement in Genesis, *know this?* What are the probabilities that an ancient writer uninspired, undertaking to give an account of the creation of the world, would hit on that order? Where else has it been done; where has it been *hinted at ?*

(*c*) The Bible affirms and explains the fact to which

all true science is tending—the unity of the race. That fact is stated and affirmed; that fact is the basis of the doctrine of universal depravity as stated in the Bible; that fact is the foundation of all its statements about the work of redemption; that fact is the foundation of all that there is in the Bible in regard to the rights of man.

But that fact of the unity of the race has been by no means apparent to men, and is a doctrine the statement of which in the Bible is most easily explained by the idea of inspiration, even if it can be explained in any other way. It is morally certain now that men will *come up* to that doctrine in their own investigations; but it is by no means a doctrine so obvious that it would be laid at the foundation of a system as a matter of course, or a doctrine in reference to which there are no scientific difficulties to be removed. The varieties of language; the varieties of complexion; the forms of the skull, and the facial angle, and many other things in the formation and anatomy of the human frame, familiar to those who have devoted their attention to this subject; the varieties in the four great divisions of the race—the Mongolian, the Caucasian, the Ethiopian, the American—all show how *daring* and *bold*, so to speak, was the doctrine laid at the very foundation of the whole book, that the races of men are all descended from one pair; that "God has made of one blood all the nations of men, to dwell on all the face of the earth" (Acts, xvii., 26); and that "the whole earth was of one language and of one speech" (Gen., xi., 1). Yet the tendency of science now is to demonstrate the unity of the human race; its tendency also is to demonstrate the original oneness of language. All the languages of the earth have been traced with very great clearness now to *three* sources, with the highest probability that they will yet be traced back to one; and it has not yet been demonstrated that the varieties of the human race in complexion and in anatomical structure are *not* susceptible of explanation on the supposition that the race was originally one.

Man, in the mean time, in the Bible, is kept wholly distinct from all the inferior creation. A line as marked as any line can be runs through the Bible between man and all the inferior races. There is no intimation that one has been developed from the other, or that the one is to be treated as the other. Man alone is a moral agent; is subject to law; is responsible. Man is a sinner; is redeemed; is immortal. Man is made in the image of God. He has a soul. He is a wandering child of God, to be governed by moral law; to be restrained by motives; to be guided by truth; to be redeemed by the blood of the atonement; to live forever with God. He is not derived or developed from the ourang-outang or the monkey; he is, in the Bible, a new *creation*, as geology now affirms him to have been.

Whence came these views and thoughts into the minds of the sacred writers? How, on subjects so difficult, and on which there was to be such variety in the opinions of men before these truths were reached by the slow process of science, did they at once anticipate all that would be established on the subject in the far-distant ages, and state *at the outset* what man *would* be led to believe *at the last ?* The simplest explanation of this is, that that Eternal Spirit that sees and knows all truth guided them *above* the exercise of their own powers to the statement of those truths to which the world would at last come, but which would be reached by men in their own investigations only after ages had passed away.

The time will not allow me to pursue this train of thought farther, or to apply it to other subjects that lie equally within its range. A farther application of the thought would relate to such subjects as the fall of man, and the fact of universal depravity; to the place which man occupies among the creatures of God here below; to the subject of death — especially death in man; to the origin of the languages of the earth, and to the dispersion of the nations. The question in regard to all these points would be whether any men would have been *likely* to have made the statements in the Bible unless they were inspired.

IV. The fourth point to which I shall advert in illustration of the subject of inspiration will pertain to the *truths* communicated in the Bible. The argument in the case will be, that those truths lie *beyond* the range of the unaided human powers.

This remark might be illustrated on a wide scale in reference to the powers of the human mind as existing any where, and, in the highest sense of the proposition, it would be that those truths are beyond the highest human intellects, or the power of such intellects to originate them, however those powers may be cultivated— beyond the reach and range of philosophy in its purest and most exalted forms. It might be questionable with some whether that could be demonstrated, but it is not necessary to consider that particular point in illustrating the proposition now before us. The real inquiry is whether those truths were beyond the natural powers of the men *actually employed* in composing the Bible. It *may be*, indeed, that the natural powers of those men were not inferior to the highest forms of intellect known elsewhere in philosophy and science; it may be that the intellects of Moses, and Isaiah, and David, and Paul were by nature equal to the great lawgivers, poets, reasoners, orators, philosophers of the world, and that, in themselves, they deserve a place by the side of Numa, and Lycurgus, and Demosthenes, and Plato, and Burke; but still the real question now is whether they, whatever were their native endowments, were competent, without aid from on high, to disclose the truths actually found in the Bible. We are to remember, too, that whatever were the native endowments of Moses, and Isaiah, and David, and Paul, they were not the *only* men employed in writing the Bible. The Bible is not *their* work alone. They are not its authors as a whole. We are to bear in mind who they were associated with, and then to inquire whether the peasants, and shepherds, and fishermen that, in fact, wrote a large part of the Bible, were competent to be associated with them in the composition of the Bible *as a whole*—whether a common stone-mason could be associated with Phidias in the design of the Minerva, or common bricklayers with Michael Angelo in the structure of St. Peter's, and in the mosaics that adorn it.

(1.) Who, then, were the men that actually wrote the Bible?

The Bible came from a land undistinguished for literature; a land not rich in classical associations; a land not distinguished for pushing its discoveries into the region of science. Chaldea had its observatory, and the dwellers there early looked out on the stars and gave them names; Egypt had its temples where the truths of science, as well as the precepts of religion, were committed to the sacred priesthood; Greece had academic groves; but Judea had neither. To such things the attention of the nation was never turned. We have *all* their literature; all their science; all their knowledge of art—and all this is in the Bible. Among the ancients they were regarded as a narrow-minded, a bigoted, a superstitious people. They did not travel abroad as Greek philosophers did, to converse with sages in other lands, nor did they ever seem anxious to obtain *any* knowledge except that which was originated in their own land. Pythagoras and Plato went abroad to converse with the wise of other lands; Herodotus to learn the facts of history; Solon and Lycurgus left their country to observe the working of the laws in other countries, and to give sanction to their own; but Moses left the court of Pharaoh and went into a desert; Isaiah, Daniel, and David never traveled to gain knowledge, and though Paul traveled much and far, it was never to *gain* knowledge, but to *impart* it to mankind. The idea is, that in the various departments of literature they could not come into competition with the classic writers of antiquity; that they made no pretensions to philosophy; that they were undistinguished in what the world regards as learning and eloquence; and, especially, that they had almost no knowledge of science as understood in the present age. They made no pretensions to what now constitutes the science of astronomy, chemistry, anatomy, mechanics; and, as compared with the philosophers of Greece, and the literary and scientific men of Germany, France, England, and our own country, the ancient Jew could have no claim to eminence, nor, in relation to these things, has he transmitted any thing that the world thinks worth preserving. It may add to the force of this consideration to remember that all the eminence of any kind which they had in ancient times ceased with the sacred writers, and that with the exception of Josephus and Philo, after the destruction of their Temple, they were of all pretended

literary people the most puerile and trifling. They
wrote no poetry worth preserving or reading; they
produced no orators or historians of any distinction;
they pushed forward no discoveries in science, and their
writings, as produced in the Talmud, are the most distinguished of all compositions for frivolous things and
for childish conceits. The writers of the Bible were
mostly shepherds, peasants, fishermen, with no other
and no better training than are now found in men of
that rank in life.

As an illustration of this point, I may refer particularly to the apostle John. He was a fisherman on the
Lake of Tiberias when Jesus first saw him, and called
him to the work of an apostle. We have his Gospel,
and we have his book of "Revelation," and, bearing in
remembrance that he was *a fisherman*, we are to ask
what would *fishermen* taken from the banks of the Del-
aware, from Marblehead and Gloucester, or from the
Banks of Newfoundland, be likely to produce if called
to compose a book on the subject of John's Gospel, or
the Book of Revelation? Suppose he were called to
delineate a perfect character; to represent an incarnate
God—living, acting, and speaking with man, and as a
man; to compose or record from memory discourses of
the profoundest character respecting God; to describe
future scenes, in the world's great changes, in pictures
and symbols, what would be likely to be the result of
such an effort? In illustrating this point, in language
better than I can use, I may be permitted here to introduce an extract from a discourse by Dr. Dwight: "The
apostle John," says he, "was born in an age when the
philosophy of his country was a mere mass of quib-
bling, its religion a compound of pride and bigotry, and
its worship a ceremonious parade. His lineage, his cir-

cumstances, his education, and his employment were those of a fisherman. On what natural principle can it be accounted for that, like the sun breaking out of an evening cloud, this plain man, in these circumstances, should, at an advanced age, burst upon mankind with a flood of effulgence and glory? Whence did it arise that, in purity of precept, discernment of truth, and an acquaintance with the moral character of man, and the attributes of his Maker, this peasant leaves Socrates, Plato, and Cicero out of sight and out of remembrance? Do you question the truth of this representation? The proof is at hand and complete. There is not a child of fifteen in this house who, if possessed of the common education of this land, would not disdain to worship *their* gods or to embrace *their* religion. But Bacon and Boyle; Butler and Berkeley; Newton and Locke; Addison and Johnson; Jones and Horseley, have submissively embraced the religion of St. John, and worshiped the God whose character he has unfolded. *Their* systems have long since gone to the grave of oblivion. *His* has been animated with increasing vigor to the present hour, and will live and flourish through endless ages. *Their* writings have not made one man virtuous. *His* have peopled heaven with the children of light. The seventeenth chapter of his gospel, written as it is with the simplicity of a child, yet in grandeur of conception and in splendor of moral excellence triumphs with inexpressible glory over all the efforts of human genius, and looks down from heaven on the proudest labors of infidelity."*

(2.) The class of truths discussed and disclosed by these men may be referred to as a second illustration of the evidence of their inspiration. A remark or two,

* Sermons, vol. ii., p. 486, 487.

without attempting now to demonstrate the truth of the remark, or to illustrate it, is all that the time will admit.

(a) All that we truly know about God is from the Bible. I say "*know ;*" I do not say *imagine* or *conjecture*. What did the Egyptians, the Persians, the Assyrians, the Babylonians, the Greeks, the Romans *know* about God? What did the ancient inhabitants of Britain, the Druids, the Celts, the Gaelic tribes? What did the Goths, the Vandals, the Gauls, the Visigoths, that came pouring down from the North on the Roman empire? What do the people of China, of India, of Tartary, or the tribes of Africa know? What do the followers of Mohammed, except as Mohammed learned it from the Bible? What has philosophy ever taught men about God? What does science teach them now? Does the telescope reach his throne? Does the microscope disclose him? They disclose something, you say; and so it may be, or at least they lay the foundation of reasoning about *some things* pertaining to God — perhaps to his existence; his greatness; his power; his knowledge. But how about those things which we are most interested in knowing—his moral character; his mercy; his justice; his goodness; his truth—about the question whether he is worthy of confidence? How long in the laboratory will the chemist toil before he will obtain from earths and alkalies—from the crucible and the blow-pipe—an answer to these questions? Just as long as his predecessors of the Middle Ages, the alchemists, would have toiled to find the philosopher's stone or the elixir of life.

(b) All that we *know* about the immortality of the soul we learn from the Bible. I say here also, all that we "*know*," not what we may conjecture and wish for.

Do philosophers disclose that? Do astronomers? Do chemists? Do scientific men, as such, even *believe* in the immortality of the soul? If they *do* believe it, do they believe it as the result of their discoveries in science? Does the chemist believe it because he has found the proof of it in his laboratory? Do mental philosophers believe it on the ground of their own reasonings? The profoundest argument on this subject in ancient or modern philosophy is undoubtedly that of Plato in the "Gorgias." And yet who is convinced by that now? Who does not rise from the perusal of that argument with the conviction—painful and sad on his mind—that if this is *all*, then, indeed, "shadows, clouds, and darkness" rest on the whole subject? You could not convince a child in any of our Sunday-schools, from that argument, that his soul is immortal. Hear Cicero again on that argument of Plato, in a passage which I have quoted to you before: "I know not how it is, but when I read I assent; but when I lay down the book, and begin by myself to reflect on the immortality of the soul, all that assent glides away."*

(*c*) All that we know about a plan of salvation is learned from the Bible, not from philosophy or science. Science does not disclose such a plan — *any* plan by which a sinner may be saved. It is not, and it is not supposed to be, a part of the province of science to reveal such a plan, and scientific men, as such, are careful to keep their own province distinct from any such plan,

---

* *Marcus.* Quid tibi ergo opera nostra opus est? num eloquentia Platonem superare possumus? evolve diligenter ejus eum librum, qui est de animo; amplius quod desideres, nihil erit. *Auditor.* Feri mehercule, et quidem sæpius, *sed nescio quo modo, dum lego, assentior; cum posui librum, et mecum ipse de immortalitate animorum cœpi cogitare, assensio omnis illa elabitur.*— *Cicero*, Tusc. Quæst., lib. i, cap. xii.

or the suggestion of any such plan. However much, in other respects, scientific men may seem to encroach on the doctrines of the Bible; however the geologist, to use a phrase derived from the law, but which may be regarded as quite expressive of the idea, may claim "concurrent jurisdiction" with the Bible over the subjects involved in its department, yet nothing of this kind is claimed or is manifest in regard to a plan of redemption for sinners, or a way of saving men. Neither the astronomer, nor the anatomist, nor the chemist claims for himself any special knowledge on this subject above other men, nor in the books published in these departments of science is there any suggestion about the way in which a sinner may be saved. Whatever may have been claimed by "philosophers," so called, in ancient times, in regard to this; whatever Socrates or Plato may have suggested, yet it is certain that the writers on mental philosophy of *these* times do not regard the matter as coming within the cognizance of their department of learning, and that, in reference to a plan of salvation for sinners, we should be as unsuccessful in our inquiries in the writings of Kant, of Sir William Hamilton, and of J. Stewart Mill, as we should in a treatise on Logarithms or Fluxions. It has somehow occurred to the writers of the Bible to state such a plan; to make it prominent; to weave it into the entire structure of the book; to make it the grand thing on which the composition of the book turns; to make it the *idea*, in fact, running through the entire *collection* of books from Genesis to Revelation, sixty in number, and composed by perhaps a hundred different authors—an idea that runs through the book as really as the wrath of Achilles runs through all the books of the Iliad, or the wrath of Juno through the Æniad, or the fall of man through the Paradise Lost — though these are respectively the production of one man—of one mind.

(*d*) All that we know about a future state is from the Bible. I do not say all that we conjecture or imagine, but all that we *know*. Science does not pertain to that world, nor does it determine any thing on the question whether there is to be a future world, or, if there is, what it is to be. The crucible and the blowpipe impart no light on that subject; the telescope has nothing to reveal in regard to it; the geologist is laboring to determine something in regard to the interminable past, but he has nothing to reveal in regard to the interminable future. The footprints of birds, and the fossil bones, and the rocks reveal something in regard to the past, but they have nothing to say about that which is to come. Nor can any man carry the deductions of his science—natural philosophy, mental philosophy, astronomy, chemistry, fluxions—a single step beyond the grave. Nor does any one come back from that world, if there is such a world, to tell the scientific man and the philosopher that there *is* such a world, and what it *is*. Apart from the Bible, we are in utter darkness—a "land of darkness and of the shadow of death; a land of darkness as darkness itself; and of the shadow of death, without any order, and where the light is as darkness" (Job, x., 21, 22).

(3.) The truths disclosed in the Bible are up to this age, and are still in *advance* of the world. Science has never come up to them; the progress made in the world in our own marvelous age has not superseded them. The Bible has not been dropped by the way, as the works of Averroes, of Galen, of Roger Bacon have been; nor has it found its place in the alcoves of the

library where lie superseded and forgotten books of
past times. It lives. It has a vitality and an energy
which it never had before—in the nineteenth century
as much ahead of the world, in its own departments, as
it was in the time when its great truths were first
preached on Mars' Hill by Paul. This remark I shall
have occasion to illustrate in the tenth and concluding
Lecture of this course, and it must now, therefore, be
taken for granted.

(4.) It remains, then, to ask how these men knew
these things; how they were able to propound these
truths, which are to live through all the changes of the
world; to influence permanently and perpetually the
nations of the earth; to survive while countless generations of men pass away?

Was it *genius* that produced the Bible? How came
these men to be endowed with such a genius? Why
has not the same thing occurred elsewhere among such
classes of men—peasants and fishermen? Where else
have such *classes* of men produced such a book? There
has been one Burns, one Bunyan, one Shakspeare—perhaps a dozen or a score more of such men of remarkable
genius—plowmen, glovers, tinkers; but if all their compositions were put together, would they make *one book;*
would there be one plan; would there be unity of design; would there be such power in the volume; would
the volume commend itself so much to all classes of
men; would it secure so permanent a hold; would it
perpetuate and extend itself so among the nations of
the earth; would it so meet the wants of man as a sinner, as a sufferer, as a dying being, as immortal?

Did the sacred writers borrow this from others?
From whom? From the Persian magi; from Chaldæan
sages; from Egyptian priests? These were the only

M

ones to borrow from at the time when a considerable part of the book was written, and they have not borrowed from them. They had nothing, and they have transmitted nothing to us which could be regarded as the *original* of which the Bible is a *copy ;* and, whatever may be said of the Bible, it is an *original book.*

Is it the production of insanity ? Something like the ravings of the Pythian priestess or the priest of Apollo; something like those great thoughts which a mind like that of Hamlet could produce, the workings of " melancholic madness of a delicate shade, in which the reasoning faculties, the intellect proper, so far from being overcome or disordered, may, on the other hand, be rendered more active and vigorous ?"* It can not be necessary to argue this. Perhaps an apology is necessary for having alluded to it again.

Is it the result of inspiration ? This is the remaining solution. This, at least, will account for the facts. This will explain all. This is the most simple and easy solution; this is what they claim for themselves; this is what has commended itself as the best solution of the facts to the great mass of mankind for these eighteen hundred years. This is *likely* to be extensively the opinion of mankind for generations to come.

That there are difficulties in the view which has now been submitted to you is not to be denied. That there are many questions which may be asked in regard to the inspiration of the Bible, which, if they do not remain to be *asked,* remain to be *answered,* is to be admitted. That there are things in the Bible apparently inconsistent with the high purpose of a revelation from God ; that there are apparent inconsistencies and con-

* Shakspearc's Delineations of Insanity, etc., by *A. O. Kellogg, M. D.,* p. 36.

tradictions in the book itself; that there are discrepancies between its statements and the statements of secular history—not determined yet which is right; that there are commands not easy to be reconciled with our notions of justice and morality; that there are statements which seem to conflict with many of the disclosures of science, no friend of the Bible can deny. That to solve these questions, and remove these difficulties, would be the meritorious work of a long life, a field worthy of the highest talent of any young man desirous of rendering the most efficient service possible to the Church of God, I most firmly believe. That there *is* no work on the inspiration of the Bible that meets all these questions, and removes all these difficulties, so that it would commend itself to a candid inquirer after truth as entirely satisfactory, be he infidel or otherwise, I think any one must admit who has had occasion to examine what has been written on the subject.

But these admitted facts do not affect the reasoning in this Lecture, if the reasoning has any value. The difficulties of science yet unexplained, and that seem, as many of them do, to lie beyond the compass of the human mind, do not affect the general course of argument in regard to astronomy, chemistry, geology, anatomy. The apparent inconsistencies and contradictions in the movements of the heavenly bodies are not allowed to set aside the deductions which seem to be clearly established. Time does wonders in all sciences. One after another difficulties are removed; a thing that seemed to jar is shown to be, in fact, in harmony; what seemed to be irreconcilable with something else is shown to be, in fact, essential to the very existence, and to the proper action of that "something else." How many difficulties, contradictions, discrepancies, thus si-

lently vanish as light advances in the world, and as the
real harmonies of the universe are better understood!
Thousands of hearts, and heads, and hands are thus
successfully toiling in removing the difficulties in nature; intellects not less profound, learning not less extensive, hands not less active, are toiling in like manner,
and with as much prospect of success, in removing the
questions of difficulty in regard to the Bible.

It is said that much of the Bible relates to common
matters; to trifles; to things that men could learn
without a revelation; to things that are of no great
consequence; to things low and insignificant.

Much of this *is* so; and the same is as true of the
world as God *made* it as it is of the Bible that He has
revealed. Atoms; molecules; germs; infusoria; worms;
reptiles; insects made to torment and annoy; centi-
pedes; tarantulas; vermin — why all these things?
Would the God that revealed the great truths of human redemption "reveal," if revelation it can be called,
so many trivial things in the Bible? Would the God
that made the sun, the stars, the milky way, the millions—the numberless millions of suns that flame in the
far distant realms of space, make and care for these
things so trivial; so annoying; so noxious?

It is said that there are discrepancies; inconsistencies; contradictions.

It is so, apparently. Are there none in nature that
science has not yet taught us how to reconcile and harmonize? There was a discrepancy in the movements
of the planet Uranus, lying, as was supposed, on the
outer circle of the planetary worlds. It did not work
well. It did not keep its course. It bent out of its
way. It was not in harmony with the rest; nor could
astronomers tell *why.* Le Verrier and Adams simulta-

neously gave their minds to the solution of the difficulty, and each suggested that there was another planet, as yet unseen by man, far in the region beyond it.
The astronomer at Berlin pointed his telescope to the
spot where they said it would be found, and the harmony of the planetary system was restored.

Who knows what time may do in removing apparent
inconsistencies and contradictions? Listen to a remark
of Mr. Hume: "No priestly dogmas ever shocked common sense more than the infinite divisibility of exten-
sion, with its consequences."*

It is said that there are things taught, commanded,
and done in the Bible, as the command to Abraham to
offer up his son Isaac, and the command to destroy the
nations of Canaan, which it is difficult to reconcile with
our notions of morality.

This, also, is so; and the same thing· is true of much
that God does in our world, and of much that he per-
mits. Who has explained these things? Who has been
able to show exactly *how* the things that occur on
earth under the divine administration — by the order-
ings of His providence, and by His own hand, are consistent with our notions of justice and right; our views
of morality; our conceptions of benevolence? When
there are any fewer difficulties in the *facts* in our world
than there are in this respect in the statements of the
Bible, then it will be proper, on this account, to make it
a *special* objection to the Bible as a work of God; when
men have succeeded in explaining the difficulties in the
facts as they occur under the divine administration, and
in showing how they are consistent with our notions of
justice, goodness, and morality, then it will remain to
inquire whether *possibly* the same explanation might

* Philosophical Works, vol. iv., p. 182.

not remove all the difficulties from the same source pertaining to the word of God. The entrance of sin; the sorrows and woes of earth; the inequalities in the human condition; the destruction of the innocent—of women, and old men, and infants by the plague, by pestilence, and by famine; the desolations of war, not less savage and barbarous than the wars of Canaan; the divine vengeance taken on nations through the agency of the wicked passions of men—the love of conquest, revenge, and ambition—O for the coming of some one, gifted above all mortals hitherto, that shall be able to explain these things, and to tell *how* they are consistent with the character of a just and holy God; with our conception of what is right, and of what would be for the best; with our notions of benevolence, equity, righteousness—O for some gifted mind to tell how sin, and woe, and death came into the universe at all! *Till* such an appearing, what better can we do than to suppose, in either case, that there *may* be principles at present beyond our grasp that may explain the one and the other; that the principles which would be applicable to the one *may* be applicable to the other; that the God of nature *may* be the God of the Bible.

These things constitute no great difficulty in the practical affairs of life; they need constitute no great difficulty in the practical matters of religion. They do not prove, in the one case, that the world is not the workmanship of a pure and holy God; they do not prove, in the other, that the Bible is not from the same pure and holy Being.

Have we reached a conclusion on this subject which will be satisfactory to your minds? Perhaps I ought not to venture to affirm what I would hope may be true. Have we removed all difficulties from the subject? Assuredly this has not been done; nor, in a world so full of difficulties on kindred subjects, could we hope that this could be done. But, notwithstanding these things, it may have been shown that the Bible is a book whose origin is not to be accounted for by a reference to human genius; and that the most simple and philosophical explanation of the facts in regard to it is, that it is given by INSPIRATION OF GOD—as the most satisfactory explanation of our world, after all, with all its difficulties, is, that it is THE CREATION OF GOD.

LECTURE VIII.

THE EVIDENCE OF THE DIVINE ORIGIN OF CHRISTIANITY FROM THE PERSONAL CHARACTER AND THE INCARNATION OF CHRIST.

THE question which, in history, has agitated the world more perhaps than any other, is that which was asked by Pilate, "What shall I do with Jesus which is called Christ ?" (Matt., xxvii., 22). In history the question has been, What view shall be taken of his person ? What origin and rank shall be ascribed to him ? What place shall he have among those whose life and teachings have materially affected the condition of the world ? Shall he be regarded as a mere man, "naturally as fallible and peccable as other men ?" Shall he be regarded as a mere man, but, unlike other men in this respect, that he was absolutely perfect and pure ? Shall he be regarded as a phantasm, appearing in the form of humanity, and living, suffering, dying in appearance only ? Shall he be regarded as a being of a higher order actually descending to the earth, and living among men—an angel; an archangel; a loftier being still, as near to God as a created being can be, sent into the world to accomplish a great work for men ? Shall he be regarded as the most highly endowed in genius of any of our own race; forming some great plan; and accomplishing his work by the mere greatness of his genius ? Shall we regard him as a mythical being, and all that has been said of him as embodying only the conceptions of men forming a system of imposture or delusion around him as a nucleus, and arranging the ideas of that system as if they had been expressed in his life? Shall we regard him as God himself in his own essence incarnate; or as a person *in* the essence of God incarnate; or as a form of the mere *manifestation* of the Deity in our world? Shall we regard him as having one nature or two; one will or two; as a perfect man having a "reasonable soul" as well as a body, united with the divinity; or shall we regard him as a man only as he had a bodily form in which God, as such, performed all the functions of the soul? Has the world come to any settled views on these subjects, or is it likely that it ever will? Enemies and friends; sages, fathers, priests; synods and councils embracing the learning and piety of the world; good men and bad men; historians and philosophers; the orthodox and the heretical, have endeavored for eighteen hundred years to answer the question which so much perplexed Pilate, "What shall be done with Jesus?" Men of profound erudition, assuming that there was a real personage who bore the name, have brought, as Strauss has done, the vast resources of their learning to the inquiry whether all else in regard to him could not be explained on the supposition that his religion is a "myth;" men of brilliant imaginations, entering the field of romance, like Renan, have inquired whether all that occurred in his life can not be explained on the supposition that he was a young man of marvelous genius, awaking gradually to the consciousness of his own great powers, and himself deluded with the idea of a universal empire. The "orthodox" world has believed that his true place in history can be assigned only on the supposition that he was the only perfect man that has ever trod the

M 2

earth since the first Adam fell, and that he was the incarnate Son of God.

Pilate was perplexed. An honest man would have
settled the question at once. The world has been perplexed. Can we now, after the lapse of eighteen hundred years, so determine what is to be "done" with him
as to find evidence in his character and claims that he
was sent from God, and that his religion is true?

The subject of this Lecture, therefore, will be, The
evidence of the divine origin of Christianity from the
personal character and the incarnation of Christ.

As preparing the way for this argument, it may be
proper to refer a little more fully to the nature of the
perplexities which have been felt on the subject, and to
the various answers which have been given to the inquiry involved in the question of Pilate.

The Gnostics regarded him as an æon or "emanation"
from God, "the first and brightest emanation of the
Deity, who appeared upon earth to rescue mankind
from various errors, and to reveal a *new* system of truth
and perfection."* He was, in their apprehension, neither
truly God nor truly man. "Not truly God, because
they held him, though begotten of God, to be yet much
inferior to the Father; nor truly man, because every
thing concrete and corporeal they believed to be in-
trinsically and essentially evil; so that most of them
divested Christ of a material body, and denied him to
have suffered for our sakes what he is recorded to have
endured." He was a *phantasm* that appeared first on
the banks of the Jordan, and lived, and suffered, and
died in appearance only.†

According to Arius, he is "totally and essentially

* *Gibbon*, Decline and Fall, i., 256.
† *Mosheim*, Eccl. Hist., vol. i., p. 111, 171–181.

distinct from the Father; the first and noblest of those created beings whom God the Father formed out of nothing, and the instrument which the Father used in creating the universe, and, therefore, inferior to the Father both in nature and in dignity."* "Though the Son of God was united with human nature on the birth of Jesus, yet that Son of God was a κτίσμα [creation]. He indeed existed long before that birth, but not from eternity."†

To the Monarchians, or Patripassians, he was the true God inhabiting the body of Jesus, the divine nature occupying the place and performing the functions of the human soul—"the man Christ was the Son of God, and to this Son the Father of the universe so joined himself as to be crucified and endure pangs along with the Son."‡ They asserted "the true and proper Deity in Christ's person, but denied his humanity. The one single person of the Godhead, the true and absolute Deity, united himself with a human *body*, but not with a rational human soul."§

Nestorius and his followers sought to answer the question by assuming the fact that there were in Christ two natures, a proper divinity and a proper humanity, but that they *remained* distinct and were not united in one person — "in a single self-conscious personality." "Instead of a blending of the two natures into only one self, the Nestorian scheme places two selves side by side, and allows only a moral and sympathetic union between them. The result is, that the acts of each nature derive no character from the qualities of the

* *Mosheim*, Eccl. Hist., vol. i., p. 343.
† *Shedd's* Christian Doctrine, vol. i., p. 393.
‡ *Mosheim*, Eccl. Hist., vol. i., p. 182.
§ *Shedd's* Christian Doctrine, vol. i., p. 394.

other."* The problem to be solved was whether all the statements in the New Testament, and all the acts of the Redeemer, could be explained on this supposition.

The Eutychian or the Monophysite Christology explained, or tried to explain, the statements in the New Testament, and the facts in the life of the Redeemer, on another and an opposite supposition, in answer to the question "what shall be done with Jesus." That system asserts the unity of self-consciousness in the person of Christ, but loses the duality of the two natures. Eutyches taught that in the incarnation the human nature was *transmuted* into the divine, so that the resultant was one person and one nature. For this reason the Eutychians held that it was accurate and proper to say that "*God suffered.*"†

Sabellius sought to answer the question by supposing that there was but one "person" in the divine nature; that, according to the different manifestations, as Creator, Redeemer, Sanctifier, that one person was designated by different *names*, implying a distinction not in nature, but in the manifestation that there was a "certain *energy* put forth by the supreme parent, or a certain portion of the divine nature being separated from it, because united with the Son, or the man Christ; that there was but one divine person; that while there was a real difference between the Father, Son, and Holy Ghost, that difference was neither an essential nor a personal one; the divine three were not three distinct persons, but three *portions* of the divine nature, all depending on God; and that that portion which united with the man Christ, in order to redeem men, is the

* *Shedd's* Christian Doctrine, vol. i., p. 397.
† *Ibid.*, vol. i., p. 397.

Son," and that by this theory all that there was in the person and work of Christ can be explained.*

Paul of Samosata and his followers—the Paulians—supposed that they could explain the mysteries of the person of Christ on the theory that the Son and the Holy Ghost exist in God as reason and the operative power do in man; that Christ was born a mere man, but that the reason or wisdom of the Father descended into him, and enabled him to teach and to work miracles; and that, on this account, it was proper to say that Christ was God, though not in the proper sense of the word.†

Julian, the emperor, greatly perplexed and embarrassed in regard to Jesus, and the progress which his religion had made in the empire, attempted to solve all the mysteries in regard to him by saying that "Jesus, having persuaded a few among you [Galilæans, as he contemptuously called the Christians], and those of the worst of men, has now been celebrated about three hundred years, having done nothing in his lifetime worthy of fame—ἔργον οὐδὲν ἀκοῆς ἄξιον—unless any one thinks it a very great work to heal lame and blind people, and exorcise demoniacs in the villages of Bethsaida and Bethany."‡

Socinus sought an explanation by assuming that Christ was a mere man, but a good man; Dr. Priestley

---

* See *Mosheim*, Eccl. Hist., vol. i., p. 241, 2. There is some confusion in the statement of Mosheim on this subject, and there has been some doubt whether he has given the correct account of the sentiments of Sabellius. His views are examined in a long note by Dr. Murdock. I have endeavored, from the text and the note, to state, as clearly as possible, what were probably the views of Sabellius.

† *Ibid.*, vol. ii., p. 244.

‡ *Lardner's* Works, vol. vii., p. 628, ed. London, 1838.

in the idea that he was a mere man "naturally as fallible and peccable as any other man."

Chubb supposed that he could explain all by the following statement: "In Christ we have an example of
a quiet and peaceable spirit; of a becoming modesty
and sobriety; just, honest, upright, sincere; and, above
all, of a most gracious and benevolent temper and be-
havior. One who did no wrong, no injury to any man;
in whose mouth was no guile; who went about doing
good, not only by his ministry, but also in curing all
manner of diseases among the people. His life was a
beautiful picture of human nature in its native purity
and simplicity, and showed at once what excellent creatures men would be when under the influence and
power of the Gospel which he preached unto them."*

The solution by Rousseau is so well known that it is
necessary only to refer to it. "Is it possible," says he,
"that the sacred personage whose history it [the Bible]
contains should be himself a mere man? What sweet-
ness, what purity in his manner! What an affecting
gracefulness in his instructions! What sublimity in his
maxims! What profound wisdom in his discourses!
What presence of mind, what subtlety, what fitness in
his replies! How great the command over his passions! Where is the man, where the philosopher, who
could so live and so die, without weakness and without
ostentation? The death of Socrates, peacefully philoso-
phizing among his friends, appears the most agreeable
that one could wish; that of Jesus, expiring in agonies,
abused, insulted, and accused by a whole nation, is the
most horrible that one could fear. Socrates, indeed, in
receiving the cup of poison, blessed the weeping execu-

* True Gospel of Jesus Christ, sec. viii., p. 55, 56, quoted by Dr.
Schaff, Person of Christ, p. 282, 283

tioner who administered it; but Jesus, amidst excruci-
ating tortures, prayed for his merciless tormentors.
Yes, if the life and death of Socrates were those of a
sage, the life and death of Jesus are those of a God."*

Strauss assumed that Jesus was a real personage—
that there was such a living Teacher, but that the
things ascribed to him are in the main mythical; that
is, that certain ideas and conceptions have been made
to have the appearance of a living form and reality by
being represented as in connection with him, or as acted
out in his life. The problem was, assuming that there
was such a real personage, to .explain how those ideas
could be represented as embodied in his life, or what
those ideas would be if represented as acted out by a
living man. "This Christ," says he, "as far as he is in-
separable from the highest style of religion, is *historical*, not *mythical;* is an *individual*, not a mere *symbol.*
To the historical person of Christ belongs all in his life
that exhibits his religious perfection, his discourses, his
moral action, and his passion. He remains the highest
model of religion within the reach of our thought, and
no perfect piety is possible without his presence in the
heart. As little as humanity will ever be without religion, as little will it be without Christ; for to have
religion without Christ would be as absurd as to enjoy
poetry without regard to Homer or Shakspeare."†

Renan takes a different view, and aims to explain his
life on different principles. ' I will assume,' is the idea
—not his exact language—' the main facts about him,
as stated by the Evangelists, especially in the Fourth
Gospel, to be true, and I will write his life anew—that

* Emile on de l'Education, lect. iv., quoted at length in *Dr.
Schaff's* Person of Christ, p. 286–296.
† Quoted by *Dr. Schaff*, Person of Christ, p. 340, 341.

life as seen especially by a contemplation of the scenes
where he lived and died.   I will make that life as attractive as possible by all the charms of fancy, romance,
poetry.   I will go and visit the place where he was
born, the place where he was trained, the places where
he dwelt, and there, studying his character, inquiring
how it was developed at that time and in those scenes
—the influences that bore on his childhood, his youth,
and his riper years—the successive ideas which he cherished in regard to his own powers, and the unconscious
illusions under which he was brought in regard to himself, and the plans which he formed under those illusions, I will set forth his life as the most beautiful and
attractive that the world has seen.   I will see what I
can do with this 'young man of profound originality'
(p. 125); of 'perfect idealism' (p. 140); 'who developed
his own powers the more he believed on himself' (p.
148); this young man of extraordinary genius, awaking slowly to the consciousness of his great powers;
forming his plans, under an, innocent enthusiasm, on
'false views,' as Columbus and Newton did (p. 138),
but deeply and permanently affecting the world.'   "In
the first rank," says he, "of the grand family of the
true sons of God, we must place Jesus.   Jesus had no
visions; God does not speak to him from without; God
is in him; he feels that he is with God, and he draws
from his heart what he says of his Father.   He lives in
the bosom of God by uninterrupted communication; he
does not see him, but he understands him without need
of thunder and the burning bush like Moses, of a revealing tempest like Job, of an oracle like the old Greek
sages, of a familiar genius like Socrates, or of an angel
Gabriel like Mohammed.   He believes that he is in direct communication with God; he believes himself the

Son of God. The highest consciousness of God which ever existed in the breast of humanity was that of Jesus." " Christ, for the first time, gave utterance to the idea upon which shall rest the edifice of the everlasting religion. He founded the pure worship—of no age—of no clime—which shall be that of all lofty souls to the end of time. If other planets have inhabitants endowed with reason and morality, their religion can not be different from that which Jesus proclaimed at Jacob's well. The words of Jesus were a gleam in a thick night; it has taken eighteen hundred years for the eyes of humanity to learn to abide by it. But the gleam shall become the full day; and after the passing through all the circles of error, humanity will return to these words, as to the immortal expression of its faith and its hopes." "Repose now in thy glory, noble founder! Thy work is finished; thy divinity is established. Fear no more to see the edifice of thy labors fall by any fault. Henceforth, beyond the range of frailty, thou shalt witness, from the heights of divine peace, the infinite results of thy acts. For thousands of years the world will defend thee. Banner of our contests, thou shalt be the standard about which the hottest battle will be given. A thousand times more alive, a thousand times more beloved since thy death than during thy passage here below, thou shalt become the corner-stone of humanity so entirely, that to tear thy name from this would be to rend it from its foundations. Complete conqueror of death, take possession of thy kingdom, whither shall follow thee, by the royal road which thou hast traced, ages of worshipers." " Whatever may be the surprises of the future, Jesus will never be surpassed. His worship will grow young without ceasing; his legend will call forth tears without end; his sufferings will melt the noblest hearts; all ages will proclaim that, among the sons of men, there is none born greater than Jesus."*

Nothing has been, also, more perplexing in secular history than the question what place shall be assigned to Jesus and his religion. Mr. Gibbon, as I have remarked in a former Lecture, found it indispensable to dispose of this question, and he gave the best efforts of his mind to it. The problem with him was how to account for the spread and the power of his religion on the supposition that it was an imposture and an illusion. The course of his history would have flowed much more freely, and the task of the great historian would have been greatly lightened, if it had not been for the difficulties involved in the solution of this question.

To the world now—to Rationalists; to Socinians; to Unitarians; to skeptics; to worldly men; to the Westminster Review; to philosophers, is there any one subject more difficult than that involved in the question of Pilate, "What shall be done with Jesus?" Ages have passed away since he lived, and now the question is revived with a power which it has never had before, and more learning is employed on the question than there has been at any former period of the world. At his birth it was said of him, "Behold, this child is set for the fall and rising again of many in Israel; and for a sign which shall be spoken against; *that the thoughts of many hearts may be revealed*" (Luke, ii., 34, 35). This was true in his own age; it is true in history; it is true in our own times; it bids fair to be true to the end of the world.

The inquiry as it pertains to us in this course of Lec-

* Life of Jesus. New York, 1864, p. 50, 51, 104, 215, 351, 376.

tures, with reference to the argument for the truth of his religion, especially in the nineteenth century—after his character has been before the world for eighteen hundred years—is, whether that character furnishes evidence that he was from God, and that his religion is divine, or whether all that there was in his character can be explained on the supposition that his claims were false, and that his religion is an imposture.

The argument now divides itself into two parts: that derived from his personal character, and that derived from his incarnation.

I. THAT DERIVED FROM HIS PERSONAL CHARACTER.

(1.) The foundation of this argument is, that the character of Jesus, as drawn by the Evangelists, is PERFECT. If that were denied, and as far as it was denied, the argument would fail.

It might, at this stage of the argument, almost be *assumed* that that character is perfect. It has been admitted by all, or so nearly by all, that as in certain mathematical propositions small fractions may be left out of the account as not affecting the result, so here the number of those who have called the perfection of that character in question has been so small, and the points have been so unimportant, if not inappreciable or doubtful, that these need not be taken into the account. The ancients did not call the perfection of his character in question. Neither Celsus, Porphyry, nor Julian expressed a doubt on the subject. The argument which they urged was not based on a denial of the perfection of Jesus; it was founded on the alleged fact that the character of others—of Socrates, and of Apollonius of Tyana—were not less perfect.

It is only in modern times that the perfection of that

character has been called in question, and the fact that
it has been done, and the manner in which it has been
done, have shocked the Christian world.

Dr. Priestley, indeed, asserted that "Christ was *naturally* as fallible and peccable as any other man," but
he did not venture to suggest that his character, in fact,
was not actually perfect, or that he was in any sense a
sinner, though he would not have been restrained from
doing it if there had been any thing in his conduct or
character to which he could have referred as proof—for
he was not restrained from saying that he had found
defects in the reasoning of the apostle Paul. It was reserved for others to take the additional bold step of
specifying what they regard as defects in the character
of the Saviour.

The "acute and candid" author of the work on "The
Soul" and the "Phases of Faith"* understood very well
that "a perfect type of character is the essence of a
practical religion," and that, if the Christian type was
perfect, it would be hopeless to set up a new religion
beside it. Accordingly, it became necessary to show
that there were imperfections in the character of Christ,
and the imperfections which he specifies are two in
number. The first is the exhibition of indignation
against the hypocritical and soul-murdering tyranny of
the Pharisees; the second is the absence of mirth, and
of laughter as its natural and genial manifestation."†
This is all.

Strauss also denies the sinlessness of Jesus. This,
however, is done not so much from the specification of
any actual facts, as on the *à priori* philosophical argument of the impossibility of sinlessness, or the panthe-

* Mr. Newman.

† Lectures on the Study of History, by *Goldwin Smith*, p. 139, 140.

istic notion of the inseparableness of sin from all finite existence. The only exegetical proof that he urges is the declaration of the Savior (Matt., xix., 17), "There is none good but one, that is God."[*]

A French writer—F. Pecaut—(*Le Christ et la Conscience*, Paris, 1859) likewise denies the sinlessness of Jesus. He refers to the following facts as evidences of imperfection: the conduct of Jesus toward his mother in his twelfth year; his rebuke administered to her at the wedding feast of Cana; his expulsion of the traffickers from the Temple; his cursing of the unfruitful fig-tree; the destruction of the herd of swine; his bitter invectives against the Pharisees; and his own rejection of the attribute "*good*" in the dialogue with the rich youth.[†]

Such objections as these it would not be difficult to answer, and it will be assumed here, in accordance with what may be regarded, with these slight exceptions, as the universal judgment of mankind, that the character of the Savior was perfect. If this is admitted, it will be admitted, also, with exceptions not more numerous, or that will not more vary the judgment of mankind, that the character stands alone. It would be as easy to dispose of the few cases — not more than two or three in number—that have been set up as being also perfect, as Socrates and Apollonius, for example, as it is to dispose of the specified objections in regard to the perfection of the Savior. The general judgment of mankind on the subject of human perfection is undoubtedly in accordance with the expressed opinion of Cicero: "In whom truly there shall be absolute perfection we have not as yet seen; we have seen no one perfect; it has only been expounded by philosophers

* *Schaff*, Person of Jesus, p. 209.　　　　　　† *Ibid.*

what such a one *would be*, if there should be such a one."*

(2.) To see the full bearing on the argument of the remark now made, it is necessary to keep in mind the fact that that character has been regarded as equally perfect in all those eighteen centuries which have elapsed since his appearing; among all nations where he has been made known; by all ranks and conditions of society. This is an ordeal through which a character claimed to be perfect must necessarily pass. It is not that the character is regarded as perfect in one age, or among those of a certain rank or condition in life, but that it commends itself to those of every age and of every condition, and that when examined in view of all the phases of opinion which exist among men, and of all the standards of perfection which are set up, in reference to what it would be if reproduced in a particular age and among a particular class, it is still found to be without a flaw. For, abstractly, there are great varieties of opinion among men about what is perfect in character; there are different standards of morality; there are different views in philosophy; there are different customs and opinions; there are different things aimed at in life; there are different attempts to draw a perfect character. That which would seem to be perfect in one age, and according to the mode of judging in that age, might be seen to be very far from being perfect when men should have more enlarged and correct views of what constitutes perfection; and that which would come up to the demands of that more advanced age might still show defects in an age still more

---

* In quo vero erit perfecta sapientia quem adhuc nos quidem vidimus neminem; sed philosophorum sententiis, qualis futurus sit, si modo aliquando fuerit, exponitur.—Tusc. Quæst., lib. ii., cap. 22.

advanced, and might fail to meet the general judgment of mankind as to a claim of absolute sinlessness.

The claim set up for the Savior, and universally conceded, with the few exceptions which I have noticed, is that it commends itself equally to every age; to every class of persons; to the learned and the unlearned; to sages, to philosophers, and to those in humble life—to all as absolutely free from sin. On this fact my argument now is based.*

(3.) Assuming now that the character of Christ is perfect or sinless, it will be proper, in order to see the force of the argument, to consider the attempts which have been made to draw or describe a perfect character.

One of two things is true in regard to the character of Christ, as exhibited in the New Testament:—it was either real, or it was the work of the Evangelists—a work of fiction.

If it was real, then the question is settled; for if he was perfect and sinless, then he was what he claimed to be, and was the Son of God sent down from heaven—for he undoubtedly claimed this.

If it was the work of the Evangelists, then we have to show how it was that such plain men as they were, and very imperfect men themselves, should have been able to set before the world a perfect imaginary character; how four or more men of such rank as they were

---

* The following works may be referred to on the general subject of the character of the Savior: *Dr. Ullmann,* Die Sundlosigkt it Jesu; *Dr. Horace Bushnell,* The Character of Jesus; *John Young,* The Christ of History; *I. P. Lange,* Leben Jesu; *Dr. Channing's* Sermon on the Character of Christ, Works, vol. iv., p. 28; Lectures on the Study of History, by *Prof. Goldwin Smith,* p. 127-167; and "The Person of Christ," by *Dr. Philip Schaff.*

should have combined, in separate narratives, to produce such a character; how, moreover, they should have done it, not by direct statements, but by placing this imaginary person in a great variety of situations, and bringing him into contact with the world for a succession of years, and under every possible temptation to do wrong; and how they were able so to describe him that he never is represented as uttering a sentiment, or manifesting a feeling, or performing an action, which is not conformable to the highest standard of perfection. It will be seen at once that it is a much more difficult thing for *four* men to present a perfect character in such details than it would be for one man to carry out his own individual conceptions; as it would be more difficult for four sculptors to produce the Apollo Belvidere, in the beauty of its form and proportions, than it was for the one mind that conceived it and executed it. Moreover, the difficulty is to be explained how, on the supposition even that Christ actually *lived*, and *was* perfect or sinless, such men had the ability so to draw his character, and so to represent him, in such a variety of situations, that his character should commend itself to all ages as absolutely sinless.

The simple fact in the matter, whether the character was real, or whether it is the creation of the imagination, is that they have done what was never before done, and what, even with this model before them, has never since been done.

The attempts made by men to draw a perfect character have been of two kinds: from real life; and from the imagination — real characters, and fictitious characters.

The former attempts have failed, because there have been no perfect characters, and because it has been the work of the historian to describe men as they are.

Themselves imperfect men, and portrayed by imperfect men, they stand before the world *as* imperfect men.

The design of fiction, in poetry and romance, is to describe men and women as they are, or human nature as it is. Such works, so far as they relate to human conduct, lose all their value when they fail to describe human nature as it is—living men and women—acting their parts on the great theatre of human life. Those works come nearest to perfection, as works of art, when they describe human nature most accurately. Shakspeare does not describe perfect characters; it may be doubted whether he ever attempted it, or designed to describe one. The characters in novels, as the characters in history, are not perfect characters; and if any one has attempted to draw such a character, it is easy at once to see, whatever else it may be, how unlike it is to the character of Jesus Christ. Where *is* there a character, in fiction, that can be held up to all the world in all ages; that can represent man in all relations and circumstances; that can be a sinless model in conduct alike toward God and toward men; that can be a model for kings and princes, sages and philosophers, the humble, the unlearned, the lowly, the down-trodden—in prosperity and in adversity; in joy and in sorrow; in benevolence, in purity, in gentleness, in the love of truth, in the love of justice; in childhood, in youth, and in middle age; under obloquy and reproach; in dealing with crafty and unprincipled men; in abandonment and persecution; in the severest form of death, and under all that could shake the firmness of virtue—where is there, where has there been, such a character, in reality or in fiction, except in the person of Jesus Christ?

I do not affirm that it has *never* been attempted. We

N

have seen that there has been, in two or more instances, a claim set up to perfection of character that would be a set-off against the claim in favor of Jesus Christ. I do not deny that writers of fiction have designed to draw a perfect character, nor that they have supposed that they have done it—just as artists have designed to present a perfect human form in the Apollo and the Venus de Medici, and perfect beauty in the Madonna. I do not deny that the attempt has been made—where, in fact, it has most signally failed—in the description of the gods appearing in human form, a fact which we shall see in another part of this Lecture bears vitally on the argument before us.

(4.) But let us look a moment at the difficulties which have attended such an undertaking.

(a) First, then, there has been no living model from which men could draw in forming such a character; no one that would be recognized universally as constituting such a model.

(b) There has been no agreement among men as to what would be such a standard of character. The idea would differ in different ages and among different nations. A Hebrew would have set up one standard; an Egyptian another; a Greek another; a Roman another; a Persian another; an inhabitant of China now has one ideal standard, a Hindoo another, a New Zealander another. A nobleman has one idea, a philosopher another, a priest another. A Mandarin has one idea, a Brahmin another, a Turkish mufti another. A Pharisee had one, a Sadducee another, and one of the sect of the Essenes another. Antony in Egypt and Benedict in Italy, founders of the monastic system, one, Ignatius Loyola and Xavier another. A Catholic priest has one idea, a Protestant minister of religion another. A peasant of

Galilee could hardly be supposed to have the same standard which would be approved in Corinth.

(c) The ideas of morality and manners change in different ages. There are very low views of morality in one age, and very stringent ones in another; there are things cultivated in one age which are disregarded in another; there are things which in one age are considered to be lofty virtues, which in another age cease to be considered as virtues at all. In the days of chivalry and knight-errantry there were things regarded as indispensable, as entering into character, which a change of social customs has rendered at best obsolete; things, too, then regarded as lofty virtues, which might now be considered as, at least, of doubtful morality. The remark of Cicero, before referred to (p. 286), may here be borne in mind when speaking of a character in which there would be " perfect wisdom"—*perfecta sapientia*—he says that such a character had hitherto existed only in the imagination of philosophers: they had described not what *had been*, but what *would be* if such a character should appear.

(d) There was this special difficulty in the case, also, that the work was to be done, not by one person, who could carry out his own conceptions, but by several persons, either acting in concert, or acting independently of each other. One man — Homer, Virgil, Milton, Shakspeare, can easily carry out his own conceptions, and secure unity and concinnity in an epic or a tragedy, however long it may be, or however many characters are introduced. The writer of the epic can place his hero in a great variety of situations, and still have before him the *same* hero, acting in conformity with his character; the writer of the drama can place any variety of characters in different situations, and lead them forth in a great variety of action, and still can so preserve his plan, and keep up the identity, that Hamlet, and Lear, and Othello are always recognized when they speak. But the case would be much more difficult and complicated if it were supposed that the Iliad, the Æniad, the Paradise Lost, or Hamlet, were respectively the production of a society or combination of poets. One sculptor can carry out his own conceptions, and produce symmetry, concinnity, harmony in his statue; for the statue is in his mind, and he can copy it as it is there combined in its proper proportions. But suppose a company of artists to have undertaken to execute the statue of Minerva or the Apollo, it is easy to see how the matter would be complicated, and how improbable it would have been that statues with such beauties of proportion and form would ever have existed.

In the case of the life of the Savior, if no such being ever existed, then the difficulty is in seeing how four, or five, or more persons could combine to form such an idea, and how they could combine in carrying out the conception. If he *did* really exist, then the difficulty would be to see how four, or five, or more persons could so write his life, with or without concert, as to produce separate and independent narratives, and yet preserve the unity of the idea through the whole.

(e) It is to be borne in mind, also, that the plan was, as appears, not to represent him as an *abstraction*, or not to present the abstract conception of a perfect man, but to place him in an almost endless variety of situations, and to show how he *acted* there; with no comment on his conduct with reference to the question whether it was consistent or not, and manifestly with no anxiety on that point; without even *saying* that he

was perfect—for that was not affirmed by the Evangelists themselves, but was reserved for later writers*—
but to describe him as *acting*, leaving the world to
judge *from* his actions whether he was a perfect being.
Accordingly, he appears before us in all the variety of
circumstances in which a human being can ordinarily
be placed; in such an endless diversity that the character, whatever it was, could not but be developed. He
makes a thousand speeches; he performs a thousand
actions; he meets with thousands of people; he is
placed in situations of temptation and of provocation;
he is among friends and among foes; he is with the
wicked and the good; he is with the sick and the dying; he addresses great multitudes in public; he warns
and denounces the wicked, and he pours consolation
into the hearts of those that weep in private.

To see the difficulty, and the nature of the argument,
let us return for a moment to the supposition already
suggested. The statue of Minerva; the Apollo Belvidere; the Venus de Medici, and the still more complicated Laocoon, are respectively the work of one artist.
One mind formed the conception; one hand carried out
the conception; one idea runs through the entire work
as a work of art.

But suppose that any one of these, either the most
simple or the most complicated, were the work of different men—the production of a society of artists, and
not of an individual, either with or without a common
agreement or understanding. Suppose it be left to one
man to form the head; to a second the hand; to a third
the foot; to a fourth the body, each according to his
different ideas of beauty. Or suppose, in one case, that
it was left to independent workmen to carry out an

* 1 Pet., ii., 22; Heb., vii., 26; ii., 10; v., 9.

idea of perfection already agreed upon, and to be produced by their joint labors; suppose, in another case,
that four men should undertake, without a concerted
idea, to form independently, by working on different
parts of the statue, the image of a perfect man.

And yet this would present but a small part of the difficulty in drawing such a character as that of the Savior
—perfect as a man; perfect and complete as the incarnate Deity. For *there* is a block of marble to be moulded at will. It is cold; passive; subject wholly to the
control of the chisel. It has no will; no passion; no
feeling; no character. It has no *complications* of fancy,
intellect, affections. You can make it what you please;
and when any part is made, it remains the same. The
idea rises before you with nothing to disturb you, and
when complete, there it stands as you intended it
should. *Here* there is will, and feeling, and purpose,
and mind, and heart, and action, all varying, and all
producing endless complications.

(5.) Assuming, then, that it has been done, the question is, How is this to be accounted for or explained?

(*a*) It is not a work of fiction. It bears all the marks
of real life. The life of Christ is *not* a fiction. Christ
is a real historical personage—as real as Cæsar or Alexander. You can make nothing of history; of nations;
of opinions; of philosophy; of the world; of any thing
in the past, if this is denied. All history is connected with that life; all history, for eighteen hundred
years at least, turns on that life. The fact that he
lived, and founded the Christian religion, is recognized
by Josephus, by Tacitus, by Pliny. It is not denied
by Celsus, by Porphyry, by Julian, as it would have
been if it could have been done. It is not denied by
Mr. Gibbon, but is assumed in his labored argument ev-

ery where. It is not denied by Strauss; it is not denied by Renan.

(*b*) It is not a work of genius. Genius has never drawn such a character; genius has never drawn a perfect character at all. Besides, his biographers, the fishermen of Galilee, were *not* remarkable for genius, unless the fact of portraying the life of Chrst proves that they were. They did nothing else remarkable. They wrote no poetry. They promulgated no new system of philosophy. They composed no works of fiction, unless this is one. They wrote no dramas to make them immortal, as Sophocles, Terence, and Eschylus did. They gave the world no inventions in the arts. They made no discoveries in science. They suggested no improvements in architecture; in ship-building; in the implements of agriculture; even in their own employment—in the methods of fishing. They would have lived and died unknown—all of them—forgotten just as soon as they had died, if it had not been for their life of Christ. Not a stone would have marked their graves; not one of them would have been heard of a hundred years after their death. Nothing else that they did would have made a ripple on the great flowing stream of the world's events. Fishermen are not commonly immortal.

(*c*) Moreover, if it were supposed that they undertook, by combination and concert, to engage in such a work as this, we should certainly not have had *this* life. We should either have had a character intensely and thoroughly *Jewish*—which the character of Jesus is not—with Jewish conceptions; a narrow, bigoted, Jewish Messiah; a prince; a conqueror; a deliverer; a Judas Maccabæus; a restorer of the pomp and pride of the ancient monarchy, in accordance with the Jewish conceptions of the Messiah, or we should have had a biography full of trifles and small conceits; of foolish marvels; of improbable stories — a biography that might have rivaled the Arabian Nights' Entertainments, such as the writers of the Jewish Talmud would have been likely to produce. We never should have had the Life of Jesus of Nazareth as we have it now in the New Testament.

(*d*) It is to be remarked, also, that in thus drawing the perfect character of Christ, the Evangelists, or the disciples who followed him, did not always themselves *see* that his character was perfect, or that he was always acting in the wisest manner. On that point they often had doubts; but they recorded the *facts* as they occurred, and time has shown that his conduct was perfect and wise. Thus, on one occasion, they said to him, when he proposed to go to Bethany, where Lazarus was, "Master, the Jews of late sought to stone thee, *and goest thou thither again?*" (John, xi, 8). On another occasion, when he announced to his disciples that he must go up to Jerusalem and die, it is said, "Then Peter took him, and began to rebuke him, saying, *Be it far from thee, Lord; this shall not be done unto thee*" (Matt., xvi, 22).

The argument which I have thus far, in this Lecture, submitted to you, relates to the perfect character of Christ—the fact that he had such a character, and that it has been so drawn by the Evangelists, demonstrating that he was from God. That he had such a character proves that he was from God, for he claimed that he was; whether his character was real or whether it was imaginary, it was above the power of such men to draw and describe it. The supposition that it was real, and that they were under a supernatural influence in describing it, explains all.

II. The other form of the argument which I proposed to submit to you IS THAT DERIVED FROM HIS INCARNATION.

I have occupied so much of the time on the former part of the subject, that what remains must now be presented in few words.

(1.) There has been a general belief or impression among men that an incarnation of the Deity is possible, and would occur. This idea or impression has been so prevalent as to show that somehow the idea does not *shock* men, or strike them as absurd. At first view it would seem that it would be likely to do this. So far exalted must God be above men; so unlike men must he be; so strange would seem to be the fact that two beings, wholly unlike and distinct, should be combined in one; so impossible is it to explain the mode in which this could be done, that it might be presumed that this would never occur to the mind as possible; that, however exalted one being or one class of beings might be above another, the extremes could be combined in one; that the highest intellect in the universe—God, could be united permanently with the lowest—man. It is to be admitted at once that it requires the highest exercise of faith to believe that this could be so. Yet somehow the belief that the gods do come down in the forms of men has been so common that the idea does not startle or amaze mankind. When, at Lystra, Paul healed a cripple, and the people lifted up their voices and said of him and Barnabas, " The gods are come down to us in the likeness of men" (Acts, xiv., 11), they expressed only what has been in accordance with a general belief. They were not shocked; they hastened to

N 2

bring oxen and garlands, that they might render them appropriate homage as gods.

This general faith of mankind in the doctrine of an incarnation of the Deity has been manifested in every way possible. It has been incorporated into legends, myths, and fables. It has been embalmed in tradition. It has been expressed in the highest conceptions of poetry. It has been made the foundation of epics and tragedies. It has suggested the noblest conceptions of sculpture. It has been uttered in the profoundest sayings of philosophy. It has been laid at the foundation of most of the religions of the world, for there is scarcely one form of religion among men in which some trace of the conception can not be found.

This universal belief in the doctrine of an incarnation of the Deity may be referred to as one among a thousand arrangements in our nature, and in the forms of belief among men, shadowing the truth; preparing men to expect and to receive the truth—arrangements in our nature which can be explained only on the supposition that there *is* truth of which this belief is the shadow, and that there is to be revelation for which this faith was to prepare the way. It may be doubted whether the revelation of an incarnation of God would not have so shocked mankind that it would at once have been rejected as impossible if the minds of men had not been prepared for its reception by this universal faith in an incarnation. At all events, this universal belief in what would seem so improbable, proves that the idea is *not* repugnant to the human mind. The doctrine of an incarnation of the Deity is not to be *dislodged* from the mind of man. It is not to be driven from it by argument. He does not argue safely, nor will he argue with permanent success, who

argues against the universal convictions of men on any
subject. The faith will find a substance corresponding
to it; the belief is to be satisfied by some revelation in
accordance with it; and the only question is whether
that is found in Christianity, or whether it is to be in
some form of heathenism already existing, or whether
it remains to be met in some hitherto undeveloped form
of religion.

(2.) The attempt has been made in almost all countries to describe the actions of an incarnate God, or to
tell what he would be. It may be said that the highest
efforts of genius and philosophy have been exhausted on
the attempt. The world has no higher genius to be
employed on any subject than has been employed on
this. Plato went to the utmost limit of his powers in
describing the Trinity of his conception—it may be said
to the utmost limit of the powers of *man ;* for who can
bring to the subject a mind more richly endowed than
his? Homer exhausted the powers of poetry in describing the gods as they came down to mingle in the
strifes of battle. The Greeks, in sculpture, accomplished all that, in this respect, the human mind could be
expected to do.

In a previous part of these Lectures I have remarked
that the highest powers of the human mind have been
employed on the subject of religion, in endeavoring to
ascertain the truth about God; the immortality of the
soul; the plan of recovery for lost men; and the realities of the future world. I remarked, in substance, that
it seemed not improper that there should be one national mind created and endowed as if with special reference to such inquiries; one people with whom the solution of the question whether man could accomplish without a revelation all that the race needs, could be safely

intrusted. I remarked that such a mind was found eminently in the *Greek* mind, and that the experiment had
been fairly made there. In subtlety; in depth; in
acuteness; in the power of analysis; in keenness of penetration; in metaphysical acuteness; and in the possession of a language unrivaled in its adaptation to such
inquiries, I remarked that it seemed as if God had prepared that mind especially for such inquiries; that the
question as to what man could do by his unaided powers might be regarded as fairly determined there; that
the result was a demonstration that man was unequal
to the task of solving those great questions, and that a
revelation was indispensable for the race.

I call your attention now to the fact that God seems
to have, in like manner, created and endowed another
national mind with special reference to the limitations
of the human powers on the subject of an incarnation
of the Deity. I refer to the Hindoo mind.

The human race, in modern times, has been divided
into certain classes, founded on certain "types" or peculiarities from the anatomical structure, complexion,
or form, as the Caucasian, the Mongolian, the Ethiopian, the American "types." A classification not less
remarkable, not bounded by the same limits, might
perhaps be made from the *mental* characteristics of
men, and it might be found that these are sufficiently
marked to constitute a distinction as real among the
people of the earth. The classes of mind most distinguished might be arranged in the following order: The
Greek mind; the Teutonic mind; the Arabic mind;
the Hindoo mind—unless the order of the last two
should be reversed, and the Hindoo mind be assigned
a place nearer the Greek. In acuteness; in subtlety;
in the power of discrimination; in an adaptation to

mental and mathematical pursuits; in poetry, the Hindoo mind, commonly supposed to belong to the classes of inferior mind in the world, has its appropriate place, as endowed by nature, with the other three classes which I have mentioned, and has exerted an influence on mankind perhaps scarcely less limited than the others that I have specified.

I have said that the Greek mind seemed to have been created almost with the design to show what the human intellect, unaided, could do in finding out God and the truths of religion, and, by its failure in the inquiry, to show the necessity of revelation. In like manner, I now observe that the Hindoo mind seems to have been made to show what man could learn by nature about the Trinity and the Incarnation, or what the doctrine of the Trinity and the Incarnation would become if intrusted to such a class of mind. For the Hindoo mind has been devoted to the inquiry. Its utmost powers have been exhausted on the subject. The representation of the Trinity and the Incarnation has constituted the very essence of its theology. The system of religion there is perhaps the most perfect system in the world of a theoretical religion carried out into minute details under the power of acute and penetrating genius.

What that system is, the time would not allow me to describe, nor would it be necessary. By the labors of Christian missionaries, it has been made familiar to the world. For puerility, for extravagance, for absurdity, no system ever proposed to mankind on the subject of religion has ever equaled it; and as the Greek mythology, "elegant" as it was, showed the limit of the best type of the human mind on the general subject of religion, so the Hindoo doctrines on the Trinity and the In-

carnation show the limit of the human mind when exercised on the problem what God would be if he should
become incarnate.

As we, therefore, compare the statements in the Gospels with the writings of the Greek philosophers on the
general subject of religion, so we may compare the details of the Hindoo theology on the Trinity and the Incarnation with the statements in the New Testament
on the life and character of the incarnate Son of God.
If it had been left to man to select the mind that was
best fitted to describe what an incarnate being would
be, it is probable that no one could have been selected
more fitted to the task than the Hindoo mind.   The result is before the world.

(3.) What, then, are the difficulties on the subject
which have placed it so far above the unaided human
powers?   I have, in the former part of this Lecture, adverted to the difficulties in describing the character of
a perfect *man*, and to the fact that all efforts to do this,
except the attempt in the Gospels, have failed.   I now
advert more particularly to the greater difficulties of
describing the actions of an *incarnate* being—of God in
human form.

(*a*) In considering this part of the subject, it is proper to remark that it is undoubtedly the fact that it was
the design of the writers of the New Testament to describe such a character; that they had such a character
before their minds in portraying the character of Jesus;
or that they undertook to write the life of one whom
they regarded as God in human form.

This was, beyond all question, the view of the Evan-
gelist John, for he begins his Gospel by saying that "In
the beginning was the Word, and the Word was with
God, and the Word was God.   And the Word was made

flesh and dwelt among us (and we beheld his glory, the glory as of the only-begotten of the Father), full of grace and truth" (John, i., 1, 14). The difficulty was in describing the character of one who was believed to be God, and who was known to be a man.

(b) If there was, as we have seen in the former part of this Lecture, great and intrinsic difficulties in describing the character of a perfect man, there was, in the case of the incarnation, this additional difficulty, which would seem to be almost insuperable, of describing the actions of an incarnate being—of one in whom the divinity and the humanity were united. We know what a *man* will do; how he thinks, speaks, acts. But how do we know what God will do—how *he* will think, speak, act? Still more, how do we know how the divine and the human could be so blended that the actions of each and of both could be represented as the actions of one person? The difficulty was in putting fit words into the mouth of one regarded as God, and of describing what he would do as the incarnate divinity, and at the same time of describing him as in union with, or in combination with human feelings, tenderness, sympathies, compassions—one who could weep, as a man, over a friend sleeping in the grave, and at the same time, by a word, restore him to life, as God. For this there was no model—no example. None of the descriptions of the actions of the gods in the heathen mythology would do for an example; none of the descriptions in the poets could be the basis for the biography of a combined human and divine person. If it was the work of fancy, it was to be mere fancy; if the life had been real, there was still the difficulty of describing that life so that the divine and the human would appear in the proper proportions; so that in the one there would be nothing inconsistent with the other; so that there would be nothing incongruous, monstrous, or absurd. The difficulty was that of describing God and man as one united being; acting as such; speaking as such; suffering as such; dying as such—the difficulty of describing the things pertaining to his divine nature as *naturally* as those pertaining to his human nature; the difficulty of describing this mysterious being performing a miracle as naturally as he performed any other action—making him, if I may so speak—as *natural* when he stilled the tempest on the sea, or when he raised Lazarus from the grave, as when he broke the bread at the last Passover, or when, in words of sympathy and love, he comforted the weeping sisters of Lazarus: to preserve the individuality, the separate consciousness, the expressions of will, of affection, and of feeling; to describe the actions of the *divinity* in language appropriate, and the actions of the *man* in language appropriate; to describe such a mysterious being in language as appropriate when raising the dead as when conversing on ordinary topics of life; when stilling a tempest on the Sea of Galilee by a word as God, and when communing with the two disciples on the way to Emmaus. Who can describe such a being, in very varied actions in life, and in a great diversity of circumstances, and yet do it so that all shall recognize its fitness? How could this be done by unlettered fishermen? How could it be done by four or more such fishermen, not acting in concert, and yet drawing out the details of such a life in a manner that would be harmonious, and so that its concinnity would be preserved?

(4.) It has not been done elsewhere than in the Gospels; not in the poetry of the Greeks; not in the in-

carnations of Vishnu.   As far as the east is from the
west are all those representations from what *must* be
the character and the life of an incarnate Deity ; and as
it may be presumed that in the efforts of these two
classes of mind—the Greek and the Hindoo, the first
minds of earth—the power of man on that subject was
exhausted, it may be affirmed now that it can not be
done.   Among the Greeks there was no bad passion of
men that was not represented as developed in their incarnate deities; among the Hindoos there is nothing
absurd, puerile, monstrous, extravagant, wild, improbable, or even wicked, that is not represented in their in-
carnations of the Deity.

On the question respecting the ability of man to describe, in a proper manner, the actions of an incarnate
Deity, we are not left to conjecture, for we actually
have two distinct classes of biographers of Jesus—both
claiming to describe him as incarnate — that of the
Evangelists, and that in the " apocryphal Gospels."
No writings in the world are more unlike each other
than these ; nothing, perhaps, could more clearly demonstrate that there has been a supernatural guidance
in portraying the character of Jesus in the Evangelists
than a comparison of the one with the other.

One of those " Gospels" relates to the " infancy of
Jesus," and the attempt has been made, assuming the
fact of his incarnation or his divinity, to describe him
when a boy.   Of such an attempt, it has been well remarked by Dr. Bushnell (Nature and the Supernatural,
p. 280), " If any writer, of almost any age, will undertake to describe not merely a spotless, but a superhu-
man or celestial childhood, not having the reality before
him, he must be somewhat more than human himself if
he does not pile together a mass of clumsy exaggera-

tions, and draw and overdraw till neither heaven nor earth can find any verisimilitude in the picture."

"These apocryphal Gospels," it has been well said, "are related to the canonical Gospels as a counterfeit to the genuine coin, or as a revolting caricature to the inimitable original." According to the representation in those Gospels, even dumb idols, irrational beasts, and senseless trees bow in adoration before the infant Jesus on his journey to Egypt; and after his return, when yet a boy of five or seven years, he changes balls of clay into flying birds for the idle amusement of his playmates, dries up a stream of water by a mere word, transforms his companions into goats, raises the dead to life, makes by miracle a piece of cabinet-work which his father Joseph could not make, and performs all sorts of miraculous cures through a magical influence which proceeds from the very water in which he washed, the towels which he used, and the bed on which he slept.*

(5.) But that in which men have failed every where else has been accomplished in the Gospels. No one can show that, on the supposition that Christ was divine—God as well as man—there is in his recorded life, in the sentiments which fell from his lips, in the actions which he performed, in the feelings which he manifested, even one thing inconsistent with such a supposition. That he was, as described, a perfect *man*, we have seen. The life which he lived was that of a perfect man. The death which he died was that of a perfect man. At the same time, the sentiments which he uttered were such as became God—those profound truths; those perfect rules of morality; those sublime doctrines; those de-

---

* The particulars, with ample illustrations, may be seen in *Rud. Hoffman's* Leben Jesu nach den Apokryphen, p. 140-236. See *Dr. Schaff's* Person of Christ, p. 31-33.

scriptions of God; those representations of man; those representations of the future state—the resurrection—the judgment—heaven and hell.` The miracles which he wrought were such as God only can perform, and the language which he used in healing the sick, in opening the eyes of the blind, in stilling the storm, and in raising the dead, is as simple and appropriate as that which he employed in his ordinary intercourse with his disciples and friends. For he is described as uttering those great truths as naturally and as easily as conversing on the ordinary topics of life, and the description of his raising the dead is a description of an act as natural and easy as the most ordinary action of life. We may safely challenge any one who denies the fact of the incarnation to show, on the supposition that there was an incarnation, what there is in the whole of the four Gospels that is inconsistent with such an idea, or that strikes the mind as incongruous on such a supposition. And even with this model before us, let it be attempted again, even by the most cultivated intellect of the world, to represent an incarnate God, and we should have a representation of the gods of Greece and Rome, or the puerilities and absurdities of the Hindoo incarnations, or a very imperfect copy of Jesus of Nazareth.

(6.) How, now, is this to be accounted for? If the case was real, and if there was a real incarnation in the person of Christ, and if these illiterate men were inspired to give a just account of his life, then the whole matter is explained; if neither of these were true, then the mystery remains as yet unsolved, and will remain unsolved forever.

LECTURE IX.

THE CHRISTIAN RELIGION AS ADAPTED TO THE WANTS
OF MAN, AS ILLUSTRATED IN THESE EIGHTEEN HUND-
RED YEARS.

AFTER the lapse of eighteen hundred years, in which
Christianity has had a fair opportunity, with other religions, to make a trial of what it is, we ought to be
able to show that it meets a want in man, and that the
manner in which it does this is proof of its divine origin. The argument would be the stronger if it could
be shown that other forms of religion have failed to
meet this want, and that they, in this respect, leave the
race as they find it. The direct argument for the divine origin of Christianity, as derived from this source,
would be that God has endowed man with certain
wants and necessities as a religious being, and that, in
the failure of all other systems, the system which would
actually meet those wants must have had its origin in
Him who has thus endowed the human soul.

It may be assumed now that the ancient religions of
the world did not meet those wants, and that for this
reason they have been suffered to die out. The Hebrew religion did not do this; for, although it has remained in the world, and is, in fact, found in almost all
nations, it does not so commend itself to mankind as to
make them desire to revive it, and to rebuild the Temple; and, but for some purposes which can be best explained on the supposition that the prophecies in the
Bible respecting it are to be fulfilled, it would have

died out long ago, and would be now reckoned with the religion of the Egyptians and the Babylonians as among the things that are past.

The religion of the Chaldæans, of the Egyptians, of the Assyrians, of the Persians, of the Greeks, of the Romans, did not meet the wants of mankind, and have been suffered to die. The religion of the Egyptians was dead, not to be revived again, when Christianity appeared. The same was true of the religion of Babylon and Nineveh. The religion of Zoroaster was dying away. The religion of the Greeks had lost its power, and that of the Romans was following in the same line of decline and extinction. Those religions were becoming effete and obsolete; and whether a new religion should come or not to meet the wants of mankind, there was nothing that could revive *them*, and restore to them their former ascendency. They have now, in fact, died out, and nothing can revive and restore them. Julian brought all the power of the empire to bear on the expressed purpose of restoring paganism, endeavoring to reanimate it by incorporating into it, in some measure, the spirit of Christianity; for he "beheld with envy," says Mr. Gibbon, "the wise and humane regulations of the Church; and he very frankly confesses his intention to deprive the Christians of the applause, as well as the advantage, which they had acquired by the exclusive practice of charity and beneficence."* He failed, and the attempt was decisive and final. No one of imperial rank has ventured on the experiment since, and the world has shown no disposition to recall to life the ancient religions of Egypt, of Babylon, of Nineveh, of Persia, of Greece, of Rome. Not an idol of the ancient religions has been restored to its place. Not a

* Decline and Fall, vol. ii., p. 31.

temple of ancient paganism is occupied as a place of worship. There are no augurs, flamens, priests, or vestal virgins; there are no restored altars and no sacrifices. Those priests are disrobed; those altars are destroyed; those temples, immortal works of art, stand as noble ruins, to tell what the religion was in its palmy days, but no one, denizen or foreigner, visits them now to worship the gods once honored there. The Parthenon is in ruins; the Pantheon is a Christian church, in honor of the Virgin Mary; Minerva is no more adored in the one, and the gods of the nations are no longer set up in the other. These ancient religions did not meet the wants of human nature, and they have been suffered to die away, to be revived no more.

It is a fair question whether Christianity has become, or ever will become, thus antiquated and obsolete, and whether, in the advanced period of the world which we have reached, it shows that it is not adapted to the nature of man, and is to die away, to be superseded or not by some other form of religion; whether the time has come, or will soon come, when, whatever it may have done hitherto, some new system — say the "positive philosophy," shall be substituted in its place. "Christianity, we are told," says Professor Goldwin Smith, "like other phases of the great onward movement of humanity, has its place, and that a great place in history. In its allotted epoch it was progressive in the highest degree, and immense veneration and gratitude are due to it on that account; but, like other phases of the same movement, it had its appointed term. That term it has already exceeded. It has already become stationary or retrograde; it has begun, instead of being the beneficent instrument, to be the arch-enemy of human progress. It cumbers the earth; and the object of all

honest, scientific, free-thinking men, who are lovers of
their kind, should be to quicken the death-pangs into
which it has manifestly fallen, and remove once for all
this obstruction to the onward movement of the race.
Confusion and distress will probably attend the final
abandonment of 'the popular religion;' but it is better
at once to encounter them than to keep up any longer
an imposture which is disorganizing and demoralizing
to society, as well as degrading to the mind of man.
Let us at once, by a courageous effort, say farewell to
our old faith, and, by a still more courageous effort,
find ourselves a new one."*

In illustrating the argument which I propose to submit to you at this time, it will be proper, in the first
place, to make some inquiries, and to lay down some
principles, in regard to *man*, considered with reference
to religion, or to the necessities of his nature as demanding a religion; and, in the second place, to consider the
question whether Christianity satisfies the wants of our
nature in this respect; or, in other words, how far in
eighteen hundred years it has commended itself to man
as meeting those wants, and as thus showing that it is
from God.

The entire argument will be stated in view of the fact
that there has been a practical trial of Christianity on
these points for a period now extending over more than
eighteen hundred years.

I. The first point relates to human nature—to man—
considered with reference to the necessity of a religion.

It may be assumed that a system of religion claiming
to be from God, in order that it may be received by
man, *must* be in accordance with the moral nature of
man, and with his innate convictions of what is true

---

* Lectures on the Study of History, p. 118.

and what is right. In other words, a revelation will not contradict what our nature has taught us to believe to be true and right, but such a revelation will be in the line of such convictions, and will *add* to them, not *ignore* or *deny* them.

This is a point to which the infidel may hold us. If the pretended revelation is not of this character, he has an argument against it which we can not well answer; if it has this character, we have an argument for its truth to which he may find it not less difficult to reply.

(1.) The first point to be considered here is, What is the "end" of life? What is man made for? What, if the object of his creation were accomplished, or fully carried out, would be secured, so that we could say that the purpose or end of life was fully obtained? These questions are equivalent to that which, to most of us, was proposed in our early childhood, as being proper not only to our age then as entering on life, but as lying at the foundation of every just system of theology, "What is the chief end of man?" The framers of our Westminster Catechism felt that *that* was the first subject on which it was proper to instruct a child; the man of mature or advanced years will feel that that is the great question which is to be before him alike in the middle and at the end of life.

Can we look into the nature of man, and find an answer to this question?

Men answer it according to their own philosophy; their propensities; their pleasure. The Epicurean was ready with his answer; the Stoic with his; the Platonist with his. The votary of the world; the child of gayety; the disciple of mammon; the aspirant for fame, each is ready with his. There is *something* which, being accomplished, would be to them the "end of life;"

which would meet, as they suppose, all the aspirations of their nature, and which, being obtained, would be an answer to the question. For what purpose were they made? Why were they endowed with the faculties which have been conferred upon them? Why have such hopes and aspirations been implanted in their souls?

To furnish a just answer to the question, let us look at the following things:

(a) There *is* such an "end" or object contemplated in the creation of man. There are so many aspirations; so many hopes; so many desires—there is, if the expression may be used, so much *machinery* in the mental construction of man, that we look for an end or object, just as we do in the watch or the steam-engine. There is a stimulus prompting to *something*, of which the main-spring in the one, and the steam in the other, and the arrangements for distributing and directing the power in both, would be a faint illustration. If there *is* no such end or object, all the complexity of wheels and springs, so nicely adjusted in the one, and all the arrangements of boilers and valves in the other, would be a mere waste. In our moral nature there is much of this. There is clear proof of design. There is great skill displayed. There is a very nice adjustment of our different mental powers to each other. There is no confusion. The powers of our nature are never displaced. There is more in the *variety* of those powers than in the most complicated machinery; there is more skill in the adjustment. There has been a vast *expenditure* of wisdom in our mental constitution. Can we believe that it has been for naught—for no "end" or purpose?

(b) Whatever that "end" may be, considered as characterizing *man*, it must be *common* to the race. If the

O

race is one, we shall find it under all the types of humanity. If the Caucasian, Mongolian, Ethiopian, and American varieties constitute one *race*, we shall find it the same in all; if these different varieties are different *races*, we shall find some such "end" pertaining to each of those races respectively; if we find that there *is* some one end common to all these varieties, it will be difficult to set aside the argument from that fact that these varieties *are* one race, and that the Bible account of the origin of man, as derived from one pair, is true. The inquiry is, What is the "end" of *man*?—not of the *brute*. There is an "end" or purpose in their creation, but we should not be satisfied on being told that the end of *our* creation is the same as theirs. That is a philosophy not to be recognized in this place as true philosophy which makes no distinction between man and the brute.

(c) Whatever that "end" or purpose may be, it must relate to the future. As far as we have the means of judging, the brute creation, so far as consciousness is concerned, if that term may be applied to a brute, acts only with reference to the present. Brutes make no calculations; they form no plans; they have no "ends" of living which extend into that which is to come. There is nothing in their nature which, being developed, will find its complement or fulfillment in any thing lying in the future. The arrangement by which the beaver builds its dam, and the bee hoards its stores of honey, and the squirrel gathers nuts and acorns for the winter, and the bird makes its nest, is an arrangement of instinct, not of thought—whatever that instinct may be. However in other respects man may resemble the brute, yet he differs in this—that his plans *do* pertain to the future, and that those plans are not the result of instinct, but of conscious thought. There is something in the future in which our happiness lies. It is not in the present.

(*d*) That arrangement looks on to a future state. What I mean is, that there is that in the mental constitution of man which looks to a continuance of being beyond death; which would not be found in man if he were not to exist there; and which can be explained only on the supposition that he is immortal—unless it shall be alleged that the Maker of man has deceived and beguiled him by unfounded hopes and fears: that is, unless a watchmaker had made a watch with no purpose that it should keep time, or a machinist had made a steam-engine with no purpose that it should ever accomplish any end in the cotton factory, on the railroad, or in the steam-boat. This arrangement is in the very nature of man, and it extends to all the results of human conduct. The plans of men relate to the future. The results of their actions strike into the future. Those results are indefinite in regard to the future; and as it is said that the circle of the wave made by the pebble may expand indefinitely over the ocean, or the slightest vibration of the air by speech may affect the whole atmosphere of the globe, or any change on the earth's surface, or in the earth's interior, may affect all the worlds of matter, so it is certain that human conduct, in its results, will extend indefinitely into the eternity of the future. Those results travel over all the changes of this life to meet us when *those* changes are passed through, and will meet us in the world where there is no change. Nothing interrupts those results. The deeds of youth travel on to meet the old man bending over the grave; the crimes committed in one land travel over continents and oceans to meet him on the other side of the globe;

the conduct of yesterday comes over the slumberings of the night, and meets us to-day. Sleep does not interrupt that course; time does not; distance does not; and there is no reason to think that death will, for death is not an interruption to life and consciousness— no, not so much as a night's sleep.

There is, therefore, some "*end*" for which man was made, and that end relates to the future.

(2.) There is a *religious* want in man that must be met in a revelation from God. Man is a religious being, and unless a pretended revelation meets and satisfies the wants of man *as* a religious being, it can not be received as a revelation from God.

This want in man as a religious being exists in two forms: (*a*) as essential to his nature, and (*b*) as a fallen being.

(*a*) As man; as essential to his nature.

This is an original principle of our nature, and is universal. It is not the result of culture; it is not originated as the world advances from barbarism to civilization; it is not detached from society as a relic of barbarism when the world makes those advances; it does not characterize exclusively any one race of men; it is not among the things which enter into the formation of the different "types" of mankind; it does not serve in any way to distinguish the Caucasian, the Mongolian, the Ethiopian, and the American races; it is not connected with the origin of species, or with the development of species. Every where it exists, from the lowest form of fetichism to the highest forms of devotion in which homage is rendered to the one infinite and independent God.

The desire of knowledge is universal in man; the desire of society is universal; the desire of happiness is

universal; the principle of acting for the future is universal. The existence of will, and imagination, and
memory, and reason is universal—in the lowest "types"
of humanity, and in the highest; in the Ethiopian, the
American, the Mongolian, and the Caucasian races.
The mind of the Caucasian does not differ from the
mind of the Ethiopian in this respect. In neither case
is it the result of culture; in neither case has it sprung
from the change from barbarism to civilization; in
neither case can it be classed among the "artificial"
wants that have been originated by an advanced state
of society; in neither case is it detached by progress
in civilization. Nothing has been added in respect to
these qualities of mind by civilization; nothing has been
dropped as the world has advanced. There never has
been a tribe of men found, in the lowest forms of humanity, where these things do not exist; there never
has been such an advance made in civilization that any
new faculty or power has been added to the human
mind. All these are original endowments; all are the
work of the Creator.

Just so it is in religion. He who forms a theory of
human nature on the supposition that man is not a religious being, and has not a religious want to be supplied, forms just such a theory as he would should he
assume that man has not a will, or is not endowed with
memory or with reason. He who attempts to meet the
wants of the world without recognizing the religious
principle, acts just as wisely as he would who should
attempt to meet the wants of society on the supposition that man has no desire of knowledge; that he has
no social propensities; that he has no will to be governed; that he has no rational nature to guide him;
that he has no passions to be restrained.

That religious want must be met and satisfied in a pretended revelation. If this is not done, the race will sooner or later throw the system off—as the old systems of Greek and Roman mythology have been thrown off, as not meeting the wants of man.

(*b*) There is a religious want in man as a fallen and sinful being. It is in vain to deny that the race is sinful, for all laws proceed on that supposition; all history has recorded the fact. Tribunals of justice, prisons, police arrangements, and the human consciousness, all proclaim that man is a fallen being.

The remedy for this is somehow to be found in religion. Such is the universal belief of man. The conviction of depravity takes this form, and is illustrated by the religions of the world. There are no religions on earth for perfectly pure and holy beings; there are none which are not founded on the conviction of human depravity; there are none which do not make arrangements, in some form, for deliverance from sin.

All the religions of the world are religions of sinners. With the exception of a few Pharisees, Philosophers, and Deists—Lord Herbert, the first and the best of British Deists, is not, however, one of these, for he made " repentance for sin" one of the ten articles of universal belief as entering into religion — with these exceptions, all the religions of the world are the religions of sinners. They are religions of sacrifice; of penance; of pilgrimages; of self-inflicted tortures designed to propitiate the gods, and to secure safety and forgiveness. Hecatombs of victims have been offered, and rivers of blood have flowed to make expiation for human guilt.

There is no conviction more nearly universal in our world than that the nature of man is sinful, and that a religion to meet his wants must be a religion that will propose an expiation for sin, and that will give peace to a guilty conscience.

This universal conviction may be regarded as the basis of our argument on this subject, and as final in the case. It is vain to argue against universal convictions of the human mind. It is vain to attempt to set them aside. He never argues safely who argues against those universal convictions; and however specious or plausible a system of philosophy may be, it will ultimately be set aside unless it is founded on those universal convictions.

It may—it must be assumed, therefore, that a religion to meet the wants of men must be a religion adapted to sinners, or must be based on the supposition that there is not only a religious want in man founded in his original nature, but also in the fact that he is a sinner.

(3.) There are some principles pertaining to these facts which the friends and the enemies of revelation must alike admit to be true. They are such as the following:

(a) *There is such a thing as truth.*

Truth may be regarded as comprising two things:

First. Truth as spoken, stated, represented; that is, as exhibited by words, by signs, by pictures, by statuary. In this sense, truth is *the representation of things as they are.* A painting, in this sense, is true if it is a proper representation of a landscape, of a waterfall, of a historical scene, or of the human countenance. A drama or a novel is true if it correctly represents human nature, or is a just delineation of the passions of man. Astronomical truth is a correct representation of the heavenly bodies; geological truth, a correct representation of the world before the creation of man, as disclosed by rocks and fossils; historical truth, a correct representation of events as they have occurred in past ages; mathematical truth, a correct representation of facts in regard to number and quantity.

Second. Truth considered as existing in the reality of things, or in the events and facts which are thus represented, or which lies at the basis of such representation. In all truth there is not only a *representation*, but a *basis* for the representation, or something on which the representation is founded, and to which it must conform. Thus, if the statement is made that two and two make four, or that all the angles of a triangle are equal to two right angles, the *statement* of these facts is truth as *represented;* but there is truth as the *basis*, or as the *foundation* of this statement. These facts or realities remain the same whether there is any representation of them or not; whether they are known or unknown; whether the representation of them by words, or signs, or symbols, is true or false.

(*b*) *There is that in man which responds to truth, or which is a just ground of appeal in regard to truth.* The mind is so constituted that an impression is made upon it by truth different from the impression made by error. It is so made that it may be an element of calculation in endeavoring to influence others; that they may be, and will be, affected by truth if it is fairly brought before their minds; so made that it is fair to assume that there will be a *uniform* result in regard to the same individual, and in regard to different individuals, by the proper exhibition of truth. Wherever man is found, civilized or savage; whatever language he may speak; under whatever government he may live; whatever laws he may obey, or whatever form of philosophy or religion he may embrace, so far as truth makes any impression, it is always the same impression, for it always finds that in the mind which responds to it in precisely the same way. This fact, not indeed capable of demonstration, we always *assume* as a maxim, or as an elementary thought in our endeavors to influence others. We have the fullest conviction that to two boys in a school, the proposition that two and two make four conveys to them, as boys, precisely the same idea, and conveys to them now the same idea which it will when they reach middle life or old age. We can not doubt, also, that it conveys to those boys the same idea which it did to Newton in the maturity of his powers, or that, to an American savage, or to a wandering Bedouin, or to a New Zealander, it would convey precisely the same impression. In like manner, also, although we may not be able to demonstrate it, we have the fullest assurance that the impression or image conveyed to the mind by a tree, a landscape, a waterfall, a flower, is the same; the same to the individual mind in all its changes; the same to all minds, whether civilized or savage. And, on the same principle, so far as the minds of men are enlightened to appreciate truth, the same thing occurs in regard to moral truths. That a parent should love his child; that a child should venerate its parent; that ingratitude is base; that treachery is wrong; that to do good to others is right—all these, and similar propositions, we have every reason to suppose, convey exactly the same idea to every mind. We may *suppose*, indeed, that it might have been otherwise; that, for example, the eyes of men might have been so made that what to one conveys the idea of white might have conveyed to others the idea of red; that men might have been so made that what to one seems to be a triangle would seem to another to be a quadrangle; that what

O 2

seems now to be virtuous and honorable to one, might have seemed dishonorable and wicked to another; but it is evident that, in that case, the world could not have moved on in harmony at all, any more than it could at the confusion of tongues at Babel. All would have been disorder; language would have been useless; any communication of ideas from one to another would have been impossible; society would have been impracticable; speech, schools, writing, printing, painting, statuary, would have been useless, and the world would have a universal, though temporary Babel, for it would soon have come to an end.

(c) *Truth depends, for its reception by the mind, on its being perceived as truth.*

The mind *sees* or *perceives* it to be true. When the truth referred to is an axiom, it is perceived at once without any medium; when it is the result of a demonstration, the process of the demonstration merely puts the mind, in reference to the truth demonstrated, in the same state in which it is, without any such process—as it is in reference to an axiom or self-evident truth.

In illustration of this, it may be remarked that it is possible to conceive that the power of perceiving truth as intuitive, or without the aid of reasoning, might exist to almost any extent in created beings, as it exists in an absolutely unlimited extent in God. We may suppose that there might be, and that there actually may be now, created intelligences to whom all that is now perceived by the highest intellects on earth as the result of the profoundest analysis may be seen to be true at a glance, and may be, in fact, to their minds, *maxims* or self-evident truths, lying, in their investigations, at the foundation of a vastly higher method of reasoning than is yet possible to man, and bearing the same relation to a system of truth which is not now conceivable by us, which the maxims of geometry do to the highest forms of mathematical reasoning known among men. It is said of Newton that he read the propositions of Euclid as if they were maxims or self-evident truths, as being too plain and obvious to need demonstration. Even the celebrated forty-seventh proposition of the first book he did not pause to demonstrate, for he saw at a glance the truth of the proposition, and it can not be doubted that there *may be* minds to whom the highest discoveries, even of Newton, would be perceived at once to be *axioms* or *self-evident* truths, from which they would start off on a higher career of reasoning than would be possible for any intellect known to us. Then there is the mind of *God*, high above all, to whom *all* truth is self-evident—the mind of One who sees all truth as we perceive the simplest maxims of geometry; who never *reasons*, but sees and states things at once as they are.

(*d*) *There is a distinction between right and wrong, and this distinction is founded in the nature of things.*

A thing can not be both right and wrong at the same time; or now right and now wrong, as the result of appointment; or made right or wrong by mere will. An object can not be black and white at the same time; or now white and now black, as the result of appointment; or made white or black by mere will. That can not be made right to-day which in precisely the same circumstances was wrong yesterday, and that can not be right for one class or order of beings which in precisely the same circumstances would be wrong in another. A lie can not be truth, nor can truth be falsehood; honesty can not be fraud, nor fraud honesty; love can not be hatred, nor hatred love; and as these can not be

transmuted into one another, so by no authority can
they, in precisely the same circumstances, be made obli-
gatory in one case and be prohibited in another. No
one can believe that *justice* in God or man depends on
mere will, or that it would be proper for either to perform any act which he chose, and call it *justice*. In like
manner, no one can believe that *truth* in God or man depends on mere will, and that it would be proper for
either to make any statement which he chose and to
call it *truth*, or that it would be right to call one utterance to-day *truth*, and to call it to-morrow *falsehood*.
Every man is somehow so made that he *can not* believe
that the contrary of this would be true, or that, under
any circumstances, it would be proper for even God to
reverse things in such a way that it would be right for
Him to do what he now denounces and condemns as
evil, false, and wrong, or that the mere act of his doing
it would make it right. Every conception which we
can form of the Supreme Being implies that, by His own
eternal nature, he *is* just, and holy, and true, and good ;
not that he has *made himself* to be so by an arbitrary
act, or that the contrary *would be* just, and holy, and
true, and good, if found in Him. Account for it as we
may, we are so constituted that we must believe this,
and can not believe the contrary; and this fact demonstrates that it was *designed* by our Maker that it *should
be so.*

(e) *There is that in man which responds to the distinction of right and wrong.* .

This proposition is almost too plain to admit of illustration. All men instinctively act on it in their treatment of others; all legislators assume it to be true; all
parents regard it as indisputable in their treatment of
their children; all authors who write on the subject of

morals take it for granted; and all preachers of the Gospel make it the ground of their most solemn appeals and most earnest exhortations. To Jews and Gentiles alike — barbarians, Scythians, bond and free, the apostle Paul could say of his preaching, " by manifestation of the *truth* commending ourselves *to every man's conscience* in the sight of God" (2 Cor., iv., 2), nor could we preach at all if we did not assume that this could be done.

(*f*) *A revelation from God will not contradict any truth, on any subject, however that truth may be made known.*

This, too, may be assumed as an axiom, and is. too plain to admit of argument. "*All* truth is from the sempiternal source of light divine." One truth can not contradict another, and God can not contradict in his word what he has declared in any other way to be truth.

A revelation will not contradict *its own teachings*— that is, it will not deny in one place what it affirms in another; a revelation will not contradict *scientific* truth —that is, God will not, in his word, contradict what he has revealed to men through their own reason or by his own works; a revelation will not contradict *historical* truth—that is, God, in his word, will not contradict what has actually occurred and has been properly recorded; a revelation will not contradict *moral* truth— that is, the word of God will not contradict what has been clearly made known as right or wrong by the constitution of the mind as he has made it. These points are mere illustrations of what is said in the Bible of God: "He can not deny himself" (2 Tim., ii., 13). The infidel has a right to hold us to this proposition when we urge the claims of a revelation; the defender of such a revelation is bound to show that the Bible does not contradict itself, and that it does not contradict any truth, from any other source, communicated to man.

(*g*) *A pretended revelation which should contradict established truth could not be received by mankind.*

This, also, is so plain as not to admit of demonstration. Two opposite statements could not both be received as true. No conceivable evidence in favor of a revelation could be stronger than the conviction that two and two make four, or that all the angles of a triangle are equal to two right angles. The mind must believe these things. That mind is not in a sound state which does not believe them.

In the application of this rule it is implied (1) that, if faith in a professed revelation be demanded, it is right to require that all its statements shall be fairly *consistent* with the ascertained facts of science; and (2) it is equally implied that it is proper to demand, on the other hand, that if there is any alleged conflict between the statements of the book and the truths of science, the facts of science *shall be clearly established.* It is right for the friends of revelation, for example, to insist, if it is alleged that man has been longer on the earth than the statements in the Bible shall warrant, that the *fact* that he has been thus long on the earth shall be established *as* a fact, and that it shall not be mere theory or conjecture; that if it be alleged that the Mosaic statement that all the races of men on the earth are descended from one pair is inconsistent with the doctrine of the separate origin of the races, the *fact* of such a separate origin shall be clearly demonstrated; that if it is alleged that the disclosures of geology are inconsistent with the statements in the book professing to be a revelation, the *facts* of geology shall be clearly established. The alleged truths of science must be demonstrated; the facts must be ascertained; the contradiction must be palpable; the discrepancy must be so great that the statements can not, by any fair rules of interpretation, be reconciled.

(*h*) *A revelation on the same line of subjects will, so far as coincident, carry forward the truth already known, not contradict it.*

The meaning of this rule is this—that a revelation *may* make disclosures in regard to truth *in advance* of what is known from other sources, or may state what will be seen to be true when the discoveries of science *come up to it*, if they ever do; in other words, that the disclosures of revelation will be in *advance of*, and not *contradictory to*, the truths otherwise ascertained. Between the two there will be no more discrepancy than between the actual though imperfect knowledge of a child and the more matured and perfect knowledge of the same child when he becomes a man; than between the lowest truths of geometry, as comprehended by the school-boy, and the highest astronomical disclosures of Newton or Laplace.

An illustration of this point may be derived from the disclosures of the telescope. Vast as are the revelations made by that instrument; far as it penetrates into distant worlds; and much as it has enlarged the boundaries of human knowledge, all its disclosures are in entire harmony with those of the naked eye, and only carry forward, on the same line, what was seen by the unaided process of vision. The telescope never penetrates regions where the laws of light are different from those which affect the naked eye. It never discloses facts in regard to other worlds which are inconsistent with the doctrine of universal gravitation. It never penetrates

into the empire of another God; and could the eye itself, now so comparatively limited in its range of observation, and to which so much which the telescope reveals is unknown, be so *enlarged* in its powers as to
take in all that the telescope reveals, it would see
things just as it does now by its aid.*

These seem to me to be just principles in regard to a
revelation; principles on which the friends and the enemies of the Bible may agree.

(4.) I proceed, then, to observe that a revelation from
God—a religion which he reveals—will, in accordance
with these principles, meet the *wants* of man; alike his
religious wants as a creature, and his wants as a sinner.
It may be demanded that satisfactory provision shall
be made for both. If provision is not made for them,
it may be at once rejected; it will, sooner or later, be
dropped, as the religions of Egypt, of Babylon, and of
Greece have been. Such a revelation must meet and
satisfy the essential religious want in the nature of
man, and it must, at the same time, meet and satisfy his
wants as a sinful and fallen being, and in both commend
itself to him as true. These are by no means the same
thing, as the provision to be made for the wants of a
sick person and a person in health are by no means the
same.

For the former of these there is the demand for a
God to be worshiped; there is the want of that which
will answer the question "What is the end of life?" or

* These points seem to me to deserve a more extended illustration
than would have been possible in a single Lecture, and I may be permitted, therefore, to refer to a work entitled "Inquiries and Suggestions in Regard to the Foundation of Faith in the Word of God,"
published by Parry & McMillan, 1859, from which these remarks have
been abridged, p. 5 -36.

why man was made—some object worthy of the powers which have been called into being; there is the necessity of some statement or promise which will meet
the desire of immortality; there is the need of an affir
mation that there will be a world beyond the grave,
where the soul may forever expand in power and in
knowledge; there is the need that there shall be a range
of truths and objects that shall correspond with the
greatness of the human soul.

For the latter of these the demand would be for a revelation of some system that would in its arrangements
contemplate man as a fellow-being, and meet and sat-   *f-?????*
isfy his wants as such.   Thus, in studying the works of
nature with reference to the question whether the world
has been fitted up so as to meet the wants of man, there
are two distinct questions: the one, Whether there are
arrangements to meet his wants *as a creature of God*,
considered without reference to the question whether
he is liable to disease? and the other is, Whether there
are arrangements to meet his wants considered *as* liable
to disease and as a sufferer?   These are by no means
the same questions.   The arrangements might have been
complete in regard to the one, while no provision should
have been made for the other.   The one is the inquiry
which would have occurred to man when in the Garden
of Eden, and when a stranger to disease; the other is
an inquiry which could not but occur to him when rejected from Eden, when driven forth to encounter disease, and when death was in prospect.   The former inquiry might have been easily answered.   The first Paradise, in its arrangement, presented an answer at once.
But what would the man have discerned there which
would have contemplated the latter?   Even if there
were such things there, until he had become a fallen be-

ing, and was brought into circumstances when he needed them, they must have passed for things whose use was unknown.

As a matter of fact, however, there is in nature just such an arrangement; an arrangement made in the beginning of the creation, and in anticipation of the fact that man would be subject to disease. It is to be remarked, also, that, so far as appears, the one is entirely independent of the other; the one is in no manner necessary to the other. The world, as a world, might have been complete without attaching healing properties to plants and minerals; certainly without creating things whose *only* properties of value are *healing* properties. If mercury could not have been so made as to have been of value in the arts *without* also the appendage that it might be a medicine, yet certainly there was no necessity for creating the Peruvian tree whose only value is the bark, and the only value of whose bark is the cure of fevers.

In fact, the arrangement for healing is an entirely independent system, and yet as essential to man as the arrangements for the supply of his wants in health. The wonderful process by which a broken bone knits itself together was in no wise necessary for the *making* of a bone; the process by which a severed vein or artery will plow for itself a new groove, and lay down a new artery or vein for the blood, was in no wise necessary for the making of a vein or artery originally, nor for the original and healthful purposes of either—for arteries and veins for conducting the blood from and to the heart would have been perfect without this arrangement; the creation of the materials of the *materia medica* of the healing art was in no wise necessary for the production of food for man. It is a separate arrangement. The one is not necessary to the other. The one does not explain the other. The one is of importance to man every where; the other is the foundation of a distinct profession—the medical profession.

But the world as it is would not have been complete without both, any more than a system of religion for man would have been complete for man alike as a creature adapted to worship, and as a sinner to be redeemed and saved, without both. A system of arrangements for man *in health* would not have met the wants of man *in sickness*, and a system which did not contemplate the latter, and which did not make provision for it, would . not have been adapted to our world as it is. Hence it was, that in the very structure of the creation, there was an *underlying system* in anticipation of the fact that man would be a sufferer—a system doubtless existing in paradise, and a system certainly now extending all over the world—for the arrangements for healing diseases are found on all the continents and in all the islands, and in every land there are men endowed with peculiar faculties to study nature with this view, and to apply these remedies to the ever-varying forms of disease.

Precisely of the same nature, though on a higher scale, is it true that there was need of an arrangement which would contemplate man as a sinner, and which would make provision for his wants as such; and as the world of nature could not be regarded as adapted to the wants of man as he is without the arrangements to alleviate pain and to cure diseases, so the arrangements for religion would not have been complete without a remedial system for sinners.

II. We come, then, to what must be the main inquiry on this subject, the question whether Christianity is a

religion which thus meets and satisfies the wants of
man; or, in other words, how far in eighteen hundred
years it has commended itself to man *as* meeting those
wants, and as thus showing that it is from God.

(1.) Considered as a *religion*, it meets the essential
wants of man. We have seen what those wants are as
every where indicated in our world—as essential; as
deep-laid in our nature; as characterizing man. Man
wants a religion. He wants a God. He wants an object of worship. He wants the hope of another life.
He wants the assurance that the soul is immortal.

Certainly all these are found in Christianity. It is a
"*religion.*" It is nothing else. That is its essential
idea. It is not philosophy; it is not science; it is not
a political theory; it is a *religion*, and meets the wants
of the soul only in regard to religion. It reveals a God,
an object of worship. In the God of the Bible there is
all that can enter into the mind in the conception of a
God. He is infinite; he is uncreated; he is almighty;
he is the maker of all things; he is a Being whose
agency is every where; he is the Ruler of the universe;
he is holy, just, pure, merciful. All that the soul can
demand in the idea of *worship* surely — of adoration,
homage, reverence — is to be found in the God of the
Bible.—Man wants some just view of what is the proper "end" of life. Christianity declares it. It reveals
an "end" of living worthy of the powers with which he
is endowed, for it brings before him, as the main object
of life, the idea of living for eternity.—Man wants the
hope of another life. Christianity reveals such a hope,
and sets it before him as that which is in advance of
all others, and which is to crown all.—Man wants the
assurance that the soul is immortal. What he can not
find in the argument of Plato; what he can not find in

any other religion, he finds here, laid at the foundation of the whole system, that the soul is to live forever.

(2.) It meets the wants of man as a sinner—as a fallen being. We could not regard it as of value; we could not receive it as a religion, if it did not. It meets that want. (a) It is the main idea in Christianity, running through the entire system, and, more than any other feature, constituting its peculiarity. (b) It is a special and distinct arrangement, as much so as the arrangement for healing disease is in the departments of nature. There are things in Christianity, entering into its very nature, which would not have been there, or which would have had no place, if it had not been supposed that man was a sinner, just as there are arrangements in nature which would not have been there, or which would have had no place, if it had not been supposed that man would be a sufferer, and the one without such a supposition would be as inexplicable as the other. (c) The system makes ample provision for pardon. It bears on its face the assurance that the arrangement is such that any and all may be forgiven. It excludes no one by the idea that its power can not reach the case, or that it was not intended for such a sinner, or that it is exhausted, as no one, under any form of disease, is shut out from the hope of a cure by the idea that no medicinal remedies were provided in the secrets of nature for such a case, or that the medicines of the world are exhausted. It excludes no one by the idea that the sin is so great that it can not be forgiven, and in the proclamation of amnesty it makes no exceptions. Human governments often do. In the times of the American Revolution, Samuel Adams and John Hancock were excepted by name in the royal proclamation of amnesty; in our own great rebellion

large numbers were excepted by proclamation from
the offer of pardon. (d) It contains provisions for pardon that are honorable to God and honorable to man.
Man, even guilty man, could not accept it if it were not
so. A child offending could not wish to be forgiven if
the pardon could not be extended to him without dis-
gracing his parent; an offender against human law
must demand that the pardon in his own case should
not be dishonorable to the government and to his country. So man, even a sinner, could not receive a religion as coming from God if it were essential to the
idea of the religion that God was regardless of truth,
of justice, and of law; that he had no concern about
his own character; that his veracity was of no consequence; that his law could be set aside at will; that it
was his nature to treat virtue and vice, truth and falsehood, rebellion and allegiance, both alike. Who could
put confidence in such a God? Who could embrace a
religion founded on such assumptions? Now something
like this *does* occur, and always occurs in pardon as extended to the guilty under a human government. The
pardon of an offender, justly convicted—and there is no
other proper idea of pardon—is *always* a proclamation
that in some cases crime may be committed with impunity; that in some cases the law is to be disregarded,
and the decrees of justice to be set aside; that guilty
men may go at large for whose crimes justice has received no atonement—no satisfaction. Pardon in such
a case always does just so much to weaken the strong
arm of the law; is just so far a proclamation that crime
may be committed with impunity. There is not a government in the world that could safely make the proclamation of universal forgiveness as it is made in the
Gospel; that could throw open the doors of all prisons;

that could invite all convicts—burglars, counterfeiters, thieves, and murderers, to come out and roam at large over the land. Who would feel that his house or his life was safe? (e) Again: The system of pardon proposed in Christianity is honorable to man—to those who have offended. It requires no needless humiliation; no mortifying concessions or confessions; no conformity to rites and ceremonies that would tend only to debase and degrade. It might have been otherwise; and we could not have rejected it with safety if it had been so. If it had required men to gird themselves with sackcloth; to cast dust on their heads; to sit down in ashes; to clothe themselves in habiliments of squalid poverty; to put on robes such as they wore who were condemned by the Inquisition—with tongues of fire and pictured demons; to go in solemn procession with some symbol of eternal death as deserved by sin; to pass thus through life humbled and degraded, man could not have proved that this would be wrong; he could not have shown that it would not be wise and well to accept of pardon and life even on these conditions. In the reign of Edward III. of England (1347), when Calais was besieged, Edward required as a condition in surrendering the city when it could hold out no longer, that "six of the most considerable citizens should be sent to him, to be disposed of as he should think proper; that they should come to his camp carrying the keys of the city in their hands, bareheaded and barefooted, with ropes about their necks, and on these conditions he promised to spare the lives of the remainder."* So, at least for the sake of illustration, we may conceive that God might have required all men to appear before him in some similar manner as a sign of submission and re-

* *Hume's* History of England, vol. i., p. 577.

pentance, and as a condition of pardon. But he has done no such thing. There are no degrading and debasing rites in the Christian religion; there are no humiliations required for the mere sake of humiliation; there are no arrangements merely to mortify men. There are no mummeries; there are no painful postures or processions; there are no requirements like those of letting the nails grow in the clenched hand till they cut into the flesh; fixing the arm in one position till it becomes rigid; swinging on hooks fastened in the muscles; standing on lofty columns in heat, and cold, and storm; or withdrawing to caves and solitudes far from the haunts of men. All these are the inventions of men themselves; they show, perhaps, what men would willingly have submitted to if such degradations had been required; they show what men regard as the proper representations and symbols of the evil and degradation of sin. But in the Gospel there are no degrading, no dishonorable acts required. Let us suppose, for the sake of illustration, that there had been. The son of an honorable father is guilty of a crime. He is told that he may be pardoned if he will perform some dishonorable act. He is to betray his father, and deliver him up to death. 'No,' says he, with generous indignation, 'I do no such thing. I can not purchase life on any such condition. I am indisputably guilty; but I can not add to that guilt a baser crime that I may live. I will not add meanness, and ingratitude, and filial impiety to my crime for the sake of saving my life. Welcome the rack; welcome the thumb-screw; welcome the gibbet, rather than that I should be guilty of such a crime!' God requires nothing of this. He asks no self-inflicted tortures; no painful pilgrimages; no renunciation of the dignity that belongs to a man, that he may be saved. He asks that he shall repent of sin and forsake it—for it is that which debases and degrades; he asks that he shall accept of the offer of mercy on the terms which he proposes—for that is the way in which we receive all the blessings which come from his hand; he asks that he shall lead a pure life, and hereafter keep his Maker's law.

(3.) The religion is *on a line* with all that exalts and adorns the race; with the solution of the problems which men are endeavoring to work out in regard to law, to liberty, to happiness. It *attaches* itself, by a natural affinity, to all that ameliorates and civilizes society; to all that is stricken out in the progress of the world that raises men to a higher elevation. There are religions which hold men as they are; there are religions which are obstructions to the advancement of the race; there are religions which are to be removed if the race shall make progress; there are religions which foster vice; there are religions which debase and degrade mankind. There was much in the religion of Greece that tended to encourage vice—for "it was not for every man to go to Corinth"*—refined, in many respects, as Corinth was; there is every thing in the Buddhist religion to fix society where it is, and to prevent progress; there is much in the Hindoo religion which must be removed if true science makes advances, for its *religion* and its *science* are identical—disclosed in the same books, and sanctioned by the same authority; there is every thing in the monastic system to hold men in degradation; there is much in the Roman Catholic system generally that has tended to retard the progress of mankind. It was not by an accident that Galileo was imprisoned; it is not by an accident that

* ὀυ παντὸς ἀνδρός τἰς Κόρινϑον ἰσίν ὐ πλους.

P

the Bible, under that system, is not spread abroad in
vulgar tongues.

I am not ignorant that it has been affirmed that
Christianity has retarded the progress of mankind, nor
are you or I ignorant of the arguments which have been
referred to on this subject.

It is not for me now, and in this place, to attempt to
prove that Christianity has been connected with the
progress of the race. In the fullest blaze of Christianity, and at the same time surrounded with the highest
developments of society in intelligence, in literature,
in the sciences, and in the ornamental and useful arts;
in an age and a country where, under the influence of
Christianity, the comforts of life have been carried to
the highest point hitherto reached; in a land of freedom, made free under the best developments of the
Christian religion, it would not become me to pause,
even were there time, to attempt to prove that Christianity is not inimical to the highest development of society; that it is *on the line* of all that adorns and exalts the race.

There have been, indeed, other civilizations; there
has been progress in other lands than those where
Christianity has prevailed.

But it is to be remarked that there has been no "*sustained historical progress*" except that which has been
confined to Christian nations. "Where," it may be
asked, "is the brilliant monarchy of Haroun Alras-
chid? How ephemeral was it as compared even with
that old Byzantine empire into whose frame Christianity had infused a new life under the very ribs of death;
a life which the fatal bequest of Roman despotism, extending itself to the Church as well as to the state,
could scarcely quench, and which, through ages of Mo-

hammedan oppression, has smouldered on beneath the ashes, to burst out again in reviving Greece. Even in the Moorish communities of Spain, the flower, as they were, of Mohammedan civilization, internal corruption had prepared the way for the conquering arms of Ferdinand and Isabella. Mohammedanism, however, whatever the degree of progressive energy displayed by it may have been, was not a separate and independent religion, but a debased offspring of Judaism and Christianity. Turning to the remoter East, we find that its history has not been a history of progress, but of the successive descents of conquering races from the more bracing climate of the North, subjugating the languid inhabitants of the plains, and founding a succession of empires, sometimes mighty and gorgeous, but always barren of nobler fruits, which, when the physical energy of the conquering race was spent in its turn, at once fell into decay. China advanced at an early period to a certain point of material civilization, but, having reached that point, she became a by-word of immobility, as Egypt, the ancient China, was in a former day. The civilization of Mexico is deplored by certain philosophers, who seem to think that, had its career not been cut short by Spanish conquest, it might have attained to a great height, and confirmed their views of history. But what reason is there to think that Mexico would ever have advanced beyond great buildings created by slave labor, human sacrifices, and abominable vices ?"*

But need I attempt to prove that Christianity is connected with the progress of the race; that it originates much that is connected with that progress; that it attaches itself to all that is connected with progress? Look at the press. If Christianity did not originate the

* Lectures on the Study of History, by *Goldwin Smith,* p. 121, 123.

discovery of the art of printing, yet that discovery was
not made in China, where it might have been supposed
it would have been; where, from time immemorial, they
had the art of printing solid pages from solid blocks of
wood, and where all that was necessary to complete the
art was to saw their blocks into separate letters—and
yet Chinese genius was exhausted when it had invented
the block; Chinese stolidity arrested the progress there,
and left the invention to be stricken out, as God intended it should be, in connection with the Christian religion.   If, too, the Bible was not the first book that was
printed, it was *one* of the first; and it has been, and
is even now, the book most frequently printed since.
Look at a missionary ship.   The missionary himself
goes as among the best representatives of Christian
lands, and of the highest form of Christian civilization—trained in Christian civilization, educated in the
best schools, imbued with the best forms of learning, instructed in science and the arts.   We know what he
will take with him to the benighted lands to which he
goes—the press, the telescope, the quadrant, the compass.   We know what he will do when he gets there.
He will set up the press; he will create a written language if there be not one existing; he will open a
school; he will found a college; he will introduce the
arts of life; he will preach the Gospel—the source of
all that which has transformed Huns, and Vandals, and
Goths, and Saxons, and Celts into the civilized nations
of Europe, and which has made Germany, and France,
and Holland, and England, and Scotland, and our own
land, what they are.*

* For a farther and a more full illustration of the subject, going into
details which the time would not permit in this Lecture, I may refer
to the Lectures on the Study of History, by *Goldwin Smith*, p. 146-

I have not exhausted this subject. I have scarcely entered on it.

I might dwell on the argument derived from the fact that the Gospel does not, like other religions, become effete, obsolete, and die out; that it imparts peace and comfort to the sorrowing and the sad—an arrangement in its very nature based on the idea that man is a sufferer; that it gives peace to the troubled conscience— an arrangement also in its very nature based on the idea that man is a sinner, and that the consciousness of sin gives a peculiar form of distress to the soul; and that it gives peace in the hour of death—an arrangement also in its very nature based on the idea that man must die—lighting up the dark valley, and taking away its "sting" from death, and its "victory" from the grave.

But there is one point involving the necessity of so much illustration that it can not be entered on now, and yet which is so essential to the argument that it could not be made complete without it. It is the relation of Christianity to the present stage of the world's progress in science, civilization, and the arts. That point will be reserved for the next, the closing Lecture.

Meantime, the inference which I would wish to draw from the argument presented this evening is, that such a religion must be from God.

This is an argument which we may use now, but which the apostles could not have used, and which could not have been employed by the early "apologists" for Christianity as it can be now. The experiment as to the actual adaptation of the scheme to the wants of man had not then been made. With them it was mainly theory, and there was as yet no experience to which

156. I may also refer, for general illustrations of the whole subject, to *Lecky* on the History of Rationalism in Europe, vol. ii., p. 222- 357.

they could appeal. With all that could be alleged from miracles, and prophecy, and the character of the Founder of the system, and the evidence of his resurrection from the dead and of his ascension to heaven, still it might be said that its adaptation to the real wants of man as a creature and a sinner had not then been tried. Who could tell whether, in the more advanced periods of the world's history; in the changes which would be made in human affairs; in the development of the powers of man in the future; in the progress in science and in the arts which the world would make in future ages, this religion, with all that seemed to them to be fitted to the wants of man, might not show itself insufficient to meet those wants, and pass into forgetfulness, as many systems of philosophy had then done, and as most of the religions of the world were then doing? Who, without the gift of prophecy, could then tell whether this religion would be found to be so adapted to the nature of man as to meet him with what would be needful in these new situations, and still maintain its position in advance of all that philosophy, science, and art could do for him?

We now are in a situation to answer these questions.

Eighteen hundred years have passed away, and they have been such in the changes occurring in society; in the progress of the race; in the developments of the human powers, that it may be assumed that if the religion has been found to be adapted to the wants of man in those eighteen centuries, it will in all the centuries to come.

The sum of what I have said in this argument is this: That the system of Christianity is based on a profounder view of human nature, and of the wants of man, than has been taken in any other system of religion, or than in any system of philosophy; that the arrangements which have been disclosed in the system are such as man *would* make if he had the wisdom and the power to make them himself—such as he has been struggling for and panting for in all ages, and all over the world; that these arrangements are, for the most part, wholly beyond the reach of the native powers of man—involving the necessity of an atonement for sin which man could not make; anticipating the wants of our nature in every new age of the world, and in every new phase of society; keeping up with the world in its progress, and still in advance of it—in the fact that unnumbered millions of the race, in all situations and ranks, have found in it an answer to the questions which men so naturally and properly ask about God and eternal things; in the fact that it has given peace in hundreds of millions of instances to consciences troubled by sin; in its influence on society—on woman, on slavery, on domestic comfort, on the arts of life, on liberty, on governments and laws, on habits, manners, and customs; in the fact that it has, from numberless eyes, wiped away the tears of sorrow, and that it has given support, peace, triumph in hundreds of millions of cases on the bed of death. Perhaps I might have made the argument much shorter. I might have staked all on this one point—*as I do now*—A RELIGION THAT WILL PRE-PARE A SINFUL MAN TO DIE, AND THAT WILL GIVE PEACE ON A DYING BED, MUST BE FROM GOD.

LECTURE X.

It has been remarked that "a system which would unite in one sublime synthesis all the past forms of human belief, which accepts with triumphant alacrity each new development of science, having no stereotyped standard to defend, and which represents the human mind as pursuing on the highest subjects a path of continual progress toward the fullest and most transcendent knowledge of the Deity, can never fail to exercise a powerful intellectual attraction."[*]

There is no doubt that the human mind desires such a system of religion; that it is endeavoring, in this age, in an eminent degree, to find it; that it will not be satisfied without such a system. In other words, it is undoubtedly true that a system of professedly revealed truth will not be received permanently by mankind unless it accords with this desire of the mind; unless it welcomes every new discovery in science, and each new invention in the arts; and unless it attaches itself to every thing that goes into the real civilization and progress of the world. To find, or to found such a system, is the present effort of Rationalism, and it is a fair question whether Christianity so meets and satisfies this demand of the human mind that it will continue to keep its place as the world makes advances.

[*] History of Rationalism in Europe, by *W. E. H. Lecky*, vol. i., p. 182.

The closing Lecture in this course will be designed, in some measure, to answer this question—a question which the world has a right to ask, and which we are bound to answer—a question on the solution of which the reception of what is otherwise adduced as evidence of the divine origin of the Christian religion will in a very material degree depend. The argument in the Lecture will be founded on the idea that a system originated long since—eighteen hundred years ago—which will meet the condition of all future ages; which began ahead of the world, and which keeps itself abreast or ahead of the world, must be from God. It is capable of easy demonstration that there is no such system unless it be Christianity.

It was assumed, of necessity, by Christianity, that it had truths to disclose of great importance to mankind, which the race, at the time when it was revealed, had been unable to discover.* Man had, indeed, made great progress in science, in civilization, and in art. The best talent in the world had been employed in investigating the works of nature, and in inquiring into the relations of man to the Creator and to another state of being. When Paul stood on Mars' Hill, he was, in respect to all that contributes to human comfort, and that marks the progress of the race, almost in a different world from what one would have been in the rude age of Tubal Cain, Jabal, and Jubal. A period of four thousand years had elapsed since the creation, and all that man had accumulated on the subjects of religion, philosophy, and the arts had culminated in Greece, and was represented by the objects around him, and by the men that stood before him. The experiment, continued for so long a time, and under such circumstances, whether man could

* 1 Cor., i., 2.

P 2

find out the knowledge of God and a way of salvation, might be regarded as having been fairly made. If it had been submitted to man himself to designate a sufficient time to make the experiment, he himself would admit that four thousand years must be regarded as ample for the trial; if it were submitted to him to select the circumstances under which the trial could best be made, he could hardly imagine, as I have endeavored to show in a former Lecture, that the trial could have been better made than in Greece. Yet, after that experiment had been thus made, the Gospel claimed to have truths indispensable to mankind far in advance of all that man had been able to discover, and which it was assumed could not be discovered by the unaided human powers. The fact that it had such truths, and that it answered questions which had been propounded by Greek philosophers, but for which no answer had been found, will not be disputed even by those who endeavor to explain the Gospel on some other supposition than that it is a revelation from heaven. It is claimed to be a fact by all who believe that Christianity is a revelation from God; it is shown to be a fact by the progress which the race has made *under* that new system as compared with its progress under the influence of the Grecian philosophy.

Eighteen hundred years have passed away, and during that period the race, in science, civilization, and the arts, has made advances far more rapid than in any eighteen centuries before, or than in all those four thousand years. The world is, in most important respects, a different world from what it was in the days of Pericles and Plato. The telescope has extended its boundaries indefinitely in one direction, and the microscope in the other. Science is a different thing now from what it was then; civilization is different; art is different. Our houses are different; our domestic arrangements are different; our facilities for passing from place to place, by land or sea, are different; our knowledge of distant lands and oceans is different; our means of recording, transmitting, and perpetuating truth are different; our knowledge of the substances which compose our globe is different; our knowledge of the world's history before man appeared on it is different; our means of cultivating the fields, and of conducting the operations of commerce, are different. Except in architecture and sculpture, there is nothing in respect to which the world is not now immeasurably in advance of what it was in the best days of Greece. A Greek of the age of Pericles would be lost now in the arrangements of civilization around him, not less than one of the age of Tubal Cain would have been if suddenly translated to Athens. We use no Greek plows in our fields; no Greek chariots in our wars or on our journeys; no Greek implements in preparing our food, in writing our books, in transmitting intelligence from place to place; no Greek weapons of war; no Greek ships in battle. We make no use in our schools of their treatises on natural history, astronomy, medicine, scarcely in mental philosophy; nor do we copy their style of domestic architecture, or refer to them for instruction in the mechanic arts. *We* are in a different world from what the ancient Greek was, and it might be interesting to speculate how long it would take Pericles or Plato to learn to act, and move, and speak, and *live* in our age.

It is a fair question whether, admitting that Christianity was in advance of the world at the time when it was communicated to men, it still holds the same relative position? Is it still ahead of the world? Is it abreast of it? Or has it fallen in the rear? Has it been superseded by the discoveries which men have made in science; by the progress of civilization; by the advances in the arts? Has the world reached a point where it can "get along" without the Gospel? Have the powers of the human mind been so developed during these eighteen hundred years that man can now successfully grapple with questions which were too difficult for even the cultivated mind of Greece; and have the secrets of nature been so explored that the knowledge which she has to impart to man, and which eluded the inquiries in the academy, the porch, or the lyceum, can now be found in the laboratory or the observatory? Or, to put the question in a form more favorable to Christianity, and in a form in which its friends would demand that it should be put: Has Christianity itself been an important element in the progress which the race has made, and are the institutions of the present time—the forms of civilization, the advances in the arts and the comforts of life, to be traced so far to Christianity that it may claim that it has been among the direct causes in effecting these changes? If it be assumed or conceded that *this* is so, then, also, it may be fairly asked whether it has not *done* its work, and may not now be dispensed with in the farther progress of the race, and whether it is not now to take its place with the systems adapted to a ruder age, which passed away when the results had become incorporated in permanent institutions, or when they had been superseded by better systems.

These are questions which would be suggested by certain forms of skepticism different from those of ancient times, but which are likely to become the forms of unbelief in the coming age. They are not questions which would have occurred in the times of Celsus, Porphyry, or Julian; they are not the questions which Hobbes, and Chubb, and Shaftesbury, and Bolingbroke would have asked, but they are questions which lie at the foundation of the whole system of Rationalism at the present day.

There is another question, also, as suggested by these remarks, which may be asked from a Christian point of view. Assuming, as the defender of Christianity must, that Christianity was ahead of the world at the time when the revelation was made, and that in its doctrines it still holds the same relative position, it is a fair question whether, in respect to its means of perpetuity and propagation, it still maintains the same relative position, or whether the apostles had advantages in this respect which the Church has not now, or which could not be employed with success in the present condition of the world. All history has united in the record of a very rapid diffusion of the Gospel in the times of the apostles; it has described the means which were employed, and which were then successful; it has delivered such an unmistakable testimony on the subject that it required all the powers of Mr. Gibbon to furnish a philosophical explanation of the fact of its propagation on the supposition that the Gospel is an imposture. But is it true that the Church in this age, in view of the present stage of the world in civilization, in science, and the arts, can engage in propagating the system under circumstances as favorable to success as were those which existed in the times of the apostles?

These, indeed, are not the same questions, but they are in the same line, and are alike suggested by the relation of Christianity to the present age. It may be

difficult to furnish an answer to both in the same argument, but perhaps the considerations suggested in relation to the one will involve all that is demanded in the
other.

I propose, in the conclusion of these Lectures, to consider the question with reference to an argument for
the truth of Christianity, and as a continuation of the
course of thought in the last Lecture on the adapted-
ness of Christianity to the wants of man.

The points necessary to be considered, in order to
a proper elucidation of the subject, are, the fact that
Christianity, from the nature of the case, is a fixed
and unchangeable system, or that it makes no progress
from age to age; the fact that, while Christianity is
thus fixed and stationary, the world does make progress
in science, civilization, and the arts; the fact that, in
the circumstances of the case, they unavoidably come
into collision with each other; the inquiry on what subjects they are likely to come into collision now as compared with former ages; the present relation of the one
to the other; and the inquiry how far an argument may
be derived from this view in favor of the divine origin
of the Christian system.

I. The first point is that Christianity, from the nature
of the case, is a fixed and unchanging system. It makes
no progress in the disclosure of doctrines to be believed; it was perfect as a system of redemption when
the Redeemer died, rose, and ascended to heaven; it
was complete as a system to be explained and understood when the volume of revealed truth was finished
on the island of Patmos. No new facts were to be
added to the record; no new doctrines were to be revealed; no changes were to be made to adjust it to a
future condition of the world; nor were the doctrines

to be modified to adapt them to new views in science or philosophy. The system for all time to come is to be found in the New Testament; and the system, when the last record was made there, was precisely what it will be in the last and most cultivated periods of the world. The work was ended when that volume was completed, for man then had all that he ever would have as constituting the record of Christianity. No new books were to be added; no new prophets or apostles were to be sent; no additional work was to be done to supplement the atonement. Whatever consequences may follow from this position, the defender of Christianity is bound to maintain it, and, in the utmost strictness of the expression, the enemy of Christianity may hold him to it.

It is not necessary to argue this point, for it springs out of the very nature of the system. It is, moreover, fairly implied in the New Testament itself. I believe that the Book of Revelation was the last book of the New Testament that was written, and that it occupies its appropriate place as the closing book in the revelation of God to mankind; and that, although the solemn passage with which that book closes undoubtedly had immediate reference to the book itself, yet that it is not improper to regard it as applicable to the entire Bible: "I testify unto every man that heareth the words of the prophecy of this book, If any man shall add unto these things, God shall add unto him the plagues that are written in this book: and if any man shall take away from the words of the book of this prophecy, God shall take away his part out of the book of life" (Rev., xxii., 18, 19).

If this is a true position, the defender of the Christian system can not, as is done in other systems, avail him-

self of the progress which the world makes to relieve
himself of difficulty, and to adjust the system to new
discoveries and inventions. A system of astronomy, of
chemistry, of anatomy, or of geography, may be adjusted from age to age. Erroneous views long entertained
in regard to the circulation of the blood, or the movements of the heavenly bodies, or the elementary substances of nature, may be detached from the system,
and the new views made to occupy their place, though
it may require that long-cherished and honored systems
shall be abandoned, and names long regarded with reverence shall cease to be among those which influence
mankind. Such has been, in fact, the progress of the
sciences; nor is there any one science that can now be
regarded as so fixed that it may not be modified or revolutionized by new discoveries. If a fact is discovered
that is at variance entirely with a prevailing theory of
astronomy, anatomy, or chemistry, it is not fatal to the
science itself. The system may be at once adjusted to
the new fact, and the change constitute an epoch in the
advance of the science. Not so, however, in regard to
the Bible and to the Christian system. If the world in
its progress discloses facts that are irreconcilable with
the Bible on just principles of interpretation, it is fatal
to its claim as a revelation from God. We can not go
back, as in the case of astronomy, and *adjust* the historical or doctrinal statement in the Bible to the new
discoveries.

It follows from these views (a) that the proper work
of man in regard to Christianity is to ascertain, by a
fair interpretation of language, what the system *is*,
not what it *should* be. The work of the Christian theologian is to sit down to the New Testament simply as
an interpreter of language, as the learner in science sits

down to the study of the works of nature, to learn what nature *is*, not to determine what it *should be ;* to *explain* a world, not to *make* a world. The principle suggested by Lord Bacon in the first maxim of the Novum Organon* is as applicable to Christianity as it is to nature, and lies as certainly at the foundation of all just views of theology as it does of all just views of science. By the proper study of language, according to the received laws of exegesis among men, the theologian is to ascertain what the system *is*, and, having done that, his work is ended. (*b*) It follows, farther, that the friend of revelation is not at liberty to modify the system; to accommodate it to prevailing theories in philosophy; or to adjust it to new facts as they shall develop themselves in the progress of human affairs. No power can change the system but the power which originated it; and the authority to modify it so as to adjust it to human belief, or to facts as they are developed in science, has not been intrusted to mortals. Truth is unaccommodating and unbending. It will not yield. It can not be made different at one time from what it is at another. The proposition that in a right angled triangle the square of the hypothenuse is equal to the sum of the squares on the two sides, is a truth not peculiar to one age or nation; nor to be expressed in one language only; nor to die away among obsolete maxims in the advancing periods of the world; nor to be modified or changed though truths of surpassing magnitude on other subjects are disclosed to human view; nor to be treated as a falsehood though there may be theories to be established that may seem vital to science or to the

* Homo, naturæ minister et interpres, tantum facit et intelligit, quantum de naturæ ordine, re vel mente observaverit; nec amplius scit, aut potest.

good of mankind. So the Christian theologian is bound to believe in regard to revealed truth; so the unbelieving world may require, in regard to each and every portion of the revealed truth of God, that he shall hold it precisely as it is in the Bible.

There are, however, one or two remarks which may be made, to show that this rule is not quite as rigid, in its actual application, as it may seem to be. In another part of this Lecture I shall show that, in fact, the rule is as rigid and stern in regard to science as it is in respect to theology.

It is not to be assumed, then, by the Christian or the infidel, that we have in fact, in our creeds and in our interpretation of the Bible, *precisely* the system which was revealed. That we have the true *record* in the Bible we are to believe, and the infidel may hold us to that; but that we have the proper *interpretation* of that record is not to be assumed as certain. Christianity has been transmitted to us from a far-distant age. It has come in contact with all the philosophical systems in the world. Its outward form has been much moulded by philosophy—much by its alliance with the state. The synods and councils which have determined the creeds of the Church have been, like other assemblies, composed of imperfect men—often of men more under the influence of philosophy than religion; often ignorant of the plainest rules of exegesis; and often seeking rather to establish a hierarchy than to promote the kingdom of Christ. As a matter of fact, we know that during that long period there is almost no absurdity of doctrine or interpretation which has not been embraced by the Church; almost no error which has not been sanctioned by synods and councils; almost no truth the belief of which has not exposed him who held it to persecution by the Church itself. Christianity has thus come down to us through a descent of eighteen centuries, collecting in its progress whatever of good or bad there might be that could in any way be made to adhere to it; adopting as its own the opinions in mental philosophy, and the doctrines of science, true or false, which have prevailed in the world; and uniting all in its symbols of faith—taking the Church at large, a vast and monstrous conglomeration of original sacred truth, and of the errors and absurdities which the world has accumulated in the lapse of ages. It is a ship, not now just sailing out of port, fresh, and new, and clean, but one that has sailed afar, and that has collected in distant seas whatever of barnacles and sea-weed that could be made to adhere to it. Those barnacles and that sea-weed must be detached from it if the ship is to be made to traverse safely distant seas again.

A great part of the work of the Church in modern times has been to *detach* from it the errors and corruptions which it had accumulated in the long period of its history. This was, in fact, the main service which Luther rendered to the Church, restoring it in a great measure to its pristine beauty, purity, and vigor. This is the service which has been rendered by modern sacred criticism; this is the work to be done by the efforts to secure a correct text of the Bible; this the work to be done by the application of the canons of criticism to the Word of God.

Luther, indeed, performed a great work; for Christianity in the Protestant form is a different thing from what it was as it had been presented to the world for a thousand years. But we are not to *assume* that the work was wholly done by him, or that in the Westminster, the Helvetic, and the Savoy Confessions, in the

Thirty-nine Articles, or in the Heidelberg Catechism, we have Christianity *precisely* as its Author designed to communicate it to mankind. We are not to assume that all the received views in the Church are true views, and are in no manner to be modified. We are not to assume that the texts of Scripture which the Westminster Assembly affixed to the Larger and Shorter Catechisms are all properly applied, and are to be held as proof-texts now in order to "soundness in the faith," or that the doctrines which they are designed to defend *are*, in fact, doctrines of the Scripture at all. We are not to assume that the views held in the Church, even to our own times, in regard to the past records of our earth, or the interpretations which, in defense of those views, the Church has attached to certain statements in the Bible, are therefore correct. It is not to be held that the past interpretations of the first chapter of Genesis are necessarily true; nor are we to assume that the pastor of the Church in Leyden was in error when he said that "God had yet many more truths to break forth out of his holy word."

All this is matter of fair inquiry still; and when a new fact is discovered in science that seems to come in conflict with a statement in the Bible, or when an old record in Egypt is deciphered, or a new bone is exhumed in fossil remains, that seems to carry the history of man back to a remoter period than that assigned by Usher, we are at perfect liberty to inquire whether the common interpretation of the Bible, though received for ages, is the correct interpretation; whether, as in the case of astronomy in the time of Galileo, the Church has not been mistaken in its views on the subject; and whether the Bible, by the fair rules of exegesis, may not be capable of being reconciled with the new discovery in science, or with the new historical fact that has been disclosed to the world. This "*play*," therefore, if I may thus express myself,* is open to the friends of Christianity, while the statement is still held true in its most rigid form that, in itself, it is a fixed and unchangeable system, incapable of progress or change.

II. While Christianity is thus fixed and unchangeable, the world makes progress in science, civilization, and the arts. It is bound by no such rigid laws as those which pertain to an unchangeable system; it holds no theory in philosophy, and no creed in regard to the sciences, which may not be modified and adjusted to the highest advances which the race can make. As a matter of fact, the world makes progress. It drops erroneous systems by the way. It readily incorporates new facts into the systems of science. The old Ptolemaic system, not without a struggle, indeed, gives way to the Copernican system in astronomy, and in the new system there is no difficulty, without changing its character, in assigning its place to each new planet that may be discovered; to any number of comets, shooting stars, and asteroids; to new systems of worlds lying beyond our own planetary system; or to any number of nebulæ floating in the distant ether that may be now resolving themselves into worlds. There is nothing, therefore, like a fixed and unchangeable system that seems to bind the race in its career of discovery. In science man seems to be free; in religion he seems to be a fettered slave.

While this statement, however, is made in regard to science, civilization, and the arts, it is important to understand precisely in what sense it is true, in order that

* "The *play* of a wheel or piston."— *Webster*.

we may appreciate the manner in which one comes in collision with the other.

Science, then, in itself, in the highest sense of that term, is as really fixed and unchangeable as Christianity. The business of science is not to *create*, it is to *discover*. The maxim of Lord Bacon, already referred to, represents man as merely the "*minister* and *inter-preter* of nature." The student of nature does not create the truths in his department any more than the theologian does in his; nor is he any more at liberty to change or modify the facts in his department than the student of the Bible is in his. Moreover, each and all the sciences, using that word in the largest sense, save the science of history, were in themselves as perfect and unchangeable at the beginning of the creation as they are now, and the struggles, the changes, the errors, the advances, the stoppages, the modifications recorded in Whewell's History of the Inductive Sciences are quite parallel with the history of theological science—with the toils of plodding theologians; with the deliberations of synods and councils; with the breaking out of new light here and there, overthrowing old systems and creeds; with the struggles, the changes, the errors, the advances, the stoppages, the modifications in developing the system of Christian theology as it now exists in its best forms. A treatise on any one of the sciences, if correctly prepared at the beginning of the world, would be a correct treatise now, just as a creed that would have fairly represented Christianity when the volume of inspiration was finished would be a correct creed now. There are no new truths; no new facts; no new principles that have been introduced in the one case any more than in the other. A correct treatise on astronomy, for example, written when "the morning stars sang together, and all the sons of God shouted for joy," or when the Chaldæan sages looked out on the heavens, and mapped the world above us with strange figures and forms, would be a correct treatise now. The worlds are the same; the laws of their movements are the same; their magnitudes, distances, periods, and revolutions are the same. Kepler did not create the great laws, the discovery of which has given immortality to his name; Galileo did not bring into existence the satellites of Jupiter; nor did Newton originate the principle of universal gravitation. So far as known, no new worlds have been added to the system; so far as known, no worlds have been certainly destroyed—it is absolutely certain that no modifications have occurred in the laws by which the system is governed.—A treatise on anatomy in the time of Galen, if correct then, would be perfect now. There have been no changes in the structure of man that would demand a revision or a modification of the system. Not one new bone has been added to the human frame; not one new muscle, nerve, or tendon has been laid down; not one new channel has been grooved out for the flowing of the blood. Had Galen given to the world a true theory in his time of the circulation of the blood, it would have been as correct now as is the theory of Harvey. —A treatise on chemistry when, under the Caliphate at Bagdad, the followers of Mohammed were on the point of such great discoveries, would be a correct treatise now. No new substances have been added to the sixty or more of which the universe is composed, nor have there been any new laws in respect to the proportions in which they combine, and the chemical changes which occur in the air, the earth, and the water.—The treatises of Solomon, when " he spake of trees from the cedar-tree

that is in Lebanon even unto the hyssop that springeth
out of the wall, and of beasts, and of fowls, and of creep-
ing things, and of fishes" (1 Kings, iv., 33), if they were
correct treatises then, and stated the true laws in his
time in the vegetable and animal kingdoms, would be
correct representations in natural history now, and, if
they had been preserved, would have rendered needless
the toils of Linnæus, Buffon, Cuvier, and Agassiz.—The
electric fluid, when it glittered and played on the mast
of the ancient mariner, was the same that it is now,
when, arrested and guided, it makes its way over hills
and plains, and along the bed of the ocean, conveying
thought from land to land, and lighting up the world
with intelligence.—In like manner, a system of metallurgy when Tubal Cain became the "instructor of every
artificer in brass and iron" (Gen., iv., 22), or of music in
the time of Jubal, "the father of all such as handle the
harp and the organ" (Gen., iv., 21), or of agriculture in
the days of Jabal, "the father of such as dwell in tents,
and have cattle" (Gen., iv., 20), would be a correct system in each department now. The instructions of the
schools have added nothing to the principles on which
the metals are spread over the earth, nor have they increased or diminished the quantity. Mozart and Han-
del have added nothing to the laws of the octave, nor
has Liebig introduced one new substance as entering
into scientific agriculture, or modified one on which
success depends.

Yet, in the ordinary sense of the word *science*, the
world does make progress, and in reference to science
as *known*, and to theories which are regarded as just
expositions of nature, the world is immeasurably in advance of what it was when the Gospel was revealed to
mankind. All the old treatises on science have passed

away. They are valuable now only as marking the progress of the race, and as enabling us to compare the present with the past. No one feels bound to defend these ancient expositions of nature as the Christian feels bound to defend the ancient records of his faith in the Bible; no one is charged with heresy in science if he discards the teachings of the ancients altogether. The friend of science *is* free. He is bound by no ancient exposition of nature; nor does he hesitate, on the discovery of a new fact in nature — in astronomy, in anatomy, or in chemistry—to lay aside at once all that in the received systems is inconsistent with that fact, and to set himself at work to *adjust* the system to that new revelation. He does not create the fact, and, therefore, he does not create the science; he modifies the system as received so as to be in accordance with that fact, and allows it to exert its full influence in forming the opinions of mankind in all time to come. He *discovers*, he does not *make.* Columbus *discovered* America, he did not *create* it, and the fact of its existence was the same before he discovered it as afterward, and would have been the same if he had not lived. Adams and Le Verrier indicated the place of an unknown planet in the heavens, they did not create it. Its existence was the same before they made it known as afterward, and would have been the same if they had not suggested the fact of its existence to mankind. From the beginning of the creation, that distant star had walked its rounds on perhaps the outer limit of our solar system, unobserved by men before, but, when disclosed, men forthwith set themselves to adjust the astronomical system to the fact that there *was* such a star, and that its movements should be allowed to explain and modify existing views.

Q

Thus science advances. Not that it changes. Not that it has any new facts. Not that new matter is created, or that new properties are given to the particles that compose it, but that the original great laws and facts of science, in themselves as fixed and unchangeable as were the truths of the Christian system when the New Testament was completed, are arranged, explained, and properly located in the respective systems of science, displacing the errors of the past, and advancing to that state where "man, the minister and interpreter of nature," shall have brought the systems of science, as far as the human powers will permit, into harmony with the system as it reposed eternally in the mind of the Creator.

III. Such being the facts in regard to the two systems, it was inevitable that they should come into collision, and that they should be liable, at any time, to cross each other. The nature of that collision must depend much on the false views which are at any time attached to the Christian system—as the sailing of the ship, before referred to, would be much affected by the barnacles and sea-weed attached to it—and by the views of philosophy and science that prevail at any time in the world. The work of adjusting the two, therefore, must vary from age to age, as the nature of the conflict between the two must vary in different periods of the world. The battle, under a new form, may be to be refought in each successive generation. The triumph of Christianity at any one time is by no means a permanent triumph, or even, in itself, a proof of permanent triumph at all; and the apparent triumph, at any time, of infidelity is by no means a demonstration of permanent and ultimate victory. Celsus, Porphyry, and Julian act their part, and disappear; Hobbes,

Chubb, and Morgan follow, and then vanish from the stage; Volney, Gibbon, Hume, attack the system, and retire from the conflict; Strauss and Renan, Hegel and Comte, follow after. A host of scientific warriors rushes on the arena for an attack on the religion that is fixed and unchangeable, deriving their means of attack from a system that is as fixed and unchangeable as Christianity itself, and the warfare assumes new forms, and is to be fought with new weapons. Whether these two systems, equally fixed and unchangeable, are *really* in conflict, or will be found ultimately to coincide and harmonize, is the question which is now before this age, and which is, perhaps, to be before the world in the developments of future ages. It is too early to determine with absolute certainty that the two will ultimately agree. The Christian theologian believes assuredly that it will be so; the scientific skeptic is not less confident that the prospect of ultimate harmony, if it ever existed, has now vanished forever.

For my purpose in these Lectures, it is important to designate, in few words, the *varying* nature of this conflict; for it has not always been the same, nor is it likely to be always the same that it is now.

Historically, the conflict may be divided into three periods: from the time when the Gospel was first preached to the age when it became permanently established in the world; the Middle Ages — the times when, amidst much darkness in science, and much error in religion, the human mind was struggling into light; and the present age.

In the first of these periods, the nature of the conflict was marked and definite, and the conflict, in that form, is never to be renewed. The systems with which the Gospel came into conflict have passed away, and are not to be revived.

That conflict was between Christianity and Judaism on the one hand, and Christianity and the Greek and Roman philosophy on the other.

In Judæa, Christianity came into collision with religion alone. The Jews had no literature besides their sacred books; they had no science, no philosophy. Beyond what is in their sacred records they have contributed nothing of value to the progress of mankind, in war or in peace; and the collision, therefore, in Judæa was wholly on the subject of religion. The views which were then regarded as antagonistic to Christianity have ceased to influence the world beyond the small number that constitutes the remnant of the Hebrew people, and the conflicts which Christian apostles waged with the Jewish doctors have ceased forever.

In Greece and Rome the conflict was of a different nature. It was partly with religion; partly with priestly power; partly with the state; partly with philosophy. It is only in the latter aspect that the subject demands notice now—the conflict with philosophy. It was, in fact, a conflict with "*philosophy*," not with *science*. The Greeks had little science, the Romans less. It is not too much to say that in respect to the physical sciences, the most eminent of the Greek philosophers would not have been qualified for admission into the lowest class of any American college;* nor have they contributed any thing that now enters into the instructions in our laboratories or schools. The conflict, therefore, in Greece, and the same was true in Rome, was with an acute and subtle metaphysical philosophy. It was not on questions started in the laboratory or the observatory, but in the Academy and the Porch. In Judæa it was substantially about the atonement; in

* Compare *Whewell's* History of the Inductive Sciences, vol. i., b. i.

Greece it was the whole question about the elevation of the race. The Greek philosopher knew of but one way of reforming mankind, of meeting human ills, of elevating the race, of obtaining the favor of the gods. It was by mental culture; by development; by instruction; by conformity to a just standard of morals. Christianity proclaimed that in this way man could neither be elevated, nor obtain the divine favor, nor be prepared for a future world, but that the entire hope of the race for reformation, elevation, and salvation was in the doctrine of Christ crucified. That was foolishness to the Greek. It was not on the line of his views in regard to the means of elevating men, and he spurned and rejected the system.

Those old controversies have passed away. All that there was in the philosophy of Greece that opposed Christianity has ceased to influence mankind, and that philosophy will not be revived. Celsus and Porphyry have done their work, and they did it well; and except as they are exhumed to illustrate the history of the Church, or are explored by some theological teacher who regards all wisdom as found among the "fathers," the whole has gone into the "extinct controversies" of the past.

The second of these periods embraced the Middle Ages; the times when, amidst much darkness in science, and much error in religion, the human mind was struggling into light. The history of this is a history of nearly all the persecutions under the Papacy. The peculiarity of this period, so far as there was a collision between Christianity and science, civilization, and the arts, was, that the Church adopted certain interpretations of the Scriptures as infallible; that it regarded the Bible as making statements on the structure of the universe, as well as on the plan of salvation, which were equally to be received as a part of the creed of Christendom, and which were to be defended in the same manner as any other articles of the creed of the Church; that it claimed jurisdiction over all the subjects of knowledge, as it did over the wealth and power of newly-discovered countries; and that to doubt the authority of the Church on subjects of science was a heresy of the same nature as to doubt the doctrine of the Trinity or the Incarnation. Each successive discovery in science, therefore, brought the Church into contact with the world, and led to persecution. The collision was not with Christianity as such, but with Christianity as it was embodied in the prevailing interpretation of the Scriptures, and in the articles of a church claiming to be infallible. Thus, in the case of Galileo, his offense in holding the doctrines of the Copernican system was not against the Bible, for the Bible, properly interpreted, has revealed nothing on the subject, but was against the *interpretation* put on the Bible by the Church. The Church had adopted the Ptolemaic system of astronomy, and to call the truth of that system in question was, in the judgment of the Church, an attack on the Bible itself. Thus, through this long and gloomy tract of ages, science struggled in dark and obscure places, restrained and intimidated by the fear of a collision with the the Church, as freedom struggled every where at the same time, restrained and awed by the fear of the papal power. The one was held in check as really as the other. Here and there, a solitary individual, like Roger Bacon, pursued his studies alone. Each new discovery involved the danger of a conflict with the Church; each advance made was imperiled by the apprehension of impinging on some article of faith.

Nature was explored with the apprehension of a revelation there that would be in conflict with the infallible revelation as interpreted by the Church, and each new discovery was made by *stealth*, and with the fear of the rack or the stake before the eyes. Science emerged into light and freedom only when those shackles were burst asunder, and men acted on the idea that science was to be pursued in an independent manner, and that the observation of the stars, and the examination of the component elements of matter, were not to be restrained by any interpretations which had been affixed to the Bible. The world was slow to learn this. In fact, the lesson is not yet wholly learned. The investigations of modern astronomy, as in the time of Galileo, have been pursued in the face of an extensively prevailing belief that these disclosures are against the teachings of revelation; and all the investigations of geology have been made, on the one hand, by a hope that the results would be found to be in conflict with the Bible, and, on the other, by a fear that it would be so. Geology and astronomy have achieved their triumphs only by setting aside interpretations of the Bible which have been received in the Church for ages; and the inquiries which are now pursued in regard to the work of creation, the antiquity of man upon the earth, the origin of the races of men, are pursued on the one hand with the hope, and on the other with the fear, that the result will be found to be in conflict with the teachings of the Bible. It has been, and is, a slow work for man to learn that his *interpretation* of the Bible is not necessarily the *teaching* of the Bible; that to detach a false interpretation from the Word of God is not necessarily an assault on the Bible itself, and is not to be regarded as heresy.

We have fallen, in the third period, on other times.

A new era is opened upon the world, and Christianity
and the world now come into collision in a form wholly
different from the collision in the times of the apostles
and in the Middle Ages. The defender of Christianity
has a different work to do from what he had in the time
of Porphyry and Celsus; in the time of Morgan and
Chubb; in the time of Volney, Gibbon, and Hume. To
the Church at large; to the Christian ministry; and to
those especially whom I am called to address in these
Lectures—those preparing for the ministry—nothing
can be of greater importance than to understand the
nature of the conflict which is to be before the Church
in the next age.

A few remarks here seem to be necessary to place
this part of the subject in a proper light:

(1.) It is, as before intimated, always a fair question,
when there is an apparent collision between the Bible
and science, whether the collision is, in fact, between
the scientific truth and the *Bible*, or between that truth
and the prevailing and received *interpretation* of the
Bible. The one is by no means to be assumed as sy-
nonymous with the other. To the utmost extent which
the proper laws of interpreting language will allow, the
friend of Christianity is to be permitted to apply those
laws to determine whether the received interpretation
of the Bible is the necessary and the fair one. The
Bible is not, indeed, to be made a "nose of wax," but it
is equally true that the infidel is not to be permitted to
assume that the interpretation which *he* puts on the
Bible is the true one, or that *any* interpretation found
in the creeds, or in treatises of theology, is necessarily
the correct one. The whole question about the integrity of the text; about the agreement of manuscripts;
about the changes in the use of words; about the mean-

ing of language as modified in any particular country, among any particular people, or at any particular time, is a fair and open question—a question of simple *interpretation*, as it is in inquiring into the meaning of Homer or Herodotus. To the utmost extent to which the fair canons of criticism are applicable to any ancient book, the friend of the Bible may avail himself of those canons to *detach* a false interpretation from the Word of God—to remove another barnacle from the ship that has, in long voyages, vexed many seas. Even if, which is almost demonstrably impossible, the followers of Lepsius, Gliddon, Nott, and Bunsen, could establish the fact that man has been upon the earth for a period of twenty thousand years, it would still be an open question whether the Bible, by fair interpretation, teaches the contrary, and whether the common interpretation of the Church, though received for ages, may not have been founded on erroneous *data* in determining what the Bible teaches on the subject, or whether it teaches any thing. There is, indeed, a limit to this; but it is a limit to be determined in the case of the Bible, as in the case of any other ancient book, by a proper application of the rules of exegesis.

(2.) The warfare in our time between Christianity and the world in respect to science, civilization, and the arts, has changed. The old modes of attacking the Bible have been abandoned, and the old modes of defending it are therefore to be abandoned. On all matters pertaining to the progress of our race there are many "extinct controversies"—old volcanoes that have been burned out—leaving nothing but scoriæ and ashes, and on no subject is this more true than on the subject of theology. Around those extinct volcanoes men wander now safe, but with nothing to relieve the desola-

tion. Time was when all was commotion there. The
mountain heaved; the flames belched forth; the sky
was lurid; rivers of burning lava flowed in every direction. All was consumed. Nor city, nor hamlet, nor
tree, nor shrub, nor flower, nor spire of grass was
spared; and perhaps no living thing will ever grow
again on the fatal spot. So with many of the old controversies in philosophy; in science; in religion. What
could more resemble the scoriæ of such an ancient volcano than the huge tomes of the schoolmen? What
could more resemble such a volcano in action than the
heat, and fire, and zeal of Thomas Aquinas, and John
Duns Scotus? What shrub, tree, flower, or living thing
can be culled from those blackened remains?

It is a material point thus gained when one is girding on the armor to fight the battles of his own age, to
know exactly where he starts, and what is precisely the
nature of the warfare in which he is to engage. It is
much to know what is settled, and what is open still.
That soldier now would spend his time to very little
purpose who should furbish some piece of ancient armor; who should see that his helmet, and his shield,
and his greaves, and his spear were in good condition;
or who should, as in other days, incase his horse in armor, and move into battle reflecting around him the
rays of the sun. Those ancient suits of armor for horses
and men do well in old baronial halls, for they have an
appropriate place there as memorials of other days and
other men, as old volumes on extinct controversies have
an appropriate place in the alcoves of vast libraries—
memorials of the past.

There have been battles in regard to Christianity
in its collision with the world which have been well
fought, and which are not to be renewed in our time,

or ever onward. Porphyry, in his day, had his field; Celsus his; Julian his. In neither case was it science or sacred criticism. It was the ancient philosophy as then held, coming into contact with a new religion— with Christianity. Those men did their work well. They did all that acute philosophers, sustained, in the case of Julian, by the might of imperial power, could do to prevent the spread of the new system. That battle is not to be fought over again. The philosophy which they held, like the men themselves, has long since passed away, to be revived on earth no more. So, in his time, Volney had his field, and he did his work well. Seated amidst the "ruins" of ages, and surveying the empires and systems that have passed away, he inferred that in the course of events there must be a succession of "ruins" to the end of time, and that the existing empires and systems of philosophy and religion—Christianity among the number—would be added to the ruins of the past, and be numbered among extinct systems. No one could do his work better than he has done, and that attempt will not be made again. Thomas Paine, in his time, had his field, and he did his work well. With talents, indeed, eminently fitted to be useful when vindicating the "Rights of Men;" with a power of noble language almost without a parallel for popular appeal,* but, also, with a still more unequaled

* Chief Justice *Marshall* says of him (Life of Washington, vol. ii., p. 399) in relation to the causes which led to the Declaration of Independence, "Many essays appeared in the papers calculated to extend these opinions; and a pamphlet under the signature of Common Sense, written by Thomas Paine, an Englishman, who had lately come over to America, had particular influence. He possessed a style and manner of saying bold things, singularly well fitted to act on the public mind, to enlist every feeling with him; and very often, especially in times when men were greatly agitated, to seize on the judgment itself."

acquaintance with the *Billingsgate* of the English tongue, and in this surpassed by none, he undertook to drive the Bible from the world by ribaldry and abuse. That battle has been fought. Whoever attempts hereafter to attack Christianity in that manner, will find that the work has been already better done than he can do it himself, and that the great point has been settled forever that religion is not to be driven from the world by scorn, ribaldry, and vulgarity. In his day, too, Voltaire had his field—satire, learning, poetry, philosophy. He did his work well. Who is to surpass him? Who is to equal him? Who shall hope to succeed in destroying Christianity by such weapons when the great Frenchman has failed? What can remain in that line but to reproduce his criticisms, to republish his philosophy, to repeat his sarcasms? Mr. Hume had his field, and he has done his work well. By most subtle sophistry; by great calmness; by a spirit of apparent candor; by perplexing and involving a subject so as, even to this day, to exercise the ingenuity of the world to show *where* he was wrong, when the great body of men feel that he *was* wrong, he attempted to show—to *prove* —that a miracle could not be demonstrated to have been wrought. Where Thomas Brown and Dugald Stewart have exhausted their powers to detect the sophistry, leaving it doubtful whether it has been detected, and where many a theologian has attempted to show that it *was* sophistry, and yet has left the impression of Mr. Hume's argument more deeply imbedded in the mind than it was before, it can not be supposed that *that* argument will be presented in a more embarrassing form, or that, as a metaphysical argument against miracles, it is to gain any new strength in coming ages. Mr. Gibbon had *his* field, and well he has

worked it. His province was history, and his investigations led him, as a *skeptic*, as he probably intended
they should, over the entire period when Christianity,
from the feeblest beginning, made its way over the Roman world, and "sat down on the throne of the Cæsars;" when, during the long and eventful ages of the
decline of the empire, Christianity was seen moulding
society, directing wars, founding empires, modifying
opinions, changing the arts of life, introducing revolutions into manners, dress, dwellings, schools; when it
controlled the government and influenced the people;
when it founded monasteries and colleges; when it
poured its embattled legions on the Holy Land, and
when it had identified itself with all the forms of civilization in Europe. It was Mr. Gibbon's task to show,
contrary to the opinion of the Christian world, and the
general judgment of mankind, that all this could be,
and yet the religion not be of God. He did his work
well. He did not leave it to be alleged, even by the
friends of Christianity, that his aim was to falsify history for the sake of skepticism. As a historian he
was among the most true, and honest, and faithful of
men. There is not the slightest evidence that his skepticism, bitter as it was, ever led him, in a single instance, to pervert or falsify a *fact*, however much it
might be opposed to his own views on the subject of
religion, or however much ingenuity it might require
to escape, as a skeptic, from the legitimate *inferences*
from the fact. By unwearied study; by great learning;
by an unrivaled command of language; by patient toil;
by a comprehensive grasp of his great subject, he has
placed himself at the head of historians, and from the
time of Thucydides down to the present age there has
not been a man more upright, stern, honest, unbending,

in recording the facts of history. Yet, faithful as to his facts, he traversed the entire field with a *sneer* on his countenance, and with a purpose to make the *facts* as they existed do all that they could be made to do to destroy the confidence of mankind in the divine origin of the Christian religion. No one hereafter, if he attempts to do that work at all, will do it so well, and in *that* method of destroying faith in the Christian religion no more remains to be accomplished.

IV. These controversies have passed away, and these methods of attempting to destroy Christianity are fast ceasing to exert an influence on mankind. The collision now between Christianity and the world is substantially a new form of collision; the attack is from a new quarter, and with new weapons; the questions involved are deeper than those with which the Church has heretofore grappled; the results of the conflict, so far as we can see, are to be final.

The points on which Christianity is now coming into collision with the world in its present stage of progress in science, civilization, and the arts, are principally the following:

First. The inspiration of the Bible — the question whether a "book-revelation" is possible, and whether, if possible, the Bible is such a revelation, and is infallible.

Second. The antiquity of the human race—the question whether, according to the commonly received teaching of the Scriptures, man has been upon the earth *about* six thousand years, or whether his history stretches back for a period of ten or twenty thousand years, or to even a remoter period.

Third. The origin of the race—whether the different types of men upon the earth have had a common origin, and have been derived from a single pair, or whether, as is maintained in regard to the inferior animals, men have sprung up in different centres, either as developed from inferior orders of beings, or from independent created "heads" of the different varieties upon the earth — the Caucasian, the Mongolian, the Ethiopian, and the American; in other words, whether the varieties in the human family can be reconciled with the undoubted doctrine of the Bible that the whole human family is descended from a single pair.

Fourth. The whole question of miracles — whether miracles are possible; whether a record of a miracle could be believed; or whether the laws of nature are so fixed and unchanging that there never has been, and never can be, sufficient evidence of the direct interposition of the divine power to justify the belief that any events have occurred in the history of our globe that are not traceable to those laws, or that those laws have ever been set aside.

Whether, in this course of Lectures, any remarks have been made to throw light on these points, or to assist those who are to be defenders of the truth in their studies, it is not for me to express any opinion. The consideration of these points has, either directly or indirectly, entered largely into these Lectures, and these points have, in fact, been constantly before my own mind in preparing them. It can not be assumed now that they are definitely and forever settled on either side, so that the discussions on them can be ranked among the "extinct controversies." They are to be among the active subjects of controversy and inquiry in the next age, and, in order that their importance and their bearing on the whole subject of Christianity may be perceived—a bearing well understood by the enemies of Christianity, a few additional remarks may not be improper.

For the first of them—the inspiration of the Bible. It is clear that the whole question about a revelation at all, and about Christianity in particular, depends on this. Nothing can be plainer than that the Bible *claims* to be a supernatural revelation from God; that its teachings are above human teachings; that the real author of the book is the Holy Ghost speaking through inspired men; and that its teachings constitute an infallible guide for man. Deny this; deny that it is inspired in any other sense than Homer, or Ossian, or Shakspeare were inspired, and it is clear that the book at once loses its authority, and the system which it contains is placed on the same level as the system in the Koran, the Zendavesta, or the Shasters.

For the second of these—the antiquity of man upon the earth—it is plain, also, that the question *may* assume such a form as to involve the whole question of revealed religion. It may, indeed, be a fair question whether the Scripture record extends back precisely to the period of six thousand years, or whether, *if* it were demonstrated that man had been upon the earth ten or even twenty thousand years, the proper interpretation of the Bible would be found to be consistent with such a fact; but, beyond all question, there *is* a limit, probably much within the twenty thousand years of man's residence upon the earth, according to the Bible. The Bible *is* a history—a history of man. It professes to go up to the beginning—the period of his first appearance upon the earth. It traces the origin of nations; records the dispersions of the race; accounts for the origin of languages. In that history of living beings—of man—there *can* be no such long periods of suc-

cessive repose, of slow development, of destruction, of
new creations, and of sweeping off entire races from the
earth, as occur in the mere geological history of the
world, when an interval, unexplained, of a thousand, or
a million of years, is scarcely to be taken into the account. In other words, by no possible propriety, by no
fair rules of interpretation, can the liberty be allowed
in regard to the history of *man* which is conceded on
all hands to the student of geology in reference to the
transformations on and within the earth before man appeared on it. The earth itself, so far as the account in
the Bible goes, *may* have existed any number of millions of ages; man, according to the Bible, is a recent
visitant to this world, and the time is not remote in the
past when he was formed by his Creator to occupy a
world made ready for his abode.

For the third of these points—the question whether
the human race is derived from a single pair—it is manifest that the whole question of the truth of revelation
and of redemption turns on this. The Bible records
the creation of a single pair, and no other. It records
the migrations and wanderings of the descendants of
that one pair to all parts of the world, and of no others
(Gen., x.). It treats the race as one. It regards that
one pair as the head of the entire race, and affirms that
the disobedience of that one pair affected all the dwellers on the earth as one race—not the Caucasian race
only, or the Mongolian, the African, or the American,
but the entire race. "In Adam all die" (1 Cor., xv., 22).
"By one man sin entered into the world, and death by
sin" (Rom., v., 12). "By one man's disobedience many
—*οἱ πολλοί*—*the* many—were made sinners" (Rom., v.,
19). These expressions comprehend the race; and the
entire doctrine of depravity and of death, according to

the Bible, is identified with the fact that there was a single pair at the head of the race. The same is the Scripture doctrine in regard to redemption. The race, according to that plan, is one—one in origin; one in apostasy; one in guilt; one in death. The work of redemption is not Mongolian, or Caucasian, or Ethiopian, but it pertains to man as man. In redemption, as in the fall, there is one Head—the counterpart of the other, each acting for the race. "As in Adam all die, even so in Christ shall all be made alive" (1 Cor., xv., 22). "Since by man came death, by man came also the resurrection of the dead" (1 Cor., xv., 21). "As by one man's disobedience many were made sinners, so by the obedience of one shall many be made righteous" (Rom., v., 19). In reference to this point, also, it is certain that it is indispensable to proper faith in the Bible. By no fair rules of exegesis; by no possible torture of language, can the teachings of the Bible be made consistent with the belief that the different "races" of men upon the earth have each had a separate origin. "God hath made of one blood all nations of men, for to dwell on all the face of the earth" (Acts, xvii., 26). This fact is not only affirmed, but every where implied, and well do the men who are assailing it understand its bearing on the question of the reception or rejection of the Bible in the world.

As to the fourth point—the question whether miracles are possible, this also is vital to all faith in the Bible. Mr. Hume understood this, and attempted, by a most ingenious metaphysical argument, to put the question about miracles, and faith in the Bible, to rest forever. It comes before the Church and the world now in a different form; not less difficult to be met; more likely to affect scientific men; more likely to be popular. The doctrine that miracles are impossible as held now is founded on the alleged stability of the laws of nature. At first, in science, nothing seems more fluctuating or unsettled than those laws. The varying seasons; the clouds; the storms of ocean; the march of disease; the wantonness of the lightning's flash; the play of the aurora borealis; the irregularity of the term of human life; the movements of comets and meteors, all these seemed to be independent of any fixed laws, and these movements were explained in the early periods of the world, as Comte (Positive Philosophy) has stated, by the supposition of supernatural agencies. Silently and gradually, however, these irregularities have been reduced to order and law, and man has approached, what Comte regards as the last stage, the Ultima Thule of science, the Positive philosophy : — the point where no supernatural agency is to be recognized; where no events are to be traced to an " unknown metaphysical cause;" but where all that is known—all that exists— is an antecedent and a sequent, with no real causation, and, as far as known, no God.* That, apart from such speculations as those of the Positive philosophy, there is a tendency in our age to this result, there can be no doubt. Thus far in the progress of science, the tendency has been, undoubtedly, to find fixed and unchanging laws prevailing, and the object of science is to ascertain and apply those laws. The studies of the astronomer proceed on this supposition; the investigations in the laboratory; the arts of navigation and agriculture; even the doctrines of tides, and winds, and storms, proceed on the supposition of the existence of unvarying

* See the elaborate and very able article on "The Positive Philosophy of Auguste Comte," by *J. S. Mill, Esq.*, in the Westminster Review for April, 1865.

laws. By all, therefore, that there is in such a tendency to universality; by all that is done to reduce that
which in former ages seemed to be irregular to the control of fixed laws; by all the affirmations which scientific men make that the laws of nature *are* fixed and
unchanging, there is an approximation, consciously or
unconsciously, to the conclusion that miracles have
never occurred; that all the well-established *facts* which
have taken place in the history of our world are reducible to the operation of fixed laws; and that all the alleged facts that can not thus be reduced are to be
classed among myths and fables.

And yet it is clear that no man *can* receive the Bible
who does not believe in the exertion of miraculous
power in our world. From the beginning of the book
to the end, it proceeds on the supposition that God has
often interfered in human affairs by his own direct
power; that there have been cases innumerable where
all there *was* in the case was an event, and the will of
God behind it. The reader of the Bible walks in the
midst of signs and wonders. He is in a supernatural
world. He is in the constant presence of Deity—God,
in his sovereignty creating the world itself; forming
man upon it; conversing with man; giving law in calm
conversation, and amidst thunders and tempests; res-
cuing his people from bondage by his own power; making a path for them through the sea; overwhelming
their enemies; shaking the nations; sending conquerors
and prophets supernaturally endowed, until the whole
is consummated by the appearance of the God incarnate—giving sight to the blind and hearing to the deaf;
healing all manner of disease, and raising up the dead
—himself raised from the grave to life, and borne up to
heaven. Who *can* believe in Jesus Christ who does

not believe in miracles? Who *can* believe that the Bible has the slightest claim on the faith of mankind if it is maintained that the laws of nature are so fixed and unchanging that a miracle is impossible?

V. It remains to inquire, in accordance with the main design of this Lecture, and in the conclusion of the whole subject, what is the relation of Christianity to the present stage of the world, in its progress in science, civilization, and the arts?

In this part of the inquiry, it must be assumed, as was stated in the beginning of this Lecture, that when the Gospel was announced to mankind it had truths of great importance to communicate in advance of what the world then possessed. Assuming this, the inquiry now before us presents itself in two forms: (1) whether the Gospel is, in this respect, still in advance of the world, or whether the world has so come up to it, or gone ahead of it, as to supersede it; and (2) whether, admitting that it is still in advance of the world in its disclosures, it has kept up with the race in its means of propagating itself, so as to be able, in this respect, to maintain its advanced position. These inquiries do not differ so materially that they can not be pursued together.

(1.) The first material point in this part of the subject is, that while the world has made great progress in other things, it has made none whatever on the subjects which constitute the peculiar teachings of Christianity. In reference to what the Gospel claims as its own, the world has struck out no light; has removed no difficulty; has answered none of the questions which, in past ages, have so perplexed mankind. The effort to find out a knowledge of God; to find a medium of access to him; to find a method by which the race may

be elevated, and to find evidence of the immortality of
the soul, seems to have exhausted itself in Greece. The
Greek mind, as has been remarked before, was perhaps
better fitted for these inquiries than any other that God
has made; the Greek taste sought and found gratifica-
tion in these inquiries; the Greek language afforded a
better medium for pursuing those inquiries than any
other language which has been spoken among men. If,
of all the tribes of men, we were to select that to which
we should most confidently intrust the question, How
much man by nature can find out about God? we
should unhesitatingly select the *Greek* mind as best fitted to solve the problem.

It is not undervaluing the science of astronomy, of
anatomy, of chemistry, of natural philosophy, of geology, to say that, to this hour, they have made no disclosures on those points which so occupied the attention of the ancients, and on which Christianity assumed
that it had truths in advance of all that the world had
known. The astronomer points his glass to the heavens; penetrates the deep blue ether; reveals worlds
and systems far beyond the reach of the naked eye;
discerns nebulæ lying behind nebulæ in the vast regions of unmeasured space, but does he see God? Does
he look upon his throne? Does he tell us, however
long or intently he may gaze, whether God is a merciful Being; whether there is a plan of redemption for
the fallen and the lost; whether there is a way of peace
for a troubled conscience; whether the soul is immortal; whether

> " The dread of something after death—
> The undiscovered country from whose bourn
> No traveler returns,"

shall make us

> "Rather bear those ills we have,
> Than fly to others that we know not of?"

Does he answer these questions so that the mind of
Plato — so that the mind of Hamlet would be calm?
Forever may he look through that tube, and not a ray
of light will visit his soul from those distant worlds
about what man is so anxious to learn, and in respect
to that on which he feels himself so much in the dark.
Who goes to the astronomer to learn how a sinner may
be saved, and how he himself may be prepared to die?
In the laboratory of the chemist, brilliant as are his discoveries, who expects to learn any new truths about
the way of redemption, and about the nature and em-
ployments of the soul in the future world? The earth,
too, is explored to its utmost limits and its utmost
depths, but what has the traveler and the miner, after
these wanderings and diggings, to tell about God? Is
wisdom found by the miner now any more than it was
in the days of Job?

"He [the miner] cutteth out rivers among the rocks,
and his eye seeth every precious thing. He bindeth
the floods from overflowing, and the thing that is hid
bringeth he forth to light. But where shall wisdom be
found? And where is the place of understanding?
Man knoweth not the price thereof; neither is it found
in the land of the living. The depth saith, It is not in
me; and the sea saith, It is not with me. It can not be
gotten for gold, neither shall silver be weighed for the
price thereof. It can not be valued with the gold of
Ophir, with the precious onyx, or the sapphire. Whence,
then, cometh wisdom? and where is the place of understanding? seeing it is hid from the eyes of all living,
and kept close from the fowls of the air. Destruction
and death say, We have heard the fame thereof with

our ears. *God understandeth the way thereof, and he knoweth the place thereof"* (Job, xxviii., 10–23).

The geologist, too, the man who has learned the history of the earth for some millions of ages, what has he to disclose that shall supersede the teachings of Christianity? What answer has he found to the questions which so perplex the human mind about the remedy for a fallen condition, and a preparation for another world?

It may seem to be a reflection on the present age, and it may require some hardihood to make the assertion, to say that, after all, if a man wished to put himself into a position where, without a revelation, he would find most that would calm his spirit, and solve his doubts, and elevate his conceptions of eternal things, he would go, not into the dissecting-room of the anatomist; not into the observatory of the astronomer; not into the laboratory of the chemist; but would visit the ancient Academy, the Porch, and the Lyceum.

On this subject, then, we claim that the Gospel is as really in advance of the world as it was when it was first communicated to men; that the world has neither gone beyond it, nor come up to it, nor made its teachings less necessary than they were eighteen hundred years ago.

(2.) Assuming, then, that the apostles had truths to communicate to mankind in advance of what the world then possessed, and that in respect to those truths the Gospel is as really in advance of the world in its present stage of progress as it was then, it remains to inquire whether, in respect to the means which Christianity now has for propagating and perpetuating those truths, it has fallen behind the world, or maintains its advanced position still?

·It is usual to represent the apostles as endowed with peculiar and exclusive powers in propagating the truths of Christianity. It is not uncommon for men to feel that the Church has lost much by the cessation of their peculiar endowments in making an aggressive movement on idolatry and sin. It is not unnatural to feel that if the Church could again be clothed with the power which it had in apostolic times, the conquest of the world to Christ would be easy and rapid, and it is conceivable that many a youthful soldier of the cross, panting for the conversion of the world, and resolving to devote himself to that great purpose in the work of the ministry, or in a missionary life, feels a sense of discouragement in the fact that he must go forth with few of the advantages which the apostles had in their work. It is important to inquire whether this is so.

The relation of the apostles to the world may be regarded as positive and negative.

(a) Positive. They had three things. *First.* The power of speaking the languages of the world; or, at once, and without study, the power of making their message known to the people of all lands. This seems to have been an unlimited power. In the case of a missionary now, the best years of his life are consumed in efforts, often imperfect efforts, to place himself in the condition in which the apostles were when they commenced their work. *Second.* They had the power of working miracles. They healed the sick; they opened the eyes of the blind; they raised the dead. This, too, seems to have been an unlimited power. *Third.* They had the advantage of freshness and novelty in the message which they proclaimed to the world. Whatever might be said in other respects in regard to the system which they preached, it could not be denied that the

R

statement that there had been a proper incarnation of
the Deity in the land of Judæa; that the Son of God in
human form had trod those hills and vales; that he
had moved with a healing power through the land;
that in his presence the insane had become sane, the
blind had been made to see, the deaf to hear, the lame
to walk, and the dead to leave their graves; that he
had died on a cross as an atoning sacrifice for men;
that he had risen to life again, and had reascended to
God—that all these were statements that were *fitted* to
arrest the attention of men. Such statements had never
fallen on human ears before.

(*b*) Negative. We are to remember, in order to form
a correct estimate of the relation of the apostles to the
world in the effort to spread the Gospel, the following
things: *First.* It was an experiment; a trial not yet
certain except to faith. There had been no past experience in regard to Christianity; there was no history
which could be referred to; there was no influence as
yet on the world that could be an argument why men
should receive it. It was a new system, whose adapt-
edness to the wants of men was yet to be tried. *Second.* There was, as yet, no public sentiment in its favor
which could be appealed to, or which could be *assumed*
as a ground of appeal. On the contrary, the entire sentiment of the world was against it. *Third.* There was
no *press* for the rapid diffusion of their doctrines beyond
the power of the living voice. We can scarcely put
ourselves, even in imagination, in this respect, in their
circumstances. Accustomed as we are to the press;
the printed page; the power of defending our sentiments through the press, and of arguing with men
through the press, we can scarcely conceive what it
would be if that power were withdrawn. *Fourth.* The

apostles had no Christian literature. Beyond the books of the New Testament—and, in the beginning of their work, not even these were written, and, in the end of their work, not yet collected into a volume—there was nothing to explain, to illustrate, and to defend their doctrines; there was nothing to edify the Church; there was nothing to instruct and guide the young. *Fifth.* There were no schools, colleges, or seminaries of learning under Christian influence, and designed to train up a generation for Christ. All the schools that existed were Jewish or heathen; nor was there one where a Christian youth might be instructed in the ways of the true religion, or that contemplated the training of a generation for the service of God. *Sixth.* There was, as yet, no established organization of believers into churches, designed to bring a united influence to bear upon the world. All this was the slow work of time.

It is to be remembered, also, that, whatever were the advantages of the gift of tongues, and the power of working miracles, the immediate effect was not the conversion of sinners. In the life of the Savior himself, there is no evidence that a single sinner was converted by his miracles, nor in the labors of the apostles is there proof that one was converted by the miracles which they wrought, or by their power of speaking foreign languages. This was, indeed, a proof of the divine origin of their religion. The multitude that came together on the day of Pentecost " marveled," were " amazed," and were " confounded"—συνεχύθη (Acts, ii., 6, 7), " because that every man heard them speak in his own language;" but the three thousand were converted, as other men are, by the preaching of Christ crucified. Miracles converted no one. Thousands saw the miracles of the Savior who joined in the cry " Crucify him."

Mere eloquence converted no one. "And my speech
and my preaching was not with enticing words of man's
wisdom, but in demonstration of the Spirit and with
power" (1 Cor., xi., 4). "And I, brethren, when I came
unto you, came not with excellency of speech or of wisdom, declaring unto you the testimony of God."

The sole ground of reliance by the apostles for the
conversion of men was the great truth that Christ was
crucified for the sins of the world, accompanied by the
power of the Holy Ghost.* In not a single instance do
they trace the conversion of a sinner to miracles, to the
power of speaking a foreign language, to eloquence. In
each and every instance it is the power of truth as applied by the Holy Ghost.

That power—that ground of reliance—we have now
as much and as really as the apostles had—as much
and as really—no less; no more. The truth is unchanged; the power of the Holy Ghost is undiminished; the promises that He will apply the truth when
properly presented are as full and as fresh now as they
were then. Each minister of the Gospel, in Christian
or in heathen lands, may go to his work as fully under
the influence of this feeling, and as fully armed with
this power, as the apostles; and as the power from this
source was entirely in advance of what the world possessed in the time of the apostles, so is it equally in advance of the world in the stage of its present progress
in civilization, science, and the arts.

(3.) I refer next in proof that the Gospel has not fall-
en behind the world, that it has now the advantage of
the *trial* made by it during the long period of eighteen
hundred years. Like every other system, it started, of

* Compare Acts, ii., 16-21; x., 44; xi., 16; xvi., 14; 1 Cor.,
iii., 5, 7.

course, without this advantage; like every other system, it may now avail itself of all that can fairly be derived from its history in vindication of its truth, and in aiding in its diffusion.

It has a history—a long, a peculiar, a definite, a very marked history. It had its origin at a time when the great empire that had so long ruled the world was tending to decay; it lived through all the changes which occurred in its "Decline and Fall" as traced by Mr Gibbon; it has been connected, in many cases closely identified, with the origin and growth of the great kingdoms which now control the world. It has a history as bearing on individuals; on families; on nations; on the course of events. It has a history in regard to trials; to conflicts; to persecutions; to death. It has a history of confessors, saints, and martyrs; a history in regard to its influence on domestic life, on education, on customs and laws. That history is now before the world, and can not now be changed.

It is true that, in close connection with real Christianity, often so apparently close as to be mistaken for it, there has been a history of false Christianity—a system of persecution, blood, and fire. The friends of Christianity are not insensible to that fact; they do not attempt to conceal it. In nominal connection with Christianity there have been wars, corruptions, vices, oppressions, persecutions. But these doings are not Christianity, nor is Christianity responsible for them. If, however, a man should strangely say, lost to all great principles of history and philosophy, that Christianity *is* responsible for these things, we ask, Why? How? Are these things prescribed and commanded in the book which embodies the laws and doctrines of the system—the New Testament? Did they characterize

the life of its Great Founder? Were they enjoined by
the teachings of his apostles? There *can* be no mistake on this subject. The nature of the system, as laid
down in the New Testament, can not be misunderstood.
The enemies of religion can tell what the religion requires as well as its friends, and often the best judges
of what it demands are those who complain of the inconsistencies of its professed friends, and who hold them
to the observance of a rule which they themselves seem
little inclined to obey.

We know what the effect of Christianity is—its effect
on the child, the wife, the man. We know what is its
effect on domestic peace, industry, comfort. We know
what is its effect in elevating woman, under nearly all
other systems sunk in deep degradation. We know
what is its effect on intelligence, industry, and liberty.

We know what are its *affinities;* with what it naturally combines. We are very imperfectly acquainted
with the elements of matter until we know with what
they will combine, and what will be the result of the
combination. Each of the sixty or more elementary
substances that compose our world has its own properties, and we do not understand the nature of matter
itself until we understand what the properties of those
individual substances are, and with what other substances, and in what proportions, they will combine.
There is the power of attraction and repulsion; there
are laws of chemical affinity that produce all the forms
of matter, either when united with life or when inorganic, which make up our beautiful world. We do not
understand the nature of oxygen or nitrogen; of phosphorus, of carbon, or of calcium—of any of the metals,
until we know with what they combine, and in what
proportions.

The same is true of systems of morals and religion. We know not what they are until we know what their *affinities* are—with what they most naturally combine.

No man is surprised to find Mr. Hume, under the notions of religion which he cherished, proclaiming that "justice is not a natural, but artificial virtue, depending wholly on the arbitrary institutions of men, and previous to the establishment of civil society not at all incumbent; that moral, intellectual, and corporeal virtue are all of the same kind; that adultery must be practiced if men would obtain all the advantages of this life; that, if generally practiced, it would soon cease to be scandalous, and that, if practiced secretly and frequently, it would by degrees come to be thought no crime at all; that the life of a man is of no greater importance than that of an oyster, and as it is admitted that there is no crime in diverting the Nile or the Danube from their courses, so there can be none in turning a few ounces of blood from their natural channel, or that suicide is lawful."* His *principles* led to such results, and he had the hardihood and the honesty to avow it. No man is surprised to learn that the horrors of the French Revolution followed the promulgation of the doctrines of the French Encyclopædia. All the blood shed in the French capital; all the crimes of the Revolution, were the regular results of the doctrines defended by Voltaire and his fellow-laborers. No man was surprised at the results reached in "New Harmony." The seed sown produced its appropriate harvest.

The same principle is applicable to Christianity. Like the chemical elements in nature, and like the systems of infidel philosophy, it has its proper laws of affin-

* See the proof that Mr. Hume held these opinions in *Magee* on Atonement and Sacrifice, p. 425–429.

ity; and its nature is not known till those laws are understood. After an experience of eighteen hundred years, the world has learned what those laws are. Christianity combines every where with pure morality, with chaste living, with refined manners, with domestic peace, with temperance, with industry, with order, with law, with learning, with liberty. The press, colleges, schools, the courtesies of refined life, charity to the poor, to the needy, and to the outcast, find a natural ally in Christianity, and, wherever it goes, we know that these will be found in its train. What it has gained in this respect is a part of its capital, and is not to be transferred to any other system.

(4.) I refer next, in proof that Christianity has not fallen behind the world, and as illustrating its relation to civilization, science, and the arts, to what, for want of a better name, may be called its *radiations*. I mean by that term to denote the influences which have gone *beyond* the direct agency of the system, and which have passed over on other systems, and made them, in a great measure, what they are. The idea is, that the condition of the world has been materially modified by Christianity beyond its direct influence, and that, to understand its exact nature and value, the extent of that influence should be known.

I have endeavored to show in this Lecture that the world has made great progress since the Gospel was first made known; that it is in many respects a different world from what it was when Paul stood on Mars' Hill in Athens; that a Greek of the age of Pericles, if he should now appear again, would find himself in a different world from that in which he lived. The remark which I am now making is, that this change has been produced in a very considerable degree by what

I refer to as the *radiations* of Christianity; by those influences which have passed beyond its immediate sphere in the Church, and which have affected surrounding objects. I refer to those things which make a Christian nation different from other nations; to those things derived from it which could not now be *detached* from civilization without destroying the entire fabric.

It is probable that there is not one thing that now pertains to us in a Christian land, and which we value as a part of our civilization, which has not been made in a great manner what it is by the silent and accumulating influence of Christianity. The laws under which we live are different from what they would have been. The methods of administering justice are different. The ideas of punishment are different. The securities for life, liberty, and the pursuit of happiness are different. The manners and customs of those among whom we live are different. Our domestic arrangements are different. The provisions made for the poor and the needy; for the sick and the wounded; for the blind, the deaf, and the insane, are different.

Now it is impossible to ascertain how much of this is due to Christianity, for no man can *prove* that the world would not have made progress in these respects if Christianity had not been revealed. But no man can deny that a very considerable portion of the comforts which we enjoy from day to day are to be traced to the *radiating* influences of the Gospel. Apart from what is its *religious* teaching, and apart from its influence in saving the soul, the world is different now from what it would have been if the Christian system had not been revealed.

We claim all this as belonging to Christianity, and as indicating its source. And in estimating the rela-

tion of Christianity to the world in its present stage of
progress in science, civilization, and the arts, we ask
that all that it has done in making science, civilization,
and the arts what they are, should be taken into the account; and we hold that the question whether Christianity is still ahead of the world, or whether it is
abreast of the world, or whether it has fallen in the
rear, and can now be dispensed with, can not be determined unless we could detach from the institutions of social and civilized life all that they have derived from
the Christian religion, and survey them as they would
be then.

(5.) I refer, in illustration of the relation of Christianity to the present age and to future ages, to what, for
want of a better term, also, I may call the *appliances* of
Christianity. I refer to the question whether it has
kept its relative position in regard to the means of
propagating and perpetuating itself on the earth.

We have seen, in the previous remarks, that there
was little in this respect in the time of the apostles;
that Christianity had no press, no literature, no schools,
almost no organization.

In reference to the means which the world now has
of perpetuating and extending what it has secured,
there is a difference as great between the apostolic age
and the present as there is in the things which have
been secured at one period and the other. Whatever
may have been done in regard to ancient literature, to
scientific discoveries, to valuable works of art, to civilization, to the means of prosecuting war, as to the question of perpetuating these things, it is certain that
nothing, in all time to come, will now imperil their existence. Those great discoveries are secured in libraries, in public monuments, in the very necessities of

common life. What now can destroy a great poem, a valuable historical work, or a treatise on medicine or astronomy, multiplied as it is by the art of printing? What can destroy the printing-press, the compass, the quadrant, the steam-engine, the magnetic telegraph? Society, in striking out these inventions, has made them self-perpetuating, and has secured the means, in the things themselves, of their preservation, of their diffusion over the earth, and of their transmission to future times. Has Christianity, in its movements, kept its relative position in this respect also?

Christianity, more than science, has secured the press. It early seized upon it as a most important auxiliary; it made it tributary to its own great work in diffusing the doctrines of the Reformation; it now employs it in the work of diffusing the truths of revelation in a large part of the languages spoken on the earth. It takes the press with it wherever it goes; it forms no plan for its own propagation or perpetuity except in connection with it.

Christianity has a literature of its own, as large, as important, as powerful on public sentiment as the literature of any other department of thought and action. One would, perhaps, be surprised, in attempting to remove what is properly a Christian literature from the alcoves of a great library, to find how large a part of the library would be removed by such an attempt; how many vacancies would be made on the shelves—to see how much of that literature has been *created* by Christianity; how much that once controlled the world has been removed into a comparatively obscure and unfrequented part of the library by the changes which have been made by Christianity in public opinion.

Christianity has done much to control the literature

which it has not directly created, and has made it different from what it would otherwise have been. A large part of the books of history, poetry, philosophy, and science are different from what they would have been if they had had their origin in lands remote from the Christian religion. Even Mr. Hume's History of England was moulded and modified by the fact that he wrote of a Christian nation; Mr. Gibbon's History is not what it would have been if he had not been called upon to record the influence of Christianity in remoulding the nations of Europe during and after the decline and fall of the Roman empire.

The great names which adorn Christian literature are quite on a level with those which pertain wholly to the world. In history, in poetry, in eloquence, in close and powerful reasoning, the names which Christianity claims as its own are on a level, at least, with those which are claimed by the world. In poetry, is there a greater than John Milton? In profound reasoning, is there a greater than Jonathan Edwards? In imagination, is there one superior to Jeremy Taylor? In eloquence, has the world any superior to Massillon or Bourdaloue —to Robert Hall or Thomas Chalmers?

Christianity has surrounded itself with colleges and schools. It plants them wherever it goes. Taking the world at large, the colleges are, at least, under a nominal Christian influence. Edinburgh, St. Andrew's, Glasgow, Cambridge, and Oxford; Bonn, Heidelburg, Halle, Göttingen, are, to a great extent, under Christian influence. In our own country there is not one avowedly infidel college; nor could such a college be sustained. There *was* one founded under the auspices of a great state, and under the patronage of one that at one time wielded more influence than any other man in the United

States, but its own internal peace demanded the influence of religion, and, in this respect, it has taken its
place by the side of the other colleges of the land.
There is not a Legislature in our land that would char-
ter an infidel college as such, nor could it live a year if
it were thus chartered.

Christianity has originated a new form of literature
wholly its own; a literature not known under any ancient form of mythology; not known under any form
of modern heathenism; not known to infidelity; not
known to philosophy; and it has, at the same time, originated an institution most effective for applying that
literature, and for securing its own influence over the
young.   I allude to the Sabbath-school, and to the literature which has been originated by that institution.
This, if there were nothing else, would show that Christianity, in its efforts to perpetuate and propagate itself,
is quite abreast of the world.   The literature of the
Sabbath-school may not be, in respect to quality, all
that could be desired, but it may be doubted whether
there is any other department of literature that is exerting as much influence on the destinies of mankind.
Infidelity has no peculiar literature for the young, nor
has it any institution where to inculcate its sentiments
on the young.   Mohammedanism and Buddhism have
no peculiar literature for the young, nor have they any
peculiar institution for training up the young in those
views of religion.   Science, with great difficulty, pre-
pares books for the young, but its literature in astronomy, botany, chemistry, designed to guide the young,
as compared with the literature of the Sabbath-school,
is meagre in the extreme.   The Sabbath-school, and the
Sabbath-school library, stand by themselves.   Both capable undoubtedly of great improvement, they are,

nevertheless, exerting a vast power on the coming generation, and it is difficult to see how a religion that has such an agency as the Sabbath-school *could be* exterminated from the world. One day during each week, of every month in the year, the children of this nation are brought directly under Christian instruction, with all the advantages, in theory at least, of calling into the service the best talent, the highest intelligence, the warmest piety, the most devoted zeal, existing in the churches. Through all the states of the Union, and in all the territories, by agencies of its own, that literature is placed in the hands of the young, before other influences are brought to bear on them, to form their opinions, to make their hearts pure, to teach them to believe the Bible, and to love and serve God. Whatever else the world may do in its progress, we may be certain that it will not be in advance of this arrangement of Christianity to diffuse and perpetuate itself upon the earth.

The argument which has been submitted to you in this Lecture, as the conclusion of the course, is founded on the idea that a religion starting in advance of the world, from such a region, and such a source as that in which Christianity was originated, and which, through ages of wonderful progress in civilization, science, and the arts, still, after the lapse of eighteen hundred years, maintains that position; a religion which has lived through all forms of furious and fiery persecution; a religion which has originated much of that which now enters into the ameliorated condition of the world in customs, manners, laws, and modes of life; a religion which, by elective affinity, has attached itself to all that is good and valuable in human discoveries, and has refused a permanent connection with evil; a religion which now, in its own means of perpetuity and propagation, is still in advance of the world, can be best explained on the supposition that it is what it claims to be, of divine origin, and that it can not be explained on any other supposition. The argument is, substantially, that it must have been founded on a knowledge of the future which is above the unaided powers of man; on the fact that man can not *adjust* any system *to* the future in its varying and uncertain changes; on the fact that in all human systems there must be arrangements for making changes to adapt them to unforeseen developments and the progress of the world—as in governments providing for "amendments" to their Constitutions, as in our own, or silently submitting to changes forced upon them by time, as in the British Constitution; on the fact that in architecture, in the arts, in agriculture, in navigation, in all the great departments of human progress, the things which are adapted to one age must silently give way in the progress of events— as in naval warfare the Greek *triremes* would be useless now, and wooden ships are superseded by iron-clad vessels, and in land service the buckler, and the shield, and the breastplate, and the coat of mail have been laid aside; on the fact that no *creed* originated by man can be adapted to every coming age of the world and to every land; on the fact that the old arrangements for preserving the memory of past events and the discoveries in science, by wax, and metal plates, and the stylus, become useless when the art of printing is made known, and are laid aside. Since, of necessity, all these things pass away, how was it that Christianity was adjusted, at the outset, to all the possible changes in the world; to all the progress which mankind could make in science, in civilization, and the arts? The simplest solution is, that it was originated by an Omniscient One, and is therefore divine.

Whatever may be thought of this argument, there *is* an inference from the whole subject in which all will agree, and the statement of which is peculiarly appropriate to this place, and as the closing remark of these Lectures. It is, that such a religion is to maintain its position only by *keeping* abreast or ahead of the world. The men who are to defend it in this age and in coming generations are to be men who are "up to their age." The arguments by which the philosophy of the Epicureans and Stoics could be met at Athens do not constitute all the arguments which are needed now. The weapons which led to victory in the contests of the "fathers" with Celsus and Porphyry will not necessarily lead to victory now. The methods of the schoolmen are not all that is needed now. The weapons which seemed so formidable in past ages might not be formidable now. Old weapons of war—greaves, and shields, and spears, and catapults, were useful, but there comes a time when they are laid aside, and find repose in ancient halls and towers. There is a "living age," and it is much for a young man entering on life, and especially in a position where he will be called to defend Christianity as the main business of his life, to know that there *is* such an age, and *what* it is. Theologians must deal with living men and with living opinions, and if they are not prepared for this, they are not prepared for the work of their age. The ministry must be prepared to meet men—living men—on the question of the inspiration of the Scriptures, and with arguments that will commend themselves to those trained in the principles of profound criticism; on the question about the antiquity of the race on earth, and with arguments not derived from synods and councils; on the whole question of miracles, and of a supernatural influence in the affairs of men. A more deep and subtle Pantheism in the form of Rationalism or Positivism lies at the foundation of the sciences of this day, as they are held, than the great mass of the friends of Christianity are aware of, and against all this, it may be unconsciously, the friend of Christianity struggles and contends when he attempts to impress its truths on the minds of men. No true friend of Christianity could wish that the ministers of religion should be less pious, or less imbued with Biblical learning; but let them go prepared to meet the world as it is, and not go clad in the armor of a past generation, only to find that the enemy which that kind of armor is fitted to subdue has long been wandering in the land of shades among the knight-errants of the past.

It can not, therefore, but be regarded as a very auspicious circumstance that in this seminary a movement should have been commenced, suggested by, and sustained by laymen, with a view to this state of things; to connect the seminary more with the world around it; to draw to its aid what may be of advantage in this respect from those engaged in other departments of learning, and those engaged in the active duties of pastoral life; and it is an auspicious circumstance—what those laymen well knew would be the case—that such a movement has the entire concurrence of the professors of the seminary, and is hailed by them as materially aiding them in their great work. Other things being equal, that seminary of sacred learning only which thus feels the contact with the living world will meet the wants of the coming age; those institutions which do not feel this, and which resist such influences,

will exhaust their power in perpetuating a dead ortho-
doxy in the Church, and will leave the world around
to the influence of Rationalism, Positivism, and Pantheism.

APPENDIX,

In the delivery of these Lectures on the Evidences of Christianity, there was a very important point which, if not wholly passed over, was not discussed with the fullness which the nature of the subject demanded. Of this I was myself deeply sensible when the Lectures were composed, and of this I presume my hearers were painfully sensible at the time when they were delivered. I can not doubt that there were persons in the audience who would have been desirous of asking me questions, as I should have been if I had been listening to a course of Lectures on that subject, and I can not deny that questions might have been easily proposed which I could not have answered, and it may have excited some surprise that inquiries which could have been so easily made, and which would have seemed to be so obviously proper, were not more fully considered in the Lectures. These inquiries might have been made by two classes of persons, and if proposed by both or by either, they would seem to be such as to have a claim to a candid answer. (*a*) It is probable that they may have occurred to the theological students for whom the Lectures were especially prepared, and who might feel that they would be likely to encounter the very difficulties involved in such inquiries in the work of the ministry, and who might have desired to be furnished with the means of allaying doubts which perhaps were suggested by the Lectures, and of removing difficulties which they could easily foresee they would be likely to meet in their professional life ; and (*b*) they are inquiries which would have been made by those who are not believers in the truth of Christianity, if such were present, and who might have found a secret satisfaction in the fact that the difficulties were not met, and that the questions which they would have asked were not solved, and in the belief that the fact that they were not adverted to was, in their apprehension, a tacit confession on the part of the lecturer that the difficulties could not be removed.

These difficulties pertained especially to the subject of miracles—the subject particularly discussed in the fifth Lecture, though often alluded to in the other Lectures.

The difficulty would be expressed, in few words, in the following questions: What evidence is there in favor of the miracles of the Bible *stronger* than that which can be alleged for witchcraft, necromancy, sorcery, divination, and demonology: for the miracles practiced among the heathen; for the miracles of the early Christian Church subsequent to the time of the apostles, and for the miracles of the Roman Catholic communion? Since, in the progress of the world; in the diffusion of science; in the advances of civilization; in the careful examination of historical testimony, the world has been disabused of belief in these things, or is tending to universal skepticism in regard to them, why should not the same result be reached in regard to the alleged miracles of the Bible, and to all that is claimed there to be supernatural? In other words, why should not the principles of Rationalism, which have been made so effective in relieving the world of superstition, and of unfounded claims to the supernatural, be applied to that which is claimed in the Bible to be supernatural, and the race be effectually delivered from all that remains that is supposed to be a departure from the established laws of nature?

For the omission in not considering this inquiry there were two reasons:

One was the difficulty of prosecuting the inquiry in a course of Lectures designed to be in their main features of a popular character, in such a manner as to make it interesting to the audience that was to be addressed. The course of Lectures, by the terms of the foundation, was, indeed, designed mainly to be for the benefit of the students of the seminary, and the course prescribed was to be on such subjects as would come before them in their preparation for the ministry, and in this view the points now adverted to would have been eminently appropriate, difficult as it might have been to make the discussion interesting in a public Lecture; but the course was also designed to be, in some measure, a connecting link between the seminary and the public, and it was contemplated that the Lectures should be of such a character as would be interesting to a popular audience, and it would have been difficult to present an argument on these points which would be interesting to such an audience. An argument on the subject, to be of value, must be somewhat abstruse. Such an argument could not have been compressed into a single Lecture, and could not have been appended to the Lecture devoted to the subject of miracles, without protracting it to a length that would have violated all the rules of propriety. It might have been difficult, moreover, before such an audience, to present the subject in such a manner as not to create more doubts than would have been allayed, and the subject, therefore, was passed over in silence.

The other reason for the omission was, that if the questions had been proposed to me, I should have been constrained to admit that there were difficulties on the subject which I could not then solve.

In reference to these difficulties I made the following remarks in the course of the Lecture on Miracles:

"I confess that of all the questions ever asked on the subject of miracles, this is the most perplexing and the most difficult to answer. It is rather to be wondered at that it has not been pressed with more zeal by those who deny the reality of miracles, and that they have placed their objections so extensively on other grounds. From the fact that it is so seldom referred to by skeptics, it is manifest that it does not strike them as it strikes me, and that they, from some cause, are not disposed to use it as I would, if I had no faith in miracles; and perhaps it may savor more of apparent candor than of wise prudence for a believer in the reality of miracles even to make the suggestion.

"The argument might be made very strong, and if there were time to present it here, it might be done in such a manner that it might *seem*, at least, to be impossible to meet and refute it."*

I might, indeed, have taken refuge from the difficulties adverted to under the plea that on *any* subject questions may be asked which can not, in the present state of human knowledge, and perhaps with the limited capacities of the human mind, be answered; that it is no certain evidence of the falseness of an opinion, or the weakness of an argument, that such questions can be asked; and that if we were to pause in our investigations of truth at the exact point where a question might be asked which we could not answer, the range of our inquiries would be narrowed down to the smallest conceivable dimensions. Such an answer, however, would not have satisfied an inquirer, and the impression could scarcely have been avoided in such an answer that there was a consciousness that there was something in the question which *could* not be answered; for while it would be admitted by all persons qualified to judge in such inquiries that questions may be asked on any subject which no one can answer, it must be admitted that questions may be asked on most subjects which, if *not* answered, will be fatal to an argument. In such a case as that before us, under such circumstances, the inference would be *likely* to be drawn that this was one of those subjects.

The argument on miracles, therefore, would not be complete if, after having referred so often in the Lecture to this as constituting perhaps the most important point in the evidences of Christianity in the nine-

* Page 161.

teenth century, and after having, perhaps, suggested doubts which might not have occurred to others, I should allow the Lectures to go forth in a volume, perhaps much beyond the circle of those who heard them, without an attempt, at least, to solve the difficulty, though in doing it I may have occasion on some points to avail myself of the admission that there are difficulties which I can not solve, and that questions may be asked on this subject, as on any other, which we might be compelled to admit that we could not answer.

The point of difficulty, and the question to be solved, may be made apparent by a few remarks :

(a) In a course of Lectures on the Evidences of Christianity in the Nineteenth Century, it was impossible *not* to advert to the great changes which have occurred in the opinions of the world on the subject of the supernatural and the marvelous in the course of eighteen hundred years—in other words, to the progress of " Rationalism" in that long period. The fact of such a change is apparent on the face of history, and the progress of " Rationalism" becomes a very important part of history, alike in secular and sacred matters, for the principles of Rationalism have been applied as fearlessly to Grecian records and to Roman history as to the Bible. Eighteen hundred years ago there were numerous subjects then supposed to pertain to the region of the supernatural which are now well understood to be connected with the operation of the regular laws of nature, as eclipses, meteors, comets, storms, diseases ; and there were numerous other subjects then supposed to be connected with the supernatural, as divination, necromancy, witchcraft, and sorcery, which have been detached from the faith of mankind, and which have taken their place with myths and legends. So far as the *facts* in regard to this change of opinion are concerned, and so far, in the main, as the *causes* of this change are concerned, the history has been given to the world in our own time in a work of great learning, with great attractiveness of style, and with a full acquaintance with the subject—a work which leaves nothing in regard to the history of this change to be desired.* It was impossible, in a course of Lectures on the Evidences of Christianity in the Nineteenth Century, not to advert to this history, and not to inquire into the bearing of this change in the sentiments of mankind on the evidences of the miraculous and the supernatural in the Bible. The history of this change I have, therefore, more than once adverted to. The fact of the change can not be called in question ; its tendency, as relating to the question of the evidences of revealed religion, is one of the most important inquiries now before the Church and the world.

* History of the Rise and Influence of the Spirit of Rationalism in Europe, by *W. E. H. Lecky, M.A.*, in 2 vols. N. York: D. Appleton and Co., 1866.

(*b*) The effect of this change, as related to the subjects discussed in these Lectures, are such as the following:

1. A great number of things once regarded as matters of true history are now reduced to the place of legends, myths, fables. One has only to look into Grote's History of Greece, or into Niebuhr's History of Rome, or indeed into any history that professes to trace events in the past to their origin, to see, if the expression may be allowed, as derived from the classic writings, that the "god Terminus" has removed the point where authentic history commences very far *within* what was once regarded as the true boundary, and that the intelligible and reliable accounts of the affairs of the world have their beginning very far *within* what was once regarded as the proper point from which to reckon the progress of human affairs. It is a very natural inquiry whether the same process of *elimination* may not properly be applied to the Bible, as well as to the Egyptian, Persian, Greek, and Roman histories.

2. Many things once regarded as supernatural and miraculous, as I have more than once observed, have been reduced to the operation of the regular and established laws of nature. Portents, wonders, comets, eclipses, meteors, diseases, have been taken out of the region of the supernatural, and placed under the rules of natural science, and now constitute subjects of regular instructions in the schools, instead of being regarded with superstitious dread, or made subjects by which one class of men can secure an ascendency over another, or by which the errors and impositions of false religions, under the control of a priesthood, can be kept up in the world. It is a fair question, and one which this age is asking, whether the same principles of explanation can not be applied to all those cases recorded in the Bible which have been commonly relied on as miracles.

3. The world has been disabused, so far as sound science has gone, of its belief in divination, necromancy, demonology, witchcraft, sorcery, and the region of the supernatural has been narrowed to an extent which we can not well estimate by the withdrawal of these things from the causes which affect the progress of human affairs and the destiny of mankind. It is a question which we can not avoid in contemplating this course of things, whether the wonders of the Bible can not be reduced to the same class of events, and may not be explained as those ancient wonders that exerted so much influence on mankind may now be explained, and take their places with the things that derived their influence from the fears, the credulity, and the superstitions of the early ages of the world.

4. There has been a great change on the subject of faith in the miracles in the early Christian Church subsequent to the time of the

apostles. If a disbelief in those miracles is not absolutely universal, yet it may be said that it is rapidly becoming so, and that that result is morally certain. For a long time the faith in those miracles was undoubted, and, even among Protestants, the question was not whether such miracles were actually wrought, but at what time they ceased. So universal was the belief in those miracles, that even Mr. Locke consulted Sir Isaac Newton on the question, not whether such miracles were wrought, but at what time they ceased. In one of the letters of Sir Isaac Newton to Mr. Locke there is a somewhat hesitating passage on this subject: "Miracles," says he, "of good credit continued in the Church for about two or three hundred years. Gregorius Thaumaturgus had his name from thence, and was one of the latest who was eminent for that gift; but of their number and frequence I am not able to give you a just account. The history of those ages is very imperfect."—Brewster's Life of Newton, p. 275. The prevalent belief on this subject among the Christian "fathers," to which I may have occasion to advért again, may be learned from St. Augustine, the ablest and most clear-headed of those fathers, and a man of undoubted piety. He solemnly asserts that in his own diocese of Hippo, in the space of two years, no less than seventy miracles had been wrought by the body of St. Stephen, and that in the neighboring province of Calama, where the relic had previously been, the number was incomparably greater. He gives a catalogue of what he deems undoubted miracles, which he says he had selected from a multitude so great that volumes would be required to relate them all. In that catalogue there are no less than five cases of restoration from the dead. —De Civitat. Dei, lib. xxii., c. 8. See, also, Sermons of Augustine (Serm. 286, § 4); and his Confessions.—B. ix., vii., p. 16. Since the time of Middleton, and his attack on the veracity of the fathers,* the faith in these early miracles of the Christian Church has to a great extent died away, and the question is an obvious one why the same reasoning which has destroyed the faith of mankind in *those* miracles should not also be applied to the miracles of the Bible?

5. The belief in the reality of the Roman Catholic miracles, once so universal in Europe, and made so extensively the basis in maintaining that religion in those countries where it is established, and of extending it among the heathen, has, in the more enlightened and scientific portions of the world, almost wholly passed away. Of course, no such faith is entertained by any of the Protestant nations. No such faith is entertained by scientific men as such. To a great extent, also, there

* A Free Inquiry into the Miraculous Powers which are supposed to have subsisted in the Christian Church from the Earliest Ages through several successive Centuries, by *Conyers Middleton, D.D.* London, 1749.

is a general incredulity on the subject among the most intelligent and scientific of the Roman Catholics themselves. On this point, Mr. Lecky, in remarking on the former belief in the supernatural in Europe, makes the following remarks: "All this has now passed away. It has passed away, not only in lands where Protestantism is triumphant, but also in those where the Roman Catholic faith is still acknowledged, and where the mediæval saints are still venerated. St. Januarius, it is true, continues to liquefy at Naples, and the pastorals of French bishops occasionally relate apparitions of the Virgin among very ignorant and superstitious peasants; but the implicit, indiscriminating acquiescence with which such narratives were once received has long since been replaced by a derisive incredulity. Those who know the tone that is habitually adopted on these subjects by the converted in Roman Catholic countries will admit that, so far from being a subject of triumphant exultation, the very few modern miracles which are related are every where regarded as a scandal, a stumbling-block, and a difficulty. Most educated persons speak of them with undisguised scorn and incredulity; some attempt to evade or explain them away by a natural hypothesis; a very few faintly and apologetically defend them. Nor can it be said that what is manifested is merely a desire for a more minute and accurate examination of the evidence by which they are supported. On the contrary, it will, I think, be admitted that these alleged miracles are commonly rejected with an assurance that is as peremptory and unreasoning as that with which they would have been once received. Nothing can be more rare than a serious examination, by those who disbelieve them, of the testimony on which they rest. They are repudiated, not because they are unsupported, but because they are miraculous. Men are prepared to admit almost any conceivable occurrence of natural improbabilities rather than resort to the hypothesis of supernatural interferences; and this spirit is exhibited not merely by open skeptics, but by men who are sincere, though perhaps not very fervent believers in their church." —History of Rationalism, vol. i., p. 159, 160.

The general result of this state of things, or the prevalent feeling on the subject, may be stated in the words of Lecky: "If we put aside the clergy, and those who are most immediately under their influence, we find that this habit of mind is the invariable concomitant of education, and is the especial characteristic of those persons whose intellectual sympathies are most extended, and who therefore represent most faithfully the various intellectual influences of their time." "All history shows that, in exact proportion as nations advance in civilization, the accounts of miracles taking place among them become rarer and rarer, until at last they entirely cease." "The plain fact is, that the

S

progress of civilization produces invariably a certain tone and habit of thought which makes men recoil from miraculous narratives with an instinctive and immediate repugnance, as though they were essentially incredible, independently of any definite arguments, and in spite of dogmatic teaching."—*Ibid*, p. 161, 162. To what this change may tend may be illustrated by a remark of the Rev. Frederick Temple, D.D., Head-master of Rugby School, in a sermon before the University of Oxford on "The present relations of Science to religion"—a remark that may, without impropriety, be regarded as expressing the sentiments or the *fears* of many in the Church. He says, "The student of science is learning to look upon fixed laws as universal, and many of the old arguments which science once supplied to religion are in consequence rapidly disappearing. How strikingly altered is our view from that of a few centuries ago is shown by the fact that the miracles recorded in the Bible, which once were looked on as the bulwarks of the faith, are now felt by very many to be difficulties in their way; and commentators endeavor to represent them, not as mere interferences with the laws of nature, but as the natural action of still higher laws belonging to a world whose phenomena are only half revealed to us. It is evident that this change in science necessitates a change in its relation to faith. If law be either almost or altogether universal, we must look for the finger of God in that law—we must expect to find him manifesting his love, his wisdom, his infinity, not in individual acts of will, but in a perfection of legislation rendering all individual action needless; we must find his providence in that perfect adaptation of all the parts of the machine to one another which shall have the effect of tender care, though it proceed by an invariable action."—Recent Inquiries in Theology, p. 489.

The great question now, as I stated in the Lecture on Miracles—*the great question of our age in regard to religion, and not less important in regard to science, is, How far this skepticism is to extend?* What is its proper limit? Is the principle to become so universal as to include *all* the facts claiming to be of a supernatural nature which have actually occurred, or which will occur in our world? Is it to embrace the whole region of the miraculous and the supernatural, so as to exclude the idea of any direct agency on the part of God, any phenomena—any changes—the antecedents in which are only the divine will and the divine power? So it is maintained by Rationalists; such, too, is the practical belief of many men whose lives are devoted to science.

The progress of things, the influences of civilization, the discoveries of science in regard to physical laws, have "*exorcised*" the world, if the expression may be allowed, in regard to sorcery, witchcraft, magic, necromancy, portents and wonders in eclipses, storms, and earthquakes; are these to "exorcise" the world in regard to mesmerism, spiritualism, spirit-rapping, and table-moving; and are they also to "exorcise" it in regard to the belief that Joshua caused the sun to "stand still upon Gibeon," and the moon "in the valley of Ajalon;" to the stilling of the tempest on the Sea of Tiberias; to the healing of the lame man at the pool of Bethesda; to the opening of the eyes of Bartimeus; to the raising of Lazarus from the grave, and to the resurrection of the Redeemer himself?

The material inquiry is, What stronger historical evidence is there of the truth of the miracles of the Bible than of the alleged facts respecting witchcraft, sorcery, divination, and necromancy; the alleged marvels in the early history of the world—as the prodigies which, according to Livy, attended the founding of Rome; the alleged miracles in the Christian Church after the death of the apostles; and the alleged miracles of the mediæval ages, and of the Catholic Church in modern times? May not the same process of explanation by which the world has been disabused of faith in these things be legitimately applied to the Bible? Skeptics and Rationalists claim that it may be so, and should be so; the existence of the Christian religion in the world depends on making out the contrary.

The proper points of inquiry, therefore, in the solution of the question would be,

I. The causes which have led to the change in the opinions of the world in regard to the marvelous; and,

II. The question whether the miracles of the Bible can not be explained in the same manner, and whether they may not also take their place with the illusions and deceptions of former ages.

These inquiries manifestly cover the whole ground.

I. The causes which have led to these changes in the opinions of the world in regard to the marvelous.

Those causes are now well understood, and may be referred to in few words.

(1.) The reduction of events which were supposed to be supernatural to the operation of natural laws. In this solution the *facts* are, of course, admitted, and the effects produced by those facts on the minds of men are admitted also. The explanation is sought in laws that are now well understood, and that imply nothing that is supernatural. Thus, as I have before remarked, eclipses, comets, meteors, that were regarded as marvelous and supernatural in the early periods of the world, indicating by their appearing the pleasure or the displeasure, the favor or the wrath of the gods, or heralding important events, are now reduced to laws that are as regular and as well understood as the ordinary laws of nature, and excite no more alarm or apprehension than the rising or the setting of the sun and the stars.

Very many things are thus *withdrawn* from the region of the marvelous, and now take their places in the ordinary course of events. The world no longer believes that the harvest-fields are under the control of Ceres; that Neptune rules on the sea; that Æolus controls the winds; that Dryads and Fawns preside in the groves; or that the healing properties of medicine are to be traced to the god Æsculapius — and the woods, and the groves, and the lakes are deserted; the temples of Ceres, and Neptune, and Bacchus, and Æsculapius are no longer crowded by worshipers, and more substantial and permanent honors are rendered to scientific men who have discovered the laws by which the phenomena are explained than were rendered to the imaginary divinities.

Science, then, just in proportion as it has made progress in the world, has contributed to this change of opinion; has relieved the world of the fears attendant on superstition; and has contributed, if not always to the introduction and establishment of true religion, at least to the removal of superstition and idolatry. The mythology of Greece can never be restored; the Parthenon can never be rebuilt; the Pantheon can never be again a temple for heathen gods and heathen worship.

(2.) The progress of civilization may be referred to as a second cause of this change. This, indeed, would include, in some measure, that which has above been adverted to, the progress of science, for that enters, of course, largely into the progress of civilization. The point to be now adverted to is that which has been dwelt upon so much by Lecky, and which springs from the nature of the case, that, up to a certain period at least, in proportion as society advances in civilization, the belief in the marvelous disappears, and that the very progress of civilization tends to prepare the minds of men to disbelieve in the supernatural altogether, or leads to Rationalism—to Rationalism in a proper use of that word; to "Rationalism," in fact, in the sense in which that word is commonly employed.

And yet, with all the concessions which should be made on that point, it would be a fair inquiry how far the *mere* progress of civilization would in fact conduct the human mind, or what, in this respect, would be its legitimate influence on the world. It could not fail to be noticed in such an inquiry that *mere* civilization has never destroyed the love of the marvelous and the belief in the supernatural; that the belief of the marvelous and the supernatural prevailed under the highest forms of civilization in Greece and Rome; that it prevails in the most civilized nations of the world at this day; and that, if one form of belief in the supernatural is banished to any extent from the minds of men by an advanced civilization, another form may take its place not more reconcilable with the sober and chastened laws of science. It can not be forgotten that in this age—an age which we regard as *more* civilized than any past period, certainly as more civilized than the ages in which a belief in necromancy, divination, and witchcraft prevailed, and, in the apprehension of many in this age, more civilized and advanced than the ages when there was a general faith in miracles, there is a wide-spread belief in mesmerism, in spirit-rapping, in table-turning, and in "spiritualism" — in actual converse with, and communication with, the spirits of departed men, and that this belief is by no means confined to those who lay no claims to a refined civilization, or who are of the most humble walks of life. Scientific men ; literary men of no mean name—judges, physicians, lawyers, and "philosophers," are found in the class of those who believe in these marvels ; and perhaps the very home of this faith may be found in the most enlightened cities of our own country, in the very vicinity of the most celebrated seats of learning, or in the most refined walks of life.* Yet, while these things are so, it can not be doubted that the advancing civilization of the world has had an important influence in narrowing the circle of the supernatural and the marvelous, nor that there is a tendency *in* such civilization to suggest the inquiry whether a perfect civilization would not remove all traces of the miraculous and the marvelous from the world.

(3.) In connection with this, it is to be observed that there has been a course of events in the world that has tended to disabuse mankind of unfounded claims to a favored and peculiar acquaintance with the secrets of nature, to a compact with powerful spiritual beings, to intercourse with the spirits of the departed, and to the special favor of God bestowed on those who were supposed to be remarkable for their piety —the "saints," and this fact has silently and imperceptibly operated to lead men to doubt the reality of *any* direct divine interposition in human affairs.

(*a*) The change in the world on the subject of witchcraft has tended to produce this. Formerly the belief in witchcraft was not less universal than the belief in miracles, and the belief was sustained by what

---

* It can not be improper to refer to the fact that the inventor of the compound blow-pipe in chemistry was a firm believer in mesmerism, spiritualism, spirit-rapping, and table-turning, and that he employed no small part of the leisure which he enjoyed in his later years in lecturing on these subjects ; in endeavoring to give a scientific form to these disclosures ; and in the mechanical effort to construct a machine, with an appropriate dial, by which the presence of the supernatural agency could be indicated—somewhat on the principle of the magnetic telegraph.

was regarded as the highest possible evidence. Faith in that has, to a great extent, passed away, and the question which men now ask is whether the belief in miracles is any better sustained.

(b) The belief in magic was once as universal as the belief in miracles, and the facts were supposed to be sustained by irrefragable evidence. That belief has also passed away. It has been removed partly by the application of science to the real explanation of the facts, and partly by the knowledge that the alleged facts were merely the results of cunning and imposture, and men, in like manner, ask the question whether the same solution is not to be applied to the whole subject of miracles.

(c) Faith in necromancy, sorcery, and divination has passed away. The world has come to believe that all the facts that were connected with such claims are to be traced to a hallucination of the mind, or to well-executed imposture, and they ask whether the same solution may not be applied to all pretended miracles.

(d) The faith of the world in regard to the reappearance of the dead, and to the visitation of the gods to earth, has passed away, and men have learned to ask whether the same result is not to follow in regard to all the divine manifestations to our world, and to the alleged resurrection of Lazarus and of Christ.

(e) The belief in the early miracles of the Christian Church subsequently to the time of the apostles has passed away, and men have learned to ask significantly what should make a difference between those miracles and the miracles of the New Testament.

(f) Faith in the miracles of the Roman Catholic Church exists nowhere outside of that communion, and to a very limited extent, apart from the priesthood, within, and the world is beginning to ask why the miracles of the Bible should not share the same fate.

Those who defend the miracles of the Bible, it is said, admit the fact that the pretended miracles of the Egyptians in the time of Moses were false; that the miracles of the early Christian Church were false; that the miracles of the Catholic Church are false—that, in fact, men have often been imposed upon in the belief of such wonders, and they ask why should not the principles which they apply so unsparingly to these pretended wonders be applied to all claims of miraculous powers.

(g) There has been, at the same time, a vast decline of priestly power and influence tending to the same result. The world has come to believe that alike among the heathen, and in the early Christian Church, and in the Roman Catholic communion, the belief in miracles has been kept up, in a good measure, by the influence and the arts of the priesthood. Outside of the Catholic Church that belief is now universal in regard to the pretended miracles in that Church, and the belief that the credit of the miracles in the early Church was to be traced to priestly power has become nearly universal.

Priestly power, as such, is fast dying away in the world—alike among the heathen, in the Roman Catholic portion of the world, in the Greek Church, and in the Protestant world. In proportion as science advances, and the world becomes acquainted with the arts which have so often characterized the priesthood of all religions, the mere power of a *priesthood* as such dies away. The power of influencing men by forms and ceremonies; by processions and benedictions; by splendid vestments and pomp; by the belief that truth flows only from the lips of an anointed priesthood and grace from their hands, dies out among men, and they are led to ask, since so much of religion has undeniably owed its power to the unfounded claims of a *priesthood*, whether the whole of it can not be resolved into such a belief.

It may be true, indeed, that the real influence of ministers of religion is advancing in other forms, and is keeping pace with the progress of the world, but it is not *as priests*, or in virtue of any supposed hereditary holiness, or of any superiority over other men as intrusted with the power of pardoning sin, or communicating grace, or delivering dogmas to mankind to be received on their authority, but it is as men who are abreast of their age in intelligence, as entitled to confidence from their moral worth, and to respect for their learning. There is a foundation in the human heart for respect and honor toward the ministers of religion when they rely for their influence on these things; all other respect for them is fast dying away, and with the *decline* of that profound reverence for a priesthood that characterizes this age as distinguished from former ages, there has been a corresponding decline on the whole subject of faith in the supernatural and the marvelous. Men refuse to embrace doctrines and dogmas in religion on different grounds from those on which they embrace truth on other subjects, not by a reference to miracles, and signs, and wonders, but as founded on reason, and as commending itself to their sober sense of what is right and true.

Perhaps the present state of the world on this subject, *as indicating an existing state of mind*, can not be better described than in the following passage from the writer to whom I have so often referred:

"Generation after generation the province of the miraculous has contracted, and the circle of skepticism has expanded. Of the two great divisions of these events, one has completely perished. Witchcraft, and diabolical possession, and diabolical disease have long since passed into the region of fables. To disbelieve them was at first the

eccentricity of a few isolated thinkers; it was then the distinction of
the educated classes in the most advanced nations; it is now the common sentiment of all classes in all countries in Europe. The countless miracles that were once associated with every holy relic and with
every village shrine have rapidly and silently disappeared. Year by
year the incredulity became more manifest, even when the theological
profession was unchanged. Their numbers continually lessened, until
they at last almost ceased, and any attempt to revive them has been
treated with a general and undisguised contempt. The miracles of
the fathers are passed over with an incredulous scorn or with a significant silence. The rationalistic spirit has even attempted to explain away those which are recorded in Scripture, and it has materially altered their position in the systems of theology. In all countries,
in all churches, in all parties, among men of every variety of character
and opinion, we have found the tendency existing. In each nation
its development has been a measure of intellectual activity, and has
passed in regular course through the different strata of society. During the last century it has advanced with a vastly accelerated rapidity;
the old lines of demarkation have been every where obscured, and the
spirit of Rationalism has become the great centre to which the intellect of Europe is manifestly tending. If we trace the progress of the
movement from its origin to the present day, we find that it has completely altered the whole aspect and complexion of religion. When it
began, Christianity was regarded as a system entirely beyond the
range and scope of human reason; it was impious to question; it was
impious to examine; it was impious to discriminate. On the other
hand, it was visibly instinct with the supernatural. Miracles of every
order and degree of magnitude were flashing forth incessantly from all
its parts. They excited no skepticism and no surprise. The miraculous element pervaded all literature, explained all difficulties, consecrated all doctrines. Every unusual phenomenon was immediately
referred to a supernatural agency, not because there was a passion for
the improbable, but because such an explanation seemed far more
simple and easy of belief than the obscure theories of science.

"In the present day, Christianity is regarded as a system which
courts the strictest investigation, and which, among many other functions, was designed to vivify and stimulate all the energies of man.
The idea of the miraculous, which a superficial observer might have
once deemed its most prominent characteristic, has been driven from
almost all its intrenchments, and now quivers faintly and feebly
through the mists of eighteen hundred years."[*]

II. Such, then, being the facts in regard to the change of belief in

* *Lecky*, History of Rationalism, vol. I., p. 194, 196.

the world on the subject of the marvelous and the supernatural, and such being the causes by which this change is to be explained, the inquiry meets us whether the miracles of the Bible can not be explained in the same manner, and whether they may not in like manner take their place with the illusions and deceptions of former ages. It is clear that if they *can* thus be explained, and if there is no stronger historical evidence in their favor than could be adduced for those things which have been referred to, they will soon, in the estimation of mankind, take the same place, and faith in the supernatural will wholly cease among men. Whether they can thus be explained is the point now to be considered. If they *can not* thus be explained, then the evidence commonly relied on for their support will be unaffected by the changes which have occurred on other subjects, and will remain in all the force attached to undisputed evidence on other well-attested historical facts in the past.

(1.) The miracles of the Bible can not be explained by the operation of natural laws, or, in other words, can not be brought within the range of natural laws. I mean by this, that, if the *facts* are admitted, there are no powers of nature known to man that would explain or account for them; that is, they could not be arranged and classified under any of the natural sciences. If Lazarus was raised from the grave; if Christ rose from the dead; if the blind were restored to sight by a word or a touch, there are no laws of science—chemistry, natural philosophy, galvanism, electricity, or magnetism to which such facts can be shown to belong; there is no power in connection with those sciences to produce such effects now; there are no principles suggested by those sciences which will explain them.

On this point I made the following remarks in the Lecture on Miracles, which it seems necessary to repeat here, in order that a connected view may be taken of the subject:

Science has *not* advanced so far as to explain the miracles of the New Testament on any known principles, as it has in these matters, nor has it made any approximation to it. Nay, just so far as it has gone it has demonstrated that those miracles can not be explained on any principles known, or likely to be known, to science—gravitation, attraction, repulsion, electricity, galvanism, or the healing properties of vegetables or minerals. The chemist does not open the eyes of the blind by a touch; he does not heal the sick by a word; he does not raise the dead by the blow-pipe or by galvanism. In the language of Mr. Mansel, "The advance of physical science tends to strengthen rather than to weaken our conviction of the supernatural character of the Christian miracles. In whatever proportion our knowledge of physical causation is limited, and the number of unknown natural

S 2

agents comparatively large, in the same proportion is the probability that some of these unknown causes, acting in some unknown manner, may have given rise to the alleged marvels. But this probability diminishes when each newly-discovered agent, as its properties become known, is shown to be inadequate to the production of the supposed effects, and as the residue of unknown causes, which might produce them, becomes smaller and smaller. We are told, indeed, that the 'inevitable progress of research must, within a longer or shorter period, unravel all that seems most marvelous;'* but we may be permitted to doubt the relevancy of the remark to the present case, until it has been shown that the advance of science has in some degree enabled men to perform the miracles performed by Christ. When the inevitable progress of research shall have enabled men of modern times to give sight to the blind with a touch, to still tempests with a word, to raise the dead to life, to die themselves, and to rise again, we may allow that the same causes might possibly have been called into operation ten thousand years earlier by some great man in advance of his age. But, until this is done, the unraveling of the marvelous in other phenomena only serves to leave these works in their solitary grandeur, as wrought by the finger of God, unapproached and unapproachable by all the knowledge and all the power of man. The appearance of a comet or the fall of an aerolite may be reduced by the advance of science from a supposed supernatural to a natural occurrence, and this reduction furnishes a reasonable presumption that other phenomena *of a like character* will in time meet with a like explanation. But the reverse is the case with respect to those phenomena which are narrated as produced by *personal agency*. In proportion as the science of to-day surpasses that of former generations, so is the improbability that any man could have done in past times, by natural means, works which no skill of the present age is able to imitate."†

In addition to these observations, I would now, for the farther illustration of the subject, make the following remarks:

(*a*) If the miracles of the New Testament *were* in themselves susceptible of explanation in this manner, it is plain that the authors of the Bible, or those who wrought the miracles, were not, in fact, so far in advance of their own age, or that they had no such knowledge of scientific principles—of the laws of nature—as to enable them to make use of this knowledge in working the alleged miracles. There were events in the Middle Ages, in connection with "magic," which *seemed* to the masses of men to be miracles; which surpassed all their power of producing or comprehending them; and which conveyed, designedly or undesignedly, to the multitudes the impression that those who

* Essays and Reviews, p. 109.   † Aids to Faith, p. 21, 22.

wrought them were in league with higher intelligences, or were endowed with supernatural powers. Those events are now susceptible of an easy and natural explanation, as has been shown amply by Sir David Brewster in his work on "Magic." Roger Bacon, for example, was so far in advance of his age in the sciences, that, on the ground of this, he might readily have obtained a reputation for being able to work miracles; and if we were to suppose that Roger Bacon, or any of his contemporaries, had the knowledge which is now possessed by those skilled in chemistry; or could have exhibited the wonderful and sudden transformations of matter now exhibited in the laboratory of the chemist; or that they had the power of multiplying copies of books, with the strictest exactness, almost in an instant; or that they could have multiplied accurate impressions of the human countenance, or of hills, and vales, and trees, and animals, by the action of light; or that they could have transmitted thought and language in a moment over hills and vales, across rivers and along the beds of oceans, it would have been easy for such men to have established the reputation of being workers of miracles. But, apart from all other considerations, now, the authors of the Bible had no such pretensions to knowledge in advance of their age. They were not in a land distinguished for science. They had received no scientific education. They had, so far as appears, no scientific genius. They had nothing which constitutes the "apparatus" of science now. All accounts agree in the fact that they were plain, unlettered men; nor does any thing which they ever said, or wrote, or did, indicate that they had any acquaintance whatever with even the very lowest rudiments of scientific knowledge.

(*b*) The principles of science can not be so applied as to explain the miracles of the New Testament. Science makes no approximation to an explanation.

This remark is especially true in regard to the resurrection of the dead, and is of special importance, because a single case of restoration to life settles the whole question. If Lazarus was raised from the dead, the Christian religion is from God. Science has settled the principle so that it is now an admitted axiom among all scientific men that the production of *life* is beyond the power of mere science. Whatever life may be, and whether it will ever be true that men will be able to explain and define what it *is*, it is reduced to a certainty that men, by the application of scientific principles, can not *produce* it. No approximation has been made to the power of causing it to exist where there has not been a germ or an ovum, or where it does not already exist, though suspended. Animalcules that seemed to have been dead for ages, and that may be dried and pounded, may be made to revive by the application of moisture; a grain of wheat that may have been hidden in the folds of an Egyptian mummy for three thousand years may be made to grow, but no power of man can *originate* life; none can cause it to exist again when it has become extinct. Until that is done, it may be regarded as settled that the miracles of the New Testament can not be explained by the application of the principles of science. If such a thing is claimed as possible, we may at least demand that the same thing should be done now by scientific men; for assuredly it can not be pretended that in true scientific knowledge the apostles were superior to the scientific men of this generation. If, therefore, it could be shown, as Renan supposed, that the healing of Peter's wife's mother could be explained by some power of mesmerism, yet we have a right, in order to set aside the evidence for the miracles of the New Testament, to demand that there shall be some unmistakable act of raising up *the dead* —where there is no doubt of the death—as in the case of Lazarus and the Savior; and, to make the argument complete, that it shall be done by a *word*—by some command which the scientific man has over the dead, and the grave, and the invisible world. As it is certain that men have never done this, and as it is certain that the scientific men of this age, or of future ages, will not even *attempt* this, it may be regarded as settled that the miracles of the New Testament can not be explained by the application of any principles of science, or can not be brought under the range of natural laws.

(2.) The miracles of the Bible can not be disposed of in the way in which the belief in witchcraft, necromancy, and sorcery has been. The explanation which has been applied to these things, and which has so entirely modified or revolutionized the faith of mankind on these subjects, can not be applied to the miracles of the Bible. In other words, we can not take the explanations; the course of reasoning; the changes produced by civilization, and the results of calm and sober thinking on these subjects, by which so material a change has been produced in the faith of mankind in regard to these matters, and by the application of the same process reach the same results in respect to the miracles of the Bible.

This is a very material point in the argument; for *if* the reasoning which has changed the faith of the world in regard to the marvelous and the supernatural on these subjects is of sufficient force to change the faith of the world in *all* that is supernatural, including the miracles of the Bible as well as other things, then it is manifest that faith in miracles will soon occupy the same place as faith in witchcraft, and necromancy, and sorcery; and as it is now certain that the faith in witchcraft, necromancy, and sorcery which was once held in the world can not be restored in the present state of civilization, and still less under the advanced civilization to which the world is tending, so, if the arguments and explanations which have banished the belief in witchcraft from the world can be legitimately applied to the miracles of the Bible, it will follow that the world is tending rapidly and inevitably to the highest point of Rationalism, where *all* faith in the supernatural and the marvelous shall cease among men. That this result is desired by many there can be no doubt; that it is secretly believed by many that it will be so there can be as little doubt; and that the tendency of the statements on the causes which have led to the changes in the opinions of the world on these subjects, as they are found in the histories of Rationalism, is to lead to the apprehension that this will be so, there can be as little doubt. No man can rise up from a history of Rationalism, and of the changes which have occurred in regard to the belief of mankind in the marvelous, without asking the question whether the legitimate result of all this is not to remove *all* faith in the marvelous and the supernatural from the minds of men.

What, then, is witchcraft? What is sorcery, divination, necromancy? By what means has the faith of mankind in these things been shaken? Are the same processes of unbelief applicable to the miracles of the Bible?

Witchcraft, divination, sorcery, necromancy, though they differ specifically from each other, yet so far partake of the same general nature that they can be grouped together, and they so far resemble each other, and so far depend on the same things, that the same explanation in regard to their origin, their prevalence, and their removal from the faith of mankind will be found applicable to them all. It would be impossible that one should retain its hold on the faith of mankind if all the others, or any of the others, should be proved to be a delusion and an imposture. The question is whether the miracles of the Bible will share the same destiny.

I have stated the difficulty on this subject in the Lecture on Miracles (p. 161-165), and perhaps so stated it as to have led to the inquiry—perhaps a painful inquiry—on the minds of some, whether all that is said there might not also be said about miracles. As there can be no desire of concealment in a candid inquiry after truth on any subject, and as it is important to have the difficulty fairly before the mind, I shall copy here what was said on the subject in the Lecture.

A more material and important question still is, Whether there is any stronger evidence in favor of miracles than there is in favor of witchcraft, of sorcery, of the reappearance of the dead, of ghosts, of apparitions? Is not the evidence in favor of these as strong as any that can be adduced in favor of miracles? Have not these things been matters of universal belief? In what respects is the evidence in favor of the miracles of the Bible stronger than that which can be adduced in favor of witchcraft and sorcery? Does it differ in nature and in degree; and if it differs, is it not in favor of witchcraft and sorcery? Has not the evidence in favor of the latter been derived from as competent and credible witnesses? Has it not been brought to us from those who saw the facts alleged? Has it not been subjected to a close scrutiny in courts of justice—to cross-examinations—to tortures? Has it not convinced those of highest legal attainments; those accustomed to sift testimony; those who understood the true principles of evidence? Has not the evidence in favor of witchcraft and sorcery had, what the evidence in favor of miracles has *not* had, the advantage of strict judicial investigation, and been subjected to trial, where evidence should be, before courts of law? Have not the most eminent judges in the most civilized and enlightened courts of Europe and America admitted the force of such evidence, and on the ground of it committed great numbers of innocent persons to the gallows or to the stake?

An extract or two from Lecky, in his History of Rationalism in Europe, will show the nature of the difficulty and the force of the objection, though the remarks made by him are in no way designed to support the cause of infidelity: "For more than fifteen hundred years it was universally believed that the Bible established, in the clearest manner, the reality of the crime [of witchcraft], and that an amount of evidence, so varied and so ample as to preclude the very possibility of doubt, attested its continuance and its prevalence. The clergy denounced it with all the emphasis of authority. The legislators of almost every land enacted laws for its punishment. Acute judges, whose lives were spent in sifting evidence, investigated the question on countless occasions, and condemned the accused. Tens of thousands of victims perished by the most agonizing and protracted torments without exciting the faintest compassion. Nations that were completely separated by position, by interests, and by character, on this one question were united. In almost every province of Germany, but especially in those where clerical influence predominated, the persecution raged with fearful intensity. Seven thousand victims are said to have been burned at Trèves, six hundred by the single Bishop of Bamberg, and eight hundred in a single year in the bishopric of Wurtzburg. In France, decrees were passed on the subject by the Parliament of Paris, Toulouse, Bordeaux, Rheims, Rouen, Dijon, and Rennes, and they were all followed by a harvest of blood. At Toulouse, the seat of the Inquisition, four hundred persons perished for sorcery at a single execution, and fifty at Douay in a single year. Remy, a judge of Nancy, boasted that he had put to death eight hundred witches in sixteen years. The executions that took place at Paris in a few months were, in the emphatic words of an old writer, 'almost infinite.' The fugitives who escaped to Spain were there seized and burned by the Inquisition. In Italy a thousand persons were executed in a single year in the province of Como; in the other parts of the country the severity of the inquisitors at last created an absolute rebellion. In Geneva five hundred alleged witches were executed in three months; forty-eight were burned at Constance or Ravensburg, and eighty in the little town of Valery, in Savoy. The Church of Rome proclaimed in every way that was in her power the reality and the continued existence of the crime."

The writer from whom I have made this extract adds: "It is, I think, difficult to examine the subject with impartiality, without coming to the conclusion that the historical evidence establishing the reality of witchcraft is so vast and so varied that it is impossible to disbelieve it without what on other subjects we should deem the most extraordinary rashness. The defenders of the belief, who were often men of great and distinguished talent, maintained that there was no fact in all history more fully attested, and that to reject it would be to strike at the root of all historical evidence of the miraculous. The subject was examined in tens of thousands of cases, in almost every country of Europe, by tribunals which included the acutest lawyers and ecclesiastics of the age on the scene at the time when the alleged facts had taken place, and with the assistance of innumerable sworn witnesses. The judges had no motive whatever to desire the condemnation of the accused; and as conviction would be followed by a fearful death, they had the strongest motives to exercise their power with caution and deliberation. In our day it may be said with confidence that it would be altogether impossible for such an amount of evidence to accumulate round a conception which had no basis in fact. If we considered witchcraft probable, a hundredth part of the evidence we possess would have placed it beyond the region of doubt. If it were a natural, but a very improbable fact, our reluctance to believe it would have been completely stifled by the multiplicity of the proofs."*

In reference to this point, I now submit the following remarks:

(a) Witchcraft, sorcery, divination, necromancy, all depend essentially on one idea—the idea of a compact with *created spirits; not with God*. The idea is always that of a compact, of an understanding, or of an alliance for certain purposes, and the accomplishing of

* See *Lecky*, History of Rationalism in Europe, vol. i., p. 28, 34, 36, 37, 38, 39.

certain things to which the unaided human powers are inadequate, but which may be quite within the range of the power of such invisible beings. Thus, in necromancy, the foundation of all that is implied in it is a desire—that desire so natural to man—to penetrate the future. The knowledge necessary for this purpose is not in the power of the most gifted man among the living,[*] but it is supposed that it *must* be in the possession of the dead—of those who now reside in the invisible world, and that a compact may be made with them by which that knowledge may be imparted to those who are parties in the agreement. Thus, also, in divination, the idea is essentially the same. It is defined by Webster to be "a foretelling of future events, or discovering things secret or obscure, *by the aid of superior beings*, or by other than human means." "The ancient heathen philosophers," says he, "divided divination into two kinds, *natural* and *artificial*. Natural divination was supposed to be effected by a kind of inspiration or divine afflatus; artificial divination was effected by certain rites, experiments, or observations, as by sacrifices, cakes, flour, wine," etc. The main idea was, that there was some aid derived from spirits superior to man with whom this knowledge was, and from whom it could be obtained by favored persons by compact, or by the performance of certain rites of homage or honor rendered to them.

The same idea was at the foundation of all that there was in witchcraft—a subject in its bearing on the matter before us of much more importance than either necromancy, divination, or sorcery. Few persons, Rationalists or skeptics, would now refer either to necromancy, divination, or sorcery as having any *evidence* in their favor which would seriously affect the evidence in regard to miraculous events; the subject of witchcraft, however, as we have seen, does materially affect the whole question of evidence, and particularly the evidence in regard to supernatural events, since the proof of witchcraft was brought before courts sitting in judgment on the very cases; since that proof was so thoroughly examined by men learned in the law, and accustomed to sift evidence; since the alleged facts were supposed to be established by incontrovertible evidence; since such trials involved the question of life or death; and since so many innocent persons were actually put to death on the ground of such evidence.

A witch is defined by Webster to be "a woman who, by compact with the devil, practices sorcery or enchantment." The essential idea *always* is that of a compact or agreement with the devil, or with evil spirits, by whose aid things are done which are beyond the natural power of those who practiced witchcraft, or which could not be pro-

[*] For an illustration of this thought I may be permitted to refer to the Lecture on Prophecy—Lecture VI.

duced by natural laws, and in which the acts, therefore, are, so far, miraculous or supernatural. Witchcraft, however, is NEVER associated with the idea of *divine* help or *divine* power. It never implies a compact with *God*. It is never supposed that what is done is done by his power. It is always something within the range of beings inferior to God, but superior to man. It is, in this respect, wholly distinguished from the idea of a *miracle* properly so called, where, as we have seen, the idea is that of an event where the only antecedent is *the will and power of God*.

The following things, therefore, enter into the idea of witchcraft, and in getting rid of witchcraft by the process of Rationalism, the world has delivered itself from these, and these only : (1.) There is a compact with some spirit or spirits inferior to God, but superior to man. (2.) The spirit with which the compact is made is always a bad, or an evil spirit—as we never associate the idea of witchcraft with a good " demon," or with a holy angel. (3.) The person who is supposed to make the compact, or who is competent to enter into it, is commonly believed to be a woman, and usually an old woman. If there has been a belief in *wizards*, it has been rare, and the common idea in such a case is merely that of a juggler, a conjuror, or an enchanter. (4.) The matter which pertains to witchcraft is usually some trifling matter; some petty annoyance; some small injury done to property ; some disease brought upon cattle ; rarely, if ever, any thing that terminates in death. It never has respect to a work of beneficence or mercy ; never is employed in healing diseases ; never is alleged to be sufficient to give sight to the blind ; never lays claim to the power of raising the dead. In these respects, also, it is distinguished by broad lines of demarkation from all proper ideas of a *miracle*.

(*b*) The alleged facts in witchcraft were usually such as could, and did occur, under the operation of natural causes. All the injuries done ; all the diseases inflicted ; all the annoyances employed ; all the calamities that fell upon cattle or upon men ; all the blightings of the harvest ; all that was involved in the idea of pinching or burning—of palsy, or of withered arms or hands, or a shriveled skin—all these are things which *do* occur in the world with no necessity of supposing any intervention of superior beings. Not one of them implies, of necessity, the agency of supernatural power ; not one of them, as *a fact*, lies beyond the range of explanation from natural causes. They are, therefore, *as facts*, wholly without the range of miracles.

(*c*) The *facts* in the alleged case of witchcraft are commonly easily established, and there was no difficulty in proving them in the courts ; in the matter of miracles the main difficulty is in regard to the *facts* themselves—whether the sun and moon actually stood still at the com-

mand of Joshua; whether the lame man at the pool of Bethesda was
actually healed; whether Lazarus was actually dead, and was raised
from the dead; whether the Lord Jesus actually came to life again
after he had been put to death on the cross.   But the alleged facts as
pertaining to witchcraft are such as may be easily established—that
is, what witches are accused of *doing* may be matter of clear and definite proof.   That a person is afflicted with some form of disease; that
property is destroyed; that mischief has occurred in regard to a man's
cattle, or that there may be some form of prevalent disease among
them; that grain about to ripen may be suddenly blighted in the
field—all these may be points of fact that could be easily established,
and about which there need be no doubt.

As an illustration of this point, we may take the case of Richard
III., as it is stated in history, and as it is represented by Shakspeare.
The scene is described by Mr. Hume (History of England, vol. ii.,
p. 174) in the following manner:

"The Duke of Gloucester was capable of committing the most
bloody and treacherous murders with the utmost coolness and indifference.   On taking his place at the council-table, he appeared in
the easiest and most jovial humor imaginable.   He seemed to indulge
himself in familiar conversation with the counselors before they
should enter on business; and, having paid some compliments to
Morton, bishop of Ely, on the good and early strawberries which he
raised in his garden at Holborn, he begged the favor of having a dish
of them, which that prelate immediately dispatched a servant to bring
to him.   The Protector then left the council, as if called away by some
other business; but, soon after returning, with an angry and inflamed
countenance, he asked them what punishment those deserved that had
plotted against his life, who was so nearly related to the king, and was
intrusted with the administration of government?   Hastings replied
that they merited the punishment of traitors.   These traitors, cried
the Protector, are the sorceress, my brother's wife, and Jane Shore,
his mistress, with others, their associates: see to what a condition
they have reduced me by their incantations and witchcraft: upon
which he laid bare his arm, all shriveled and decayed.   But the counselors, who knew that this infirmity had attended him from his birth,
looked on each other with amazement, and above all Lord Hastings,
who, as he had, since Edward's death, engaged in an intrigue with
Jane Shore, was naturally anxious concerning the issue of these extraordinary proceedings.   Certainly, my lord, said he, if they be guilty
of these crimes they deserve the severest punishment.   And do you
reply to me, exclaimed the Protector, with your ifs and your ands?
You are the chief abettor of that witch Shore!   You are yourself a

traitor; and I swear by St. Paul that I will not dine before your head be brought me. He struck the table with his hand; armed men rushed in at the signal; the counselors were thrown into the utmost consternation; and one of the guards, as if by accident or mistake, aimed a blow with a poll-axe at Lord Stanley, who, aware of the danger, slunk under the table; and though he saved his life, received a severe wound in the head, in the Protector's presence. Hastings was seized, was hurried away, and instantly beheaded on a timber-log, which lay in the court of the Tower."

Shakspeare describes the scene in the following words:

> "*Gloucester.* I pray you all, tell me what they deserve
> That do conspire my death with devilish plots
> Of damned witchcraft; and that have prevailed
> Upon my body with their hellish charms?
> *Hastings.* The tender love I bear your grace, my lord,
> Makes me most forward in this noble presence
> To doom the offenders: Whosoe'er they be,
> I say, my lord, they have deserved death.
> *Gloucester.* Then be your eyes the witness of their evil,
> Look how I am bewitched; behold mine arm
> Is, like a blasted sapling, withered up:
> And this is Edward's wife, that monstrous witch,
> Consorted with that harlot, strumpet Shore,
> That by their witchcraft thus have marked me."
>
> *Richard III.*, Act iii., Scene iv.

Now, about the *fact* of the withered arm, there could have been no doubt. The evidence was at hand. No one would call it in question; no one would dare to dispute it. That fact could have been proved before any court of justice as clearly as any of the facts to which Mr. Lecky refers when he says, "The subject [of witchcraft] was examined in tens of thousands of cases, in almost every country of Europe, by tribunals which included the acutest lawyers and ecclesiastics of the age on the scene at the time when the alleged facts had taken place, and with the assistance of innumerable sworn witnesses."

(*d*) The main point, therefore, in witchcraft—the point on which the whole turned, and on which it differed from all the questions connected with miracles, was *in* CONNECTING *the accused person with* THE FACT; *in showing that the accused person was the cause of it, or the author of it.* Thus, in the case of the Duke of Gloucester, the point on which the whole turned was not the fact that the arm of the duke was dried up, or was shriveled—for of that there was no doubt, but it was whether this had been caused by the wife of Edward and Jane Shore. That the duke affirmed; that would have been the point in a court of justice; that was the only point that would have any bearing on the question of witchcraft. That point—the connection of the accused persons with the alleged and undoubted facts—*was* the point which was before the courts—the point on which so many hundreds and thousands were condemned to the flames.

And yet how could that point be properly brought before a court of justice? What evidence *could* there be that would bear on it?

It is evident that, in this circumstance, there was all that was necessary for wide-spread illusion, imposture, and wrong; for the indulgence of all that there was in a community of suspicion, malignity, and hatred against particular individuals; all that could be devised to keep up the faith of a community in the marvelous; all that was needful to feed and satisfy the desire for the belief in invisible influences, and to perpetuate a prevalent superstition. For what was demanded in the case was not the proof of certain *facts* that might be the proper subject of testimony, but the connecting of certain obnoxious persons *with* those facts; and as soon and as far as the popular idea connected such facts with a certain class of persons—as aged females—there would be no lack of witnesses to testify *to* such a connection.

It is difficult to account for popular illusions; for the fact that a whole community will be affected with such an illusion at the same time; that it may influence all classes of persons; that it will constitute the characteristic of a certain period or a certain land; that it will, for the time, break down all the ordinary and sober rules of thinking, and override all that is sacred in truth, and solemn in the forms of oaths. It would be easy to adduce now, in any court of justice, almost innumerable witnesses, of most respectable character, that would testify on oath to the alleged facts in regard to table-moving and spirit-rapping. The witnesses of these alleged facts would not by any means be found altogether or mainly among the humblest ranks, or the most ignorant in a community, nor among those who have no proper idea of the solemnity of an oath, or who are ignorant on the subject of evidence. Judges, lawyers, merchants, professors of chemistry, *clergymen* — men profoundly learned in the sciences, could be found in large numbers who would testify to the reality of the facts, and who would do it with no ascertainable intention of imposing on mankind.

It matters little what is the *thing* that thus becomes the subject of popular illusion, and it is to be admitted that if the miracles of the New Testament could be brought under this idea, it would not be less difficult to establish their reality than to establish the facts about witchcraft and spirit-rapping. Macaulay, in his History of England, refers to an epidemic of that nature which followed the successful effort of Titus Oates to excite universal alarm in England in regard to the plot to murder the king [Charles II.] ; to burn the city of London ; to revolutionize the kingdom, and to restore it to the dominion of the Papacy. "Every person," says he, "well read in history must have observed that depravity has its temporary modes, which come in and go out like modes of dress and upholstery. It may be doubted whether, in our country, any man ever before the year 1678 invented and related on oath a circumstantial history, altogether fictitious, of a treasonable plot, for the purpose of making himself important by destroying men who had given him no provocation. But in the year 1678 this execrable crime became the fashion, and continued to be so during the twenty years which followed. Preachers designated it as our peculiar national sin, and prophesied that it would draw on us some awful national judgment. Legislators proposed new punishments of terrible severity for this new atrocity. It was not, however, found necessary to resort to those punishments. *The fashion changed ;* and during the last century and a half there has perhaps not been a single instance of this particular kind of wickedness."*

Any explanation which will account for a popular illusion or a prevalent superstition will account for all the phenomena of witchcraft. The power of such an illusion has often been manifested in the world ; perhaps no one has satisfactorily explained the causes. The effect of it is easily understood. It is a species of insanity. It indisposes the mind for calm and sober thought. It gives reality in the view of the mind to that which is desired. It blunts the moral sense, and dims the perception of truth, and perverts all just notions of testimony. It gives reality in the view of the mind to that which is the creation of the imagination, and, under the force of the illusion, annihilates for the time all the ordinary feelings of kindness and humanity. It will lead to the endurance of suffering—to the spirit of martyrdom —on the part of those who embrace the illusion, and it will make them regardless of the severest sufferings of those—though of the tenderest years, and of the gentle sex—on whom the suspicion falls. To pity them in their tortures would be a crime ; to aggravate their sufferings would be a merit. In witchcraft it would be a crime of the highest nature to pity those who are in league with the devil ; to punish them is to punish the devil himself, and no amount of suffering could be beyond his desert.

(*e*) It is apparent, therefore, that there is a broad line of distinction between the miracles of the Bible, and witchcraft, necromancy, sorcery, and divination, and that the explanation which would meet the one would not affect the other. It is apparent, also, that in the one case —the case of witchcraft, necromancy, and sorcery, there may be a

* History of England, vol. iv., p. 155.

change in the public mind that will effectually banish all belief in these things, that will not necessarily, or in fact, affect the public faith in miracles. That state of the public mind—that phenomenon—is, in fact, reached now. The progress of Rationalism has been such for the past hundred years as almost entirely to banish all belief in witchcraft and necromancy from the world; it has not been shown that the change of mind on *that* subject has in reality affected the faith of man on the subject of miracles, or that they have, in fact, reasoned from the one to the other. Indeed, it may be assumed as undoubtedly true that those who *have* become skeptical in this age on the subject of miracles are not conscious to themselves that they have been led to reject the evidence for miracles *because* they have seen reason to reject the belief in witchcraft, or *because* the sentiments of the world have changed on that subject. This fact I adverted to in the Lecture on Miracles, and I can not but regard it as a remarkable fact. I do not know that even skeptics in religion, or Rationalists in any form, have urged this as an objection to the faith in miracles, or have stated it as a proposition, as indicating their own state of mind on the subject, that *because* witchcraft, necromancy, and sorcery are delusions, *therefore* the miracles of the Bible and all pretended miracles are false. The world at large would not see any connection between such premises and such a conclusion. Skeptics themselves would perceive that the world would not admit the force of such reasoning. As a matter of fact, no such conclusion has been reached from these premises. So far as appears, the faith of mankind in the miracles of the Bible has *not* been affected by the change which has occurred in regard to the belief in witchcraft, necromancy, and divination. The change adverted to, especially in regard to witchcraft, is a change which has occurred in the Church not less than in the world; for the belief in witchcraft pervaded the whole Church, Catholic and Protestant alike, two centuries ago, and the Church, as is often urged by infidels, and as a matter of fact, was most firm in the belief of witchcraft, and most active in the persecution of those who were supposed to be under its influence (see Lecky, vol. i., p. 28–34), and yet the Church, while it has changed its belief wholly on that subject, has not changed its faith in the belief of the miracles of the Bible, and it is certain that infidelity would make no impression on the Church by arguing from the one to the other.

The reasons of this are now plain. The sphere of witchcraft, necromancy, sorcery, and divination, and the sphere of miracles, is widely different. All, indeed, pertain to the supernatural, but they do not so pertain to it that the one affects the other. The one—witchcraft, necromancy, divination, sorcery—is an alliance with inferior spirits;

not with God.   It is for purposes of mischief; never for good.   The
power which it summons, and with which it combines, is an evil—a
malignant power.   The facts in the case are susceptible of explanation from natural causes.   The effects on a community can be traced
to a popular illusion.   The whole operation—the agents employed, the
manner in which they are supposed to effect their marvels, and the
effects themselves, are all beneath the dignity of philosophy, beneath
religion, beneath God, and beneath the rules of sober reasoning.   In
reference to the great change produced in the world in our age on the
subject of witchcraft, there is undoubtedly much force in the following
remarks of Lecky, and those remarks may furnish one cause to show
why faith in the miracles of the Bible has *not* been extensively affected by this change of belief.   He says, "If we ask why it is that the
world has rejected what was once so universally and so intensely believed—why a narrative of an old woman who had been seen riding on
a broomstick, or who was proved to have transformed herself into a
wolf, and to have devoured the flocks of her neighbors, is deemed so
entirely incredible, most persons would probably be unable to give a
very definite answer to the question.   It is not because we have examined the evidence and found it insufficient, for the disbelief always
precedes, when it does not prevent, examination.   It is rather because
the idea of absurdity is so strongly attached to such narratives that it
is difficult even to consider them with gravity" (vol. i., p. 34).   It will
instantly occur to the mind that no such process of thought can be applied to the healing of the sick, to the restoration of the blind to sight,
or to the raising of the dead.

I infer, therefore, that the process of thought by which the world
has been delivered from faith in witchcraft, necromancy, sorcery, and
divination, is not applicable to the miracles of the New Testament,
and that the miracles of the Bible can not be disposed of in the way
in which the belief in witchcraft, necromancy, and sorcery has been.

(3.) The third point in the argument relates to the inquiry whether
the miracles of the Bible can be *disposed of* in the manner in which
the miracles alleged to have been wrought in the early Christian
Church after the time of the apostles, and at subsequent periods, can
be.   This inquiry would also embrace the Roman Catholic miracles
which are claimed to be wrought in our own times as proofs of the divine origin of the Roman Catholic faith, and in defense of the Roman
Catholic Church.

The inquiry is, whether what would be a proper explanation of the
one would also apply to the other ; whether, on the supposition that
these claims in regard to the miracles of the Church subsequent to the
times of the apostles are false, the same process of reasoning would

show that the miracles of the Bible are false? In other words, the inquiry is, whether, on the supposition that the world will settle down into a universal skepticism in regard to the miracles alleged to have been wrought *since* the time of the apostles, and especially those claimed to have been wrought in the Roman Catholic Church, as it probably will, the process of thought by which that conclusion will be reached will carry with it *necessarily* a universal skepticism in regard to the miracles of the Bible? It is clear that if the same explanation can be given to the one as to the other, the conclusion will be inevitable that they are equally false; if there is no stronger testimony in the one case than in the other, on the supposition that the world has been under a delusion in reference to the facts alleged, then the same conclusion in regard to both classes of miracles is inevitable. It is a great question, therefore, whether the present *tendency* of the world to Rationalism, as affecting this point, as it undoubtedly exists in the scientific world, in the Protestant churches, and even, as we have seen, in the Roman Catholic communion, is in fact a *tendency* toward Rationalism or skepticism on the whole subject of miracles, and will lead to the denial of miracles altogether.

It is not necessary to advert farther to the great change which has occurred in the world in reference to the miracles which were alleged to have been wrought in the times subsequent to the apostles. Up to a recent period, the inquiry in ecclesiastical history has been, not whether such miraculous powers *existed* in the Church, but *at what exact point* that power ceased. The general impression among Protestants has been, that that power ceased when miracles were no longer necessary for the defense and the diffusion of Christianity. The prevailing opinion on the subject has been undoubtedly expressed by Archbishop Tillotson : "That on the first planting of the Christian religion in the world, God was pleased to accompany it with a miraculous power; but after it was planted that power ceased, and God left it to be maintained by ordinary ways."*

It would not conduce to any proper view of the point before us to state farther the changes which have occurred in the opinions of men on the subject; to inquire at what time the power of working miracles in the Church, if it ever existed, ceased; or to consider the question whether such miraculous powers existed or not. The sole inquiry is, whether the miracles of the Bible can be disposed of in the same way as the alleged miracles in the Church subsequent to the time of the apostles; whether an absolute skepticism in regard to the latter of necessity involves an absolute skepticism in regard to the former; whether the two stand or fall together?

* Sermons, vol. iii., p. 488, ed. 1735.

On this inquiry I submit the following remarks:

First. If miracles were actually wrought in the primitive Church subsequent to the time of the apostles, and continue to be wrought still in the Roman Catholic Church, this would not *prove* that the miracles of the Bible were false. That one thing has been done does not prove that another has not been. Moreover, in such a case and on such an admission, the *possibility* of miracles would be established, and the presumption, therefore, would be that they *may* have occurred as recorded in the Bible. Indeed, if they have occurred in such numbers as it has been claimed that they have done in the Church, then, so far from its being true, as Mr. Hume alleges, that "a uniform experience has established the stability of the laws of nature," the very reverse of this has been established. The admission of the fact of such miracles would destroy the whole argument of Mr. Hume.

Second. If the miracles referred to were *not* wrought in the primitive Church, and if they are *not* wrought in the Roman Catholic Church, that does not prove that the miracles of the Bible are false. Obviously it *may* be possible to account for the prevalence of a belief in false miracles, and for well-executed impostures in one case, by explanations which would not be applicable to the other. Illusions in one instance do not prove that illusions extend to every thing; imposture in one case does not prove that it exists in all cases; that there are deceivers at one time and in one place does not prove that they exist at all times and in all places; the fact that there is counterfeit coin does not prove that there is no genuine coin; that there are false religions in the world does not prove that there is no religion that is genuine. It is clear that the pretended miracles in the primitive Church, and in the Roman Catholic communion, should be examined on their own merits, and be embraced or rejected as the evidence in the case shall demand. If there is reason to reject them, that fact does not prove that there may not be reasons why the account of other miracles should be embraced as true. No amount of testimony in regard to the alleged fact that the dead were raised subsequent to the time of the apostles, whether for or against such claims, could demonstrate that Lazarus was not raised from the dead; nor should Rationalism and skepticism make a hasty stride from one to the other.

Third. It is possible to account for all that is said to have occurred in the primitive Church after the time of the apostles, and in the Roman Catholic Church, without supposing that there were real miracles wrought. It might be that tricks and jugglery were practiced; it might be that there was collusion and concert in performing the alleged miracle; it might be that the witnesses did not say that they saw

T

the miracles, but that they were reported to have occurred; it might be that no record was made at the time, but that the belief grew up in a subsequent age; it might be that the alleged miracles were manifestly wrought to sustain a particular form of religion, or a party in the Church, or the claims of a priesthood to a divine appointment, or the truth of a particular doctrine, or to honor a particular saint; it might be that there were rival churches, and that the miracles were manifestly wrought to sustain the one against the other; it might be that there was a susceptibility in the public mind, or in the prevalent belief of the age, which received such accounts without calling them in question; it might be that the belief in the miracles was on the same ground as the belief in prevalent superstitions—as of ghosts, apparitions, witchcraft, table-turning, and spirit-rapping; it might be that the alleged witnesses were not credible witnesses, and that they were never subjected to any test or trial which would show that they were sincere witnesses for truth, and were not impostors. Without affirming now that these things *were* so, it is affirmed that it is conceivable that they *might* be so; and the world is undoubtedly coming to that belief in regard to all the pretended miracles in the Roman Catholic Church; all the marvels of the Middle Ages; and to no small part, at least, of the alleged miracles of the primitive Church after the time of the apostles.

Fourth. The philosophical mode of accounting for the alleged miracles of the primitive Church after the time of the apostles will not explain the facts in regard to the miracles of the New Testament. This remark, for the purpose of the argument, and without in any way affecting injuriously the general conclusion, may be confined to the alleged miracles in the period immediately succeeding the apostles— for it is there that the strength of the argument must lie. If those miracles are disposed of there can be no difficulty in regard to those that follow.

The following facts, then, have been established so as to admit of little or no doubt in regard to those miracles:

(a) That the "apostolic fathers"—as they are commonly called— those who lived in the time of the apostles, and who had, some of them at least, conversed with the apostles, advance no claim to any such miraculous powers, and make no affirmation that such miracles were wrought by any in their own age who were not apostles. Those "fathers" embrace Barnabas, Clement, Ignatius, Polycarp, and Hermas, some of whom survived for half a century after the death of the last of the apostles.* "Here, then," says Middleton (p. 9), "we have

* For the proof of what is affirmed here and in the remainder of this argument about the alleged miracles in the Church, I refer to the work of Middle-

an interval of about half a century, the earliest and purest of all Christian antiquity after the days of the apostles, in which we find not the least reference to any standing power of working miracles, as existed openly in the Church, for the conviction of unbelievers; but, on the contrary, the strongest reason to presume that the extraordinary gifts of the apostolic age were by this time actually withdrawn."

(*b*) It is also true that none of the early "fathers" of the Church, succeeding this time, who declare that the power of working miracles existed in the Church, "have any where affirmed that either they themselves, or the apostolic fathers before them, were endowed with any power of working miracles" (Middleton, p. 21). They affirm, indeed, that "such powers were actually subsisting in their days, and were openly exerted in the Church; that they had often seen the wonderful effects of them; and that every body else might see the same, whenever they pleased," but they do not affirm that *they* had the power, or that *they* had seen the miracles, nor do they specify the names, the dates, or the persons by whom, or on whom, the miracles were performed. Origen, speaking of the miracle of casting out devils, says that "it was performed by laymen." Mr. Whiston remarks on this subject that "this gift was wholly appropriated by the Savior to the meaner sorts of Christians, with an exclusion even of the clergy, so that after the days of the apostles none of the sacred order ever pretended to it."[*]

Something, perhaps, may be learned respecting the *character* of those who pretended to work miracles from the uniform statements of the enemies of Christianity. It is certain that they were always regarded as pretenders and impostors, and were always charged with the practice of fraud. Thus Lucian says that "whenever any crafty juggler, expert in his trade, and who knew how to make a right use of things, went over to the Christians, he was sure to grow rich immediately by making a prey of their simplicity."[†] In like manner Celsus represents all the Christian wonder-workers as mere vagabonds and common cheats, "who rambled about to play tricks at fairs and markets; not in the circles of the wiser and better sort, for among such they never ventured to appear, but wherever they observed a set of raw young fellows, slaves, or fools, there they took care to intrude themselves and to display their arts."[‡] Cæcilius calls them "a lurking nation; shunning the light; mute in public; prating in corners."[§]

In view of all the statements among the ancients respecting those

ton: A Free Inquiry into the Miraculous Powers which are supposed to have subsisted in the Christian Church from the Earliest Ages, by *Conyers Middleton, D.D.*, ed. London, 1749. [*] Account of the Demoniacs, p. 52.

[†] De Mort. Pereg., t. ii., p. 568.   [‡] Orig. Con. Cels., l. 6, p. 284.

[§] Minuc. Fel., p. 7. Middleton, p. 22, 23.

who were supposed to work miracles, Middleton makes the following remarks: "The celebrated gifts of those ages were generally engrossed and exercised by private Christians, who used to travel about from city to city to assist the ordinary pastors of the Church and preachers of the Gospel in the conversion of the pagans, by the extraordinary gifts with which they were supposed to be endowed by the Spirit of God, and the miraculous works which they pretended to perform" (p. 24).

In accordance with this view, it is stated that the pretended power of working miracles was committed, not to those who were intrusted with the government of the Church—not to bishops, martyrs, and the chief defenders of the Christian cause, but to boys; to women; to private and obscure laymen; to even those of abandoned moral character:

Νυνὶ δὲ καὶ δι' ἀναξίων ἐνεργεῖν ὁ θεὸς εἴωθε.

Chrysostom, t. iii., p. 66.

Ut intelligamus, quædam miracula etiam sceleratores homines facere, qualia sancti facere non possunt.   *Augus. Oper.*, t. i., p. 71.

(c) The character of many of the Christian fathers for credulity and for the want of veracity is such as to render their testimony on this point of great doubt and of little value. They undoubtedly adopted the principle that the Christian religion was true; that it was indispensable for the salvation of men; and that *all* means were to be employed to propagate it, to convince men of its truth, and to induce them to turn from idolatry to the service of the true God. If the *result* was reached, that result was, in their apprehension, of much more importance than the *means* of reaching it. In accordance with this, it is undoubtedly true that false histories were early forged; false and weak interpretations were given to the Scriptures; false narratives of events were given to the world—until the world became full of the legends of the saints and martyrs. If it be true that, as historians of ordinary facts and ordinary events, they report such facts accurately, it is also true that there were numberless narratives in those early ages which were based wholly on fiction, and true also that these were employed in the propagation of religion. Middleton (p. 36–71) has placed these facts beyond question, and these facts would go far to explain the accounts of the early miracles in the Christian Church.

(d) It is a very material fact in regard to these pretended miracles, alike in the early Christian Church, in the Middle Ages, and in the modern Roman Catholic Church, that the testimony is not usually given by contemporaries, or those who lived at the time—so far as names and dates are concerned, but by writers of a later age. This is true alike of the pretended miracles of the early Christian Church, of the miracles of the heathen as referred to by the enemies of Christianity, of most of the miracles attributed to the sacred relics of the saints, and of most of the miracles of the "saints" who have been "canonized" in the Roman Catholic Church. Thus miracles are attributed to Pythagoras, not by his contemporaries, but by Porphyry and Iamblichus, who wrote his life three hundred years after his death; the prodigies in the History of Rome are recorded, not by persons who lived at the time, but by Livy, who lived many centuries afterward; the miracles ascribed to Apollonius of Tyana, of which so much has been made by the enemies of Christianity, were not recorded by any one living at the time, but the belief in them rests solely on the single assertion of his biographer, Philostratus, who lived a hundred years after the death of Apollonius; the accounts of the miracles of Gregory, bishop of Neocæsarea, called Thaumaturgus from the number and character of the miracles which he wrought, is found only in the writings of Gregory of Nyssen, who lived a hundred and thirty years after him; and a great part of the legendary miracles of the Popish "saints" depend for their credibility on the certificates presented at their "canonization," a ceremony which seldom takes place till a century after their deaths.

A single case will illustrate this point, and show its real force in the argument. It is that of Ignatius Loyola, the founder of the order of the Jesuits. His life, written by a companion of his, was published about fifteen years after his death. In that life, the author, so far from ascribing any miracles to Ignatius, carefully states the reasons why he was *not* invested with any such power. That life was republished fifteen years afterward, with the addition of many circumstances, which were the fruit, the author says, of farther inquiry and of diligent examination, but still with a total silence about miracles. When Ignatius had been dead nearly sixty years, the Jesuits, conceiving a wish to have the founder of their order placed in the Roman calendar, began, for the first time, to attribute to him the power of working miracles, and specified a large number which could not then be distinctly disproved, and which there was, in those who governed the Church, a strong disposition to admit on the slenderest proofs.*

It is clear that these circumstances constitute a broad line of distinction between these alleged miracles and the miracles of the New Testament, and that, so far as these cases go, the explanation of the one would in no manner constitute an explanation of the other.

(e) It is material, also, to remark, that a large part of the miracles alleged to have been wrought in the early Church, and nearly all of those wrought in the Roman Catholic Church, were wrought, not by

* The authority for these statements is *Paley*—Evidences of Christianity, Works, ed. 1824, vol. i., p. 182, 183.

the persons themselves while living, but by their *relics*, and many of them hundreds of years after the death of the "saints" themselves. The Ecclesiastical History of the Middle Ages and of the Romish Church is full of such wonders, and our own age has been edified with the accounts of numberless such miracles as were wrought by the "Holy Coat" at Treves. Even Augustine, the ablest and most clear-headed of the fathers, and a man of undoubted piety, solemnly asserts that in his own diocese at Hippo, in the space of two years, no less than seventy miracles had been wrought by the body of St. Stephen, and that in the neighboring province of Calama, where the relic had previously been, the number was incomparably greater. He gives a catalogue of what he deems undoubted miracles, which he says he had selected from a multitude so great that volumes would be required to relate them all. In that catalogue we find no less than five cases of restoration of life to the dead (De Civit. Dei, lib. xxii., c. 8). In his Confessions (b. ix., viii., 16) he relates the case of miracles wrought by the dead bodies of Gervasius and Protasius, which were discovered by Ambrose of Milan, and which were removed to the Ambrosian Basilica, particularly the restoring of sight to a blind man who was allowed to touch the bier with a handkerchief. Of this miracle, and of numerous others of a similar kind, he says, "Of which so great glory of the martyrs I also was a witness. I was there—was at Milan; I knew the miracles wrought, God bearing witness to 'the precious death of his saints,' so that through those miracles that 'death was precious' now not 'in the sight of the Lord' only, but in the sight of men" (De Civit. Dei, lib. xxii., c. 8, 32). It is clear that whatever explanation is given of *these* miracles, the explanation would not be applicable to the miracles of the New Testament.

(*f*) It is farther to be remarked that the testimony on these subjects among the fathers, and in subsequent times, involved no sacrifices; led to no persecutions; was not attended with the loss of place or property, or with peril of life. All that is required in such cases is what Dr. Paley calls "an *otiose* assent." They are employed for the maintenance of doctrines already embraced; or in defense of a priesthood already established; or for the credit of an "order" of religionists, like the Jesuits; or in honor of a particular monastery; or to commemorate some particular virtues of a saint, or to attract men to his shrine. Such things require no sacrifices. They demand no abandonment of country, of friends, or of home. They lead to no perils by sea or land. They involve no dangers of persecution. They are not believed and defended with the apprehension of fearful tortures; of being thrown to wild beasts; of being scourged or stoned; of being burned at the stake, or put to death on a cross. They belong to the same class of marvels, in this respect, as the belief in apparitions, ghosts, table-turning, spirit-rapping. Whether men *would* suffer persecution on their account might be a fair question; it is certain that they do not.

But it is hardly necessary to advert to the fact that all this is different from the miracles of the New Testament, and the treatment of the apostles consequent on their faith in those miracles. Those miracles, if real, decided the most important questions conceivable in regard to the destiny of mankind. The belief in them led to an entire change in the religion of the world. They were not wrought to establish any *existing* system of religion, but they led to the overthrow of all the systems of religion that *did* exist, in all lands, involving all that there was of property, and position, and influence, and traditionary sacredness in those religions; all that there was that was mighty, and sacred, and venerable in a priesthood; and all that was held sacred in the laws. The belief in those miracles involved the necessity of parting with friends; of encountering the perils of land and ocean; of meeting with opposition, contempt, persecution, and death in its most terrific forms; of bidding adieu to all that was attractive in this life, and of enduring all that could be made fearful to human nature while living, and all in death that could be made terrible.

I infer, therefore, that the explanation which must be given of the miracles of the early Church after the time of the apostles, of the miracles of the Middle Ages, and of the miracles of the Roman Catholic Church, is *not* a philosophical explanation of the miracles of the Bible.

(4.) The fourth point in the argument relates to the inquiry whether the miracles of the Bible can be *disposed of* in the same way as the miracles alleged to have been wrought among the heathen; or, more generally, the miracles which are referred to by those who reject the claims of the Bible. These may, of course, embrace a part of those which have already been referred to, but they may properly, so far as they are appealed to by the rejectors of the Bible, be again noticed with reference to their direct bearing on the argument.

It would have been wiser undoubtedly for the rejectors of the miracles of the Bible to base the argument for their rejection on general principles and on abstract reasoning, and not to peril their argument by bringing other miracles into comparison with those of the Bible. Mr. Hume's celebrated Essay on Miracles would have been stronger by far if he had omitted all reference to other miracles in comparison with those in the Bible. It is, therefore, an advantage in the argument *for* the miracles of the Bible that an attempt has been made to bring others into comparison with them. If, now, an explanation can be given of *those* alleged miracles which *can not* be applied to those in the Bible, or which will not satisfactorily account for them, the argument for the reality of those miracles will remain in all its proper force.

In such an argument on the part of those who reject the miracles of the Bible, they who make the appeal have, as Dr. Paley has remarked, an undoubted right to select their own examples. We may presume that they would select the strongest instances which the world has furnished to bring into comparison with the miracles of the Bible, and all the proprieties of the case will be complied with if, in the argument, the attention is confined to those examples to which they have referred. The friends of religion can not be supposed to be bound to furnish, if they could, stronger instances than those which have been actually selected.

In particular, it may be presumed that Mr. Hume would select those which, for his purpose, could be best brought into comparison with the Scripture miracles. Of the rejectors of revelation, few, if any, have been more acute and learned than he; none probably have had a larger acquaintance with history, or could make a better selection of the miraculous events on which the argument might be made to rest.

From the wide range of pretended miracles in the world; from the almost innumerable cases of such pretensions; from those marvels which have been regarded as miracles in the heathen world, in the early Christian Church after the time of the apostles, in the Middle Ages, and in the Roman Catholic Church in more modern times, he has selected *three* on which he seems willing that the argument shall rest. They are the following:

I. The cure of a blind and a lame man of Alexandria, by the Emperor Vespasian, as related by Tacitus;

II. The restoration of the limb of an attendant in a Spanish church, as told by Cardinal de Retz; and,

III. The cures said to have been performed at the tomb of the Abbé Paris in the early part of the last century.

The circumstances in these cases, and the argument, can be best expressed in his own words: "One of the best attested miracles in all profane history is that which Tacitus reports of Vespasian, who cured a blind man in Alexandria by means of his spittle, and a lame man by the mere touch of his foot; in obedience to a vision of the god Serapis, who had enjoined them to have recourse to the emperor for these miraculous cures. The story may be seen in that fine historian, where every circumstance seems to add weight to the testimony, and might be displayed at large with all the force of argument and eloquence, if any one were now concerned to enforce the evidence of that exploded and idolatrous superstition. The gravity, solidity, age, and probity of so great an emperor, who, through the whole course of his life, conversed in a familiar manner with his friends and courtiers, and never affected those extraordinary airs of divinity assumed by Alexander and Demetrius; the historian a contemporary writer, noted for candor and veracity, and, withal, the greatest and most penetrating genius, perhaps, of all antiquity, and so free from any tendency to credulity that he even lies under the contrary imputation of atheism and profaneness; the persons from whose authority he related the miracle, of established character for judgment and veracity, as we may well presume — eye-witnesses of the fact, and confirming their testimony after the Flavian family was despoiled of the empire, and could no longer give any reward as the price of a lie—utrumque, qui interfuere, nunc quoque memorant, postquam nullum mendacio pretium — to which if we add the public nature of the facts as related, it will appear that no evidence can well be supposed stronger for so gross and so palpable a falsehood.

"There is also a memorable story related by Cardinal de Retz which may well deserve our consideration. When that intriguing politician fled into Spain to avoid the persecution of his enemies, he passed through Saragossa, the capital of Aragon, where he was shown in the cathedral a man who had served seven years as a door-keeper, and was well known to every body in town that had ever paid his devotions at that Church. He had been seen for so long a time wanting a leg, but recovered that limb by the rubbing of holy oil upon the stump; and the cardinal assures us that he saw him with two legs. This miracle was vouched by all the canons of the Church; and the whole company in town were appealed to for a confirmation of the fact, whom the cardinal found, by their zealous devotion, to be thorough believers of the miracle. Here the relater was also contemporary to the supposed prodigy, of an incredulous and libertine character, as well as of great genius; the miracle of so singular a nature as could scarcely admit of a counterfeit, and the witnesses very numerous, and all of them in a manner spectators of the fact, to which they gave their testimony. And what adds mightily to the force of the evidence, and may double our surprise on this occasion, is that the cardinal himself, who relates the story, seems not to give any credit to it, and consequently can not be suspected of any concurrence in the holy fraud. He considered justly that it was not requisite, in order to reject a fact of this nature, to be able accurately to disprove the testimony and to trace its falsehood through all the circumstances of knavery and credulity which produced it. He knew that, as this was commonly altogether impossible at any small distance of time and place, so was it extremely difficult, even where one was immediately present, by reason of the bigotry, ignorance, cunning, and roguery of a great part of mankind. He therefore concluded, like a just reasoner, that such an evidence carried falsehood upon the very face of it, and that a miracle supported by any human testimony was more properly a subject of derision than of argument.

"There surely was never a greater number of miracles ascribed to one person than those which were lately said to have been wrought in France upon the tomb of Abbé Paris, the famous Jansenist, with whose sanctity the people were so long deluded. The curing of the sick, giving hearing to the deaf, and sight to the blind, were every where talked of as usual effects of that holy sepulchre. But, what is more extraordinary, many of the miracles were immediately proved upon the spot, before judges of unquestioned integrity, attested by witnesses of credit and distinction, in a learned age, and on the most eminent theatre that is now in the world. Nor is this all; a relation of them was published and dispersed every where; nor were the Jesuits, though a learned body, supported by the civil magistrate, and determined enemies to those opinions in whose favor the miracles were said to have been wrought, ever able distinctly to refute or detect them. Where shall we find such a number of circumstances agreeing to the corroboration of one fact? And what have we to oppose to such a cloud of witnesses but the absolute impossibility or miraculous nature of the events which they relate? And this surely, in the eyes of all reasonable people, will alone be regarded as a sufficient refutation."*

Of the first of these alleged miracles, the account by Tacitus is as follows:

"One of the common people of Alexandria, known to be diseased in his eyes, by the admonition of the god Serapis, whom that superstitious nation worship above all other gods, prostrated himself before the emperor, earnestly imploring from him a remedy for his blindness, and entreating that he would deign to anoint with his spittle his cheeks and the balls of his eyes. Another, diseased in his hand, requested, by the admonition of the same god, that he might be touched by the foot of the emperor. Vespasian at first derided and despised their application; afterward, when they continued to urge their petitions, he sometimes appeared to dread the imputation of vanity; at other times, by the earnest supplication of the patients, and the persuasion of his flatterers, to be induced to hope for success. At length he commanded an inquiry to be made by the physicians whether such a blindness and debility were vincible by human aid. The report of the physicians contained various points; that in the one the power of vision was

* Essays, vol. ii, p. 115-118.

not destroyed, but would return if the obstacles were removed; that in the other, the diseased joints might be restored if a healing power were applied; that it was, perhaps, agreeable to the gods to do this; that the emperor was elected by divine assistance; lastly, that the credit of the success would be the emperor's, the ridicule of the disappointment would fall upon the patients. Vespasian, believing that every thing was in the power of his fortune, and that nothing was any longer incredible, while the multitude which stood by eagerly expected the event, with a countenance expressive of joy, executed what he was desired to do. Immediately the hand was restored to its use, and light returned to the blind man. They who were present relate both these cures, even at this time, when there is nothing to be gained by lying."*

What, now, is the real force of the argument from this alleged miracle? What were the facts in the case? Was it believed by Mr. Hume? Can it properly be brought into comparison with the miracles of the New Testament?

It is plain that if the miracles in the case of Vespasian *were* actually wrought, this would not *prove* that the Savior did *not* restore Bartimeus to sight, or heal the impotent man at the pool of Bethesda. There would be no incompatibility between the miracles, for there is no necessary conflict. *Suppose* that in one case a miracle was wrought *as a work of benevolence*, and in another *for the establishment of the truth of a divine mission*, there evidently would be no such conflict between the two as to prove that either was false.

In reference to these alleged miracles of Vespasian, it is to be remarked (a) that the account by Tacitus was given twenty-seven years after they were said to have occurred; (b) that he recorded in Rome what was said to have occurred in Alexandria; (c) that he did not profess to have seen the miracles himself, but wrote from report; (d) that he manifestly did not believe in the reality of the miracles; (e) *that the whole affair is liable to a strong suspicion that it was the work of illusion and deception.* In other words, all that there was in the case *can* be explained on the supposition that there was collusion between the patients, the physician, and the emperor. This explanation is admissible for these reasons: (1.) It was not uncommon, then, to believe that such miracles could be wrought, just as in later times in England it was believed that scrofula, or the "king's evil," could be cured by the touch of the king.† (2.) It would be for the interest and

---

* Tacit., Hist., lib. iv.

† Charles the Second, in the course of his reign, "touched" near a hundred thousand persons. In 1682 he performed the rite eight thousand five hundred times. James the Second, in one of his progresses, touched eight persons in

credit of the emperor that such a belief should be entertained in regard
to him. (3.) The miracles were achieved in the midst of the emper-
or's flatterers and followers; in a city and among a people devoted to
his interest, and to the worship of the god Serapis; and where it would
have been treason and blasphemy to have contradicted the fame of the
cure, or to have questioned it.   (4.) It is to be observed, also, that the
report of the physicians is just such a report as would be made in a
case in which no external marks of the disease existed, and which,
consequently, was capable of being easily counterfeited, to wit, that in
the one case the organs of vision were not destroyed, and that the
weakness of the second was in the joints.   (5.) There is little force in
the remark of Tacitus that they who were present continued even then
to "relate both these cures, when there was nothing to be gained by
lying." The particular point of importance is the state of mind of the
witnesses, and the circumstances *at the time*, and not whether the
story would be likely to be repeated.   It is also of importance to remark, that if there was nothing " to be *gained* by lying," it is a question of much more moment whether there was any thing to be *lost*, or
any thing to be *suffered* by continuing to repeat the story.   *Would* the
witnesses have done it if it would have involved them in trouble and
losses; if it had subjected them to persecution; if it had exposed them
to death in most horrid forms?   (6.) To make this case parallel,
therefore, with the miracles of the New Testament, all, or nearly all
of these circumstances must be reversed.   If these marvelous cures
had been performed in the presence of cavilers and enemies; if those
who were present were incredulous, and had no previous disposition to
believe such a fact; if every circumstance was watched with a jealous
eye; if nothing was to be gained by it at the time or afterward; if the
case was removed as far as possible from all appearance or possibility
of collusion; if they who professed to be witnesses of the transaction,

the choir of the Cathedral of Chester. The reality of these cures—the efficacy
of this touch—was attested by much stronger evidence than that adduced by
Mr. Hume for the miracles of Vespasian; than that referred to by the Cardinal de Retz; and than those performed at the tomb of the Abbé Paris.
"Theologians of eminent learning, ability, and virtue gave the sanction of
their authority to this mummery, and medical men of high note believed, or
affected to believe, in the balsamic virtues of the royal hand. We must suppose that every surgeon who attended Charles the Second was a man of high
repute for skill; and more than one of the surgeons who attended Charles
the Second has left us a solemn profession of faith in the king's miraculous
power." William of Orange committed an almost unpardonable offense by
"sneering" at the practice, and refusing to lend his sanction to it. "It is a silly
superstition," said he, when, at the close of Lent, his palace was besieged by a
crowd of the sick. "Give the poor creatures some money, and send them
away."—*Macaulay*, History of England, vol. iii., p. 432–435.

and who gave circulation to the report on the strength of what they saw, gave up their former cherished hopes, changed their whole course of life, abandoned all their plans, and all the opinions in which they had been trained, and sacrificed their ease and their reputation ; if they went forth on the ground of this to meet every form of trial, and bore patiently the most cruel tortures, and met death itself rather than change their testimony on the subject , and if the belief of such miracles actually changed the religions, the customs, and laws of the world, producing changes that could be traced through eighteen hundred years, making the world different from what it was, and modifying its customs and laws, then, and only then, would it be proper to allege that the miracles of Vespasian were an offset against the miracles of the New Testament.*

The second case referred to by Mr. Hume is the restoration of the limb of an attendant in a Spanish church, as told by Cardinal de Retz.

It is evident from the narrative, as given by Mr. Hume, that the cardinal who relates this story did not himself believe it; and it is manifestly adduced by him *because* the cardinal did not believe it, and with a design to leave the impression that *all* miracles should be treated with the same degree of incredulity. Undoubtedly there have been thousands of pretended miracles in the Roman Catholic Church, as well as elsewhere, that *should be* treated in this manner, and that are precisely parallel with this. The *reasoning*, however, so far as there *is* any reasoning in the case, would not be far from that where, if a man saw one counterfeit note, he should infer that all notes were counterfeit, or where, if he met with one case of imposture in a community, he should infer that all the transactions in society were imposture and delusion. In fact, nothing *can* be more easy than to account for all that is here said by Cardinal de Retz. The substitution of an artificial leg would account for all that he says. What he *says* is, that the man, "who had served seven years as a door-keeper, and was well known to every body in town, had been seen for so long a time wanting a leg," but that "*he* saw him with two legs." He indeed affirms that he had "recovered that limb by the rubbing of holy oil upon the stump," and that "this was vouched by all the canons of the church;" but the only fact to which *he* bears testimony is, that "he saw him with two legs." There was, manifestly, no examination : there was no comparison of the two there is even no statement that he was seen walking; and every thing that the cardinal *saw*, and which is, therefore, the subject of his testimony, could be explained on the supposition that an artificial leg had been made to supply the place of the one that had been lost—a thing certainly not unusual, and not

---

* Compare *Paley's* Evidences of Christianity, Works, vol. i., p. 108-291.

involving a miracle. It is to be remembered, also, as Dr. Paley has remarked, that "the ecclesiastics of the place would, it is probable, favor the story, inasmuch as it advanced the honor of their image and the church. And if *they* patronized it, no other person at Saragossa, in the middle of the last century, would care to dispute it. The story likewise coincided not less with the wishes and preconceptions of the people than with the interests of their ecclesiastical rulers, so that there was prejudice backed by authority, and both operating on extreme ignorance, to account for the success of the imposture."*

The only thing, in fact, remarkable about this case is, that a man of Mr. Hume's acuteness in argument should ever have referred to such a case as an offset against the miracles of the New Testament—the healing of the blind, the deaf, and the lame by the Savior, the stilling of the tempest on the Sea of Tiberias by his command; and the raising of Lazarus from the grave, and that he should have been *willing* to peril the cause of infidelity by an argument so manifestly weak.

The third case referred to by Mr. Hume is derived from the cures said to have been performed at the tomb of the Abbé Paris.

The *argument* in the case, as stated by Mr. Hume, rests on these points: (*a*) The *number* of the miracles: "There surely never was a greater number ascribed to one person than those which were lately said to have been wrought in France upon the tomb of the Abbé Paris." (*b*) The fact that these were "every where talked of as usual effects of that holy sepulchre." (*c*) The fact that these miracles were immediately proved to be true "What is more extraordinary, many of the miracles were immediately proved upon the spot, before judges of unquestioned integrity, attested by witnesses of credit and distinction, in a learned age, and on the most eminent theatre that is now in the world." (*d*) The fact that the Jesuits, enemies of the Jansenists, in whose favor the miracles were said to have been wrought, "though a learned body, supported by the civil magistrate, and determined enemies to those opinions, were never able distinctly to refute or detect them."

In regard to this case, and the arguments in favor of these miracles, considered with reference to a comparison with those of the New Testament, the following remarks may be made.

(1.) The *number* of the miracles said to have been wrought was, in fact, exceeding small. Mr. Hume says there "never was a greater number ascribed to one person." That, however, is not true, for a much larger number has been "ascribed' to Jesus of Nazareth. The number of cures at the tomb of the Abbé Paris, as actually recorded by historians, was *nine* only. These were *all* that the zealous and inde-

* Works, vol I., p. 202.

fatigable Montgoron claimed to produce vouchers for, or claimed to have been proved to have been wrought at the tomb.* These were all that were pretended to be cured out of the crowds of the infirm and the sick who came or were brought to the tomb. It is true, indeed, that another author who has given a record of those miracles, referred to by Mr. Hume under the title of Recueil des Miracles de l'Abbé Paris (Essays, vol. ii., p. 441), has mentioned a much larger number, but they were miracles wrought, as he says, in the private chambers of the sick, by virtue of the relics of the Abbé, or by images of the saint, or by earth brought from under his monument.† As Mr. Hume confines the argument to miracles wrought at the "tomb," it is proper to notice those only.

What is particularly remarkable, however, in regard to these alleged miracles is the small *number* out of the whole that are claimed to have been cured. Many thousands of such persons — the afflicted in all forms — visited the tomb. *Nine* only are vouched for as actually cured. Now there has been no form of pretended miracles, or of deception and imposture in medicine, in which a greater proportion have not been restored to health—*cured*—than in this case. Under the application of mesmerism, or "quack" medicines of any kind, more marvels than these have been accomplished—more cures effected. Many more cases of cure—probably many more in proportion to the whole number — occurred undoubtedly in the "touch" for the "king's evil" during the time when faith was exercised in the efficacy of that "touch," that is, there were more cases of cure where, under the influence of the imagination, persons were "touched;" or where the disease was imaginary and was thus removed; or where a restoration to health had been already commenced under the power of medicine, or the recuperating power of nature; or where, from any cause, a recovery to health was dated from such a touch. It is impossible to suppose that this superstition could have been kept up from age to age if such had not been the case. It is not difficult, in most or all of these cases, to account for these facts without supposing that the quack medicine has genuine restoring properties; that the nostrum is valuable; that mesmerism is founded in truth; or that there was *real* efficacy in the "touch" for the "king's evil." Many of these diseases would be healed by the mere course of nature; many were nervous complaints, and would be allayed and removed by a belief in the efficacy of the medicine; many would be healed under the influence of the imagina-

* Mons. Montgoron, the reporter of these miracles, was, as Mr. Hume says (Essays, vol. ii., p. 441), a "counsellor or judge of the Parliament of Paris, a man of figure and character, who was also a martyr to the cause."

† *Dr. Campbell*, Examination of Mr. Hume's Essay on Miracles.

tion; many would be cases which would not bear a rigid examination, but would be cases where the healing was apparent, and where
there would be seen to be imposture at the foundation.

It is unnecessary to remark how unlike all this is to the miracles of
the Savior. Many thousands of cases came before him. ALL—not
the proportion of "nine" to thousands, but *all*, according to the account in the New Testament, were healed (Matt., v., 24; xii., 15;
xiv., 14; xvii., 15; Luke, xxii., 51. Comp. Acts, iv., 14; v., 16;
xxviii., 8).

(2.) Many of the cases at the tomb of the Abbé Paris were such as
could be cured by natural causes. One of the cures referred to by
Montgoron was that of Don Alphonzo de Palacios, who had lost one
eye, and who was afflicted with an inflammation in the other. The
inflamed eye was cured, but the lost eye was not restored to sight.
Had the lost eye been restored to sight, there could have been no
doubt that a miracle was wrought. An inflamed eye might be restored by natural causes. In another case—that of Peter Gantior—one
of his eyes had been pricked with an awl. It is certainly possible that,
while there was temporary blindness, nature would have restored the
sight. Many of the cases at the tomb were cases of paralytic and drop-
sical disorders—cases where nature, in numerous instances, produces
temporary if not permanent relief. It does not appear that any one
of the "nine" was a case which could not be accounted for in that
way.

(3.) It was a fact that many of the devotees at the tomb, and some
of those who were asserted to have been cured, had been using medicines before, and continued to use them even when there. "That the
Spanish youth had been using all the while a medicine prescribed by
an eminent oculist was proved by the depositions of witnesses: that
Gantior had begun to receive his sight before he had recourse to the
sepulchre was attested not only by his uncle, but even by himself,
when, as the Archbishop of Sens informs us, he signed a recantation
of what he had formerly advanced."[*]

(4.) None of the miracles at the tomb were *instantaneous*. All
that Christ and his apostles wrought were. The blind saw at once;
the lame man leaped as an hart when told to walk; the paralytic took
his bed and walked immediately; the young man of Nain sat up in-
stantaneously in the bier; Lazarus came forth, at the very moment of
the command of the Savior, from the grave. Not so at the tomb of
the Abbé Paris. "All the worshipers at the tomb persisted for days,
several of them for weeks, and some for months successively, daily imploring the intercession of the Abbé, before they obtained relief from

---

[*] *Dr. Campbell*, Hume's Essays, vol. II., p. 588.   [†] *Id. Ibid.*

their complaints; and the relief which they received is, in most cases, acknowledged to have been gradual."†

(5.) In view of these facts, and of the strong presumption in the nature of the case that there might have been collusion and designed imposture practiced to establish and maintain the credit of the "saint" and of the tomb, we are prepared to see what is the *real* force of the remark which Mr. Hume so exultingly makes in the text of his Essay, and which he labors to confirm in a note appended to it, that the testimony in this case was above suspicion, and that it could not be refuted. Thus he says, in the Essay, "What is more extraordinary, many of the miracles were immediately proved upon the spot, before judges of unquestioned integrity, attested by witnesses of credit and distinction, in a learned age, and on the most eminent theatre that is now in the world. Nor is this all; a relation of them was published and dispersed every where; nor were the Jesuits, though a learned body, supported by the civil magistrate, and determined enemies to those opinions in whose favor the miracles were said to have been wrought, ever able distinctly to refute or detect them."*

Thus he says, also, in a note: "Many of the miracles" [the word "*many*" here means *nine*] "of the Abbé Paris were proved immediately by witnesses before the officiating or bishop's court at Paris, under the eye of Cardinal Noailles, whose character for integrity and capacity was never contested even by his enemies." "No less a man than the Duc de Chatillon, a duke and peer of France, of the highest rank and family, gives evidence of a miraculous cure, performed on a servant of his, who had lived several years in his house with a visible and palpable infirmity." "I shall conclude," says he, "with observing that no clergy are more celebrated for strictness of life and manners than the secular clergy of France, particularly the rectors or curés of Paris, who bear testimony to these impostures."†

The sum of the whole matter in regard to these alleged miracles is this: We may surely and safely admit all the *facts* which are alleged in the case. The *facts* are these: (*a*) That great numbers of persons, afflicted with various kinds of diseases, visited the tomb with the hope of a cure. (*b*) That we may suppose that a part or all the cases of those who are alleged to have been healed were cases of real disease, or were not feigned. (*c*) That there was, in a few instances, a real and permanent restoration to health. (*d*) That this occurred at the tomb of the Abbé Paris, or after visiting that tomb. (*e*) That the cases were examined before judges deemed competent to decide such matters. (*f*) That the witnesses were credible witnesses, and were, in many instances, above suspicion. (*g*) That it *was* impossible for

* Essays, vol. ii., p. 117.   † Id. Ibid., p. 242, 244.

the Jesuits to disprove these facts, and that they were constrained to admit that these cures were actually wrought.

The material point, however, is *not* reached and affected by these admitted facts—that all this was done by the saint; by his tomb; by his virtues; or by God in attestation of his virtues, or in defense of the party to which he belonged. If the remarks above made furnish a *plausible*, or POSSIBLE explanation of the facts in the case—of all that occurred—then the case does not amount to a miracle, and, *therefore*, whatever else may follow from it, it does not follow that Christ did *not* raise Lazarus from the dead, or that he himself did not rise.

And these are *all*. These are the strongest cases which have been referred to as parallel to those in the New Testament, and as having strength sufficient to neutralize the argument for the divine origin of Christianity as derived from miracles. These are *selected* from the wide range of supposed supernatural agencies in the heathen and in the Christian world; and it may be presumed that the best selection has been made. The inquiry as to the cases which *should* be selected embraced the entire period from the remotest ages to the time of Mr. Hume himself, and was made by one who was an accomplished historian, and who was, perhaps, as familiar with the facts of history as any man then living. Nothing new has been added to the argument since his time; no more decided cases of miraculous agency have been referred to; none have been furnished in heathen lands, or in the Papal church, that would contribute more strength to the cause of infidelity. It may be assumed now that no stronger cases *will* occur in future times. If, therefore, these do not neutralize the force of the testimony in favor of the miracles of the New Testament, then that testimony remains in its full force.

The conclusion which we have reached is this: If the miracles of the Bible can not be resolved into facts to be explained by natural laws; if they can not be philosophically placed on the same foundation as witchcraft, divination, sorcery, mesmerism, and spirit-rapping, and explained in the same manner; if they can not be disposed of as the alleged miracles in the Christian Church after the time of the apostles may be; and if they are not on a level with the miracles referred to by skeptics as parallel cases, and are not to be explained in the same manner, then the argument for the miracles of the Bible which has been so satisfactory to a large part of the world for eighteen hundred years is as strong as it can be supposed to have been in the first century, and the evidence is to be regarded as placed on the same foundation as that for well-attested historical facts that have gone into the history of the world.

It is to be borne in mind that the real facts of history *have* gone into the history of the world, and have made the world what it now is. Those facts, and the proper influence of those facts, can not now be *detached* from history, or from the present condition of the world. The facts in regard to the miracles of Christianity, also, have gone into the history of the world, and can not be detached from it. The civilized world is what it is now, and the whole world will be what it will be in coming ages, because Christ was believed to have wrought miracles, and to have been raised from the dead. Those facts were attested by men who saw them; who recorded them; who had no special interest to promote by them; who abandoned all the opinions in which they had been trained because they believed in them; who sacrificed all their prejudices on the ground of that belief; who met reproach and calumny, persecution, peril, and death in its most fearful forms, in attestation of the truth of those miracles; who never wavered in their statements, who could never be induced by terrors or by bribes to give utterance to a doubt about the truth of those events; and of whom not one—no, not one—ever breathed a suspicion that he had been himself deceived, or that those with whom he was associated had conspired to deceive the world. In a most intelligent age; in the very centre of learning: among the most cultivated people, and in cities where the talent and power of the world were concentrated, they bore their testimony, and their testimony was believed. The religion was propagated on the ground of these miracles. The religions of the world were changed, and a new order of things, sending its influence onward for eighteen hundred years, was instituted on that ground. Altars were forsaken; temples were abandonded; priests were disrobed; laws were changed; customs of long standing passed away on that ground. A new spirit was breathed into the literature of the world on that ground; and philosophy took a new form on that ground. Men were changed from vice to virtue on that ground; and thousands of martyrs from all ranks of people—the rich, the honored, the gay, the refined—on that ground sealed their faith with their blood. The alleged miracles of Vespasian and those at the tomb of the Abbé Paris have done nothing—literally *nothing*—permanently to affect the faith, the religion, the hopes, the intelligence, or the morals of mankind; the miracles of Christ have changed the world. Myriads of the human race, among the most intelligent and pure, have believed that those miracles demonstrated that he came from God; there is nothing *yet* to lead us to doubt that this will be still more prevailingly the faith of the world in the ages to come, and that perpetuated faith in those miracles will determine the condition of the nations of the earth in the winding up of human affairs.

THE END.

HILDRETH'S UNITED STATES. History of the United States. FIRST SERIES: From the Discovery of the Continent to the Organization of the Government under the Federal Constitution. SECOND SERIES: From the Adoption of the Federal Constitution to the End of the Sixteenth Congress. By RICHARD HILDRETH. Popular Edition, 6 vols. in a Box, 8vo, Cloth, with Paper Labels, Uncut Edges and Gilt Tops, $12 00. Sold only in Sets.

MOTLEY'S DUTCH REPUBLIC. The Rise of the Dutch Republic. A History. By JOHN LOTHROP MOTLEY, LL.D., D.C.L. With a Portrait of William of Orange. Cheap Edition, 3 vols. in a Box, 8vo, Cloth, with Paper Labels, Uncut Edges and Gilt Tops, $6 00. Sold only in Sets. Original Library Edition, 3 vols., 8vo, Cloth, $10 50; Sheep, $12 00; Half Calf, $17 25.

MOTLEY'S UNITED NETHERLANDS. History of the United Netherlands: from the Death of William the Silent to the Twelve Years' Truce—1584-1609. With a full View of the English-Dutch Struggle against Spain, and of the Origin and Destruction of the Spanish Armada. By JOHN LOTHROP MOTLEY, LL.D., D.C.L. Portraits. Cheap Edition, 4 vols. in a Box, 8vo, Cloth, with Paper Labels, Uncut Edges and Gilt Tops, $8 00. Sold only in Sets. Original Library Edition, 4 volumes, 8vo, Cloth, $14 00; Sheep, $16 00; Half Calf, $23 00.

MOTLEY'S JOHN OF BARNEVELD. The Life and Death of John of Barneveld, Advocate of Holland: with a View of the Primary Causes and Movements of "The Thirty Years' War." By JOHN LOTHROP MOTLEY, LL.D., D.C.L. Illustrated. Cheap Edition, 2 vols. in a Box, 8vo, Cloth, with Paper Labels, Uncut Edges and Gilt Tops, $4 00. Sold only in Sets. Original Library Edition, 2 vols., 8vo, Cloth, $7 00; Sheep, $8 00; Half Calf, $11 50.

GOLDSMITH'S WORKS. The Works of Oliver Goldsmith. Edited by PETER CUNNINGHAM, F.S.A. From new Electrotype Plates. 4 vols., 8vo, Cloth, Paper Labels, Uncut Edges and Gilt Tops, $8 00. Uniform with the New Library Editions of Macaulay, Hume, Gibbon, Motley, and Hildreth.

HUDSON'S HISTORY OF JOURNALISM. Journalism in the United States, from 1690 to 1872. By FREDERIC HUDSON. 8vo, Cloth, $5 00; Half Calf, $7 25.

SYMONDS'S SKETCHES AND STUDIES IN SOUTHERN
EUROPE. By JOHN ADDINGTON SYMONDS. In Two Volumes. Post 8vo, Cloth, $4 00.

SYMONDS'S GREEK POETS. Studies of the Greek Poets.
By JOHN ADDINGTON SYMONDS. 2 vols., Square 16mo, Cloth,
$3 50.

TREVELYAN'S LIFE OF MACAULAY. The Life and Letters of Lord Macaulay. By his Nephew, G. OTTO TREVELYAN,
M.P. With Portrait on Steel. Complete in 2 vols., 8vo,
Cloth, Uncut Edges and Gilt Tops, $5 00; Sheep, $6 00;
Half Calf, $9 50. Popular Edition, two vols. in one, 12mo,
Cloth, $1 75.

TREVELYAN'S LIFE OF FOX. The Early History of Charles
James Fox. By GEORGE OTTO TREVELYAN. 8vo, Cloth, Uncut Edges and Gilt Tops, $2 50; 4to, Paper, 20 cents.

MÜLLER'S POLITICAL HISTORY OF RECENT TIMES.
Political History of Recent Times (1816–1875). With Special
Reference to Germany. By WILLIAM MÜLLER. Revised and
Enlarged by the Author. Translated, with an Appendix covering the Period from 1876 to 1881, by the Rev. JOHN P. PETERS, Ph.D. 12mo, Cloth, $3 00.

LOSSING'S CYCLOPÆDIA OF UNITED STATES HISTORY. Popular Cyclopædia of United States History. From
the Aboriginal Period to 1876. By B. J. LOSSING, LL.D. Illustrated by 2 Steel Portraits and over 1000 Engravings. 2
vols., Royal 8vo, Cloth, $10 00. (*Sold by Subscription only.*)

LOSSING'S FIELD-BOOK OF THE REVOLUTION. Pictorial Field-Book of the Revolution; or, Illustrations by Pen and
Pencil of the History, Biography, Scenery, Relics, and Traditions
of the War for Independence. By BENSON J. LOSSING. 2 vols.,
8vo, Cloth, $14 00; Sheep or Roan, $15 00; Half Calf, $18 00.

LOSSING'S FIELD-BOOK OF THE WAR OF 1812. Pictorial
Field-Book of the War of 1812; or, Illustrations by Pen and
Pencil of the History, Biography, Scenery, Relics, and Traditions of the last War for American Independence. By BENSON
J. LOSSING. With several hundred Engravings on Wood by
Lossing and Barritt, chiefly from Original Sketches by the Author. 1088 pages, 8vo, Cloth, $7 00; Sheep, $8 50; Roan
$9 00; Half Calf, $10 00.

PARTON'S CARICATURE. Caricature and Other Comic Art, in All Times and Many Lands. By JAMES PARTON. 203 Illustrations. 8vo, Cloth, Uncut Edges and Gilt Tops, $5 00; Half Calf, $7 25.

MAHAFFY'S GREEK LITERATURE. A History of Classical Greek Literature. By J. P. MAHAFFY. 2 vols., 12mo, Cloth, $4 00; Half Calf, $7 50.

DU CHAILLU'S LAND OF THE MIDNIGHT SUN. Summer and Winter Journeys in Sweden, Norway, and Lapland, and Northern Finland. By PAUL B. DU CHAILLU. Illustrated. 2 vols., 8vo, Cloth, $7 50.

DU CHAILLU'S EQUATORIAL AFRICA. Explorations and Adventures in Equatorial Africa: with Accounts of the Manners and Customs of the People, and of the Chase of the Gorilla, Crocodile, Leopard, Elephant, Hippopotamus, and other Animals. By P. B. DU CHAILLU. Illustrated. 8vo, Cloth, $5 00; Sheep, $5 50; Half Calf, $7 25.

DU CHAILLU'S ASHANGO LAND. A Journey to Ashango Land, and Further Penetration into Equatorial Africa. By P. B. DU CHAILLU. Illustrated. 8vo, Cloth, $5 00; Sheep, $5 50; Half Calf, $7 25.

DEXTER'S CONGREGATIONALISM. The Congregationalism of the Last Three Hundred Years, as Seen in its Literature: with Special Reference to certain Recondite, Neglected, or Disputed Passages. With a Bibliographical Appendix. By H. M. DEXTER. Large 8vo, Cloth, $6 00.

STANLEY'S THROUGH THE DARK CONTINENT. Through the Dark Continent; or, The Sources of the Nile, Around the Great Lakes of Equatorial Africa, and Down the Livingstone River to the Atlantic Ocean. 149 Illustrations and 10 Maps. By H. M. STANLEY. 2 vols., 8vo, Cloth, $10 00; Sheep, $12 00; Half Morocco, $15 00.

BARTLETT'S FROM EGYPT TO PALESTINE. From Egypt to Palestine: Through Sinai, the Wilderness, and the South Country. Observations of a Journey made with Special Reference to the History of the Israelites. By S. C. BARTLETT, D.D., LL.D. With Maps and Illustrations. 8vo, Cloth, $3 50.